Spring Wind

The Story of the Japanese Martial Arts

David McCullough

Kitayama Books

© David McCullough 2013

ISBN 9781490394145

For Michael and John

Chapters

1. The Final Battle — 7
2. The Samurai — 17
3. The End of War — 35
4. Miyamoto Musashi — 63
5. The Swords of Edo — 86
6. The Last Days of the Samurai — 111
7. Yamaoka Tesshu — 141
8. Bushido — 160
9. The Birth of Judo — 191
10. Okinawa — 217
11. Karate Becomes Japanese — 233
12. Aikido: The Divine Art — 247
13. Total War, Total Defeat — 264
14. The Way Back — 279
15. GodHand — 305
16. Into the World — 323
17. The Modern Age — 340

Introduction

My discovery of Japan came as a young undergraduate when I wandered into a karate class for the first time. The room was full of activity but very quiet. Several dozen students in white outfits and colored belts were warming up and stretching. And then a man wearing a black belt entered. Everyone scurried to take their place in a series of rows. We kneeled and bowed, touching the tips of our fingers together on the ground in front of our heads. My nose wrinkled at the smell of the bare feet just in front of me.

As we stood up the teacher spoke to us. He was not Japanese but issued instructions in the language of that country. He made the unfamiliar words clear by demonstrating each movement to us. We imitated his actions, counting in Japanese as we moved. Everything was very controlled and patterned. The teacher was not friendly with the students, in fact he was rather brusque. He expected compliance and the students followed his instructions with great vigor. It was all very different from anything I had experienced before.

Several years later I found my way to the outstanding karate club where I would spend ten years undergoing the hard and often painful training that is required to acquire a black belt. It was a place where I would have some of the most important and intense experiences of my life. My fellow students were from all walks of life. We trained together in an atmosphere that was certainly martial, and occasionally aggressive, but almost always devoid of bad feeling.

This very special martial arts club was the creation of two men who are friends and collaborators. On the surface they are very ordinary individuals, holding down jobs and raising families. But in the confines of our club they were extraordinary. Physically gifted and powerful for sure, but also possessed of something that seemed to me to be much more interesting and important than strength. There was something about their values, about their humility and their presence that made me want to dig beneath the surface.

Both of my teachers had learned their karate from a true expert, one of the first Japanese martial artists to settle in the United Kingdom. Tatsuo Suzuki arrived in London in 1965, a prematurely balding man in his late thirties. As he stepped down from his plane Suzuki was holding a single suitcase. But he also carried with him an intangible treasure, the history and the traditions of an entire culture. It was this rich legacy that for the next fifty years enabled him to command the attention and devotion of thousands of students. What were the ideas, the philosophy, and the history that sustained that karate teacher as he arrived alone in London? This book is my attempt to answer that question.

The Japanese martial arts are, perhaps, the most important way in which Japanese culture has spread around the world. Tens of millions have taken up karate, judo, aikido and the other Japanese fighting arts and have gained enormous physical and mental benefits from doing so. In fact, since the Second World War, it has become customary to think of the martial arts as peaceful paths to self improvement. But medieval Japan was no different from most other countries. It was a world of violence, a world where death and cruelty were commonplace. And yet even in those times when blood seemed to flow in rivers the Japanese martial tradition presents us with much to admire. The samurai were capable of stirring displays of honor, bravery, loyalty and skill in the midst of all their butchery. War shone a magnifying glass onto the Japanese spirit, bringing the most noble as well as the most debased instincts of the warriors into sharp relief. It is hard to tell this story without being drawn toward moral judgements. And there are important questions to be asked. But they must remain largely beyond the scope of this book.

The recorded history of the warrior arts in Japan stretches over more than one thousand years. Consequently, this book can only provide a summary of the most important events and is not an exhaustive account. Many of the incidents I describe were originally passed down in oral form or were recorded in a number of conflicting ways. Where different interpretations of historical events are possible I have simply aimed to present the most likely, or most commonly accepted, version. A great number of Japanese place names and terms appear throughout the book. For the sake of readability I have given prominence to English translations of Japanese terms. Whenever possible I have also included romanized versions of the original language in parentheses.

In several places I have quoted from the translations of authors whose understanding of the Japanese language and of Japanese history greatly surpasses my own. I hope that readers who enjoy this book will take time to explore the fine writings of John Stevens, Hiroaki Sato, William Scott Wilson, Steven Turnbull, Karl Friday, Kenji Tokitsu, John Dower, Mary Elizabeth Berry, Mark Ravina, Stanley Pranin, Graham Noble and the many other authors whose work has been invaluable to my research. I am deeply grateful for their inspiration.

1. The Final Battle

He was tall for a seventeen year old, just over six feet. And even at five in the morning there was something different about him, something in the eyes that set him apart from the other troops as they began to shake the sleep from their bodies. He was fully awake, dressed in a light armor breastplate and holding a long spear. This quiet and intense young man was destined to become, in his lifetime, the most famous warrior in Japan. And that fame would outlast him, burning bright for centuries in the memory of his nation. He was Miyamoto Musashi, the most remarkable individual in the long story of the Japanese martial arts.

But, for the moment, he was nobody. All around him lay the shadows of a great horseshoe of hills and stretched along the slopes of those hills a huge army of eighty thousand soldiers and their horses preparing for battle. Down below in the valley, hidden by the dark and the October fog, was the opposing army, an army that had trudged over narrow country roads for hours to take up positions during the night. Glimmers from the campfires far below twinkled through the mists and Musashi could hear the shouts of commanders as they roused their men from a brief and uncomfortable sleep. More than one hundred and fifty thousand fighters had packed themselves into this narrow bowl among the mountains. And every one of them carried weapons that had been designed to maim another human being - bows, swords, spears and muskets. All of these men knew that as soon as the sun rose they would be close enough to kill their enemies, or to be killed.

The place is Sekigahara, the year 1600. These armies waiting for the sun to rise would soon begin to fight the greatest and most important battle of the samurai era. But most of the soldiers at Sekigahara were unaware that the day ahead was going to be anything more than just another clash. They had no way of knowing that their nation had reached a decisive turning point. After more than a century of chaos and violent confusion, the outcome of the next few hours would usher in a long period of peace and unified government for Japan.

The samurai at Sekigahara were all tough soldiers. Most of them had been to war several times. Many of them had journeyed over the seas to Korea together and had fought there in two exhausting and ultimately unsuccessful wars of conquest. Warfare was the only constant in their lives. It was what they trained and lived for. It was what made them samurai.

These fighters had travelled to Sekigahara from every corner of Japan. They made their way in local detachments, the samurai forces of the lords who controlled the provinces. These small outfits assembled into patchwork armies, unruly crowds of warriors that were so diverse that inspiring them to unite in battle would be a severe challenge for even the most experienced general.

For the last thirty years one great and brilliant man, the dead leader Hideyoshi, had been able to bring the samurai warriors of the entire nation together as a single army. From nowhere, some even said from a peasant family, he had outfought and outthought his opponents as he rose to become the supreme ruler of a Japan that was growing tired of war. Hideyoshi had been a wonderful leader, so astute and so determined that no one dreamed of challenging him. But he was dead and the same generals who had so recently kneeled in front of Hideyoshi taking vows to maintain the peace were now at the head of two great armies preparing to fling themselves at each other.

As the warlords of Japan squabbled over the succession to Hideyoshi they gradually formed into two loose coalitions. One group had its heart in Edo, the eastern capital and one was based in Osaka, in the west. There was a bitter enmity between these two sides that erupted in a series of skirmishes, pitched battles and sieges. Over time most of the regional lords and their samurai armies were drawn into the conflict. Almost every warrior in Japan joined the ranks of one side or the other as the two great forces gathered for a final settling of the scores.

For Musashi the violence of 1600 was entirely welcome. Like all ambitious young samurai who had come of age in sixteenth century Japan he was sharply aware that his future depended on finding an opportunity to prove himself as a fighter. War was a chance for a junior samurai to "borrow the battlefield" to demonstrate his courage and skill. Musashi had already tasted mass combat on two occasions. But the huge gathering of samurai at Sekigahara was on a different scale to anything he had seen before. It was a moment of great power. Terrible killing would take place as soon as the sun rose. Musashi was dimly aware that he was not afraid. He was excited, and determined to make his name.

First Blood
Musashi had been close to violence all his life. As a boy he had lived in the country home of his father Munisai, a noted martial arts instructor who had mastered several weapons systems. Munisai was a prominent swordsman in his youth but he had failed to secure a plum position in one of the large towns. Perhaps the father was a frustrated man, he was certainly an angry and aggressive individual. Relations between the boy and his father were difficult and they finally fell to pieces when Musashi's father divorced his mother. One day Munisai, in a fit of temper, threw a dagger and then a short sword at his son. Musashi took the hint and fled from his father's home to live with his uncle, a temple priest. In these quieter surroundings Musashi followed the course of study that was expected of a samurai youth. He

read the Chinese classics and learned the rudiments of calligraphy and painting. Later in life he would become a great artist. But first he would become a fighter.

One morning in 1596 the thirteen year old Musashi, on his way home from a lesson, spotted a notice tied to a fence post outside the village. The hand written message offered a duel to anyone in the vicinity who was willing to fight. It had been posted by a wandering swordsman named Kihei. He was a shugyosha: one of the thousands of young men who were drifting from town to town in the violent world of sixteenth century Japan in search of the fame and fortune that came to those who could win recognition as outstanding fighters.

Rising through the ranks of Japan's class conscious society was extremely difficult. Boys who were born into the closed circle of aristocratic samurai families were sure of a comfortable living. They were paid a handsome salary by their local lord in return for a promise to fight in times of war. But for youths from the lower ranks of the samurai the only honorable way to acquire wealth and fame was to take part in combat. Wars meant opportunity but wars came and went. Young, ambitious samurai would therefore take the enormous risk of confronting a recognized sword fighter and demanding a duel. These face-offs, known as tachiai, were only attractive to young men who had great confidence in their own ability. The duels might be fought with steel swords or with wooden practice swords but in either case terrible injuries to one or both fighters were the most likely outcome.

Kihei posted his notice in the hope that a notable local samurai, perhaps even the well-known father of Musashi, would be tempted to face him in a duel. But it was Munisai's teenage son who accepted the challenge. Musashi had just completed a calligraphy lesson and still had his writing brush to hand. Across Kihei's notice he scrawled these words: "Miyamoto Musashi, who lives at the local temple, will fight you tomorrow."

News of this impetuous reply soon buzzed through the village and finally made its way to Musashi's uncle. The shocked priest immediately rushed to the inn where Kihei was staying and began to apologize for the ridiculous prank that had been played by his young nephew. The boy was only thirteen years old, his uncle pleaded. Kihei knew that he had little to gain by thrashing a child and so replied that he would forget the insult as soon as a formal apology was offered.

The following morning Musashi, holding a long walking staff in one hand, appeared at the inn with his uncle. Kihei stepped outside and was standing waiting for an apology when the boy suddenly ran straight towards him. The startled samurai drew his sword and attempted to defend himself but before he could make a single swing the boy seized Kihei in a surprisingly powerful grip. They struggled for a while and then, in front of a number of astonished villagers, Musashi threw Kihei down onto the dusty ground. The boy picked up his staff. With a wild look in his eyes he beat the swordsman until he was dead.

The sudden violence of this attack, the confidence and surprise of it, foreshadowed the way that Musashi would fight as an adult swordsman. He would go on to make ample use of unexpected tactics and overbearing aggression in most of the sixty duels that he would fight and win during his lifetime. Kihei became a footnote in history. It was Musashi who would win a glorious name as a fighter. Just three years after this first taste of blood Musashi himself decided that he would set out in search of adventure as a wandering samurai, a shugyosha.

The sixteen year old Musashi climbed up into the hills that surrounded the village of his birth. He had already given away all of his possessions and had renounced any right of inheritance on his father's property. There was no thought in his head of ever returning to this place. He climbed to a pass in the mountains accompanied by one of his dearest friends. After pausing briefly for one final look back at the village he presented his staff to the friend. Then he walked away from his childhood home and into a future of imagined fame and glory.

Two Armies
Within a year of leaving home Musashi had seen plenty of combat. The civil war between the West and the East was rapidly moving towards a climax and the entire country had been drawn into the struggle. It was easy in those dangerous days for the young man to find a place in the army of a local lord. Musashi enrolled with a small regional force that was soon swallowed up by the great army of the West. He fought in two battles and was part of the huge force that took the high ground at Sekigahara.

The western army had arrived in the valley first, tramping over rice fields to occupy the most advantageous position that stretched across two hills overlooking the valley floor. As the fog began to lift with the first glimmers of predawn light the samurai of the Western army were looking forward to the battle. The other army was roughly equal in size but the West held the high ground. And justice was on their side. They had come here to defend the legacy of Hideyoshi, their dead ruler. Tokugawa Ieyasu, the leader of the Eastern army, had betrayed the memory of Hideyoshi. It was time to bring him to heel.

Ieyasu was the lord of the great flatlands that surround modern-day Tokyo and he was the richest man in all Japan. He was fifty eight years old, extremely overweight and dressed for war in European armor that made him so heavy that he could only be supported by the strongest of horses. Ieyasu was a fearless samurai. Since his teenage years he had been leading men into battle through the most dangerous and violent period of Japanese history. He had personally climbed onto his horse fifty times to ride into combat. And yet despite his undoubted bravery he was a cautious leader, a general who preferred using brainpower rather than violence to win victories. Ieyasu had spent decades negotiating treaties to restrain powerful enemies while he concentrated his forces on overwhelming weaker opponents. He never entered a battle unless he was confident of winning. And yet here he was, seemingly holding the weaker position against an enemy whose army at least matched the strength of his own. What had provoked him to lead his troops into this narrow valley?

Lost in his own thoughts Ieyasu sat in a rough tent on a small hill some way back from the bulk of the Eastern army. Directly in front of him were thirty thousand troops and samurai generals who were loyal to him personally and to the Tokugawa family. Ahead of the Tokugawa army, stretched across the entire valley, were the smaller forces of some twenty lords who had decided to back Ieyasu. Several of these lords had travelled here because of the friendship and personal ties they had with Ieyasu. Others had joined his army because they were sure that he was destined to be the future leader of Japan. These men were making a deliberate gamble. If they fought for the winning side in this civil war they were certain to receive enormous increases in their land and wealth. Yet another group of lords were backing Ieyasu because they regarded him as simply the lesser of two evils. They could not face the prospect of rule by the men who led the Western army.

Looking down on the Tokugawa forces from higher ground was that huge Western army. Just three kilometers of ground separated the two forces and the Eastern generals stared uneasily at the enemy campfires twinkling on the hills on either flank of their army. But although it held a weaker position the Eastern army had one great advantage. Among the Western army there was no single general who could command the unquestioned loyalty of the diverse groups of samurai from different parts of western Japan. Hideyoshi did have a son but that heir to the leadership of Japan was still only a small child, too young to even symbolically lead an army in his father's name.

In the end, the task of assembling the Western coalition had fallen to Ishida Mitsunari, an unconvincing general. Hideyoshi had raised this man to the very heights of Japanese society but Mitsunari had not been promoted for his fighting skill. He was a brilliant peacetime administrator who many viewed as a schemer, a politician who pretended to be fighting on behalf of Hideyoshi's son but who actually hoped to seize national power for himself. Despite his political skills Mitsunari was dependent on the military strength of others. He personally commanded only six thousand troops at Sekigahara.

Instead, the true fighting heart of the Western army was a proven general, the aggressive Ukita Hideie. This young samurai, who was still only twenty eight years old, had often led troops into battle during the doomed invasion of Korea. As the Eastern army stumbled its way through the dark and the driving rain to take up position on the plains of Sekigahara it was Hideie who bristled with eagerness for the fight. He sent a message to Mitsunari calling for an immediate charge down the hillside to rout the unprepared enemy. His requests were ignored.

Mitsunari had good reason to be cautious. He was uncomfortably aware that his army was in reality a coalition of detachments from different regions. It could not easily be persuaded to act as a single unified force. So he waited for the daylight that would allow him to clearly determine which lords were present and how many were ready to fight on his side. In fact all of the warlords who had travelled to Sekigahara from the length and breadth of Japan were anxiously measuring the strength of the rival armies. The winner of this battle was likely to punish any losing lords who remained alive by confiscating their lands, or by forcing them into exile. And losing the battle could be a matter of life or death for even the most senior generals. Ambitious young samurai competed to be the first to enter the enemy camp and remove the head of a commander. As the battle approached there was great uncertainty on every side. Some of the provincial lords switched their allegiances on the muddy roads that led to Sekigahara. Some arrived without having made up their minds.

At the centre of the confused loyalties that surrounded this battle was Kobayakawa Hideaki. He was a young man of only nineteen years of age who had already become one of Japan's most important leaders. Hideaki was an adopted son of Hideyoshi and at the raw age of fifteen had been appointed by his father as the commander-in-chief of the invasion force in Korea. Hideyoshi's strange decision to place a boy in charge of his massive army was extremely unpopular with the battle-hardened generals. They whispered their grievances to Mitsunari and he finally persuaded Hideyoshi to have his adopted son brought home in disgrace. But Ieyasu stepped in to protect Hideaki from the anger of his father, finally convincing Hideyoshi that the boy had done his best. Hideaki undoubtedly owed a debt to Ieyasu and had every reason to hold a grudge against Mitsunari.

As the showdown between East and West grew closer the generals of the two armies had no choice but to try to win the allegiance of Hideaki and the strong samurai army at his disposal. Ieyasu made Hideyaki an offer of two large provinces in return for battlefield support. This forced Mitsunari to make an even more extravagant offer. He would, he promised Hideyaki, make him the Regent of all Japan. As the armies arrived at Sekigahara Mitsunari seemed to have won the bidding war and Hideaki duly lined up in the ranks of the Western army. But Ieyasu was much too wily to easily give up on this prize. He had kept channels of communication open to the young lord and was now convinced that he could be persuaded to switch sides at the last moment. Hideaki was the key to everything. The choice he made at Sekigahara would decide the outcome of the battle.

The confusion created by having so many disparate groups of fighters on the battlefield was added to by the lack of any straightforward system for distinguishing the two sides. A few lords had equipped their forces with coordinated sets of clothing and armor but most groups of samurai arrived at Sekigahara kitted out in a riot of colors and designs. Some wore armor and carried weapons that had been passed down from their own fathers and grandfathers. Others were dressed in a motley collection of gear that they had scavenged from battlefields or from castles they had sacked. Many of the samurai did have flags attached to their backs that displayed their local allegiance and helped them to find each other in battle.

Behind the troops, clustered around the chief generals, were senior samurai dressed in a fantastic array of battle clothing. Their armor was of the old style, designed to make them stand out on the battlefield so that their great deeds would be remembered. The leading samurai wore dramatic helmets decorated with meter high deer antlers or huge crescent moons. Many had covered their faces in gruesome battle masks.

Samurai wars had for centuries been regarded as opportunities for individual samurai to polish their personal honor. But the huge armies of the sixteenth century required a different style of combat in which coordinated action by samurai fighting in massed ranks had become more common. In fact most of the fighters at Sekigahara were foot soldiers. These lower ranking samurai, and detachments of conscripted peasants, were organized into groups of archers, spearmen and musketeers. They wore whatever armor they could lay their hands on. Almost all had some kind of chest protector and a helmet.

But faceless battle groups were anathema to the more senior samurai. These higher ranking fighters were mounted on trained war horses and carried three meter long spears that they could drive at high speed into groups of foot soldiers. They wore armor that protected their bodies from head to foot. Samurai of all ranks carried swords at their sides to be used in the later stages of battle when the enemy was close at hand. Most carried two swords of different lengths. Thousands of guns were also carried to Sekigahara. Most samurai regarded these 'foreign' muskets with distaste. They saw little honor in killing their enemies with long range gun attacks. Nonetheless, the groups of gunmen, and their heavy, primitive muskets that fired only one shot per minute were a deadly weapon that the top generals valued highly.

Clashes at Sunrise
Well before sunrise the rice fields of Sekigahara and the surrounding hills were covered in battle groups waiting in their final positions. Here and there samurai tried to snatch some sleep in their rain soaked armor. Others laughed and drank sake around impromptu campfires. At eight in the morning the fog

began to clear, revealing to each side the breathtaking scale of the other army. There was a hush among the samurai as they stared at the crowds of enemies. It seemed almost impossibly dangerous to move towards such a huge force. But this was a thrilling moment for a samurai. There was great honor to be won by being the first group to launch an attack.

Suddenly from the middle of the Tokugawa forces the aggressive captain Naomasa led thirty horseback riders in a high speed charge towards the opposing ranks. He attacked without orders, eager to be at the head of the shock troops that opened the battle. Naomasa and his men had dressed for combat in a way that was designed to frighten and intimidate the enemy. Their armor, their masks, and even their weapons had been painted scarlet. They smashed into the Western army at full speed, thrusting spears into the defensive lines that awaited them.

Groups of musketeers loaded their guns and fired into the Western ranks, slaying dozens. For two hours clouds of black smoke rose from the guns into the morning sky. Shouts and screams could be heard from those places where hand to hand fighting had broken out. Ieyasu, sensing victory, moved his command post forward to within a few hundred meters of the fighting. He was impatient with his commanders, angry and tense, knowing that most of the opposition army had not yet taken the field.

Watching from his elevated position on the left flank of the Western army Mitsunari waited for countering attacks to come from his own massive forces. The strongest Western general, Ukita Hideie, ordered his fifteen thousand men to push back into the main body of the Eastern army. Fighting spread right across the opposing lines and the plains of Sekigahara were quickly covered with samurai and foot soldiers swinging at each other desperately with their spears and swords. Thousands of dead fighters were trampled underfoot.

The Western army was holding its ground. Strong reserves were waiting on the hillside and the day would be won if they could be brought into the fighting. Mitsunari ordered signal fires to be lit. He expected that Kobayakawa Hideaki would see the fires rising and would, as the two men had arranged, order his fifteen thousand troops to charge down the slopes of Mount Matsuo to smash into the flank of the Eastern army. The enemy would scatter and would fall into the hands of reserve forces advancing from their rear. The great Eastern army would be trapped inside a four-sided box from which there could be no escape other than death. All of them would be slaughtered and Mitsunari would rule Japan.

By noon, after four hours of continuous fighting, the rice fields had been plowed into mud as bands of samurai charged backwards and forwards. But neither Ieyasu nor Mitsunari was directing much attention to the fighting. Their gaze was fixed on the huge group of fighters high up on Mount Matsuo. What was Hideaki waiting for? Mitsunari had long since given the signal for attack, and he waited impatiently for the fifteen thousand samurai to descend from their elevated position to win the battle, and so the war, for him. Ieyasu had a very different expectation. He had spent weeks communicating in secret with Hideaki and he was sure that the teenage general would prove to be his secret card. He was waiting for Hideaki to shock the Western army by turning on his own ranks. But Hideaki did nothing, he just sat unmoved on his mountain perch.

In the end Ieyasu's legendary patience and caution deserted him. He had reached the top by carefully consolidating power, fighting only when necessary. But this time Ieyasu was so agitated that he made one of the most extraordinary decisions of his life. He ordered his gunners to load ammunition into their muskets and cannon and to begin firing at the ranks of Hideaki's samurai. This desperate move had the effect of a whiplash on the young general. At last he was startled into action and began issuing orders to his troops to prepare for battle. As Ieyasu and Mitsunari looked on, holding their breath, Hideaki and his men charged down the mountainside and smashed into the right flank of the Western army.

The right wing and even the rear of the Western army was thrown into chaos as mounted samurai charged in and among their ranks from all directions. Other generals from the Western army who had been waiting in reserve on Mount Matsuo drew their own conclusions about the way the battle was moving. They quickly joined the betrayal and launched attacks on the Western units below them. The great Western army was thrown into confusion and the battle quickly became a rout. Several groups pulled out completely from the Western army to flee over the mountain passes. Those who were brave enough to put up a fight were decimated. By two in the afternoon it was all over. Samurai from the Eastern army wandered through the rice fields finishing off wounded soldiers and taking their pick of discarded armor.

Many thousands of Western samurai, by some estimates as many as forty thousand, died on the battlefield of Sekigahara. Heads were severed from bodies and laid out to be formally inspected by the Eastern commanders. So many heads were taken, in fact, that one of the rivers where the Eastern troops cleaned their grisly trophies for presentation was later renamed as Black Blood River (Kurochigawa). The remnants of the Western army, Musashi among them, fled for their lives singly or in disorganized bands. Many who had managed to escape were hunted down and killed in the days that followed. For weeks afterwards poor farmers and then crows and rats descended on the blood soaked fields to scour the mud for the belongings and the remains of the dead.

For once in his life Ieyasu had risked everything to win this decisive battle. And he had succeeded completely. He would never again be seriously challenged for power. With his brilliant mind and a selective application of force to crush the remnants of Western power he went on to establish such complete control over the Japanese archipelago that his family would rule the nation for two hundred and fifty years. Ieyasu rewarded his friends handsomely for their support. He increased their lands and gave them positions of power. He executed many of the top leaders of the opposition and punished others by confiscating or reducing the lands they controlled. Most of the rank and file samurai who had fought for the Western army now faced an extremely unpromising future. When they made the long and difficult journey back to their home regions they found that their lords, on whom they were dependent for income and employment, had been executed and their lands given away. Some of these soldiers simply gave up on the warrior life and became poor farmers. Others became ronin, wandering samurai who walked from town to town in search of employment and opportunity.

What happened to Miyamoto Musashi during this great battle? In fact, history has no record of the part he played and we can not even be sure which of the two armies he fought for. The single piece of evidence that strongly points to his participation in the Western army is that Musashi would spend the remainder of his life on the outside of society. Like the tens of thousands of other samurai who were on the losing side at Sekigahara he faced a harsh life in the new, settled Japan that emerged from the carnage of the awful battle. For years Musashi would have nowhere to call a home. Instead he wandered from place to place depending on his wits and his sword skills to stay alive. The seventeen year old youth who escaped from Sekigahara had been born into a world that was constantly shaken by violence and war. That was the way Japanese warriors had lived for generations. Although Musashi had no way of knowing it, the age of samurai wars would soon be at an end.

2. The Samurai

Conquering the Barbarians

Miyamoto Musashi was a samurai, a member of the caste of Japanese warriors who regarded fighting in battle to be the core purpose of their lives. And Musashi, like all of the samurai who fought at Sekigahara, took great pride in his status. By 1600 the martial culture of the Japanese islands could be traced back for more than nine hundred years and it was hard to imagine a world without the samurai. Japan was not the only place in the world where warriors had seized control. But here the samurai culture was uniquely important. It had shaped the destiny of an entire nation.

The first coherent accounts of warrior life in Japan date back to the seventh century, to a time when a small group of families fought their way to secure pre-eminent positions on the main island of the Japanese archipelago. These families consolidated their rule by creating a hereditary system of power. It was a system that allowed a living emperor to hand over the leadership of the nation to a relative. In time the power struggles that had given rise to the imperial system were largely forgotten. Legends were created that enshrined the divine right of the emperors to rule the nation by suggesting that they were descendants of Amaterasu, the sun goddess who had first breathed life on the islands of Japan.

At first the Japanese emperors actually controlled only a small part of the land that we now think of as Japan, the Yamato region to the south of present day Nara. But over time they expanded their power, and the idea of a single and united Yamato people, until they controlled most of the southern half of Japan. The north proved to be a harder nut to crack. The Ainu people who lived in northern Japan were ethnically and culturally quite different from the Yamato people and they were unwilling to accept the rule of the Yamato emperors. But the court desired the territory of these 'barbarians' and so the emperor created a conscription system which obliged every able bodied man aged between twenty and thirty to serve as a defender of the nation. These young men were required to arm themselves and submit to military service.

But even when they had large conscripted armies at their disposal the Yamato emperors struggled to control the skilled Ainu horsemen. The men of the north were effective and mobile warriors who fought with lightning attacks and quick withdrawals. By the end of the eighth century the imperial court, tired by a succession of defeats, began to reorganize its armies so that a stronger campaign to subdue the north could be mounted. Foot soldiers were gradually replaced by more highly skilled horseback archers who could compete with the hit and run fighting methods of the Ainu. This shift to a mounted soldiery was expensive and the cost had to be borne by individuals who equipped themselves for war. As a result, most of these new soldiers came from families who were wealthy enough to be able to provide their sons with horses, armor and training.

The new horseback army was commanded by the sons of the most important court families and at their head was placed a single individual who had been given exceptional, if temporary, powers. The Emperor awarded this soldier the title of sei-i-taishogun, or 'great general who conquers the eastern barbarians'. Both the title and the concept of a military dictator had been copied from an old Chinese tradition of appointing a single general to subdue armed groups that threatened the centralized control of the state. The new approach to military organization proved to be effective. The north east was gradually pacified and the court, with no other major threats to worry about, allowed the system of military dictatorship to fall into disuse. But the tradition of a taishogun had been established and would become of central importance in later centuries.

As the danger of Ainu invasion faded there was no longer a need for the Yamato emperors to recruit large standing armies of tens of thousands of conscripted farmer-soldiers. But the court still needed a security force and so maintained a smaller elite corps of horse mounted solders. These were the first true samurai, the armed servants of the imperial family. Even the title given to these troops reflected their service to the court; samurai is a term descended from the ancient verb saburau, to serve. However, these early samurai were not mere puppets for the emperor. Their ranks were drawn from the sons of wealthy families and the samurai were trained, equipped and supported by their own local communities. It was, from the beginning, an order of young men who were proud of their fighting skills and who were fiercely independent.

The emergence of this class of tough regional samurai was overshadowed by the brilliance of the glorious imperial court. During the long years between the ninth and thirteenth centuries, years that are remembered today as the Heian Period, Japan enjoyed a rich cultural flowering. The court in Kyoto stood at the heart of a highly privileged aristocratic class that was composed of only five thousand people out of the total Yamato population of around five million. Some of these privileged families had pedigrees so ancient that any trace of their connection to the military lay hidden in the distant past. Other aristocratic families with rural origins had more obvious ties to the samurai. But at the Heian court the warriors and the royalty mixed and intermarried with a good deal of freedom.

The Kyoto court was a place where elegance was prized above all other things. The Japanese aristocrats eagerly scoured the great civilization of China in search of ideas that they could adapt and employ in their own society. Interchange with the Chinese empire brought about important developments in religion, architecture and literature. The court was richly aesthetic. Women whitened their faces, blackened their teeth and painted false eyebrows high on their foreheads. On formal occasions they wore elaborate, twelve-layer kimono. Sensual pleasures were delighted in by courtiers who devoted a good deal of their time to moon viewing, poetic composition and seduction. These five thousand aristocrats created a world that was both highly cultivated and thoroughly decadent. Their floating world would give way to something much tougher.

Two Great Families
The end of the rule of the refined Heian court and the rise of true samurai families to the leadership of Japan began in a bitter and complex struggle among the leading families in Kyoto. The imperial family was riven by disputes over succession to the throne and these quarrels drew in two of the strongest samurai families, the Taira and the Minamoto. In 1159 these two families joined forces to rescue the teenage Emperor from a palace coup. But the young Emperor, in a fateful miscalculation, failed to express his gratitude equally. Overlooking the Minamoto family he rewarded the Taira for their help by raising members of that family to the very highest levels of society. The family leader, Taira Kiyomori, was appointed as prime minister and the Emperor took Kiyomori's daughter as a wife. To many it seemed to be an outrageous breach of the hereditary principle. Kiyomori, who was not from the royal bloodline, had become the greatest power in the land.

Kiyomori proved to be a terrible leader, a greedy tyrant who shocked the nation by promoting his own non-royal grandson to be the next emperor. Meanwhile, the Minamoto family was watching with growing anger from the sidelines as their rivals assumed more and more power. In 1180 Yorimasa, the leader of the Minamoto family, organized a rebellion against the court. But his attempted coup ended in disastrous failure. The rebel forces were crushed and Yorimasa took his own life. It was one of the first recorded cases of ritual suicide (seppuku) in Japan.

Years later the sons of Yorimasa would avenge their father's death. But at the time they were young children who were in real peril. The boys only survived, in fact, because they were taken into exile when most of Yorimasa's extended family fled to distant corners of Japan. In rural hideaways they bided their time for twenty years.

When they were fully grown the sons of Yorimasa brought an end to the rule of the Heian court and seized the power that had been in the hands of the imperial family for centuries. Their rebellion began in Kamakura, a natural fortress to the south of present-day Tokyo that is sheltered between a ring of mountains and the Pacific Ocean. In this distant stronghold Yoritomo and his courageous younger brother Yoshitsune rebuilt the Minamoto forces until they were strong enough to challenge the Taira army. The two families then clashed in a civil war that culminated in a dramatic sea battle. The Taira and most of the leading nobles were slaughtered by the Minamoto army. The infant Emperor drowned in his mother's arms So many aristocrats had died that the power of the imperial court was fatally weakened. Control of Japan shifted to a samurai government led by Yoritomo.

Yoshitsune never took a place in the government headed by his elder brother Yoritomo. In fact, the relationship between the two Minamoto brothers was a tragic one. The bad blood between the brothers became one of the most shocking episodes in Japanese history and turned Yoshitsune into one of the nation's great romantic heroes. Although the two men were both sons of Yorimasa, they had been born to different mothers and had never actually met before they united their strength to drive the Taira out of power. They had very different personalities. Yoritomo was a planner and a schemer, a natural politician with a strong eye for strategy and organization. The younger brother, who had been sent into exile from Kyoto as a baby, was a born warrior whose use of aggressive and unconventional tactics lay behind the most important victories in the war against the Taira. Yoshitsune specialized in launching shock attacks with small groups of horse mounted samurai. In one skirmish that made his name famous throughout Japan he destroyed a supposedly impregnable enemy fortress at Ichinotani by leading his troops down the steep cliffs that led to the rear of the castle. No one had imagined that an attack from that direction was possible and Yoshitsune's samurai routed the seemingly secure and numerically superior defenders.

Yoshitsune was an unconventional general in many ways and his warriors were chosen more for their fighting skill than for their noble birth. One of the most famous of his followers was Benkei, a warrior still revered in Japan today as a symbol of heroic loyalty. Benkei was a mountain of a man who is said to have reached two meters in height at the age of seventeen. He was raised as a Buddhist monk and later became a yamabushi, a member of the sect of mountain ascetics who worship the spirits of the high peaks. Like many of the monks of his time, Benkei combined religious duty with a love of the martial arts.

The first meeting of the friends is said to have taken place on a day when Benkei had decided to practice his fighting skills by taking up position in the middle of one of the central bridges in Kyoto. Benkei demanded the sword of every samurai who wished to cross the river and fought anyone who refused. He had won 999 consecutive duels and collected 999 swords when he finally met his match in Yoshitsune. After conceding defeat to the much smaller samurai Benkei made a decision to follow Yoshitsune. He would be at the side of the general for the remainder of his short life.

The two friends ended their days as hunted outcasts. Despite his vital role in the defeat of the Taira Yoshitsune fell out of favor with his older brother who had become the most powerful man in Japan. In fear of his life Yoshitsune fled north to distant Tohoku where he was finally cornered by Yoritomo's troops. The young warrior retreated into the inner sanctum of a castle while Benkei took up position on the only bridge across the moat that surrounded the building. Time after time the giant warrior cut down any attacker who tried to get past him. In the end Yoritomo's assassins stood off at a distance and peppered Benkei with arrows. They fired dozens of arrows into the body of the solitary defender who, nonetheless, continued to stand his ground. After several hours the attackers finally worked up the courage to approach Benkei who fell to the ground at their feet. Even in death he had been maintaining a defensive posture in protection of his beloved master. Inside the castle Yoshitsune took his own life.

With his brother out of the way Yoritomo was now the unchallenged leader of Japan. Breaking with tradition he decided to avoid the decadence and subterfuge of Kyoto society by locating the military government in his base at Kamakura. In 1192 the Emperor revived the ancient title of sei-i-taishogun by naming Yoritomo as shogun but it soon became clear that on this occasion the title was to be a permanent one. Yoritomo was a military dictator who passed on the rank of Taishogun to his descendants.

It was a decisive turning point. From that time onwards Japan would have two parallel systems of hereditary rule and it was the shogunate, rather than the imperial house, that would hold the real power. The armed headquarters (bakufu), as the Kamakura government was known, lasted for one and a half centuries. It created the template for an entirely new system of government, one that placed the shogun at the head of a power structure that was supported by the samurai lords of the regions of Japan. The nation had now come firmly under the control of the samurai class, a class that would hold on to its power for seven hundred years.

The Way of the Bow
The samurai who had taken control of Japan generally thought of themselves as independent individuals who only occasionally and temporarily went to war as soldiers. Most were actually farmers who lived in villages. When they were summoned to battle they travelled to join their army with whatever armor and weaponry they had to hand. Arriving at the site of a battle these rural samurai formed up in natural units with their local comrades and with foot soldiers and camp followers from their own region. The samurai fought in small groups that felt more loyalty to each other than they did to the commanding general of the army they happened to be fighting for. They were not professional soldiers but they were enthusiastic fighters who were deeply interested in acquiring the military prestige that could add to their personal honor. Honor was highly important to every samurai because it was the key to winning recognition and rewards from the local lord. A samurai war was a splendid occasion to demonstrate bravery and even a

samurai who happened to be on the losing side could still build his reputation through acts of conspicuous valor.

Samurai combat was organized in a pattern that made it clear that the fighting was between opposing groups of essentially honorable individuals. The opening stages of a battle were often extremely formal. Challenges would be called out and important samurai would dash forward to announce their names and pedigrees. Once these introductions had been completed signal arrows were fired to whistle through the air marking the beginning of battle. Only then would the horse mounted samurai close on each other. The horses that the samurai rode were important symbols of their status but they were not particularly effective as battle chargers. The Japanese mounts were smaller and less powerful than European war horses and struggled to carry men laden with armor and weapons at a gallop for anything more than very short distances.

The chief weapon of these mounted warriors was the bow. And consequently it was skill in the use of bow and arrow that was the number one qualification for a successful samurai in medieval Japan. Japanese bows were made from composites of wood and strips of bamboo that produced a fine combination of flexibility and power. Unlike European bows they were held with a grip closer to the bottom of the bow, a factor that allowed bows of over two meters in length to be held and fired from horseback.

Skillful use of bow and arrow was a matter of great pride. In the greatest Japanese chronicle of medieval war, the Heike Monogatari, there are several tales that make it clear just how important the bow was to these warriors. In the climactic battle between the Minamoto and the Taira, the Minamoto samurai lined up on the beach of Yashima Bay to face the boats of the Taira fighters. During the customary, polite exchanges before the start of battle the Taira shouted out a challenge to the Minamoto samurai. They asked them to use their arrows to attempt to strike a fan that had been hung from the mast of one of the Taira ships. One young Minamoto samurai rode his horse into the waves and, ignoring the motion of the sea and his horse, fired a wonderful shot that split the fan in half. The incredible feat was cheered by the samurai of both sides but when one over-excited Taira samurai began to dance in jubilation on his boat the young bowman loaded another arrow and, with equal skill, shot the dancing man dead.

It was the bow, and not the sword, that medieval samurai considered the weapon of choice when a private quarrel escalated into a duel. The Konjaku Monogatari Shu includes this dramatic account of a tenth century confrontation.

> The two men started galloping toward each other, arrows ready on their bows, and made the first shots. Hoping to shoot the enemy down with the second arrow, each drew the string and shot as they galloped past each other. When they had run past each other they turned their horses around and galloped back.
>
> Again they drew their strings and took aim. Yoshifumi took aim at the centre of Mitsuru's body and shot. But because Mitsuru jerked himself sidewise, almost falling off his horse, to avoid the shot, the arrow hit the centre of his sword hilt. Mitsuru himself turned back and shot at the centre of Yoshifumi's body, but Yoshifumi twisted himself to avoid the shot and the arrow hit his sword belt. [1]

Few samurai carried shields. Instead they protected themselves from the iron tips of enemy arrows by covering their bodies with armor. This protection needed to be strong enough to resist heavy arrows but also light enough that it would not exhaust the small samurai horses. The resulting compromise, known as yoroi, was a composite armor constructed from small plates of leather and iron that were tied together with silk or leather cords. The right arm, which was needed for pulling the bow, was left uncovered and the head was shielded by an iron helmet. At his waist the samurai carried a long sword and a shorter dagger for close fighting.

Face to Face

Samurai battles in the twelfth century were fluid, individualistic affairs. They involved extensive maneuvering between highly mobile forces that tried to gain advantage by seizing higher ground and by making unexpected attacks. Horseback bow-fighting was conducted at close quarters. The arrows were rarely accurate over distances greater than twenty meters and were unlikely to penetrate armor from any distance much greater than point-blank range. A samurai who had been knocked off his horse, or had his horse killed, would fight on foot with his bow and arrow. Only when arrows were exhausted would a samurai then resort to drawing his sword. This description from the Tale of the Heike (Heike Monogatari) reveals the order of battle.

> Arikuni, having penetrated very deeply into the ranks of the foe, had his horse shot from under him, and then while he was fighting on foot, his helmet was struck from his head. By this time his arrows were exhausted, so he drew his sword and laid about him mightily, until, pierced by seven or eight shafts, he met his death still on his feet and glaring at his enemies. [2]

With so many horses charging around, foot soldiers on the battlefield needed weapons that could be used against a horseman. The naginata, a curved blade at the end of a long shaft, was a popular choice of weapon for cutting down both horses and men from a distance.

> Loosing off his twenty four arrows like lightning flashes he slew twelve of the Heike soldiers and wounded eleven more. Flinging away his bow he strode across the bridge. With his naginata he mows down five of the enemy, but with the sixth it snaps. Flinging it away he draws his tachi (sword), and wielding it in the zig-zag style, the interlacing, cross, reverse dragonfly, waterwheel and eight sides at once styles of fencing, and cutting down eight men; but as he brought down the ninth with an exceeding mighty blow on the helmet the blade snapped at the hilt. Then seizing his dagger he plied it in the death fury. (2)

As samurai dismounted they were drawn into desperate close combat where their bows and even their swords quickly became irrelevant. Coming face to face with an enemy a samurai would punch, kick and and even wrestle in his heavy, box-like armor, trying to gain an opening that would allow him to end the struggle with a quick thrust of a dagger to a vital point. The following accounts from the Heike Monogatari give an impression of the mixed set of skills and the determined violence that were required to survive in close fighting on the battlefield.

> Clutching Tadazumi he pulled him from his horse, dealing him two stabs with his dagger while he was yet in the saddle, and following them with another as he was falling. The first two blows fell on his armor and failed to pierce it, while the third wounded him in the face but was not mortal.

> Rushing upon each other, they grappled fiercely so that both fell from their horses. He gripped his adversary and pinned him down so that he could not rise but he suddenly sprang up from the ground and dealt Moritoshi a heavy blow on the breastplate with his closed fist. Losing his balance at this unexpected attack, Moritoshi fell over backwards, when Inomata immediately leapt upon him, snatched his dagger from his side, and pulling up the skirt of his armor, stabbed him so deeply thrice that the hilt and fist went in after the blade. Having thus dispatched him he cut off his head. (2)

Battles began with polite greetings, continued with bloody slaughter and usually ended with ceremonies to mark the honor and dignity of those who had distinguished themselves in the fight. These ceremonies were grisly affairs that centered around viewings of the piles of bloodied heads that had been removed from the bodies of defeated samurai. At the end of battle the victorious general would sit in a formal pose as the heads were presented to him. Some of these heads would still be impaled on the end of a sword or spear. There was great competition to collect the heads of famous samurai from the opposing army and fighters would take enormous risks, even riding alone into the camp of a general, in order to secure such a noble prize. This was one sure way of increasing one's own honor and status. After the heads had been inspected the ghoulish trophies, sometimes numbering in the hundreds, would be transported to the army's home town where they were displayed on castle walls or along the banks of rivers for the edification of the local population.

Mongol Hordes

Medieval war in Japan was a collective enterprise where individualism was highly valued. But individualism on the battlefield had limitations that were sharply exposed by the Mongol invasions of the thirteenth century. Kublai Khan, ruling the huge Mongol empire from his capital of Beijing, cast an acquisitive eye over the Japanese archipelago. When in 1274 he heard that his ambassadors had been refused permission to even set foot on the shores of Japan Khan assembled a fleet and sent twenty thousand troops to invade the southern Japanese island of Kyushu. This assault from the sea was a great shock to the samurai government. Japan had enjoyed fifty years of peace and the samurai rulers of the day had little personal experience of war. They had no idea of how to take on such a large and determined foreign army.

The first exchanges between the two sides were bewildering for the Japanese samurai who had never seen an army fight like the Mongols. The Asian detachments were brutally efficient, formed around squads of foot soldiers who marched in tight formation and sent clouds of arrows flying into the air. When the Japanese samurai lined up in their accustomed manner to issue challenges and to fire the whistling arrows that marked commencement of battle the Mongols laughed at them. Worse, when samurai horsemen charged at the ranks of the Mongols the horseless invaders simply parted ranks and then surrounded the riders in a tight mass of bodies so that both men and horses could be hacked to pieces.

The methods of the Mongols were regarded as barbaric, even by the samurai. They often marched into battle behind a defensive shield made up of a string of living Japanese prisoners of war. Even more disturbingly, the Mongols liked to decorate their boats by nailing the bodies of dead samurai, and of living Japanese women, to the outside of the hulls. Most frightening of all was a new weapon that the Mongols threw into the ranks of the samurai. The strange objects exploded with a terrifying roar, spitting out flesh-ripping shards of iron. The Mongol army had brought the first gunpowder to Japanese shores, a century after it had become a weapon of war in China.

But, however disorganized they seemed, the Japanese samurai were no cowards. They fought a determined defensive battle and were greatly assisted by a kamikaze, a divine wind that blew up and wrecked many of the Mongol boats. As his fleet disintegrated Kublai Khan reluctantly withdrew his troops. Instead, he continued to send envoys to press his demands on the Japanese rulers. Tokimune, the Shogun, had these envoys executed.

The ruler of Japan had developed the courage to be able to deal so harshly with the messengers of the great Kublai Khan thanks to a series of meetings with Bukko, a master of Zen Buddhism. At first the

Shogun had been deeply shaken by the Mongol threat. Bukko advised Tokimune to sit in meditation for some time in order to discover the original source of his own fear. After a few days of silent meditation, the Shogun rushed to see the Zen priest and announced, "Finally, this is the greatest moment of my life." "Very well," said the master, "so how are you going to face this great moment?" Without hesitation the Shogun shouted "Victory!" (katsu!). "Aha", replied Bukko, "that is the roar of a true lion." This exchange between the Zen priest and the Shogun became famous and is said to mark the starting point of the rise in popularity of Zen Buddhism among the samurai.

Following this insight Tokimune received another set of ambassadors from Beijing and once again he had them all executed. Kublai Khan, who was undoubtedly taken aback by the unusual stubbornness of the Japanese, raised a huge army of more than one hundred thousand Chinese and Korean soldiers. But the Japanese fighters were better prepared for a second assault and they fought fiercely enough to drive the invaders back into the sea. Another divine wind arrived and the thousands of hastily constructed invasion boats were smashed and scattered. Kublai Khan abandoned his plans to conquer Japan.

Japanese fighting methods had been badly exposed by the massed ranks of the Mongol army but the samurai did have one great advantage over the invaders. When it came to hand-to-hand fighting the Japanese katana, razor-sharp and with a perfect balance of strength and flexibility, was vastly superior to the Mongolian sword. The invading army had been unfortunate to arrive at a time when the Japanese sword, after centuries of improvements, was approaching its perfected form. In an earlier era samurai swords had been designed to be swung from horseback and had been straight. Over time these swords became longer and curved throughout their length. There was a period when Japanese war swords became so elongated that they were longer than a man's body. These cumbersome weapons had to be carried into battle by a servant who ran behind the mounted samurai and handed over the sword in time of need. The long swords were certainly powerful, an expert could slice through an opponent's iron armor or cut through the legs of an onrushing horse. But such extreme length was impractical. In time samurai swords once again became short enough to be carried at the waist of a horseman and to be swung, with a two-handed grip, from a standing position.

The incredibly sharp and yet resilient Japanese swords were manufactured in a range of complex and secretive processes that had been developed and were guarded by sword producing families across the nation. The process of forging battle swords varied from family to family but essentially involved folding the steel many times, a method that gave the blade great strength and allowed it to be sharpened to a fine edge. Hard steel was wrapped with a cushion of softer steel to guard against brittleness. The resulting composite would be covered in clay, leaving the edge bare for separate treatment in a further series of heatings in the forge and dousings in water. The final blades, with carved channels to allow blood to flow swiftly along their length, could be exquisite. More importantly, they were the world's most effective cutting instruments. In the hands of a skilled user a samurai sword could split open an iron helmet and slice a man in half from head to toe.

Warring States

For one hundred and fifty years the Japanese islands were controlled by a samurai government based in Kamakura. This physical separation from the aristocrats in Kyoto helped to reinforce the separate identity of the samurai elite as a governing class. But the imperial house and the courtiers in Kyoto never fully accepted their position as puppet monarchs and over the years the aristocrats made a number of attempts to regain control of the nation. In 1338 yet another uprising inspired by the Kyoto aristocrats broke out but this time the turmoil was cleverly exploited by a prominent samurai named Ashikaga Takauji who seized control of the nation for himself and returned the government to Kyoto.

The descendants of Takauji were splendid patrons of the arts but proved to be ineffective rulers. Gradually the lords of the regions were able to increase their local power and to distance themselves from the rule of the Shoguns in Kyoto. The Ashikaga family itself squandered its energies in squabbles over the line of succession. In the end the delicate balance of power between the capital and the regions collapsed completely and the strongest lords of Japan marched their troops into Kyoto to contest for national power. After battles that destroyed most of the capital the struggle spread all over Japan. There was no longer any restraint on local clashes as nobody feared intervention by the Shogun. At the opening of the sixteenth century Japan was a nation in pieces. For the peasants it was a time of hardship and terror. But for the samurai this was a golden era, the age when they attained the historical highpoint of their activity and influence.

The samurai who fought in the battles of the sixteenth century regarded themselves in much the same way as their ancestors had. They were elite, individualistic fighters. But so many soldiers were needed for the frequent, large-scale battles of this era that other groups were drawn into the fighting. Regional lords began to conscript groups of peasant farmers to serve as foot soldiers in their armies. These common soldiers were joined by bands of roving mercenaries who would fight for a wage and, more lucratively, for the chance to plunder the homes and property of a defeated enemy. As the sixteenth century progressed, and battles grew in scale, the foot soldiers (ashigaru) assumed a more and more prominent role in samurai armies. The ashigaru had historically been spear carriers but now Japanese generals began to equip them with bows and arrows. Japanese armies came to resemble the terrifying Mongolian invaders of the thirteenth century. Massed ranks of archers, marched to the best positions, could fill the sky with dark clouds of arrows. Against this kind of large-scale assault the mounted samurai, who needed to get close to the enemy to launch an arrow attack, were largely ineffective.

The elite samurai grumbled constantly about having to mix in with the despised ashigaru but it was becoming obvious that a unit of foot soldiers could easily do as much damage as any mounted warrior. By the sixteenth century it was the foot soldiers, marching at the front of armies, who used bow and arrow. Spear-carrying horseback samurai, much fewer in number, were held back as shock troops. From the middle of the century foot soldiers became even more important when primitive firearms began to appear on Japanese battlefields. The first matchlock guns had been brought to Japan by Portuguese traders in the 1540s. The Portuguese guns were quickly handed over to highly skilled Japanese metal smiths who soon began to turn out replicas and even to introduce their own design improvements.

Guns were not immediately regarded as a big improvement on traditional weapons. They were useless in wet weather and were very slow to load. A single archer could fire off fifteen arrows in the same time that it took to reload a matchlock gun for a second shot. But gunpowder did bring something new to the Japanese battlefield. Groups of foot soldiers could build defensive walls and, from relative safety, fire devastating volleys into the ranks of the enemy. Oda Nobunaga was the first Japanese general to enthusiastically adopt the use of matchlocks and they played an important role in his rise to power. By the end of the sixteenth century Japan was producing more firearms than any other country in the world. A large battle, like that at Sekigahara, could involve thousands of ranged gunmen.

The sheer scale of the violence in the sixteenth century affected every facet of life in Japan. Samurai were regularly engaged in huge pitched battles but even away from the battlefield there was a good deal of violence in the air. As the bow lost status the sword became the weapon that most closely represented the identity of a samurai warrior. A good sword had great value for its owner, the best were even given their own names, and swords were carried everywhere and at all times under the belt of a samurai. From this period onwards it was skill with the sword, and not the bow, that became the ideal for every Japanese warrior.

Wandering Samurai
A battle was the most important opportunity for a samurai to demonstrate bravery and skill in a way that could be recognized by a lord. But even samurai who fought courageously in war often found themselves on the losing side. In such a situation their lord faced the dangers of having his home castle demolished and his lands confiscated. The samurai who had served this lord would find themselves suddenly unemployed and perhaps even homeless.

In this way many sixteenth century samurai were reduced to roaming the countryside. These men scratched around for ways to earn enough money to survive and dreamed of finding some new position.

It became common for masterless samurai, or ronin, to set out on foot, traveling from town to town in search of opportunity and adventure. In the popular imagination this was a new kind of samurai identity. Traditionally a warrior had been thought of as a proud, and often wealthy, horse-mounted member of a lord's army. But now it was understood that a samurai could also be a poor but noble man who faced the vicissitudes of life with nothing but the two swords and few belongings that he carried with him. He lived a wandering life of poverty and adventure that was not a cause for personal shame but could actually be a matter of great pride. The best of the ronin were believed to be scrupulously moral and determinedly independent. Famously, they were said to always carry with them a special purse that contained enough money to pay for their funeral in the event of a violent death.

A romantic image had emerged of the wandering samurai as men who deliberately welcomed hardship in the name of character training and this idealistic conception of samurai life survived long beyond the time when it had ceased to be a common practice. As late as the nineteenth century the Goden Ryu school of military philosophy recommended that samurai in training should seek out the following hardships.

- Make cold, heat and storm your friends. Travel in the depths of the mountains.
- Sleep outdoors.
- Don't save money, put up with hunger, wear only the clothes on your back.
- Take your opportunities in battle. If you meet another samurai in combat, don't behave like a bandit.
- Become a prisoner. Use your skill to escape.
- Work in the fields along with the farmers.
- Spend time alone in lonely and spirit-haunted places. [3]

A wandering samurai sought for opportunities to prove his honor and thereby to improve his employment prospects. Word of an impending battle would bring all of the unemployed samurai in a particular area hurrying to the gathering armies where they would request permission to 'borrow the battlefield' to demonstrate their courage and skill. If no battles were on the horizon samurai looked for other ways to prove their bravery. As they criss-crossed through the towns of Japan it was a matter of course for these ronin to meet and issue challenges to each other. Defeating or even killing a well known samurai brought great honor to the victor and could catch the attention of a lord who was on the look out for skilled fighters. That is why young samurai on the make, like the man Miyamoto Musashi had killed at the age of thirteen, would post open challenges to combat. The resulting duels (tachiai) often took place on the street in front of an audience of passers by. If both swordsmen were prominent figures a more formal showdown might be arranged at the home of a local lord in front of an audience of regional dignitaries.

Serious though they were, few of these duels were fought with actual swords. A match with swords would almost always result in a death or in terrible injuries. It was much more common for a challenge to be played out with bokuto, wooden training swords that had the same dimensions and weight as a real sword. This kind of fighting was somewhat safer but the heavy wooden swords could easily break an arm, or even kill with a direct blow to the head.

Most of the homeless samurai wandering from town to town in sixteenth century Japan were anxiously seeking an opportunity to settle down in a comfortable position in a pleasant castle town. But for a small elite group the wandering life was a deliberate choice. They went on the road as a kind of pilgrimage in search of meetings with other experts that would enable them to improve their skills in actual combat. Even defeat had value. It could serve as an introduction to a more highly skilled swordsman who could be adopted as a teacher.

This kind of warrior pilgrimage, known as musha shugyo, was one of the roots from which particular styles of sword fighting gradually emerged. A samurai with a strong reputation might be accompanied on his pilgrimage by a group of admirers and supporters who would take care of his personal needs in return for lessons in swordsmanship. In this way the strongest samurai gradually became teachers who were recognized masters of the sword. These masters would hold out to their followers the prospect of inheriting the deepest mysteries of the martial way. These inner truths were written on secret scrolls that would be handed over to students who had completed a long course of training.

Different kinds of sword technique can be traced back to the middle ages and several are mentioned in the twelfth century epic, the Heike Monogatari. But it was in the fifteenth century that the structures and training methods of what we think of today as sword schools began to emerge. By the sixteenth century the masters of these schools were in great demand from regional lords who had wars to fight and wanted the best teachers to prepare their leading samurai for combat. While many sword teachers were employed as castle instructors there were other masters who established independent schools, usually in large towns, and provided training to any samurai who were thought to be worthy of admission.

All of the sword schools offered an established curriculum with a range of techniques and the opportunity to practice pair drills with another swordsman under the close supervision of the master. This type of training was much safer than the dangerous method of building skills by fighting duels on the road. The key element of sword training was suburi, the repetitive practice of designated sword movements. Most schools also expected their students to take part in kata practice - sets of pre-arranged swords movements that were either performed alone with an imaginary enemy in mind or with a real partner.

The most realistic form of training offered in these schools was sparring practice with wooden bokuto. But bokuto sparring was so dangerous that almost every teacher encouraged his students to apply the restraining technique of tsumeru. Rather than striking with full power, they were expected to be able to control their strikes just at the point of contact. This required a level of control that, in itself, represented a high level of skill. Students who could pull their blows perfectly were praised by their teacher and those who hurt their partners badly were often in trouble. Such controlled practice was far from ideal - on the battlefield samurai needed to use their swords with full power but most sword schools actually provided little in the way of realistic training for battlefield fighting. One solution began to emerge at the end of the sixteenth century when some schools introduced bamboo swords that allowed students to hit each other hard without inflicting terrible injuries.

Sword training was something that almost all younger samurai did during the sixteenth century. These men flocked to the sword schools primarily to prepare for battle but there were other reasons for sword practice. The violent atmosphere of the sixteenth century made Japan a dangerous and unruly place. Even after the end of a battle the countryside would be swept by groups of poorer samurai, peasants and bandits who were looking for ways to exploit the chaos and lawlessness of the times. In this environment the sword took on an importance that made it much more than a supplementary battle weapon. Swords were now seen as vital tools for the preservation of individual safety and the protection of family members.

The Divine Sword
Miyamoto Musashi was probably the greatest swordsman of the early seventeenth century, a time when Japan was gradually returning to peace and stability. But in the rough chaos of the sixteenth century, when opportunities for real combat were plentiful, the outstanding swordsman was Tsukahara Bokuden. The violent character of the years he lived through can be gathered from the number of duels fought by Bokuden during his lifetime, said to have been more than one hundred. Thirteen of these duels were fights to the death using real swords. He is also said to have taken part in mass battles on thirty seven occasions, personally removing twenty one heads and suffering no more than superficial arrow wounds. In the course of this fighting he is believed to have killed more than two hundred opponents. Clearly, Bokuden was both a highly skilled and a remarkably fortunate samurai.

Bokuden was born in the year 1490 in Kashima, just to the north of modern-day Tokyo. No better place could have been chosen for the birthplace of a great swordsman. Kashima Shrine, hidden by a deep forest, is devoted to a god of the martial arts. Ancient Kashima legends, stretching back to the seventh century, tell of humans who developed divine sword techniques that transcended mere physical skill. By the time Bokuden came into the world his home town had been an important centre of sword training for centuries. As a child he was able to watch the sword work of two of the greatest experts of the fifteenth century, Matsumoto and Kunii. These two men created the Kashima Divine School (Kashima Shin Ryu) of swordsmanship, a style that still exists today more than five hundred years after its creation. At the age of ten Bokuden vowed to learn all of the secrets of the sword and began to train daily with these two teachers among the towering cedars that surround Kashima Shrine.

When he reached the age of seventeen Bokuden left Kashima to set out on the first of the three long training pilgrimages that would define his life. He traveled far and wide through the provinces of Japan, seeking out great sword masters and fighting duels. On a balmy May afternoon in 1510 Bokuden made his first recorded appearance as a fighter. He had challenged Ochiai, the leading swordsman of one of Kyoto's eight sword schools, to a duel at Kiyomizu Temple. Ochiai, who was a large and powerful man of forty at the peak of his power, accepted the challenge from the young stranger and happily advertised the time and location. He must have regarded such a rash challenge as an opportunity to take another easy victory that could only serve to heighten his already peerless reputation. Crowds hurried up the steep hill to Kiyomizu looking forward to seeing the master swordsman humiliate a novice. And when the two samurai faced off there was nothing to suggest that a shock was in the offing. The young man from the north was physically unimpressive. But all of a sudden, with one flash of his sword, Bokuden knocked Ochiai to the ground. He loomed over the startled expert, pressing the flat of his blade against the man's chest. Then, to the amazement of all, he turned on his heel and strode away.

1510 was a time of war and skilled swordsmen were in high demand. Bokuden was quickly showered with offers from the lords who had heard about his victory. Even the lord who employed Ochiai invited Bokuden to his home and offered him a job. Bokuden turned the proposal down. On the following morning the young man was just about to leave the mansion when he noticed a shadow behind a screen in the entrance hall. A samurai, sword drawn, leapt out in front of Bokuden. Recognizing that the attacker was Ochiai Bokuden instantaneously took one step backwards, drew his short sword and stabbed his onrushing attacker. The great sword instructor fell dead at Bokuden's feet.

This skillful young man soon made a name for himself as an absolutely fearless and violent warrior. In battle he was notorious for storming into the command camp of the enemy, forcing his way to the centre of the officer ranks and removing the head of the enemy general. He also took place in a number of duels against famous martial artists.

On one occasion he fought with Kawajira Nagato, a naginata master who had a bone-chilling reputation. In the hands of an expert a naginata is a formidable weapon that easily outreaches the longest sword. Nagato had never been defeated by a swordsman and he had killed many. Before a duel he liked to loudly predict the precise manner of his opponent's impending death, announcing that he would remove both arms and then take the head. When a fight began he would swing his naginata in wide, sweeping circles that made it almost impossible for even the strongest swordsman to block his blade. Bokuden's friends and followers begged him not to be so foolish as to attempt a duel with Nagato. But when the two met it was the swordsman who had an easy victory. As Nagato began to swing his naginata Bokuden stepped inside the range of the sweeping blade and sliced the weapon in half. He then did the same thing to his opponent.

By the age of thirty seven Bokuden felt that he had accumulated enough experience to create his own school of swordsmanship, the Kashima New Way (Kashima Shinto) School. It is a battlefield sword style, with deep stances and attacks that are designed to penetrate the gaps in an opponent's armor. Bokuden is said to have taught a single-stroke (hitotsu-tachi) technique that required great skill and nerve. He trained his students to leave their bodies exposed long enough to convince an opponent that there was an opening for a successful strike. The technique involved waiting for that attack to begin and then instantaneously pre-empting it with a flashing swing of the sword.

Many lords would have liked to have employed Bokuden as a teacher or as an officer in their army. He preferred the independent life of a wandering samurai. After opening his sword school he set off on two more musha shugyo training pilgrimages but now he traveled as a famous man. He was no longer a ronin wandering the country paths alone and was accompanied on tour by a procession of disciples who carried his possessions and flew his beloved hawks.

At the age of sixty-six Bokuden retired to Kashima where he built a small hermitage and concentrated on passing on his sword skills to his three adopted sons. Bokuden and these three sons gave rise to the well-known story of the samurai father who decides to put the skills of his three sons to the test. Bokuden placed a wooden pillow above one of the sliding doors in his house so that it would fall on the head of anyone who attempted to enter the room. The youngest son, sensing the falling pillow, magnificently drew his sword and sliced through the pillow before it could graze him. The middle son reached for his sword but then stepped aside, dodging the falling pillow. Finally, the oldest son paused at the entrance and, smiling, extended his hand to catch the pillow as it fell. Bokuden, the story tells us, commended his oldest son as being the only one of the three to have completed his training successfully. This great swordsman lived to the age of eighty-one, a remarkable achievement given the violent circumstances of his life. In many ways he lived a life that samurai in later periods would idealize but would never be able to replicate. Japan was about to change, and to change dramatically.

3. The End of War

High and Low

Sixteenth century Japan was a terrible place. Tens of thousands of young men died on desolate battlefields; bandits roamed the countryside raiding helpless farming villages at will; social progress came to a grinding halt. And yet most Japanese people today look back on the sixteenth century as a time that was certainly fearful but also exciting and enthralling. It was an era when history seemed to move at a greater speed and when lives had real meaning and purpose. These thirteen decades, lasting from 1467 to 1600, would be known to historians as the Period of Warring States.

For the samurai who were born in later generations this time of war was remembered as the summit of their culture. It was a world where fighting skill was valued above all other things. And it was a time that changed Japan completely. The fighting lasted for so long that it destroyed the old system and allowed a new order to emerge from the chaos. This new Japan, a peaceful nation ruled by an enlightened warrior class, was created by three friends who came to the fore with great courage, willpower and intelligence. Their names were Nobunaga Oda, Hideyoshi Toyotomi and Ieyasu Tokugawa.

At the outset of the fifteenth century the power structures of Japan were strangely distorted. It was generally accepted that ultimate authority rested with the Emperor. But the imperial family was almost completely powerless and it had been so since the middle of the fourteenth century when efforts to restore imperial power had been crushed. Actual power lay in the hands of the Ashikaga family, a hereditary line of Shoguns. But the Ashikagas were unimpressive dictators. They maintained gorgeous palaces in Kyoto and devoted themselves more enthusiastically to the arts than they did to ruling Japan. With little leadership from above the regional lords had plenty of room to become both independent and proud. In 1467 the relationship between Kyoto and the lords of Japan broke down completely. The Shogun died and confusion over the line of succession encouraged several regional lords to march their armies into the capital. Kyoto quickly became the stage for an open struggle for power.

In the year 1467 Kyoto was a wealthy and beautiful city that had been home to the Emperor and his family for more than 500 years. It was a planned city, designed on a grand pattern of parallel streets that ran exactly north to south in imitation of Chinese urban planning. Nestled at the foot of the hills around the city were huge temples that were headquarters to Japan's greatest religious organizations. Scattered among these temples were dozens of luxurious villas including the dazzling Golden Pavilion, built as a retirement home for a Shogun. Right at the heart of Kyoto was the grandest estate of all, the Imperial Palace.

But the armies that marched into the city in 1467 took little interest in the architectural treasures around them. They attacked and counter-attacked through these gilded streets for ten years, reducing the city to a ruin that was finally abandoned by every citizen who had a safer place to go. Kyoto had never known such destruction; a devastation that was mourned in a contemporary poem.

> Our beloved capital has become a wasteland
> And even the sight of sparrows rising from the sunset
> Gives way to tears (4)

In the end, when there was nothing much left to fight over in Kyoto, the warlords withdrew their troops to continue fighting in other places. In the chaos that swept throughout Japan even the family of the Emperor suffered. The lands and the tribute that had always sustained the imperial family were seized by others. The Emperor's home, around which much of the fighting had taken place, was badly damaged and the broken and crumbling palace walls became overgrown with weeds and briars. When a new Emperor took up his post in the year 1500 he was so poor that he had to spend the first twenty one years of his reign struggling to raise enough money to pay for his own enthronement ceremony. Shocking rumors circulated throughout Japan that the impoverished young Emperor was behaving like a common merchant. To raise funds he was busily painting and selling samples of his own calligraphy.

At the outset of the sixteenth century there was no central power strong enough to keep the regional lords under control. The Ashikaga Shogun, Yoshimasa, was the only leader who could have prevented the chaos in Kyoto. But he spent most of his time attending poetry readings and designing a wonderful Silver Pavilion that he hoped would outshine the Golden Pavilion built by his grandfather. In this power vacuum the old social order began to collapse. Constant fighting allowed a new class of the most ambitious, intelligent and violent warriors to rise to high positions. Some of those who became lords in the sixteenth century had started their lives as mere soldiers in regional armies, or even as peasants. The speed of social change was so bewildering, so different from all that had gone before, that a word was coined to describe the atmosphere of the time: gekokujo – the overthrow of the high by the low.

By the latter part of the sixteenth century a new group of leaders had emerged to take control of the regions of Japan. These 120 lords, known as daimyo, came from a variety of backgrounds. Some were the offspring of old, powerful families; some had fought their way to the top from the most humble of beginnings. Violence was the common factor in the rise of most of these lords but brainpower and strategy were of almost equal importance. With the whole country at war the most effective lords built strategic alliances with neighboring powers that allowed them to concentrate their fighting strength in one direction at one time.

With the entire nation in chaos an ambitious daimyo was forced to regard the building and maintaining of peace treaties as a matter of the highest priority. Many lords demonstrated their commitment to agreements by making their own sisters and daughters symbolic hostages of the peace when they married them off to their neighbors and rivals. If a suitable marriage seemed difficult to arrange some daimyo took more extreme measures. They simply seized the children of the neighboring lords and held them as human shields.

At this time of rapidly shifting allegiances the rulers of Japan also had to worry about the loyalty of their best samurai. The most effective fighters could easily find employment in other armies. In most cases the lords tried to secure the loyalty of their warriors by handing out parcels of land to samurai who could in turn impose taxes on the local peasants. Land was necessary to win the backing of skillful fighters and so winning local wars was vital. It was the key to maintaining existing troop levels as well as to attracting new fighters. Loyal samurai repaid their lords by paying taxes, by fighting in battle when required and by persuading the farmers on the land they controlled to fight as foot soldiers. In later centuries a great deal would be made of the loyalty of the samurai. In the sixteenth century the most notable feature of this loyalty was that everyone believed it had a price.

Is There Anyone Alive Who Will Not Die?
Sixteenth century Japan was a world of sudden combat, negotiated truces and regular betrayal. For a leader to survive in this unforgiving environment a sharp intelligence and ferocious determination were essential qualities. No other warlord in Japanese history was fiercer or more confident than the man who finally rose above the decades of conflict to re-establish some kind of central control over his dissolute nation.

Oda Nobunaga was a young samurai who inherited the leadership of his family in 1551. He did not inherit very much more. His father was a brave fighter but controlled only one part of the small, unimportant province of Owari in present-day Aichi. Owari was a rural province that boasted no important towns and the Oda family could only muster an army of a few hundred samurai. They were overshadowed by more powerful neighbors who pressed in on them from every side.

As a teenager Nobunaga fought in many battles to help his family keep their small patch of Owari out of the hands of a number of predatory competitors. He was unknown in Kyoto and was nobody's pick for the future ruler of Japan; and yet this was a daring and ambitious young man. Nobunaga liked to fight and as he learned how to lead the small army at his disposal he attracted other young fighters. He recruited these warriors with little regard to their class background or social manners. Many young men from humble families, including the brilliant Hideyoshi, found themselves fighting at Nobunaga's side.

Less than ten years after he first became the head of the Oda clan the young Nobunaga won a startling victory that made him famous throughout the nation. On the eastern border of Owari lay the much more extensive, and wealthy, lands controlled by the Imagawa family. The Imagawa were one of Japan's greatest samurai families and the head of the family, Yoshimoto Imagawa, was at the height of his power. Yoshimoto was a successful warrior in his thirties, a sophisticated samurai who like to blacken his teeth in the style of the Kyoto aristocrats and to perfume his hair.

Like many other regional lords Yoshimoto had been keeping a careful eye on the political shifts in the capital and considering the best time to make a strike for power. In 1560 he gathered a powerful army of twenty five thousand samurai and foot soldiers and prepared to march on Kyoto. Owari just happened to be directly on the route that the Imagawa would take on their way to Kyoto. Yoshimoto had no doubt that it would be an easy task to swat the little army of Owari aside if it impeded him in any way. As the Imagawa began to march into Owari Nobunaga called a conference of his generals. They advised him to be cautious, to withdraw into the mountains, or simply to surrender to an army that was too big to defeat. But Nobunaga was twenty seven years old and he was not willing to bend the knee to anyone.

On the morning of the battle that would make him famous Nobunaga rose in a splendid mood. He began the day by singing some lines from a well-known drama: 'Life lasts for fifty years, nothing but dream and illusion. Is there anyone alive who will not die?' Then he called for his armor and sat eating breakfast in full battledress. Scouts reported that the Imagawa army was camped in a narrow gorge near Okehazama. They had spent the night celebrating a victory and many of the troops were still asleep, or suffering from hangovers that were intensified by the heat of the hot summer day. Nobunaga moved out, leaving a small force in place that he had surrounded with many banners to give the impression that his army was holding position. He then quickly and silently led most of his troops, numbering less than three thousand, to the hills above the gorge.

As the Owari samurai reached Okehazama a thunderstorm broke and the Imagawa troops who were up and about scattered to take cover under the trees. Seeing that his chance had arrived Nobunaga called the attack. His horsemen charged, seeming to appear out of the rainclouds. At great speed they raced in and among the ranks of the confused and frightened Imagawa. As the noise rose Yoshimoto mistook the ruckus for the sound of his troops continuing their party from the previous evening. He marched out from his tent to restore discipline. Out in the open he was cornered by Nobunaga's shock troops who swiftly cut his head from his body. Confused and frightened the remainder of the army scattered.

The extraordinary and unexpected defeat for the Imagawa made everyone take notice of Nobunaga for the first time. Before long the great lords of central Japan moved to sign peace treaties with him. But there was no peace treaty offered to the Imagawa family; they never recovered and by 1564 their proud history had come to an end.

Nobunaga was simply the most aggressive and determined samurai general to emerge from a generation of Japanese men who been bred to fight. His violence took him to the top. After his first great victory at Okehazama he continued to win again and again on the battlefield until, in 1568, he was ready to march on the capital. By this time the family of the Shogun was in complete disarray, their energy absorbed in internal squabbles. The rulers of Kyoto could offer no resistance to Nobunaga when he rode into their city at the head of a massive army. He was thirty four years old and he was the first general in decades who had proved to have the toughness and vision to establish some kind of control over the disorderly nation.

Cover the Earth with War
Nobunaga held onto his newly won power with great force. He happily applied violence as a tactic and shed so much blood in the early stages of his rule that the other great lords of Japan slowly came to the conclusion that they might as well accept the leadership of this upstart. Nobunaga won his battles by using new technology and new tactics. Muskets and gunpowder had just been introduced to Japan by Portuguese traders and Nobunaga immediately recognized their military value. He reorganized his armies, reducing the numbers of horse mounted samurai and replacing them with foot soldiers who could carry and fire the primitive guns of the time. In order to arm these new troops he seized control of Japan's ports and mining operations and set up factories that could provide him with a steady supply of guns.

The new ruler was proud of his reputation for violence, a reputation that proved very useful because it deterred others from attempting to challenge him. To make sure that everyone understood his purposes he had his own personal seal redesigned so that it read Cover the Earth with War (Tenka Fubu 天下布武). The samurai who marched under Nobunaga's banner fought with the pitiless resolve of their chief. They had a chilling determination to win at all costs and showed little mercy to their enemies. This description of the conclusion to a battle, written by one of Nobunaga's generals, demonstrates the attitude of his warriors.

> We lay in wait at Hachiman for our final vengeance. Three times we met them, pursuing and crushing them. We took the heads of the dead. The others we chased into the lake. (5)

If anyone was not yet convinced that Nobunaga had the resolve to hold onto power there could be few remaining doubts after his frightening decimation of the temples on Mount Hiei. This assault on one of the most treasured and sacred sites of Japanese Buddhism thoroughly shocked the Japanese who lived at that time and four hundred and fifty years later still has the power to disturb.

Mount Hiei is a broad peak that looms over the north-eastern corner of Kyoto. It had great significance for the rulers of Japan because the north-east, according to Chinese tradition, is the demon-gate, the source from which evil flows. To protect the city a great temple complex was founded on Mount Hiei in 788 by Saicho, the founder of the Tendai sect of esoteric Buddhism. The followers of Saicho eventually carpeted the nine hundred meter high peak of Mount Hiei with hundreds of temple buildings that made it one of the most important centers in Japan for the training of Buddhist monks. Many of the greatest figures in Japanese Buddhism had spent months or years in religious training on the cool mountaintop that hovered high above the muggy capital. The monks were untroubled by the secular armies below as they maintained their own army of warrior-monks known as sohei. These fighters were not always of a particularly religious disposition, most were actually conscripts or mercenaries. But the warrior monks were well organized and close enough to Kyoto to have a foot in the door of Japanese power. Frequently they marched down into the capital to burn and loot the city over what they claimed were religious disagreements with the secular authorities.

Nobunaga, who had established his headquarters just a few miles south of Mount Hiei, was unwilling to tolerate the shadow of these rebellious monks hanging over the city that he had conquered. On one dark evening in 1571 his troops completely surrounded the broad mountain. Sounding horns, they began to march up toward the summit and the ancient buildings of Enryakuji Temple, the spiritual home of Tendai Buddhism. The mountain's army of warrior monks desperately tried to stave off the attack but they were overwhelmed by Nobunaga's relentless samurai who proceeded to set fire to every building in sight. Thousands of structures were set alight and monks, women and even children were indiscriminately slaughtered. So many buildings burned, it was said, that Lake Biwa, the great inland sea to the east of Mount Hiei, grew warm to the touch. As smoke rose from the devastated mountain the skies over Kyoto were blackened for three days.

After this assault on religion Nobunaga made his next move against his strongest remaining secular opponent, Azai Nagamasa. Nagamasa was the lord of Omi, a province just to the east of Kyoto. Like many other lords he had forged a tactical alliance with Nobunaga who had responded by marrying his sister to Nagamasa to secure the deal. When Nagamasa later broke from this pact and joined forces with another enemy Nobunaga was infuriated. He assembled a large army that defeated the troops of Nagamasa at the battle of Anegawa and then spent the ensuing three years ruthlessly hunting down the leaders of the scattered opposition.

One of those leaders was the young Shogun, Asakura Yoshiaki, the man whom Nobunaga had left in Kyoto as a puppet king. Yoshiaki resented the role he had been forced to play and spent years plotting against Nobunaga. In the end, Yoshiaki threw his lot in with the remaining forces of Nagamasa. Nobunaga responded to this alliance of enemies with contempt. He raised war taxes from the residents of Kyoto to pay for a campaign against the Shogun, closing his eyes to the fact that Kyoto was, on paper, the Shogun's capital. Those who refused to pay the new tax had their houses burned to the ground.

Yoshiaki, the last of the Asakura Shoguns, was driven into exile but the rest of his family fought on in a bitter war against Nobunaga. When another Asakura, Yoshikage, joined forces with Nagamasa he was hounded by the troops of Nobunaga. They surrounded Yoshikage's castle, razed the buildings and forced him to commit suicide. In the end Nobunaga's army managed to trap the leader of the opposition, Nagamasa himself, in his castle. He too was forced to commit suicide. Nobunaga, who was determined to have no further revolts, also had Nagamasa's mother tortured and killed and meted out the same treatment to Nagamasa's son and heir. With all of his enemies dead the delighted Nobunaga carried their heads back to Kyoto where he had them displayed in public. Later, it was said, he had the head of Nagamasa lacquered so that it could serve as a grisly ornament on festive occasions.

The unrelenting violence that Nobunaga had deployed against all of his enemies shocked the country and proved a strong disincentive to any further challenge. But Nobunaga had not yet conquered Japan, in fact he now directly controlled only about one third of the nation. He did, however, rule over the most important part of Japan and here his power was absolute. Despite his strength Nobunaga showed little interest in titles or in becoming Shogun. He did deign, however, to show some sympathy for the impoverished Emperor and awarded his family enough land and income to allow them to regain some degree of aristocratic self-respect.

Nobunaga clearly felt that he had become untouchable. His egotism showed in the way he condescended to the royal family and bullied his most loyal lieutenants. The following lines from an extraordinary letter of thanks to the wife of Hideyoshi show that Nobunaga was capable of treating even his best and most important general in the manner of a rather cruel cat playing with an insignificant mouse.

> I particularly looked with admiration upon your features and your appearance which seemed doubly beautiful since we last met. That your husband is said to be ceaselessly dissatisfied is a great wrong, beyond words. However far he searches the bald rat will never again find anyone like yourself. Become strong as a wife and do not give into jealousy. It is best, in your role as a woman, to leave some things unsaid. Please show this letter to Hideyoshi. (5)

But Nobunaga was entirely focussed when it came to military action and he cleverly used his position of power in the centre of Japan to build up his armies into an irresistible fighting force. He expanded the production of muskets in his factories to a point where his army could muster three thousand foot soldiers armed with guns. They were drilled to form disciplined ranks that could rain continuous fire from one row while the other rows were reloading their gunpowder. These guns were devastating when used against the horse mounted samurai and spear carriers of the regional lords. After years of hard struggle Nobunaga was able to win his later battles so easily that he began to find some space in his action-filled life for relaxation. He built an impressive castle at Azuchi and began to revel in the civilized pursuits of the capital. The war lord from the countryside became something of a sophisticated Kyotoite. He organized elaborate performances of noh drama, held cherry-blossom viewings and recruited the greatest tea masters to lead public tea parties.

Seizing Power
Just when Nobunaga was beginning to enjoy his life at the very top of Japanese society a bitter, and perhaps fitting, twist ended his life. In 1582 he was suddenly betrayed and killed by one of his senior generals, Akechi Mitsuhide. It was a shocking treachery that has unclear origins. The prevailing theory told a complicated tale of a family whose leader had been executed by Nobunaga. The family had wrongly believed Mitsuhide to be behind the execution and had kidnapped MItsuhide's mother and tortured her to death. Crazed by grief, the explanation went, Mitsuhide decided to revenge himself in a dramatic coup-d'etat.

Nobunaga was enjoying a stay at a Kyoto temple, Honnoji, with only a small detachment of guards for security. He was practicing his beloved tea ceremony with some of the city's masters when the temple was surrounded by Mitsuhide's troops who set fire to the buildings. Nobunaga, seeing that there was no hope of escape, took his own life. At the same time in another part of Kyoto Mitsuhide trapped Nobunaga's oldest son and heir and had him killed. The dogs of war had returned to the capital. In just one day, at the very height of his power, Nobunaga had lost his life and his family had lost their position. Every lord in the land set about preparing for the battles that were sure to come.

Mitsuhide's coup had been rapid, perfectly-planned and chillingly effective. He undoubtedly expected that the death of Nobunaga would be followed by several months of uncertainty and consolidation as the regional lords considered how to respond. If he could hold on to power in Kyoto the enfeebled imperial house would come round to accepting his coup and the rest of the country would fall into line. But if Mitsuhide believed that he would be given time to settle into power he counted without the resolve and self-confidence of his greatest rival.

Toyotomi Hideyoshi, one of the leading samurai generals behind Nobunaga's dramatic rise to power, was a genius in waiting. He had been a loyal soldier in the army of Nobunaga but the sudden death of his lord gave him the perfect excuse to seize power for himself. He took his chance and did so with the brilliance and self-assurance that would enable him to completely dominate Japan for the ensuing twenty years.

Hideyoshi's counter-coup began instantly, within hours of receiving the news of Mitsuhide's betrayal. He broke off from the battle he had been fighting at the time and quickly reorganized his forces for a march on Kyoto, gathering extra troops along the way. Just eleven days after Nobunaga's death Hideyoshi fell on Mitsuhide's army. It was a completely mismatched battle that was over in two hours and Mitsuhide, as he tried to flee, was captured and killed. Hideyoshi carried the traitor's severed head to Honnonji temple where he placed it with respect and honor before the spirit of the dead Nobunaga.

Hideyoshi is undoubtedly one of the very greatest figures in Japanese history, a commander so brilliant and daring that he can be favorably compared with Napoleon. He was a great military leader but, more importantly, he played the decisive role in steering Japan through a transition away from violence to the peaceful and unified society it would remain for centuries. The scale and the speed of his achievement is breathtaking. Within eight years of Nobunaga's death he ended the terrible civil war that had dragged on for one hundred and thirty years and established settled control over the entire country. He reformed the tax system, the class structure and the administration of Japan, shaping institutions that would last for generations. He was just as aggressive as Nobunaga but in Hideyoshi brute force was combined with a strong and subtle mind, a mind that was capable of placing strategic goals above the pleasures of immediate victory. Hideyoshi had great vision and complete confidence in his own ability to achieve that vision. In the end, however, it was his supreme self-confidence that brought about his fall. Like Napoleon, he believed that his ability was limitless. But not even Hideyoshi could conquer the entire world.

Little Monkey

Hideyoshi rose to the summit of the Japanese warrior class from the most unimpressive of beginnings. He was born in 1536 into a peasant family in the province of Owari. From the very beginning his destiny was linked to the family of Nobunaga who ruled Owari. Hideyoshi's father was probably a peasant who may have gained fighting experience by combining farming with some foot-soldiering for the Oda family. But the father died early and the seven-year-old was left to the precarious fate of a fatherless boy in an impoverished rural family. Hideyoshi did not even have any of the advantages of great strength or physical beauty that might have helped a farm boy to make his way in society. On the contrary, the surviving portraits of Hideyoshi show a thin man, lined with worry. He was not a striking figure. Little wonder that the physically imposing Nobunaga had enjoyed giving Hideyoshi insulting nicknames such as 'bald rat' or 'little monkey'.

The rise of this poor farm boy, who did not even have a surname, to the rulership of Japan was an astonishing twist of fate. It was the ultimate symbol of those strange times that had been called gekokujo, times when even those of low birth could aspire to the heights. In the early stages of his rise Hideyoshi was helped by his connections to the Oda family, a family who were much more interested in fighting than they were in social protocol. Nobunaga had surrounded himself with the best fighters he could find without respect to their family pedigree. Hideyoshi first joined this democratic samurai army in 1558 and he would spend the next twenty-four years fighting as a soldier, and eventually as a general, in the same ranks.

For the first ten years of his career as a fighting samurai Hideyoshi was invisible to history. He finally appeared as a brilliant young leader in 1567, in the final year of struggle that preceded Nobunaga's seizure of power in Kyoto. When Hideyoshi was charged with the task of taking a supposedly invincible castle at Inabayama he ignored the advice of much older and more experienced generals and decided to build a rough fortress in full view of the castle defenders. This rival fort, where horses and armor could be protected, allowed Hideyoshi to assemble forces close to the point of attack and made a final victory possible.

Hideyoshi became well known for his intelligent and unconventional leadership. In 1582 he again faced the problem of seizing an impregnable castle at Takamatsu. This time Hideyoshi had a nearby river dammed so that it would overflow and create a lake around the castle that made any kind of resupply impossible. Hideyoshi was patiently waiting for the surrender of the rapidly weakening defenders when word came that Nobunaga was dead. Immediately he sent a message into the castle to the effect that he would spare the lives of the defenders and their families if the commander himself committed suicide.

The deal was accepted and the castle commander took a boat out onto the surrounding lake where he slit his belly open in full view of both armies. Hideyoshi was freed to race his troops to Kyoto.

Preserve the Nation in Peace

Just one month after Nobunaga's death a conference was called at Kiyoshi Castle to choose a new leader and to divide up the deceased leader's extensive territories. Among the generals who gathered Hideyoshi was the most powerful, and the most likely successor to Nobunaga. But several of the other generals despised him for his low birth. The kind of person they really wanted to succeed Nobunaga would be a weak figurehead who would allow them to hold onto the lands they already possessed and give them opportunities for future expansion. Accordingly, they voted to appoint Nobunaga's three-year-old grandson as his successor. But Hideyoshi was completely undisturbed by this outcome. He was sure that he was going to be the man to succeed Nobunaga. In a letter written just after the conference at Kiyoshi he made it clear that he was already planning to take supreme power and to hold it.

> I shall order my men to level the castles of the whole land to prevent further rebellions and to preserve the nation in peace for fifty years. (5)

But first Hideyoshi would have to deal with a group of generals who had aligned themselves around Nobunaga's son, Nobutaka. They were led by Shibata Katsuie, a grizzled war veteran who more than any other resented the rise of this farm boy and was eager to fight him. When the two factions finally clashed on the battlefield it was Katsuie who drew first blood, defeating the portion of Hideyoshi's army that had been sent to contain him while Hideyoshi himself pursued Nobutaka.

This was a moment of great danger for Hideyoshi and he responded with the alacrity and brilliance that typified his leadership. When the news of his losses arrived Hideyoshi instantly turned the samurai troops under his command around and marched them fifty kilometers in a single day. Drawing near the enemy Hideyoshi formed a group of aggressive mounted samurai and sent them in without warning to attack the much larger force led by Katsuie. The older general was taken completely by surprise as these raiders arrived out of nowhere. His army was scattered and he fled to take refuge in his own castle at Echizen. Hideyoshi was merciless in pursuit of this enemy and rival. He trapped Katsuie in his castle and ensured his death. Hideyosh's own account of the end of his quarry is both dramatic and chilling.

> Katsuie climbed to the ninth floor of his keep ... and declared his intention to kill himself to serve as an example to later generations. His men, deeply moved, shed tears which soaked the sleeves of their armour. When all was quiet to the east and the west, Katsuie stabbed his wife, children and other members of his family, and then cut his stomach, together with over eighty retainers. (5)

Having disposed of his most important rivals for power Hideyoshi proceeded to unify and completely pacify Japan for the first time in living memory. He achieved this great feat in just seven years using the strength of the large armies that he could now assemble and his control over imports, mining and production; a control that allowed him to arm his forces with unprecedented quantities of muskets. Many regional lords quickly recognized, as they had with Nobunaga, that Hideyoshi was simply too strong for them to challenge. They limited their ambitions to protecting and consolidating their own regional power bases. All of these lords sent family members as hostages to Hideyoshi and he adopted many of their sons as a mark of his commitment to the peace. By 1584 the daimyo of thirty-seven provinces had sworn their allegiance to his rule. Even many of those who had resisted the rule of Nobunaga signed up to Hideyoshi's coalition when it became clear that he was a leader who was inclined to be generous to his former enemies. Hideyoshi was intelligent enough to realize that cultivating the image of a benevolent ruler would make it easier for him to strike treaties and mend bridges. All over Japan provinces signed up to the gathering peace.

Hideyoshi began a grand program to bring all of the lands of Japan under a single rule. He dealt ruthlessly with those who opposed him but made grand gestures of reconciliation to anyone who quit the fight. Nobunaga had persecuted the great religious centers of Hiei, Negoro and Koya but Hideyoshi helped the monks to rebuild their temples once they had sworn to permanently forsake arms. Only one huge holdout to his power remained, the massive southern island of Kyushu which was as wealthy as it was independent. Using the support and allegiance he had secured from central and northern Japan Hideyoshi ordered every lord under his command to raise troops. He then marched on the south at the head of the largest army Japan had ever seen, by some counts over a quarter of a million strong. It was an irresistible force and within four months Kyushu had surrendered.

Hideyoshi was now if full control of almost all of the Japanese islands but his lust for power was, if anything, still growing. A letter written to his wife at this time shows how far his ambition was beginning to stretch.

> By fast ships I have dispatched orders to Korea to serve the throne of Japan...
> Even China will enter my grip; I will command it during my lifetime. (5)

Reshaping Japan
Hideyoshi dreamed that he could conquer the entire known world but first he needed to reshape Japan. The land he ruled was a disorganized patchwork of large and small domains, of religious fiefs and of areas where no one was quite sure who was in control. The sword had ruled Japan for more than a

hundred years and the threat of violence carried more weight than any law or any faith. It was a dangerous and unstable country. Hideyoshi's greatest legacy lies in the firmness and speed with which he moved Japan away from chaos and laid down a basis for the Great Peace of the ensuing centuries.

He began by confiscating the weapons of the farmers. All swords, muskets and spears, he ordered, were to be collected from the peasantry and would be melted down into raw materials that would be used to construct a great metal statue of the Buddha. The disarming of the peasantry was, perhaps, the most dramatic of all of Hideyoshi's reforms. Armed peasants had been fighting in wars for centuries and they regarded the opportunity to take part in battle as their one avenue for social mobility. When the farmers lost their swords they also lost any possibility of being able to rise into the warrior class, as Hideyoshi himself had done. Swords and other weapons were now to be restricted to the samurai. For the first time the samurai became a definite class, separated out from the rest of society.

Hideyoshi's next move was to freeze the social classes into a rigid system. Just as farmers were now forbidden to bear arms, the samurai would no longer be allowed to engage in farming or to switch their allegiance from one lord to another. Both farmers and samurai were forbidden from engaging in trade or in other kinds of labour. The movements of all classes were greatly restricted, especially for farmers who now became tied to their villages and for samurai who would be required to remain close to their lords. Up to this point many of the poorer samurai had been providing for their families by growing rice in the intervals between periods of war. Hideyoshi's orders meant that they could no longer support themselves by working the land and would be entirely dependent on their lords for both salary and accommodation. Samurai began to move out of the villages and into the castle towns. Urban samurai were encouraged to separate themselves from the lower classes both physically and socially. Rules were issued about the clothing of the samurai (silk-lined), their hairstyles, the parts of town where they should live and even the kind of food they should eat (white rice).

Hideyoshi made these huge social changes possible by gathering information from all over Japan in a series of surveys. For the first time, the acreage and production of each village was accurately recorded. With this new information the regional lords were able to impose taxes on every farmer, and the taxes were high. Whatever the wealth or poverty of a village, whatever the size of the harvest, two thirds of all production was to be handed over as tax to the local lord. It was a truly draconian tax system but the villages had been stripped of their armaments by official sword collectors and now had no way to physically oppose the tax inspectors. The lords, on the other hand, now had a permanent samurai class at their disposal and could easily provide the muscle required to enforce tax collection. Most of the taxes raised from the peasantry were used to maintain the luxurious lifestyles of the lords and their families.

The remainder was divided up among the samurai in proportion to their rank. In this way Japanese society was divided into a privileged caste of consumers and an exploited class of producers.

Hideyoshi was guarded by his own personal forces in Kyoto but when he wanted to gather a large army he was reliant on the support of the regional lords. The surveys and tax system made this a simple task. Each regional lord was responsible for conscripting, training and leading his own samurai into battle. With the information from his surveys Hideyoshi could impose martial service as a specific tax on each lord, linked to the wealth and production of his villages. These lords continued to be independent of the Kyoto government and to manage their own armies but Hideyoshi ensured his control by strengthening the old safeguards that were designed to ensure loyalty. Up to a thousand close relatives of all the most powerful lords of Japan were required to live in compounds close to Hideyoshi's palace. These aristocratic hostages formed a flesh and blood barrier to any idea of revolt and acted as a ready-made samurai aristocracy for the capital. Hideyoshi, who had grown up on a farm, was undoubtedly delighted to be able to choose his concubines from among the daughters of the greatest lords of Japan.

With the nation now at peace Hideyoshi set about the task of rebuilding Japan from the ruins of the endless war. He began with destruction - the dismantling of the hundreds of castles that crowded the countryside. These castles had made it possible for local clashes to drag on for months at a time. Hideyoshi appointed castle destruction officers who were placed in charge of clearing away fortifications and defensive structures. Without these strongpoints for rest and resupply, war became much more of a gamble for even the most aggressive generals. In place of the old forts Hideyoshi encouraged the construction of permanent castles that were designed for defense, like the gorgeous and dramatic eight-tiered Himeji Castle. These new castles were built as peacetime centers of regional administration and were very different from the rough battlements that they replaced. Hideyoshi even extended his pacification measures to the seas around Japan. He took strong measures to bring piracy to an end in Japanese waters and encouraged foreign traders to take advantage of the newly becalmed sea-lanes.

The Uncrowned King
Hideyoshi greatly relished the constructive aspect of leadership. In a relatively short period he did more to reshape Japan than any other single individual in its history. He selected important towns to become centers of administrative and business power, usually providing these towns with an elegant new castle. But it was in the devastated Kyoto, still by some distance Japan's largest and most important city, that Hideyoshi would have his greatest impact.

Hideyoshi established himself at the very centre of the capital by building a personal headquarters on part of the grounds of the Imperial Palace. His new mansion, which he named Home of Gathered

Pleasure (Jurakutei) was no rough fortress. It was a dazzling and elaborate complex that was constructed by one hundred thousand laborers from fine materials that were transported to Kyoto from the length and breadth of Japan. With its two moats, a theatre, tea rooms, moon-viewing rooms and accommodation for several concubines, the Jurakutei was designed for the comfort and leisure of a cultivated king. Sadly, the building no longer exists. In fact it only stood for seven years until it was razed by Hideyoshi himself in the gathering madness that would cloud the end of his life.

The renewal of Kyoto involved all of its citizens, from the highest to the lowest. The Imperial Palace was rebuilt and the imperial family was finally provided with sufficient income to help them forget the decades of humiliating poverty they had endured. At the foot of the hills pressing in to the eastern edge of the city Hideyoshi erected the largest building in Japan to house a massive statue of the Buddha, the very same statue that he had used as an excuse to confiscate the swords of the farmers. A great wall was built around the entire city and new bridges across the Kamo River were constructed. Hideyoshi rezoned the city, ordering monks and their acolytes to demolish dozens of temples and rebuild them in the area that he now decreed to be a teramachi, or temple town. Closer to his own mansion he moved out the commoners and created a zone to house military commanders and aristocrats. In this purposeful rebuilding of the capital we can see the same strength of mind and self-confidence that Hideyoshi had displayed on the battlefield. Under his direction Kyoto rose from the ashes of war to become once again one of the most important and beautiful cities of Asia.

Hideyoshi never officially became a shogun but in every other way he behaved as if he were the uncrowned king of Japan. Unlike the radical Nobunaga, who had despised the pomp of the aristocrats, Hideyoshi understood the reverence that almost all Japanese people still held for the imperial family. He took lessons in court etiquette and allowed the Emperor to officially appoint him as Regent, the second highest position at court. In 1588 Hideyoshi invested a huge amount of time and money in arranging a visit by the Emperor to the Jurakutei. It was a lavish event that stretched over five days and began with Hideyoshi leading the Emperor to his Imperial ox-cart to begin the very short journey between their respective homes. The splendid procession was followed by days of feasting, music, theatre, poetry readings and gift-giving.

Hideyoshi also made unprecedented efforts to win over the masses. One year before the Emperor's visit he had organized Japan's biggest ever tea party in the grounds of Kitano temple. He invited people of all classes who were serious about tea, put his own most precious tea implements on display and personally served tea to more than eight hundred citizens. Hideyoshi followed the tea party with public cherry-blossom viewing parties, visits to distant shrines and boat trips. His great love, however, was the theatre. With his usual irrepressible enthusiasm, Hideyoshi decided to become an expert in the dramatic arts. He called the greatest teachers and performers of noh theatre to his mansion and instructed them to train him to be a performer. Before long he was demonstrating his new skills in front of the Emperor.

Amid all these pleasures there was still some fighting to do. One single family had not accepted the rule of Hideyoshi. The Hojo family controlled the great plain that surrounds present-day Tokyo and to their south, blocking the route from Kyoto, was the region commanded by Tokugawa Ieyasu. They expected that they would have the support of the powerful Ieyasu and that this would give them the strength to hold out against the capital. It was a great shock to the Hojo when Ieyasu threw his lot in with Hideyoshi and marched north to attack them. The Hojo family withdrew their forces to Odawara Castle, a strong point that dominated the coastal chokepoint between the high mountains of Hakone and the ocean.

Hideyoshi made preparations for his final battle on Japanese soil with a leisurely self-assurance. He had no doubts that the Hojo army could be easily crushed and ordered the lords of Japan to provide him with two hundred thousand samurai and foot soldiers. Fleets of ships and wagons were assembled to supply the huge army from Osaka. Unhurriedly Hideyoshi moved his forces into place, surrounding Odawara with a double ring of moat and wall. "I have placed the enemy in a birdcage," he gloated as he settled in for a lengthy siege.

As the besieging army waited for the inevitable surrender of the Hojo their quarters took on something of the atmosphere of a holiday camp. Hideyoshi and his generals lived in great comfort and had their concubines installed in nearby mansions. Vegetable gardens were planted to ensure a supply of fresh food. Merchants, entertainers and craftsmen swarmed around the camp where money was being freely spent. After six months of this enjoyable phony war the resistance of the Hojo family crumbled. They opened the gates to Odawara Castle and were placed under a guard of fifteen hundred soldiers. The noble family were allowed a polite interval to bathe, to dress in their finest clothing and to compose their farewell poetry. Then, as expected, they set about the task of publicly ripping open their own bellies with sharp knives. As a reward for his support the extensive and wealthy lands of the Hojo were handed over to Ieyasu.

The Spirit of the Four Seas
By the age of fifty-four Hideyoshi had brought all of Japan under his control. Just eight years later he would be dead and those eight years were to be shrouded with obsession and frustration. The ruler of Japan had long made it clear that he had ambitions that stretched far beyond the shores of his own nation. A Jesuit priest who met with Hideyoshi at this time reported that he openly discussed launching a war to conquer the very heart of Asian civilization. As every educated Japanese person knew, this

meant China. It was undoubtedly intended to be a war that would shape his legacy. It turned out to be Hideyoshi's greatest failure.

In 1592 a huge Japanese army entered Korea. It was a tough army, steeled by decades of battles fought in Japan, equipped with thousands of muskets and tightly organized. The Korean people were helpless to defend themselves in the face of this terrifying force and scattered from its path, taking time only to burn the capital of Seoul. Hideyoshi, who thought of Korea as a mere stepping stone, laid plans for the destruction of the Chinese armies. He would, he firmly believed, bring an end to the Ming dynasty and enthrone the Japanese Emperor in Beijing. The self-confidence that had served Hideyoshi so well throughout his life was beginning to transmute into megalomania, as a letter he wrote at the time suggests.

> Throughout our nation of more than sixty provinces, I have pacified all people and governed with mercy and affection. Everything – excepting no foot or inch of land – has entered my grasp... Henceforth, even if a land be thousands of miles distant ... I shall build the spirit of the four seas as one family. (5)

The Japanese leader sent letters demanding tribute and land from Okinawa, Taiwan and the Philippines. He must be obeyed, he threatened those far away nations, as his power was divine.

> At the time my mother conceived me, she had an auspicious dream. That night a ray of the sun filled the room as if it were noontime. (5)

Whether these disturbing communications were the first signs of incipient madness or mere diplomatic saber rattling it is difficult to discern. At first all of his warnings and threats seemed to be simply bald statements of fact. The Japanese army raced north and within three months had crushed all opposition in Korea to reach the border of China itself. The Korean fighters had long since given up trying to directly challenge this huge, disciplined army. Instead they began to fight with guerrilla tactics, burning crops and attacking the long supply lines that stretched back to the southern coast of Korea. It was at sea, in fact, that the war was lost. The Japanese had no history of naval warfare and their ships were no match for the small Korean navy that was brilliantly led by the admiral Yi Sun-sin. Although they were reduced at one point to only thirteen boats the Koreans outfought the Japanese at sea and were able to greatly hamper the ability of the Japanese army to resupply. At the same time a large Chinese army drove south from their borders and retook Seoul from the Japanese.

Little more than a year after Hideyoshi had launched his glorious invasion of Asia the campaign was over and the great Japanese army returned to the homeland. This was Hideyoshi's first experience of a defeat that he could not easily reverse and he took it as a personal humiliation. In response he did his best to convince the world, and perhaps himself, that the Japanese withdrawal from Korea had been purely tactical. He sent letters to China suggesting that Korea should be equally divided between the two powers. To the Korean royal family he sent letters demanding hostages. No replies to these demands were received. Hideyoshi had finally reached the limits of his might and abilities. He could now comprehend that Asia would not easily fall to the same storming tactics he had used to conquer Japan. Reluctantly, Hideyoshi turned his gaze to home.

After straining for so many years to reshape the world about him Hideyoshi seemed to sense for the first time that even he was mortal. In the last years of his life he shifted his energies toward attempts to establish his legacy and to create a dynasty. There was a terrible warning for him in the way the Oda family had lost all of their power and position at one stroke when Nobunaga and his son were murdered on the same day. Hideyoshi wanted a different ending for his own family but he first needed to produce a suitable heir. His palace was full of attractive women and any one of them could, in keeping with Japanese tradition, have served as a suitable mother for his heir. Indeed, he had already fathered a boy with his favorite concubine Chacha but that boy had died as a toddler. What a pity, he complained about one of his adopted daughters, a spirited and intelligent child, that she was not a man.

Finally, rather reluctantly, Hideyoshi decided that Hidetsugu, the son of his sister, would inherit his power to rule Japan. This nephew, who was already in his early twenties, was groomed for the succession by being promoted to the court position of Regent. Hideyoshi even moved out of Jurakutei, his beautiful Kyoto palace, and installed his nephew in those luxurious surroundings. But Hidetsugu was not given much time to enjoy his new status as the prince in waiting. Less than two years after he had become Regent Chacha threw the succession plan into chaos by producing another son. This event not only ruined Hidetsugu's chances, it placed Chacha herself in a powerful position. Perhaps the pregnancy was not entirely fortuitous. Chacha was an extraordinary woman, a true product of sixteenth century Japan. She was the daughter of the same Nagamasa Asai whose lacquered head had been a table ornament for Nobunaga's dinner parties. Later Hideyoshi had killed her mother's second husband and had taken the most beautiful daughter, Chacha, for his own pleasure. Mysteriously, despite the fact that Hideyoshi surrounded himself with women, Chacha was the only one who ever bore him a son. In 1593 she gave birth to a boy named Hideyori and the great Hideyoshi became a doting father.

By this time Hidetsugu had settled into his position as the second most powerful man in Japan. He had gone to battle alongside his uncle and certainly expected to inherit his power. But perhaps Hideyoshi felt that there was something lacking in Hidetsugu's character. The nephew seems, even by the brutal standards of that time, to have had a cruel streak. He was said to practice his swordsmanship on condemned criminals and to conduct target practice with both bow and musket on unfortunate farmers working in their fields. Whatever the reasons, Hidetsugu lost everything before his young cousin had even reached the age of two. In a twist that is still difficult to fully understand the boundless patronage of his uncle suddenly became a murderous enmity. Hideyoshi sent his nephew into exile and, shortly afterwards, ordered him to commit suicide. Hidetsugu's young children, his relatives and his leading followers were dragged through the streets of Kyoto and executed in public. The gorgeous palace that had been Hidetsugu's home, the Jurakutei, was torn down and all of the important lords of Japan were summoned to Kyoto to take oaths of loyalty to the toddler Hideyori.

Something had changed. The brutality of Hidetsugu's removal from power was not typical of the rational way in which Hideyoshi had built his position. The ruler seemed to want to make it clear to Japan that he would not tolerate any squabbling over power when he was gone – and he publicly destroyed an entire family just to make that point. The small boy who was now designated to be the next leader of Japan was sent to live in the safest place in the nation, the huge castle at Osaka.

Hideyoshi took care of his own needs by building another massive and elaborate pleasure complex in Fushimi, close to the southern edge of Kyoto. Once again his home was designed to be a luxurious base for the pursuit of the cultivated arts – poetry, tea and theatre. Hideyoshi commissioned the greatest playwrights of the age to create a series of ten noh dramas that told the story of his life. He personally acted in the leading role and liked to order hapless citizens that he passed in the street to visit his palace to enjoy the regular performances.

But he was not to have a peaceful retirement. In 1596 Hideyoshi received the greatest humiliation of his life. He had sent communications to the rulers of China suggesting a peace treaty between the two nations. Japan and China, he suggested, should divide Korea, and the daughter of the Chinese Emperor should be married into the Japanese royal family. He waited impatiently for a reply to his suggestion, a suggestion that would at least bring an honorable conclusion to his failed invasion of Korea. Letters in the sixteenth century could take months to travel from one capital to another but at long last messengers bearing a reply from Beijing arrived in Japan and were transported with great honors to Osaka Castle.

An entire day was spent on formal exchanges of greetings and on presentations of gifts. On the second day Hideyoshi and the greatest lords of Japan assembled to listen to the counter-proposals of the Chinese Emperor. They expected substantial concessions. It was only common sense, they all felt, for Japan to now be recognized as the greatest power in Asia. A Japanese monk stood up in front of the assembled guests to read a translation of the letter from the Forbidden Palace. It was a brief and stunning message: "We hereby recognize Hideyoshi as King of Japan". There were gasps of anger. The

Chinese leadership had conceded nothing at all. They had not even taken the trouble to try to understand Japanese politics. It was an unforgivable and infuriating insult.

Hideyoshi, beside himself with rage, immediately ordered another invasion of Korea. Once again a huge samurai army was assembled and once again it wreaked havoc on the Korean mainland. So many Koreans were killed, in fact, that the Japanese army had to give up the cumbersome process of transporting entire heads back to Japan as souvenirs of their victories and instead began to remove and pickle the ears and noses of dead Korean soldiers. A grisly relic of this invasion, the Mimizuka (ear-mound) can still be visited in Kyoto today. It is said to contain the mutilated ears and noses of some thirty eight thousand Koreans. Despite all of the carnage the second Japanese invasion was no more successful than the first one had been. The Korean army and navy fought a tough guerrilla war, supply lines were compromised, and within two years Hideyoshi had been forced to once again order the withdrawal of his samurai forces.

The frustrating end to the second invasion of Korea coincided with the ebbing away of Hideyoshi's life. In 1598, lying on his deathbed, the ruler called the great lords of Japan to his palace at Fushimi and ordered them to swear allegiance and protection to his five year old son. He appointed an inner council of five of the strongest lords to protect the boy. Nothing, he protested with the last of his strength, is more important to me than the safety of my child Hideyori. And then the genius who had transformed Japan died at the age of 63. Hideyoshi had dominated Japanese society so completely that it was difficult to imagine what the future would be like without him. What, everyone wondered, could possibly take his place?

The Samurai Prince
The answer to that question had already been settled in the mind of Tokugawa Ieyasu. He was the lord of the extensive lowlands that surround present-day Tokyo and he was, in his own cool and patient way, just as great a man as Hideyoshi. Ieyasu was a brilliant, fearless and determined samurai but he was not driven by the kind of romantic belief in his own destiny that had taken Hideyoshi to the heights and then pushed him over the top into madness. In his own, measured way Ieyasu achieved the one thing that had eluded his two great predecessors. Following in the footsteps of Nobunaga and Hideyoshi he united Japan; but he also established a hereditary system of rule that would keep his family in power for centuries. Ieyasu fathered nine sons who would inherit his rule over a unified nation and he died a peaceful death in a pacified land at the age of seventy-five.

Ieyasu had been born into a very different Japan, a turbulent vortex of war and shifting allegiances. He was the product of a love match between a seventeen year old father and a fifteen year old mother that ended when the two families fell out and Ieyasu's father was forced to reluctantly return his teenage bride to her family. At the age of six Ieyasu was sent as a hostage to the Imagawa family, was kidnapped en route by the Oda clan, and was finally returned to the Imagawa at the age of eight. Although he was officially a hostage, the young Ieyasu was raised as a samurai prince by the Imagawa who were one of the most distinguished and cultured families in the nation. In the manner of the times he matured quickly, leading men into battle for the first time at the age of seventeen and fathering his first child at eighteen. One year later Nobunaga crushed the Imagawa army and Ieyasu was finally free to return to the modest territory of Okazaki where he had been born. Quickly, he made the first of what would prove to be a long series of wise strategic decisions by electing to offer his support to Nobunaga. It was an excellent choice; his alliance with Nobunaga would last for twenty-two years and would help to make Ieyasu one of the richest and most powerful lords in Japan.

For the next twenty years Ieyasu fought regularly in dangerous battles to expand and defend his own family's territory. He also fought several times in support of Nobunaga and came to know Nobunaga's best general Hideyoshi well. It is quite remarkable, in fact, how closely intertwined the lives of these three giants of sixteenth century Japan actually were. Ieyasu unhesitatingly used force when it was necessary and diplomacy when it was possible. By the brutal standards of the times he was a relatively restrained leader but he could be harsh to his enemies.

On one occasion Ieyasu's anger was aroused by the betrayal of a trusted servant. His approach to punishment was bloodcurdling. He began by crucifying the man's wife and his four children. He then had the culprit paraded through town on a horse, facing backwards, with a banner advertising his crimes. Finally, the unfortunate man was buried up to his neck in the ground, his fingers were sliced off and nailed to a board in front of his eyes. Beside the board a bamboo sword was provided for any passer-by who might like to add to the man's agonies by taking a cut out of his neck. The traitor died after seven days of this torture.

Ieyasu, like many of his contemporaries, was capable of great cruelty but he could also display an exceptional sensitivity. Even in his dealings with enemies Ieyasu could be courteous. During a siege in 1580 he surrounded a garrison that soon ran out of food. The defenders, realizing that death was near, asked Ieyasu to send a famous singer from his camp to perform for them. Ieyasu not only agreed but personally spent hours helping the singer to choose appropriate pieces for the occasion and then had him placed as close as possible to the besieged castle. The audience climbed into a tower where they listened to the singing in floods of tears. At the end of the concert one of the defending warriors left his castle to offer thanks and gifts to the wonderful singer. The following morning Ieyasu launched his final attack on the castle. It was met with a brave, determined, and completely futile defense. The garrison was slaughtered.

Ieyasu was in Kyoto in 1582 when the city was rocked by the betrayal and murder of Nobunaga. Ieyasu was among the best-known and most loyal supporters of Nobunaga and he was now in deadly danger. Kyoto was full of hostile troops so Ieyasu decided to attempt an escape to the north, an escape that required him to make a six day journey without guards through lands that were infested by enemies and bandits. It was the most imperiled week of his life. One story from his dramatic escape tells of Ieyasu's ship being boarded by agents of the enemy. Ieyasu hid himself among the cargo but was almost discovered when one of the searchers decided to thrust a spear repeatedly through the packages to make sure that no-one was being concealed. One spear thrust sliced into Ieyasu's thigh but, acting instantly, he silently placed a cloth on the spear blade to wipe away the blood as the spear was withdrawn. With no sound or blood to give him away Ieyasu remained undiscovered.

Nobunaga had not given much thought to his succession as he had certainly expected to live for many more years. After his death the two most powerful samurai in Japan were now Ieyasu and Hideyoshi. Hideyoshi was the older man by six years but it was common knowledge that he was not of true samurai blood. When it became clear that Hideyoshi intended to take power Ieyasu decided to oppose him. In doing so he presented himself as a loyal follower of Nobunaga and as a protector of Nobunaga's family, a stance that won him temporary support from many of the regional lords. The opposition of the two great men finally came to a head in 1584 when they brought their respective armies to Komaki. Warily, the generals prowled like two tigers from castle to castle but held their forces back from an all out battle. They allowed only limited clashes and constantly shifted their armies. In the face of this stalemate Hideyoshi, who had plenty of other battles to fight at the time, finally withdrew his troops.

Having come so close to an outright clash, the two men now seemed to recognize that they were faced with an opponent who was both intelligent and dangerous. Seeing clearly that a clash would only allow them to damage each other, perhaps fatally, they took steps to defuse their rivalry. In the way of the times the samurai generals took formal steps to renew their friendship. Hideyoshi offered his half-sister as a bride to Ieyasu and, after Ieyasu accepted this gesture, Hideyoshi sent his own mother to visit the newlyweds at Ieyasu's castle. Here, he subtly inferred, is a hostage so valuable that you can feel safe enough to travel to Kyoto to pay your respects to me.

When Ieyasu finally made his way to the capital Hideyoshi breached the usual protocol for a formal visit by slipping into Ieyasu's quarters on the evening of his arrival and pouring sake for him to drink. "I have come from nothing," he told Ieyasu. "If Kyoto sees you, the greatest lord in the land, paying respect to me it can only strengthen my position. I will do the same for you." At their public meeting the next day Hideyoshi was as good as his word. He placed Ieyasu's followers in better seats than those given to his own retainers. Charmed by this gesture of respect Ieyasu decided to accept the situation. He would continue to be the second power in Japan.

The two men were now partners and fought together at the siege of Odawara that led to the destruction of the Hojo family. As a reward for his help in achieving this victory Hideyoshi handed Ieyasu complete control of the eight provinces that had been under the control of the Hojo. In return, Ieyasu ceded the five provinces that he had previously governed to Hideyoshi. It was a bargain for peace. Ieyasu was pushed further north, away from Kyoto and at a sufficient distance from Hideyoshi to free himself from central control. As he surveyed the new lands he had been awarded Ieyasu decided to build his capital on the site of a small village called Edo. It was a historic decision – within a hundred years this unimpressive settlement of a few hundred houses and a small castle would become the world's largest city.

Shogun
Soon Hideyoshi was dead and the remaining lords of Japan were left to once again warily eye each other as rivals for power. Gradually the samurai of the land coalesced into two opposing camps – a Western army that declared itself loyal to the young son of Hideyoshi and an Eastern army led by Ieyasu. As soon as it became clear that there were now two rival centers of national power a series of battles and skirmishes broke out across the country. One such battle took place at Otsu, a few kilometres from Kyoto and was viewed by many of the city's residents who brought packed lunches and teapots to a hillside where they could picnic while enjoying the spectacle of samurai warriors in combat.

But there were few spectators at the great final showdown between the two armies at rural Sekigahara where the Western army was destroyed by Ieyasu's brilliant manipulation of the loyalties of the rival commanders. After the battle Ieyasu quickly set about redistributing the wealth and power of the nation. His supporters were rewarded generously while enemies were executed, exiled or had their lands stripped away. More than ninety lesser lords were completely dispossessed. Attempting to draw a line under the civil war Ieyasu made a gesture of reconciliation by marrying his seven year old granddaughter to the eight year old son of Hideyoshi. In 1603 he marked his seizure of state power by accepting the historical title of Shogun. It felt like a new beginning. Japan had been without a shogun for decades as neither Nobunaga nor Hideyoshi had wanted the title.

As Shogun, Ieyasu lived in luxury that greatly outshone that of the Emperor. He was much the richer of the two. But he was less interested in the pomp and circumstance of rule than in the information it brought to him. Ieyasu was an intellectual by disposition, a man who had a large map of the world displayed in his palace and who would often have the leading Buddhist monks and scholars of the day brought before him to debate philosophy and science. He became ruler at a time when European explorers were just beginning to brave the long, exhausting journey to the far East. Ieyasu's active, inquiring mind enthusiastically welcomed the knowledge and weaponry brought by travelers from Spain, Portugal and Holland.

There was a good deal in European learning that was new to Ieyasu but he also had much to astonish his visitors. Japan was, despite its isolation, perhaps the most civilized country of the early 17th century world. Europeans were taken aback by the elaborate manners of the Japanese and impressed by their sewage systems and daily baths, a standard of hygiene that was almost unknown in the Europe of the time. A Spanish visitor, mistakenly believing that Ieyasu was the Emperor, described with awe his visit to the court of the Shogun in 1609.

> The style and decoration of these apartments was a thing worth seeing. The ceilings were bright with gold and on the walls were paintings. On the dais the Emperor sat on a round seat of green. He wore loose robes of green satin ornamented with gold brocade. In his belt were two swords, his hair was done up in a coloured band. He was a stout, heavily built old man between sixty and seventy years old, with a most dignified bearing.[6]

Ieyasu formed one close relationship with a foreigner, a friendship that has been famously retold in James Clavell's bestselling novel Shogun. William Adams was the English navigator of a Dutch ship that had barely survived the arduous journey to Japan in 1600, arriving with most of its crew either starving or dead. Ieyasu had the remaining sailors thrown into jail and stripped the boat of its cannons, many of which he used to great effect at the battle of Sekigahara. Eventually Ieyasu freed Adams and, realizing that the sailor had a fine mind, probed him for information on geography and mathematics. The failed invasions of Korea had made it clear to the Japanese administrators that their naval technology was primitive and ineffective. Even the tiny sixteenth century vessel that Adams had sailed in from Europe was vastly superior to any Japanese ship. Ieyasu gave Adams the task of designing and building ships. The Englishman was barred from leaving Japan but was granted with an income and an estate that allowed him to enjoy the lifestyle of an upper-level samurai.

Adams was a Protestant and cleverly used his influence to make Ieyasu more suspicious of the motives of European Catholic missionaries. Ieyasu finally proclaimed a law that forbade samurai to become Christian but he never persecuted the Christian faith to the extent that later Shoguns would. He was fascinated by the outside world and strongly encouraged the creation of centers for trade between Japan and other countries. He even wrote warm letters to the kings of England, Holland, Spain and the

Philippines inviting them to engage in commerce with Japan. No one could have predicted that only thirty years later his grandson would firmly close almost every avenue of trade and contact between Japan and the outside world.

With Ieyasu at the helm of Japan Edo became the administrative centre of the nation and the Shogun set about using his wealth and power to transform that sleepy village into a capital worthy of his name. The scale of the work was astonishing. Three thousand ships were commandeered from the four corners of Japan to transport huge rocks that were used to build the outer wall of Edo Castle. Each ship could carry only two of these rocks and one hundred men were required to drag, roll and push a single rock into place. The outer walls of the castle, the same walls that can be seen today, stretched for five miles and enclosed fifty acres of grounds. Ieyasu did not stop at building a castle. Entire hills were flattened and the soil used to fill in and reclaim land from Edo Bay. Aqueducts were constructed to bring fresh water from the mountains into town. In order to guard against revolt the daimyo were ordered to make annual trips to Edo to pay their respects to the Shogun. These wealthy leaders needed suitable housing for their families and servants during these visits and so began to put a good deal of their tax incomes into the pockets of Edo merchants, entertainers and builders. A huge construction boom began in the years following Ieyasu's elevation to the Shogunate that would continue for most of the seventeenth century.

One Must Not Hurry
Ieyasu was determined to pass on the control of Japan to his descendants and he took a dramatic step toward achieving this by retiring in 1605, just two years after becoming Shogun. His son Hidetada travelled to Kyoto to receive his appointment as the new Shogun from the Emperor. Ieyasu fully intended to continue ruling from the shadows but first he had to deal with the one threat that still troubled him. Hideyori, the young son of Hideyoshi, was alive and enjoying an independently powerful and wealthy life in the greatest castle of the land at Osaka. The young prince was still only a teenager and was tied to the Tokugawa family through his political marriage to Hidetada's daughter. But the Toyotomi name and the loose alliance of samurai who still felt an allegiance to the family of Hideyoshi had not been erased by the crushing defeat of Sekigahara. Japan was still an unruly country and it was still full of restless and heavily armed samurai. Very many of these samurai were now masterless and they were anxious to see a war that would bring them employment and opportunities for glory.

Ieyasu, who was a doubly cautious man, decided that he could not live with the threat to his family that was embodied in the young Hideyori. At first he took a fiscal approach to containing his rival. Hideyori had inherited much of his father's wealth and was one of the richest lords in Japan. Ieyasu encouraged the teenager to get involved in various rebuilding schemes that included a vastly expensive project to renovate the great Buddha in Kyoto. But even as Hideyori was being distracted the supporters of the Toyotomi family began to regroup behind the scenes. They did not dream that they had the strength to directly challenge Ieyasu but it was obvious that he was aging. Perhaps his death would give them an opportunity to strike and to restore the Toyotomi rulership over Japan. Slowly they built up the massive defenses of Osaka Castle, preparing for a future struggle.

Ieyasu was not about to give the Toyotomi followers time to create a dangerous army. In the winter of 1614 he conscripted troops from all the regions of Japan and, for the first time since 1600, a huge army assembled to surround Osaka Castle. But entering the castle would be no easy task. Osaka was the largest fortress in Japan and was powerfully defended with several rings of walls and hundreds of cannon. The castle was also now packed with thousands of samurai, many of them mercenaries. It was a fortress that was too strong to be taken in haste and so the encirclement turned into a long siege. Various tactics were employed to break the will of the defenders. When a messenger rode out from the castle to request peace talks his fingers were chopped off and he was sent back into the castle with 'hideyori' branded into his forehead. On several occasions when the defenders were asleep late at night the surrounding army sent cannonballs flying in among them, hoping to shatter their nerves. Arrows carrying propaganda messages urging instant surrender were fired into the castle grounds.

Ieyasu displayed the strength of his great army on every possible occasion by lining them up in view of the defenders but at the same time he was secretly sending peace negotiators into the castle. It was a strategy that is still known in Japan today as gripping the throat while stroking the back. The defenders were under intense pressure and, when cannonballs began to crash into the living quarters of Hideyori, they decided to accept the offer of a negotiated peace. It was agreed that some of the outer defenses of the castle would be voluntarily dismantled and that the Shogun and his army would simultaneously withdraw peacefully. What the defenders did not realize as they struck the deal was that Ieyasu was playing with them as a cat plays with a cornered mouse.

The peace agreement proved to be a disaster for the defenders and is remembered in modern Japan as a good example of the foolishness of appeasement. As soon as the deal was struck Ieyasu sent thousands of workmen to the castle ramparts where they began demolishing walls and filling in moats. Their work went far beyond the very limited reduction of defenses that had been agreed in the peace pact but the defenders who had opened the castle gates were now in a hopeless position and they did not receive much sympathy from Ieyasu when they complained. Although the confrontation was officially over it soon became clear that the issue of Osaka Castle had not been finally settled. Now that the castle was in such a weakened state Ieyasu's advisors urged him to attack and destroy it for good. On Hideyori's side the generals, who still commanded thousands of samurai, argued for a desperate battle that would drive away the Shogun's forces and give the Toyotomi supporters time to rebuild their defenses and their army.

Just three months after peace had been declared Ieyasu and his son led their great army back to Osaka. The castle samurai, knowing they could never survive another siege, came out to face the much larger forces of the Shogun and fought with the ferocity of desperate men. For a while their bold counter-attack seemed to be winning the day but the sheer weight of the Tokugawa numbers finally pushed the defenders back into the castle. The leading samurai charged in behind the retreating defenders and set the inner defenses of the castle ablaze. Hideyori and his mother, trapped and hopeless, took their own lives. In the aftermath Ieyasu had Hideyori's young son, the last heir to the Toyotomi line, executed. Seventy two rebel lords and thousands of their followers were beheaded. The heads were displayed on planks on the outskirts of Kyoto - rows of severed heads, stretching as far as the eye could see. Ieyasu and his family had totally eradicated the last shreds of resistance to their rule. They would not be seriously challenged again until the nineteenth century.

Ieyasu died one year after this conclusive victory at the age of 73. As he aged he had grown corpulent but his will had never weakened. He was a man of vigor, a man who had fathered twelve children, fought in ninety battles and caused the deaths or expulsions of thousands of enemies. But the key ingredient in Ieyasu's character was his patience. He tempered the hot blood of Nobunaga and the egotism of Hideyoshi with a cooler approach. The very different personalities of these three great men are encapsulated in a rhyme that is still learned by every Japanese child:

> If a cuckoo does not sing, kill it;
> If a cuckoo does not sing, find a way to make it sing;
> If a cuckoo does not sing, wait until it does.

Ieyasu was a man who believed that self-discipline was the key to success and many of his recorded statements have an almost Puritan ring to them : "life is like a long journey carrying a heavy burden, one must not hurry"; "when ambition arises, remember the days of adversity". Ieyasu lived a life of relative restraint, indulging in few of the elaborate entertainments that were so enjoyed by Nobunaga and Hideyoshi. But there was nothing restrained about his afterlife.

Ieyasu had asked his family to build him a modest shrine in the elevated, and beautiful, mountain town of Nikko. It was a high point from which he could watch over his beloved Japan. But when his family set about building the shrine dedicated to Ieyasu at Nikko they turned it into a dramatic demonstration of Tokugawa wealth and power. The first Tokugawa Shogun was enshrined as a god in a mausoleum that was surrounded by the most elaborate and gorgeous complex of buildings ever erected in Japan. More than four million workmen made their way to this small highland town to construct the breathtaking shrine that would symbolize the new order. Japan was finally a land at peace and under the firm control of the Tokugawa family. All samurai would now have to learn to live in a nation where war was a thing of the past.

4. Miyamoto Musashi

Shining Light

By 1604 Kyoto had regained its place as the most beautiful city in all Asia. One hundred years earlier the ancient capital had been reduced to ruins by the devastating street battles of the Onin War. But it was now, thanks to the patronage of Nobunaga and Hideyoshi, once again glorious. Luxurious new mansions and temple complexes had been constructed of wood, stone and paper as demonstrations of the wealth and taste of the most powerful samurai and the nation's leading monks. Surrounded by new walls and dramatic castles the city was the richest and most important urban centre of Japan. Kyoto had undoubtedly lost some of its power thanks to the decision of Tokugawa Ieyasu to base himself in distant Edo. But it was still a magnetic place that drew pilgrims, merchants and sightseers from far and wide. They arrived to gape at the city's magnificent sights, dabble in its busy markets and enjoy the incomparable pleasures of the entertainment quarter.

Among the crowds streaming into the city in 1604 came an anonymous young samurai in faded clothing. He carried a small pack of belongings on his shoulder and wore two undistinguished swords at his side. Miyamoto Musashi was twenty one. He had somehow escaped with his life from the great battle of Sekigahara four years earlier and then disappeared from recorded history. Now he arrived in Kyoto with a daring plan that, if it worked, was going to make him famous. He would find the best swordsman in Japan's greatest city and challenge that man to a sword fight. Musashi was aiming high, perhaps too high. There had been plenty of aggressive and ambitious young samurai among the violent turmoil of the previous century. Few of them had lived very long.

Since the battle at Sekigahara Japan had enjoyed four years of almost unbroken peace. But this was still a nation shaped for war and Kyoto was still a stronghold of the martial arts. The city, which was close to the great military fortresses of Osaka and Fushimi, hosted many schools where samurai and their sons could learn fighting skills from the very best teachers. Eight important sword schools were based in the city and in 1604 these schools were at the forefront of the nationwide shift towards a new kind of swordsmanship.

Samurai had begun to think of their swords in a new way. Living in towns and cities their swords seemed more like defensive tools for everyday life than offensive battlefield weapons. The heavy, powerful techniques that had been so important in war were becoming anachronistic and the Kyoto schools were leading the nation toward a faster and more fluid style of sword fighting that better suited the modern age. The sword masters who led these schools were distinguished men with nationwide reputations. If a scruffy, pock-marked country samurai happened to hang around a sword dojo, quietly watching the practice, not one of these teachers would have given him a second thought.

The Yoshioka School, the greatest sword school in Kyoto city, had a humble beginning. Kenpo Yoshioka had been a cloth dyer and he was said to have developed a unique sword style from the practiced movements he made as he rolled his dyeing tools. In the sixteenth century it was still possible for a mere craftsman to become a famous samurai and Kenpo had made his name on the battlefield. He proved to be such a formidable warrior that the family of the Shogun, the Ashikaga, had recruited him as their professional sword instructor. This was a great social achievement for Kenpo but when Oda Nobunaga threw the Ashikaga family out of power the Yoshioka family lost a good deal of their status. Although they no longer moved in government circles their reputation as sword teachers had nonetheless remained intact and the headquarters of the Yoshioka sword school, the Heihosho dojo in the north of Kyoto city, was one of the best known and most respected training centers in the land.

At the head of this school were two of the grandsons of Kenpo Yoshioka, Seijuro and Denshichiro. They were young, distinguished swordsmen and were generally believed to be among the very strongest fighters in Japan. The older brother Seijuro was the head of the family and the master of the Yoshioka sword school. He was rumored to have extraordinary mental strength, a talent that he would practice as he wandered at night through the forests at the edge of the city. His mind was so powerful, people said, that his thoughts could fling the birds themselves out of their roosts and into the sky.

Why did Musashi, an unknown and unemployed samurai, decide to target this impressive family? The primary reason seems to have been an encounter between the fathers of Seijuro and Musashi that had taken place decades earlier. Both had been noted swordsmen of their day and were invited by the Shogun to fight a series of demonstration matches with wooden swords. The result was a humiliation for the Yoshioka school. Naokata, the Shogun's own sword instructor, was defeated in two matches out of three by Munisai, a mere village sword teacher. The Shogun praised Munisai as a swordsman without equal but for unknown reasons Musashi's father received no other honors. He returned to his obscure life as a rural samurai while Naokata Yoshioka and his family continued to enjoy the privileges of Kyoto society. Bad feeling ran thick between these two clans. If Musashi planned to make a name for himself he would take great pleasure in doing so at the expense of the Yoshioka family.

From the very beginning Musashi was actually quite different from other young samurai hotheads. He was a man who combined enormous courage and self confidence with a keen intellect. He was certainly ambitious and would willingly face great danger but his habit was to make use of every possible tactic to turn a risky situation to his own advantage. For months he lived quietly in Kyoto, observing the Yoshioka brothers from a distance and considering the best way of matching their sword technique. When he was ready to act he wrote a formal letter to issue a challenge. In the letter Musashi took some pains to present himself as an acceptable opponent. He explicitly referred to the previous meeting of their fathers and, in order to place himself on an equal social footing with the Yoshioka family, described himself as the head of the Shining Light School of swordsmanship (Enmei Ryu). The brothers had never heard of this school but they certainly remembered the country samurai who had embarrassed their father. They would be glad to teach his son a lesson.

Three Brothers

An unlikely meeting between the wealthy sword master and his unknown challenger was finally arranged. In 1604 the old tradition of using duels to settle personal grievances was frowned on by the government but men like Seijuro and Musashi were not employed by anyone and they had little reason to fear official sanction. They had more reason to fear each other; a sword duel was almost certain to result in the death or severe maiming of one of the participants. Because of this danger the majority of duels were actually fought with wooden swords that allowed participants to test their respective skills without running the risk of being sliced open. But wooden swords were dangerous enough. They could easily shatter bones or smash through a skull.

The duel took place on a May morning near the Rendaiji temple in northern Kyoto. The designated time was ten o'clock and Seijuro Yoshioka arrived well before ten accompanied by several supporters who set about preparing his swords and clothing. Seijuro was a civilized man and naturally followed the etiquette that was expected of a brave samurai on such an occasion. But even by the time he had completed his preparations there was no sign of Musashi. As Seijuro stood and waited his irritation and impatience grew. Finally Musashi arrived alone. As he approached Seijuro's supporters stared with obvious contempt as this ronin who was dressed in unkempt clothing and gave off a pungent odor of sweat. Samurai were the ruling class of Japan, they aspired to lead society. This young man was clearly a ruffian.

Both of the duelists selected wooden swords and it was agreed that the first strike would settle the match. They took up fighting stances, leaving the length of a sword between the tips of their blades. Slowly they moved back and forth watching each other carefully for the slightest sign of inattention or fear. Musashi had always trained under the sky and his straw sandals moved easily over the uneven ground of the field. In this he had a small advantage over Seijuro who was used to training on polished wooden floors.

Suddenly the space between the two men disappeared and it was Musashi who struck first. His wooden blade thumped into Seijuro's shoulder and produced an audible crack. Musashi stepped back and looked down at the sword master who had fallen unconscious at his feet. Supporters from the Yoshioka school crowded forward and tried to revive Seijuro but he showed no signs of life. They were forced to lift him bodily and carry him back towards the city. Later in the day he came round but his left arm had been badly smashed and in those pre-surgical days there was nothing to be done. Seijuro was disabled for life and his reputation was destroyed. He could never work as a sword teacher again. Eventually he retired from the leadership of his family to put on the robes of a Buddhist monk.

This had been a truly shocking turn of events for the Yoshioka family and for the many students who had committed time and money to take lessons with the school. Denshichiro Yoshioka, the younger brother of Seijuro and his equal as a swordsman, knew that he had little choice other than to exact a quick revenge. He issued a challenge to Musashi. On the appointed day Musashi once again infuriated the Yoshioka supporters by arriving late. Denshichiro was determined to badly injure Musashi this time and so selected an exceptionally long sword that took great strength to swing. It did him no good. As soon as the fight began Musashi dispensed with caution and stepped in close against Denshichiro's body. With a powerful twist of his wrist he wrenched the long sword from his opponent's grasp, raised it high and slammed it into Deshichiro's head. The second Yoshioka brother fell like a stone at Musashi's feet. The blow had killed him instantly.

Shocked and angry the remainder of the Yoshioka family and students gathered at their training hall. They had practiced hard for years and now the reputation of every person in the room had been stained by these two disastrous defeats. Musashi, they quickly decided, could not be allowed to live. Once again they sent him a challenge, this time under the name of Matashichiro Yoshioka. It was a purely symbolic challenge; Matashichiro was a boy aged twelve and could not be expected to face such a dangerous swordsman on his own. The entire school would accompany the boy with the aim of surrounding and slaughtering Musashi. When they had killed him the terrible stain on their honor could be forgotten.

On the arranged morning a large group of samurai armed with swords, bows and muskets set out for the large pine tree next to the Ichijoji temple that marked the site of the final duel. Their plan was to fall on Musashi as he arrived and to bury his body in an unmarked grave. Their target, however, was no fool. He knew that an ambush was being prepared and so he switched tactics. This time Musashi set out before dawn with the intention of arriving well in advance of the Yoshioka camp. Brave as he was, Musashi understood perfectly well that his life was now in great danger.

In the conventional way he stopped off at the nearest shrine to offer a prayer for his safety to the gods. But as he faced the holy sanctum and prepared to bow in prayer Musashi suddenly paused. " No." he told himself. "I will not rely on any external forces, I need to do this with my own strength." It was a supremely unconventional thought and a momentous turning point in Musashi's life. He did not reject religion but, from that moment forward, would follow a path of complete self-reliance and self-responsibility. He was the most unsentimental of men.

Musashi climbed the trunk of a large pine tree and concealed himself among the branches from where he could observe the Yoshioka fighters as they arrived in the faint light just before sunrise. When they walked into the clearing the Yoshioka samurai were off guard, expecting that Musashi would be as late as he had been for the two previous duels. As they milled around he quickly dropped to the ground from his hiding place and ran straight toward the boy who symbolized the survival of the Yoshioka family. Drawing his sword on the run, Musashi sliced through the body of the twelve-year-old Matashichiro with one sweeping cut. Moving constantly, never allowing himself to pause, he used both of his drawn swords to cut his way through the startled crowd of samurai and to make his escape. The Yoshioka family and their famous sword school were finished.

The Greatest Swordsman in Japan
Kyoto had seen more than its fair share of duels but these three defeats for the Yoshioka family were truly sensational events. As word of Musashi's brilliant feat raced through the tightly knit samurai community he quickly lost the advantage that he had held on arrival in Kyoto. If he was not yet an admired samurai he had ensured that any fighters who crossed his path in future would be wary. If this bothered Musashi he showed no sign of it. In fact, in letters written while he was still in his early twenties, Musashi seems to be brimming with confidence. "I am now," he flatly stated, "the greatest sword expert in all Japan."

These were years filled with violence and danger for the young swordsman. Between the ages of twenty and thirty Musashi fought in sixty duels, winning them all. His victories were based on daily practice and on the experience he gained from encounters in which his honor and reputation, and at times his life, were at risk. Gradually he became an expert in a wide range of martial techniques. He practiced with long swords, with short swords and with two swords applied in combination. He became proficient with knives and with the one weapon a traveling samurai always had to hand, the walking staff.

Musashi disdained convention. If the need arose he would even throw his sword at an opponent to startle and create an opening. He carried a supply of shuriken, small edged weapons that are designed for throwing. His chief interest was in winning fights and he was willing to use any method that worked, however graceless it might appear to a more dignified samurai. He developed a habit of preparing for a duel by studying the weapons, the fighting style and even the psychology of his opponents. He openly made use of tricks and ruses to unsettle his opponents and secure the victory. Musashi was certainly highly skilled but it was his mental approach to combat that made him exceptional. The key to victory, he wrote decades later, lies in finding an effective method and in then applying it ruthlessly.

Not a great deal is known about the many matches that Musashi fought during his youth. Some of these encounters seem to have been friendly practice matches while others were duels in which his life was at stake. One record tells of a meeting between Musashi and a warrior monk who was an expert in spear fighting. The monk used a particularly long spear with a cross blade that was designed to trap a sword and disarm the owner. A long and intense duel ensued in which Musashi was able to hold his own with a wooden sword against the much more dangerous spear. The two men then sat up through the night swapping stories about the martial arts until the sun rose.

A much less comradely encounter came about when Musashi was traveling through the region of Iga in the mountains to the south of Kyoto. Even in wartime this place had acquired a dangerous reputation as a centre for the espionage experts known as shinobi, or ninja. The warlike people of this region were known to enjoy using a wide range of home-made weapons. Musashi had been drawn to the Iga village by stories of a local man who was an expert fighter with one of the most frightening weapons of all, the kusarigama. This daunting contraption consists of a razor sharp sickle blade that is attached to one end of a steel chain. At the other end of the two meter long chain is an iron ball that can be swung in wide circles. At any moment the iron ball can be thrown to wrap itself around an opponent's limb, giving the attacker an opening to close in and wield the blade. It is a complex weapon, difficult to master but almost impossible for a samurai armed with a sword to defend against.

Musashi found that the kusarigama expert was a man named Shishido. He was an iron worker who made his own weapons and who had never been defeated in a duel. The two met in a field on the outskirts of Iga with a cheerful crowd of villagers looking on. As Shishido began to whip the iron ball in wide circles above his head Musashi increased the distance between them and searched for some stratagem to counter this strange weapon. He took both of his swords from their scabbards, but with the wrong hands, so that he held them in the reverse two swords (gyaku nito) defense. Musashi raised his short sword into the air with his right hand and began to swing the blade in circles, matching the rhythm of the spinning iron ball. This was such a strange maneuver that Shishido took a moment to wonder just what Musashi was playing at. As he paused in thought, Musashi flung his short sword so that it impaled the villager's chest. Now the end came quickly. Musashi stepped in close and finished Shishido with one stroke of the long sword in his left hand.

Musashi in Edo

By the time he had reached his mid-twenties Musashi seems to have grown tired of his wandering life and decided to try his luck in the new boomtown, Edo. This bustling city was packed with great lords from the length and breadth of Japan who had been ordered to maintain homes close to the Shogun's palace and to raise and educate their children under its walls. These wealthy samurai and their generals typically kept a full time sword instructor as part of their household staff. Musashi, who believed that he was an unrivaled swordsman, must have expected to find work with one of these lords, or perhaps even in the service of the Shogun himself.

If that was his ambition, it would remain unfulfilled. Musashi never found employment among the powerful families of Edo. Perhaps the reason for his failure to secure a distinguished post lay in his affiliation with the defeated army at the battle of Sekigahara. Memories of that terrible conflict and its many casualties were still fresh enough to keep anger and resentment alive on both sides. Or it may be that Musashi was simply constrained by his social standing. The new rulers of Edo were battle hardened veterans but, as the peace deepened, they were beginning to think of themselves as a cultivated upper class. These lords taxed the peasants in their domains harshly so that they could afford to live in great luxury during their bi-annual stays in Edo. They wore the finest silk kimono, ate exotic foods and greeted each other with elaborate courtesy. The unwashed and ungroomed Musashi may have found that it took more than pure sword skills to impress anyone in this upwardly mobile society.

During his first stay in Edo Musashi dreamed of being allowed to prove himself in a duel with Yagyu Munenori, the most important of several official sword instructors to the Shogun and his family. Munenori was in his thirties and had already attained a status much higher than that of a mere sword teacher. Most likely the social gulf between the two was simply too great for any kind of meeting to have taken place.

A meeting did, however, take place between Musashi and two of Munenori's personal students. Musashi, who was paying his bills in Edo by running a small sword school, was visited one day by the two students, Oseto and Tsujikaze. They wandered into his dojo looking forward to having some fun with this countrified samurai. Things soon went badly for both men. Oseto was getting ready to attack when Musashi stepped in and knocked him to the ground. Tsujikaze, a large and powerful man, was also preparing his first move when he felt Musashi physically crash into him with great force. He was thrown against a heavy stone jar that stood at the entrance to the dojo. Tsujikaze passed out, momentarily recovered his wits, then sank back into death. Once again Musashi had demonstrated his utter lack of interest in the prescribed etiquette for sword duels. The only thing he cared about was winning.

One other duel from this stay in Edo has been recorded, and it was a duel that would prove to have a lasting impact on the martial arts. This time the challenger was one Muso Gonnosuke, a colorful samurai who like to walk through the streets with a sign fluttering above his back that proclaimed him to be the greatest swordsman in Japanese history. The braggart made the mistake of wandering into Musashi's dojo one afternoon where he insisted on a duel. Gonnosuke quickly drew a wooden sword and stepped forward forcing Musashi to pick up the only weapon within range which happened to be a lump of wood lying in the fireplace. As Gonnosuke swung away with his sword Musashi stood his ground and finally knocked down his assailant with a single blow to the forehead.

Such a straightforward defeat was a total humiliation for "the greatest swordsman in history" but for once the defeated samurai responded with admirable determination. Gonnosuke is said to have withdrawn into a long period of retreat and study that led him towards the creation of a new kind of staff fighting (jojutsu) that employed a staff long enough to defeat any sword. This was the origin of the important jojutsu school, known as Shinto Muso Ryu, that still exists today and still honors Gonnosuke as a great martial artist.

Drying Pole
At the age of twenty-eight Musashi came to the climactic confrontation of this dangerous period of his life, his famous duel with Sasaki Kojiro. This fight shines in the Japanese imagination today as a dramatic showdown between two great swordsmen, perhaps the greatest of their age, and it has been recreated hundreds of times in manga and movies.

Kojiro had been a student of a sword master known as Toda Seigen, a teacher who insisted that his students use long swords so that he could practice the difficult art of defending himself with a short sword. Kojiro became used to the longer sword and broke away from Seigen to found his own group that he named the Rock School (Gan Ryu). Kojiro was notorious for his use of a devastating technique known as the swallow turn (tsubame-gaeshi), a technique that he liked to practice by slicing swallows in half as they flitted past his head. He was so fast, it was said, that he could anticipate the turns made by the agile birds as they swung away from the edge of his sword. In a duel the 'swallow-turn' may have consisted of a long downward swing of his sword that would suddenly reverse its course so that the blade sliced upwards into an opponent's body.

Kojiro at that time held a reputation at least equal to that of Musashi, they were both outstanding young swordsmen on the rise. He had won duel after duel fighting with a sword that was so long, more than three feet compared to the two feet three inches of the typical samurai sword, that his weapon had been nicknamed 'Drying Pole'. Unlike Musashi, however, Kojiro had settled into respectable employment as a sword instructor to Hosokawa Tadaoki, the lord of northern Kyushu. Musashi, who was well aware that Kojiro was the only other young samurai in the land whose reputation matched his own, arranged for a family friend to present a request to Lord Hosokawa that the two be allowed to fight a duel. Hosokawa was a sword connoisseur and was anxious to see such an exciting match but he was unwilling to run the risk of having his sword instructor humiliated. In the end he decided that a duel could take place away from the crowds on a small uninhabited island that lies in the straight between the great islands of Honshu and Kyushu. In this dramatic setting, in front of only a handful of spectators, the two men faced each other on the sand after traveling from the mainland in separate boats. It was Musashi who triumphed, killing Kojiro and bringing an end to the Rock School.

As with so much of Musashi's life only scant details of his encounter with Sasaki Kojiro were recorded, and these details are disputed. The most commonly accepted description of their meeting tells of Kojiro waiting on the island shore at the arranged time of eight in the morning. But Musashi was just beginning to rouse himself from slumber in his bed on the mainland. As the set time for the duel passed he dressed, enjoyed a leisurely breakfast and climbed into the small rowing boat that was waiting. On his way to the island Musashi borrowed a spare oar from the boatman and began to carve himself a long wooden sword, a sword that was even longer than the 'Drying Pole'.

On the island Kojiro was pacing up and down the beach, his irritation growing as Musashi failed to appear. At last the small boat emerged from the morning haze and Musashi stepped down into the waves. Kojiro could not contain his anger. "Why are you so late," he snarled. "Were you too afraid to arrive on time?" Musashi quietly gazed at his excited opponent who, now desperate to begin the fight, flung the scabbard of his sword into the surf. At last Musashi spoke. "Kojiro! You have already lost the match. Someone who expected to win would never discard their scabbard like that."

As Musashi undoubtedly intended, Kojiro was now beside himself. He swung his sword at Musashi's head but the samurai with his back to the sea moved simultaneously and both swords reached their target. Kojiro's sword cut through Musashi's headband but did no other damage. Musashi's blow was harder and knocked Kojiro to the ground. As Musashi stepped over the prostrate body Kojiro sliced his sword upwards. The blade cut into his opponent's clothing but Musashi had moved at the same moment to drive his wooden sword hard into the ribs of Kojiro. It was a devastating blow. Kojiro died as the waves rolled over and around his prostrate body.

Musashi Matures
In the wake of this famous victory Musashi began to reassess his life. Up to this point he had sought out experience, danger and challenge with a reckless determination. He would, he had decided at a young

age, become the greatest swordsman in the land or die in the attempt. Musashi had provoked duels with several of the strongest fighters in the country and had lived to tell the tale. But from this point in his life the hunger for fame and reputation seemed to leave him. In later duels a different Musashi appeared, a swordsman who was more interested in quietly demonstrating his technique and in subduing opponents without having to humiliate them. Later in life he wrote about the transition he had made to a more mature, more internal, approach to sword fighting.

> At the age of thirty, I reflected and saw that although I had won, I had done so without having reached the ultimate level of strategy. Perhaps it was because my natural disposition prevented me from straying from universal principles; perhaps it was because my opponents lacked ability in strategy. I continued to train and to seek from morning till night to attain a deeper principle. When I reached the age of fifty, I naturally found myself on the way. (7)

Three years after his showdown with Kojiro Musashi once again put on his battle armor to take part in the Winter and Summer clashes at Osaka Castle. These were almost the last battles of the Edo period, a series of engagements that put a final end to any possibility of organized opposition to the rule of the Shogun. Circumstantial evidence suggests that Musashi once again fought for the losing side and that he again found himself among the ranks of thousands of unemployed and poverty stricken samurai who paid the price for being part of the defeated army. This is the only interpretation of events that helps us to fully understand why Musashi would spend most of his remaining years as a wanderer. He was certainly welcomed and recognized as a great man in many places but not until the very end of his life would he be rewarded with the kind of high office that his outstanding skills seemed to deserve.

The middle years of Musashi's life are clouded by the obscurity of his situation and by his decision to avoid violent duels. The few details that have been recorded suggest that Musashi became a very different kind of swordsman from the impetuous and aggressive young man he had once been. He was now a famous man and no longer needed to challenge others. The tables had turned, in fact. It was Musashi who had acquired a reputation and who presented an attractive target for challenges from young, ambitious samurai.

One certain fact from these middle years is that Musashi spent some of this time living in one of the great castle towns of Japan as a guest of the lord of Himeji. He was not given a position but was treated as an honored friend of the lord who placed trust in him as an advisor on town planning and garden design. Even in this sheltered environment he faced challenges. Shortly after his arrival in Himeji Musashi was visited by the leading swordsman of the Himeji area, Miyake Gunbei, who showed up with three companions to see if Musashi could really live up to his reputation. Having looked the visitors up and down Musashi picked up two wooden swords and offered to take all four of them on at once.

Gunbei was maddened by this insult to his own skills. He began to attack Musashi and to search for a way to break through the impenetrable defense presented by Musashi's crossed swords. Finally, after managing to push Musashi back into a wall Gunbei sensed an opportunity to win and lowered his sword into a position from which he could impale his opponent. "Wrong!", exclaimed Musashi, as he blocked Gunbei's thrust with his short sword and delicately touched Gunbei's cheek with his longer sword. A thin line of blood appeared on the face of the disappointed local hero causing Musashi to drop his defense and produce a cloth to clean Gunbei's wound. This gentleness was almost as much of a humiliation for Genbei as his defeat had been. Later he remarked that in fighting Musashi he had felt like one man going into battle against an army. He apologized for his impudence and the four friends from Himeji became students of the master.

Musashi was regularly invited to the mansions of lords who wanted to see a great swordsman in action. In return for their hospitality he would demonstrate his skill against the top martial artists of the surrounding area. He found himself in matches with sword, spear and staff experts, always defending himself with the unique two sword style that he had himself created. In many of these fights he did not even try to attack but simply overwhelmed his opponents with a powerful aura that drove them backwards and seemed to stymie their every attempt to strike.

Musashi was not the first Japanese sword expert to fight with two swords in hand. It had long been recognized that a second sword could be drawn in order to block attacks from a longer weapon such as a spear. But Musashi does seem to have been the first expert to have developed a system based around the constant use of two swords. It was a fighting style that required great strength and the ability to employ both hands with equal skill and precision. Musashi had been trained by his father to use the jitte, a weapon designed to block and trap a sword blade, and his youthful experiences of fighting with a sword in one hand and a jitte in the other may have been the origin of the double handed method. After his death the fighting system of Musashi was carried on in schools of swordsmanship that were named after his unique style: Two Heavens as One (Niten Ichi Ryu) or Two Swords as One (Nito Ichi Ryu).

The Musashi of these middle years seemed to have lost the need to prove anything, either to himself or to others. Instead he was becoming one of the first Japanese martial artists to engage in a search for a deeper meaning for the fighting arts, one that could be relevant to the new and peaceful society that was emerging. In this new Japan samurai with administrative skills were of greater value than powerful fighters. What profit was there in studying the way of the sword? Musashi's answer was that the sword could be a vehicle for exploring what it means to be human. The intensity of his search took him to a level of skill that was far beyond that of the brilliant swordsman he had been as a young man. On one notable occasion he began a duel by dropping his sword and inviting a young samurai to attempt to strike him. After some time the young attacker, covered in sweat, admitted that he could find no way to touch Musashi. The middle-aged master seemed to be surrounded by an invisible force field.

He was undoubtedly an extraordinary man, a man so exceptional that a certain mystery still surrounds the somewhat lonely, wandering life he seems to have led for much of his life. Musashi's personality may have contributed to this loneliness. He was a proud man, a man who was ready even in his twenties to describe himself as the greatest sword expert in the land. Later in life he was less inclined to boast but there is no reason to believe that his self-belief changed in any way. Musashi was also fiercely independent and was temperamentally unable to accept any of the conventional rules of behavior if they did not correspond to his needs. Such a man, even the loyal, intelligent and skillful samurai that Musashi certainly was, would not have been easy to employ.

Neither, at a time when the samurai were becoming intensely aware of their social position as a respectable class, was Musashi a physically impressive candidate for high office. This was the opinion of several contemporaries who suggested that Musashi was simply too dirty and scruffy to be employed in service. Since childhood he had been badly afflicted by a skin condition that in adulthood made it impossible for him to shave his head in the conventional manner. Instead of a chonmage hairstyle Musashi wore his hair long, hanging to his shoulders. Even worse, in a nation where the bathroom has historically been at the centre of family life, Musashi was said to have been a reluctant bather. He would avoid the daily soaking in hot water that is so important to the Japanese and would simply wipe his body with a damp towel in the evening.

The Poised Brush
Musashi may not have been the most elegant samurai and he was not as successful in conventional terms as many of his peers. And yet he is regarded today as a truly important individual, one of the greatest of his age. This reputation is founded on his exploits as a swordsman but also rests on the quality of his wonderful painting, his calligraphy and his written works. While the existing records of his duels are rather obscure the scrolls and artworks penned by the hand of Musashi allow us to gain a direct insight into the quality of the man. He was a renaissance figure at a time when Japanese culture was blossoming. Musashi successfully turned his hand to poetry, garden design, architecture, sculpture, carpentry and calligraphy. He could master any of these arts, he believed, because he had first mastered the sword. True insight in one field gave way to a clear understanding of every human undertaking.

Of all the activities that Musashi took up in the middle years of his life it was in painting where he made the deepest mark. Working under the artistic name of Niten he created several works that are among the finest examples of seventeenth century Japanese art. Musashi worked in suibokuga, a powerful style of painting that restricts itself to the most basic elements - black ink, a single brush and white paper. This monochrome art form arrived in twelfth century Japan from China and has a close historical link with Zen Buddhism. Suibokuga paintings are executed at a high pitch of concentration and energy that has been described as a duel with the paper. Standing in silent meditation above a white sheet the artist dips his brush in the ink and immediately draws a line without pause or contemplation. Within a few short minutes the work is complete. At their best these paintings seem to transcend art. In just a few scribbled lines they get right to the essence of an object or a landscape.

Musashi painted several images of birds, usually fishing birds that, with their sharp faces, penetrating eyes and poised stances, seem to be swordsmen in disguise. In what is perhaps his finest painting he sketched a small shrike sitting in perfect stillness a the top of a long vertical branch. The English author Aldous Huxley adroitly captured the atmosphere of this impressive work:

> Perched on the very tip of a naked branch, waiting without purpose, but in a state of highest tension. Beneath, above and all around is nothing, the bird emerges from the Void [8]

It is in his painting that we can most clearly see the influence of Buddhism on Musashi's life. It had always been a simple life. He grew up on a farm and spent many of his younger years traveling alone from town to town along rough mountain paths. Only in middle age did he did begin to enjoy the more sophisticated pursuits that were typical of an educated samurai. On the occasions that he accepted hospitality from a regional lord Musashi would sing songs from Noh dramas and enjoy the tea ceremony. But his taste always ran to the austere and he was naturally drawn to the simplicity and quietude of Zen Buddhism. Late in life it became Musashi's practice to walk into the mountains with a young monk in search of a spot where they would spend hours in deep meditation. On one occasion as they sat in the hills the two silently meditating men were approached by an inquisitive snake. It slowly crept undisturbed across the knees of the young monk. But when the snake came close to Musashi it suddenly stopped and reared up in front of the swordsman before slithering away to a hiding place. Later Musashi ruefully remarked that the snake had recognized his aggression. He needed, he said, to work harder on his meditation practice.

The swordsman painted several portraits of the great Buddhist figure Bodhidharma. Known as Daruma to the Japanese, Bodhidharma is the legendary teacher who carried Buddhism to China from its birthplace in India. For students of Zen he is recognized as the founder of Chan Buddhism, the branch of the religion that subsequently made its way to twelfth century Japan and was modified into the sect we know today as Japanese Zen Buddhism. Bodhidharma was an intense and forbidding figure, a man who spent several years alone in a cave lost in solitary meditation. He was a dour character, utterly uninterested in impressing the Emperor of China during his first audience with the ruler. When he was asked by the Emperor to teach about the ultimate secret of Buddhism Bodhidharma gravely disappointed his host by replying, "Just emptiness. Nothing holy."

Painting this huge historical figure is the ultimate test for a Buddhist painter. In the simple lines of a suibokuga painting the artist must bring to life both the historical character and also the painter's own, living understanding of the Way. Musashi's paintings of Bodhidharma have all the intensity, psychological realism and earthy humor of the greatest Zen artists. The most famous of several such paintings gives shape to Bodhidharma's lumpy head with a single, amused sweep of the paintbrush. Beneath the huge forehead lies a great, hairy face with the eyeballs squinting inwards and the mouth pulled downwards in an unbreakable frown of concentration.

Musashi also painted several versions of Hotei the priest, another common subject for Zen-influenced artists. Hotei was a ninth-century Chinese monk who lived an eccentric, wandering life and paintings of the monk typically depict him as a happy symbol of the ultimate freedom to which Zen Buddhists aspire. Musashi followed this convention in several paintings of Hotei but his most interesting portrait shows the priest enjoying a cock fight. Dashed off in washes of black ink and rapid brush strokes the burly Hotei leans forward, his chin propped on a cane, watching two cocks prepare for battle. Above the corpulent chin his face seems to press through space into the birds, amused and engaged. It is a wonderfully effective presentation of the Zen ideal of complete absorption in the moment.

The Feeling of Love
Musashi spent a good deal of this part of his life in the comfortable accommodation provided by his friends and found time to enjoy a wide range of cultural pursuits. But at heart there was a loneliness to his lifestyle that was never tempered by the comforts of a family home. Despite his wanderings, however, Musashi did find time to adopt two sons, a practice common among the samurai of his time. His first son, named Mikinosuke, was offered employment with the lord of Himeji, Honda Tadatoki. This was the same lord who had sheltered and befriended Musashi in Himeji for many years and Mikinosuke rose to a fine post as sword instructor to the Honda family.

But the young man's sense of security was shattered when Honda Tadatoki died of tuberculosis at the premature age of thirty. The custom of junshi, a ritual suicide by a samurai in order to follow his master into death, was still being sporadically practiced at this time and Mikinosuke, who had been close to his young master, decided to take his own life. Musashi and his twenty-three year old son shared a painful final meal together on the eve of the impending suicide. Both men knew what was coming but they completely avoided any mention of the following day and there seems little doubt that Musashi fully approved of his adopted son's decision. It was a tragic and unnecessary death. Just seven years later the Tokugawa government would outlaw the practice of junshi.

Musashi's second son was a precocious farmboy named Iori who had dreams of becoming a great samurai. He succeeded in realizing his ambitions thanks to the support and training of his adoptive father. Iori secured an important position with the Ogasawara family, the lords of Akashi. He distinguished himself in both administration and war and rose to become a notable and wealthy samurai. In fact it was Iori who, eight years after the death of his father, erected the great stone memorial at Kokura that did so much to preserve the story of Musashi's life and deeds.

Musashi never married but his life was not completely devoid of romance. Even in his fifties he was capable of forming a passionate relationship with a lovely young woman, a girl named Kumoi who was a lowly ranked courtesan in the Yoshiwara quarter of Edo. This was the most licentious square mile in all of Japan, a sheltered area where samurai surrendered their swords at the gate to devote themselves to gambling, alcohol and the company of women. But however deep his feelings for Kumoi, Musashi was not a man to completely lose his head over a woman. In a later poem he reveals a dryly humorous approach to matters of the heart.

> If you are in love,
> Don't waste time on letters
> Or romantic poetry.
> Spend your energy
> On taking care of money.

The most important relationships of Musashi's life were not, in fact, those that he formed with family members or lovers. His deepest feelings of affection seem to have been reserved for the great lords who welcomed him into their homes as a distinguished and cultured guest. Musashi had been close to Honda Tadatoki and, toward the end of his life, he would renew another great friendship with Hosokawa Tadatoshi, the lord who had arranged his famous duel with Sasaki Kojiro.

A New Start
In 1634, at the age of fifty, Musahi travelled to Kyushu, the southernmost island of the Japanese mainland, to visit his son Iori. The young man was beginning to establish his career in service to the

Ogasawara family and it was Ogasawara Tadasane himself, the powerful ruler of northern Kyushu, who welcomed Musashi as an important guest. Tadasane was well aware of Musashi's reputation and immediately employed him as sword instructor at the family castle. By way of initiation to his new post Musashi was asked by Tadasane to give a demonstration of martial arts by sparring in public with the castle's own spear fighting instructor. In front of an audience of dignitaries the two martial arts masters squared off, Musashi holding a wooden sword and his opponent a bamboo spear. Musashi easily won the first two matches but, in the final challenge, the spear brushed against his legs. He immediately conceded defeat and praised his adversary's skill highly. Perhaps Musashi had learned to be diplomatic. "I could not touch him," the other man later said, "he acted to allow me to save face."

Musashi spent five happy years with the Ogasawara family, watching with pride as his son rose to a senior position. In 1637 the father went into battle for the last time in his life, in company with his son. A revolt had broken out in the southern part of Kyushu led by peasants who were infuriated by a punitive tax system. The uprising was soon joined by large numbers of fortune-seeking samurai. Angry at their economic plight and frustrated by the strict prohibition of Christian worship the rebel army quickly attracted enough popular support to be able to take control of a large part of the Kyushu island. It was a strange army, a democratic crowd of peasants and samurai led by a charismatic sixteen-year-old boy.

This rebel uprising was the greatest challenge that the Tokugawa government of Japan had faced in more than twenty years. It was a direct threat to the class system established by Hideyoshi and to the rule of the Shogun. The Edo government raised a huge samurai army from all over Japan with the intention of crushing the rebels. The peasant army was quickly chased from open ground and retreated to Hara Castle where it put up a desperate defense that lasted for months despite the overwhelming advantages of the attackers who used Dutch cannons to bombard the castle. In the end the brave defenders were starved into a final defeat and were beheaded by the thousand. Iori and his father Musashi both played important roles as leaders and military advisors during the siege. It may well have been Musashi's only experience of fighting a battle on the winning side. In the siege of Hara Castle he received his final battle wounds – minor cuts to the legs that were probably caused by rocks thrown from the castle walls.

Old Warrior
During the long siege Musashi had been delighted to be able to renew his friendship with Hosokawa Tadatoshi. This lord had been a great admirer of Musashi since he had organized the famous duel with Sasaki Kojiro and Hosokawa now wanted to have the company of Musashi as a guest and sword instructor. But persuading the swordsman to leave the Ogasawara family was not going to be a simple matter. Musashi was a proud, prickly man who valued his independence above all else. There is no

doubt, however, that at this stage of his life he was delighted to receive such an offer from a good friend. Hosokawa asked Musashi to write a letter outlining his demands in return for leaving the service of the Ogasawara family and transferring to the Hosokawa capital of Kumamoto. The letter Musashi wrote is deeply revealing of his feelings about the loneliness and frustrations of his life.

> Until now, I have never been officially in the service of a lord. And time has passed; moreover, in the last years I have often been sick. That is why there are not so many things that I desire ... I am an old man who has neither wife nor child. I am not concerned about a house or furniture ... From the time of my youth, I have participated in battles six times. Four times out of six, I was in the van, leading the army into battle ... I can be useful teaching the way weapons are used and what is suitable conduct on the field of battle. (7)

Musashi was welcomed to Kumamoto with great honors and was given his own castle. But he was not destined to enjoy a long retirement. He had become a sick and weakened man, slowly dying, it has been suggested, from thoracic cancer. For the first time since childhood he gave up the practice of carrying two swords everywhere and began to walk with the help of a long cane. But even in this weakened state he was still capable of performing impressive feats with a sword. Hosokawa was a connoisseur of sword play and asked Musashi to duel with him and also with the family's senior sword expert. Musashi completely dominated both men without once striking them. He simply prevented them from launching any kind of blow.

Musashi was keenly aware that he was not going to live much longer and threw his energies into passing on all he had learned to a small group of students. And then suddenly, just a few months after he had arrived in Kumamoto, Hosokawa Tadatoshi died. Musashi was devastated by this turn of events. Here at last, he had felt, was a man who truly appreciated him and who could share his feelings about the world. Miserably, he wrote:

> The late lord liked strategy, and I was able to teach him and to communicate to him the overall mind of my school. That was my greatest happiness. His death caused me to lose hope. (7)

The grief stricken sixty-year-old began to spend more and more time alone in the mountains that lay behind his castle. High in these mountains he found a cave where he could establish a simple retreat and from where he could look out across the sea to the setting sun in the west. In this dramatically private space Musashi once more took up brush and ink to compose his masterwork – The Book of Five Rings (Gorin no Sho).

The Book of Five Rings

In front of the cave where Musashi wrote his great treatise on the way of the sword are hundreds of stone towers, most of them composed of five differently shaped rocks that have been carefully heaped one on another. These are stupa, stone towers that represent the Buddhist conception of the material universe. Sometimes intricately carved, at times simply a pile of roughly shaped rocks, these stupa symbolize the five elements of the universe – earth, water, fire, wind and the void. Musashi named his book after these towers and divided the work into a five part structure, naming each part after one of the five elements.

The book was carefully transcribed on five separate scrolls as Musashi entered the last few months of his life. But although he was dying there is no sense that he was writing with one eye carefully fixed on posterity. The book, in fact, seems to have been composed with the simple aim of passing on his innermost thoughts to the few students that had gathered around him in Kumamoto and to the Hosokawa family. These people were already intimately aware of his ideas and methods. He wanted to clarify his thinking for these students rather than for a general audience and he repeatedly insists that his words are only of value to those who are engaged in intense sword practice. As a result, the book includes a good number of subtle suggestions couched in a terminology that would have been easily grasped by his friends but can be rather opaque for a modern reader. Enough remains clear, however, to make The Book of Five Rings the best known and most instructive of all the martial texts that emerged from Japanese warrior culture.

Musashi's literary style is as terse, direct and forceful as the great man must have been in person. And his writing is markedly different from the majority of medieval martial texts in the way it quickly dispenses with any notion that 'secrets' or 'mysteries' lie hidden in the sword art. Many of Musashi's contemporaries liked to dangle the tantalizing prospect of a final set of discoveries in front of students in order to encourage them to persevere with long years of hard training. After twenty or thirty years the teacher would pass on his secrets to students who had completely finished their training and had qualified for a certification of mastership. They were handed scrolls on which the innermost mysteries of their sword art were recorded and these were to be guarded with great vigilance. These students then became teachers in their own right with a vested interest in prolonging the myth of magical techniques. But Musashi strongly disagreed with the notion of any supreme secret of the martial arts. The real secret, he stresses throughout his book, is to adapt to the situation, to discover the weakness of an enemy and to apply whatever weapon or tactic is relevant. At the age of twenty one Musashi had rejected the help of all gods and Buddhas and he was an utterly practical man. Insistently he urges his students to try his ideas out for themselves.

> Read this text thinking that it is written for you ... Instead of imitating what I write, make this text yours, like a principle that you have brought forth from your own thought. (7)

Earth

The Book of Five Rings begins with the Scroll of Earth which takes as its subject Musashi himself. It is a grand statement of self-belief. I trained hard and fought hard for many years, he declares. At the age of fifty I found myself on the correct path. My long search finally ended and all of my questions were answered. My identity, he says, lies in the fact that I am a warrior. In an extended analogy he suggests that a warrior is, in many ways, like a master carpenter. Just like a carpenter a swordsman is someone who fully understands the tools of his trade, who can apply them efficiently at the right time, who can analyze a situation and take decisive action, and who can lead other men in their work. In the same way that a young man must follow an apprenticeship in carpentry, those who want to learn to use a sword must be ready to commit a great deal of time and effort. But this devotion to one's craft can produce huge benefits as mastery of the sword allows a swordsman to understand the principles of every human undertaking and craft. I am fully enlightened, Musashi implies, and I no longer have need for a teacher in any walk of life. Everything has become clear.

Water

The second section of his book, the Scroll of Water, explains how a swordsman should actually behave in combat situations. The physical intuition and skill required for expert swordsmanship, Musashi writes, needs to be centered around an unshakeable mental attitude that persists "even in the middle of a battle when everything is in rapid movement." (7) Musashi proposes a number of pointers on how to use the eyes in battle, "look powerfully, see gently"; on how to move the feet and on how to grip the sword. A good deal of this section describes sword positions and attack moves that would have been well known to the personal students of the master. Repeatedly, Musashi stresses that every body position, every block, and every movement provides an opportunity for attack. The key to superior swordsmanship lies in developing an instinct that always seeks to deliver a devastating attack. Such an attitude is more important than any particular technique.

> ... make your body into a body that is striking, make your mind into a mind that is striking. Then your hand will strike spontaneously out of emptiness, with speed and power, without taking note of the starting point of the movement. This is the strike of nonthought. (7)

Musashi was no purist. He describes several roughhouse techniques that involve using the body as a weapon against another swordsman. In one passage he describes a twist and sudden blow applied with the left shoulder to the chest of an opponent. This, he claims, can knock the opponent backwards several meters and can create surprise, injury, or even death.

Fire
In the Scroll of Fire Musashi leaves the physical side of combat behind and considers psychological aspects. He also widens his perspective, describing the importance of psychology to both individual combat and to war situations. Psychology had always been of great importance to Musashi. From his earliest duels he had used various tricks to unsettle and provoke his opponents. As he grew older Musashi began to use duels as a testing ground for his psychological theories. He would create an unshakeable defense and probe his opponents for extended periods, watching how they responded as he attempted to startle them into action or repeatedly frustrated their attacks. Musashi learned to control a duel without making a single strike. He would push his opponents around a room, watching them intently with his fearless, hawklike eyes. I have, he wrote, fought many battles and have learned what it takes to "situate oneself between life and death". (7)

Musashi begins this section with a list of practical methods that offer advantage to a fighter. A swordsman should make use of the light, take the high ground and exploit terrain to put his opponent at a disadvantage. From this conventional advice Musashi goes on to discuss the most important dimension of sword fighting, the factor that allows advanced swordsman to hold an extra edge in combat. The finished fighter, he says, can read the intention of an opponent before a strike happens. With this kind of ability a swordsman can stymie any attack at the very point where it begins.

> When your opponent means to attack, you grasp the letters att in attack, when he means to jump, you take hold of the ju in jump, when he means to slash, you seize the sla in slash. (7)

This is the key to understanding the aura that surrounded Musashi during his later duels as he circled the other fighter, pressing sword against sword. His opponents were unable to make any attack because Musashi could read their intentions perfectly and move just as they moved, killing the first breath of aggression.

The Scroll of Fire goes on to describe a number of important psychological features that determine the progress of combat. He outlines ways of surviving under pressure, of spiritually crushing an opponent, and of confusing, irritating or frightening an adversary. The other man can be forced, he suggests, into revealing his favorite sword stroke or his chief tactic. Above all, he says, a swordsman must aim to become like an unbreakable rock, impervious to any feelings or blows.

Wind

Wind, the most ephemeral element, is where Musashi chooses to place his rather scornful survey of the sword schools of his day. Each school had its own distinct style of swordsmanship, something that allowed it to stand out in the public eye from all other schools. Musashi dismisses these differences as pure advertising hokum:

> Techniques are displayed like merchandise adorned with colors and flowers, so they can be turned into a way of making a living. (7)

In the early seventeenth century every sword school needed to have a well-defined style; this was a vital part of their promotional image and was directly linked to their material wealth. In challenging the importance of sword styles Musashi was challenging the entire community of sword instructors, men who had established their professional reputations on their ability to teach something new.

Styles are a waste of time, Musashi insists. Any school that takes a definite approach to combat is making a fundamental mistake. Schools that promote the use of a long sword are in error because close fighting is sometimes required. Schools that stress the importance of brute force are mistaken, the object is actually to kill the opponent and excessive force can lead to deadly mistakes. Short sword schools are deficient as they force their student to always adopt a defensive posture when attack is often the key to victory. Schools that teach a large number of techniques are wrong because fighting is essentially simple and should not be overcomplicated. Schools that train fighters to use certain guard positions are in error because a fixed guard can cause fighters to cede the initiative to their opponents. Schools that teach a certain kind of gaze are missing the point, a fighter should fix his gaze on the mind of his opponent. Training samurai to use certain styles of footwork is foolish, combat often takes place on rough ground or in water. Finally, the boast of so many schools that they can teach secret 'depth' techniques is ridiculous. Any technique that works is relevant and is of equal value to any other, writes Musashi, adding that he does not require his own students to keep any of the secrets of his school intact. The true secret, he insists, does not lie in any technique but in the arduous process of engaging in intensive, lifelong training.

The Void

Musashi ends his book on a grand philosophical note. In the brief final scroll he reveals the influence of Buddhist thought on his resolutely practical mind. Ultimately, he writes, the way of the warrior exists in a place of emptiness, a void that lies behind and beyond mere technique or emotion. The path to this void must be discovered through determined and resolute practice.

> He should put it into practice from morning till night without tiring and without letting his mind wander. He should polish his mind and his will ... He should know that true empty space is where the clouds of uncertainty have completely dissipated. (7)

Living above the clouds in his mountain cave, gazing out over the winter sea, Musashi completed his book. He was seriously ill and the Hosokawa family sent doctor after doctor up the mountain to treat his failing body. The physicians insisted that Musashi should come down from his perch to rest and recuperate and many wondered how the intimidating old warrior would respond to such orders. In the end he did grudgingly return to his castle. But, after a period of languishing in illness and sensing that the end was near, he decided to walk back up to the cave in order to hide his "dying body from the sight of others".

In early May of 1645 Musashi began to give away all of his possessions to his friends and disciples. He had just enough strength left to compose one more document, a list of twenty one principles for living that was to be his last will and testament. He called the list 'The Solitary Path' (Dokkodo) and it rings with the loneliness and self-discipline of his life. He had lived a life that placed great value on the pursuit of essential truth, a life that took the insubstantial attachments and pleasures of the world lightly. Musashi was no ascetic; he greatly enjoyed food, drink, art, friendships and love affairs. But these things could never hold his attention for long. The comforts of the world are irrelevant, he suggested. There is something more important that we must try to find in the midst of everyday life.

> The Solitary Path
> 1. Accept everything just the way it is and always has been.
> 2. Do not pursue pleasure for its own sake.
> 3. Do not, in any situation, depend on a partial feeling.
> 4. Think lightly of yourself and deeply of the world.
> 5. Be detached from desire your whole life long.
> 6. Do not regret what you have done.
> 7. Never be jealous of the good or evil in others.
> 8. Never let yourself be saddened by a separation.
> 9. Resentment and complaint are not appropriate for yourself or for others.
> 10. Do not let yourself be guided by the feeling of love.
> 11. In all things have no preferences.
> 12. Be indifferent to where you live.
> 13. Do not pursue the taste of good food.
> 14. Do not try to preserve old possessions for the future.
> 15. Do not follow traditions and beliefs in your actions.

16. Do not collect or practice with weapons beyond your needs.
17. Do not fear death in pursuit of the Way.
18. Do not try to gather either goods or lands for your old age.
19. Respect Buddha and the gods without counting on their help.
20. You can abandon your own body but you must hold on to your honor.
21. Never depart from the Way.

Just one week after composing this ringing moral testament Musashi came to his end. Alone for much of his life, the warrior died in the company of friends, his son Iori, and his students. As he neared the moment of death the sixty two year old samurai pulled himself up into a position of readiness with one knee raised and his sword in his hand.

Musashi had decided to end his life with one last demonstration of loyalty to the family who had truly understood and truly valued him. At his own request he was buried in his war armor in a place next to the route taken by the Hosokawa family as they made their regular journeys to Edo. Even in death Miyamoto Musashi was going to perform his duty. He would watch over the family of the man who had come to be his dearest friend and his lord.

5. Swords of Edo

Urban Samurai

The bustling streets of Edo were like nowhere else in Japan for a man like Miyamoto Musashi who had lived most of his life in rural villages and small castle towns. By the end of Musashi's life this young city had surpassed Kyoto in almost every way. It was growing so fast that by the middle of the eighteenth century it had turned into the world's largest city; a thriving society of more than a million people. The city was so important to Japan that it even gave its name to an era, the Edo Period.

In these years, between 1603 and 1868 both the city and the nation were at peace. The warrior class was firmly lodged at the top of society and provided Japan with its bureaucrats, philosophers and politicians. Tens of thousands of samurai strode through the streets of Edo City, their twin swords swinging at their sides. For most of these men life was good, their social position brought both respect and a steady government income. Although they carried swords they gave little thought to preparation for war. To be a samurai had become a matter of behaving with social grace. It no longer demanded courage or even fighting ability.

The thousands of samurai in the capital were themselves stratified into a series of ranks. Those in the upper levels were directly employed by the Shogun as government officials, civil servants, inspectors, army officers and planners. They were paid for their services with a fixed annual allocation of rice that they could exchange for cash and other goods. The middle ranks of the Edo samurai vied for employment in the police, the fire service, or in local administration. At the lower end of the samurai class were men who lived a hand to mouth existence and faced periods of unemployment or even hunger. These poorer samurai made the most of any connections they had with the upper tier samurai who could help them to find work. All of these samurai who had been born in Edo were joined by thousands of rural samurai who arrived in the company of visiting lords from the regions of Japan. Another group who were attracted to Edo were the ronin, masterless samurai who came in search of employment and adventure. For these young men Edo was the best place in Japan to make contacts and to enjoy the endless delights of the pleasure quarters.

As the peace deepened and the seventeenth century gave way to the eighteenth it became clear to those who still cared about such things that the number of samurai who were capable of actually fighting in a battle had fallen into serious decline. But although the samurai became less warlike they never entirely lost their identity as members of a warrior class. Most of the young city samurai were sent to martial arts classes as children and they often continued with martial training as they entered adulthood.

The fighting training that these young men experienced in Edo was quite different from that of their grandfathers. The sense that a samurai would at some point be required to fight for his life on a battlefield practically disappeared. At the same time a new self-image was emerging among the Edo samurai. They began to see themselves more as a ruling class rather than as a collection of fighters. It was natural for a samurai to aspire to become a cultivated intellectual as well as a warrior. And as the samurai became sophisticates the martial arts slowly changed. Training became more elegant and more formal as ritualistic elements of practice came to the fore. Martial arts also tended to become specialized. In the sixteenth century it had been normal for samurai to practice all of the skills that they might need on the battlefield. By the eighteenth century martial arts schools that were based around one weapon or skill began to dominate.

By some distance the most popular and important martial art of the Edo period was kenjutsu, the art of sword fighting. In a world where it was no longer common to carry a bow or a spear in public but where every samurai man carried two swords at his side the sword was now the key symbol of samurai identity. Swords were a ready means of self-defense in a city that thronged with young men. Samurai boys were sent to sword schools to learn what it meant to be a warrior and also to learn how to take care of themselves.

Sword schools had multiplied since the sixteenth century and by the eighteenth century more than five hundred sword schools existed throughout Japan. This amazing diversity was largely the result of the prohibition on samurai changing their place of employment introduced by Toyotomi Hideyoshi. Most sword styles were created in isolation by local experts and these schools rarely spread beyond the confines of the region. But in Edo the situation was different. Styles that had been created in the city brushed up against sword styles introduced by visiting rural samurai. There was a great choice of schools and a great variety of training methods. Some schools continued to teach students who dressed in full battle armor and used steel swords. But these styles were in a minority. Most Edo period schools allowed their students to attend practice in their everyday clothes and experimented with the use of bamboo swords and full-contact fighting. The popularity of the sword fighting schools and their physical proximity to each other created a natural competition. Challenge matches between the best fighters from rival schools were common.

Many other weapons systems and martial arts were also practiced in Edo, sometimes in conjunction with the sword and sometimes as separate schools in their own right. One classification of the martial arts of Edo city in the early nineteenth century described eighteen separate fighting arts. Aside from swordsmanship, there were schools of archery (kyujutsu), staff fighting (bojutsu), spear fighting (sojutsu) and gun fighting (teppo). Jujutsu, the art of unarmed grappling, boomed in popularity during this period as it provided training in skills that could be used to stop fights or to arrest criminals. Older forms of jujutsu had been largely based on simple wrestling techniques but in the new era of peace it became a more subtle and varied art. Samurai could also attend schools that taught the practical skills of horsemanship (bajutsu), swimming (suieijutsu), throwing weapons (shurikenjutsu) and defensive skills such as the use of a truncheon (jitte). One thing that almost all of these schools held in common was the secrecy of their teachings. Students were made to swear oaths that they would never reveal the innermost secrets of their style. Some teachers would even black out the windows of their training dojos so that samurai from the rival schools could not climb up on the walls to peep inside.

Village Masters
At the very apex of the complex world of Edo martial arts in the seventeenth century was the Yagyu family. For three generations this family held positions that marked them out as the greatest experts in the land. The Yagyu were employed as sword teachers by a succession of Shoguns and took advantage of their privileged status to become both wealthy and powerful. They achieved a social distinction that no Japanese martial arts expert before or since has been able to match. Undoubtedly the Yagyu family were in the mind of the young Miyamoto Musashi as he strove to build his reputation. They were living evidence that winning fame as a great swordsman could raise a man to the very top.

And yet the origins of the Yagyu clan were humble enough. The family that came to dominate Japanese swordsmanship emerged from a tiny village hidden away among the deep mountain valleys of what is now Nara Prefecture. They were the leading samurai family of the village that had adopted their family name and were licensed by the Kamakura government to govern the surrounding area. It was a quiet place, a farming community that eventually saw its peace shattered in the uncontrolled warfare of the sixteenth century. As fighting swept through the region the Yagyu family was inexorably drawn into hard combat. Yagyu Muneyoshi, the founder of the Yagyu sword dynasty, was a mere youth of sixteen in 1544 when an army of ten thousand samurai besieged his village. Alongside his father and the thousand or so men of the village young Muneyoshi was caught up in desperate hand-to-hand fighting as the villagers struggled to hold off their attackers for three days.

When they finally surrendered to overwhelming numbers the Yagyu people were forced to accept the rule of their invaders, the Miyoshi clan. As often happened in those days of shifting fortunes Muneyoshi was recruited as a fighter for the Miyoshi army. For the next fifteen years he went to war again and again, being transformed by his experiences into an outstanding young swordsman. By the time he had turned thirty the name of Muneyoshi was known far beyond the bounds of his little village. Many believed that he was the outstanding living swordsman in central Japan. He had faced great numbers of determined warriors and had killed many enemies. He had every reason to believe in his own skill. And then one day he came face to face with something entirely new; a true genius of the sword.

The Shadow

Kamiizumi Nobutsuna was one of those irrepressibly ambitious and energetic samurai who travelled the roads of mid-sixteenth century Japan in search of challenge and adventure. One incident from his travels became enough of a legend to be featured in Akira Kurosawa's great movie The Seven Samurai. As Nobutsuna wandered into a certain country village one day he came across a group of distraught villagers. They had chased down and trapped a thief but, before they could properly restrain the criminal, he took a child hostage and barricaded himself inside one of the village houses. To the horror of his mother the thief was loudly threatening to kill the child.

Nobutsuna immediately took hold of the situation. He approached the village priest and asked to borrow his robes. He also asked the priest to take a knife and shave off his distinguished samurai hairstyle, leaving his head bald gleaming like that of a monk. In this disguise, Nobutsuna slowly approached the hut where the thief was yelling out his determination to slice the child up. Gently, Nobutsuna offered a rice ball for the child and, guessing that the criminal had not eaten for hours, tossed a second portion of food into the hut. As soon as the robber's attention had shifted to the rice Nobutsuna dashed through the door, threw the muscular thief onto the dirt floor and emerged with the unharmed child in his arms.

Nobutsuna's swift action, and utter fearlessness, were a demonstration of the supreme stillness of mind that he had acquired through systematic sword training in the Shadow (Kage Ryu) school of sword fighting. This school is historically important as the first Japanese martial school known to have paid serious attention to the psychology of combat. Swordsmen of the Shadow style aimed to keep their own mind in the shadows and to clearly perceive the mind of an opponent. The mind of a fighter, they believed, should be as empty as the still surface of a pond reflecting the moon. This stillness allowed the emotions and intentions of the opponent to become apparent and made victory a simple matter of responding instantaneously to an obvious attack. The Shadow school, was one important point of origin for the philosophical, psychological and even religious dimensions that were to become so important to the Japanese martial arts in later centuries.

The sword style of the Shadow school was based on careful observation of an opponent and was therefore essentially defensive. Nobutsuna described his attitude in battle as being like that of a sailor shifting sails in response to the wind or like a hunter who lets his hawk fly just as a rabbit is spotted bounding across a field. Swordsmen of his school were trained to never begin an attack but to wait in silent preparation for an instant response to the opponent's first move.

Nobutsuna, who had many devoted students, was an innovative teacher. Most schools of the time required their students to train with heavy and dangerous wooden swords. These swords could kill if they were swung with full force, so most teachers required their students to control their strikes at the point of contact. But Nobutsuna rejected the artificiality of this kind of practice. Students needed to learn what it felt like to hit, and to be hit. In order to make this possible he created the fukuro-shinai, a bundle of bamboo sticks wrapped in a leather bag that allowed students to strike each other with full power. Later, this innovation would evolve into the bamboo shinai that is used in modern kendo. The Shadow School, with its rejection of a first attack and the introduction of safe sparring equipment, was centuries ahead of its time.

Nobutsuna was fifty-five years old and on a journey through Nara when he was invited to fight in a challenge match with the local hero, Yagyu Muneyoshi. The agreed venue was the Hozoin Temple, an ancient centre of the martial arts, and the match attracted quite a crowd. Before an audience of monks and local samurai the delegations of the two swordsmen politely exchanged greetings. Nobutsuna, who was a new face in this part of Japan, was the focus of interest. But disappointment rippled through the crowd when the older man ordered one of his students to step forward to face Muneyoshi. The proud local hero, irritated at being asked to spar with a mere student, raised his sword. But his pride was hurt even more when the bamboo sword of the student struck him twice with bewildering speed. Muneyoshi no longer felt like 'The Greatest Swordsman of Central Japan'.

Now Nobutsuna stepped forward and took up a fighting stance in front of Muneyoshi. The younger man stared for a silent eternity into Nobutsuna's eyes. Then, to the astonishment of the crowd, he flung his sword aside. Muneyoshi fell to his knees and begged Nobutsuna to accept him as a student. Here, he sensed, was ability beyond his imagination.

Muneyoshi was determined to learn all he could from this great master and persuaded Nobutsuna to make an extended visit to the village of Yagyu so that he could give daily lessons in sword fighting. Nobutsuna stayed in Yagyu for more than a year and it soon became clear that this was an expert who had progressed far beyond the swordsmanship he had learned as a young man. The fighting style of the Shadow School was designed for battlefield combat but Nobutsuna had discarded many of the very low stances and overwhelmingly powerful sword strokes of battlefield fighting. In their place he had introduced fluid, blindingly fast techniques. He named his adapted system the New Shadow School (Shinkage Ryu).

As they practiced sword work Nobutsuna slowly introduced Muneyoshi to the most difficult and dangerous set of techniques known to the samurai – unarmed defense against a sword attack. Nobutsuna had developed an interest in this type of fighting after an incident when he had been the victim of an unexpected sword attack in a temple garden. As the attacker drew close Nobutsuna had instinctively sprung to his feet and raised his bare hands to trap the razor sharp blade before subduing his assailant. Inspired by the success of this impromptu defense Nobutsuna had gone on to make a study of all the ways that a sword attack could be delivered and had devised a series of unarmed techniques to block a sword and throw an attacker. These no-sword (muto) techniques of the New Shadow School would, centuries later, become one of the roots of modern martial arts like judo and aikido.

In the peaceful atmosphere of Yagyu village Muneyoshi trained hard under Nobutsuna. The master watched the talented Yagyu swordsman closely and he would often order one of his students to attack Muneyoshi without warning so that he could observe the young man's reaction. After a year of this intense tutorship Nobutsuna officially recognized that his student had reached the highest level of swordsmanship. Nobutsuna was ready to retire from teaching and announced that Muneyoshi would be his successor. The younger man was in full command of the secrets of the way and could take up the leadership of the New Shadow School. Nobutsuna inscribed a certificate of mastery for Muneyoshi. It began with a final command: "You must train even harder than before."

When Nobutsuna left the Yagyu village Muneyoshi stayed on, practicing his sword work daily with the other village samurai and his five sons. He continued to build on the techniques he had learned from Nobutsuna by traveling to meet and practice with other sword masters. Regular local battles also created many opportunities for Muneyoshi and his sons to test their techniques out on in combat situations. But the family paid a heavy price for their education. The fourth son was killed in battle while the oldest son was so badly injured that he was no longer capable of practicing martial arts. Muneyoshi himself survived, however, and the reputation of his sword style, now named the Yagyu New Shadow School, spread far and wide.

Throwing the Shogun
Eventually rumors about the outstanding swordsmanship of the Yagyu family made their way to one of the most important and powerful men in the land. In 1594 Tokugawa Ieyasu was living in Kyoto. In just a few years he would be Shogun but already his active, restless mind was scouring Japan for the best teachers and best fighters. After listening to regular praise of the Yagyu school Ieyasu took the step of

inviting Muneyoshi to visit him at his countryside villa to give a demonstration of the techniques of his school.

Muneyoshi, by now sixty-six years old, brought his youngest son Munenori with him to Kyoto. The two men gave a skillful display of sword kata but they really began to impress Ieyasu with a sequence of unarmed defense methods. One would attack with a sword while the other would suddenly step forward to catch the sword hand, the hilt of the sword, or even the razor-sharp blade itself. They would then demonstrate ways of disarming the sword wielding attacker.

Ieyasu had never before come across this kind of daring and risky defense. But he was not a man to be easily impressed and had encountered plenty of charlatans in his time. Ieyasu decided to find out for himself just how real the demonstration had actually been. He picked out a wooden sword and approached the older man. Ieyasu was a large, fearless samurai who had decades of combat experience. Clearly, he knew how to handle a sword.

Muneyoshi faced up to the lord of eastern Japan in a relaxed posture, his arms swinging loosely in front of his body. He was a skilled practitioner of kimiuchi, one of the grappling arts that would later provide the basis for jujutsu. Suddenly Ieyasu raised his sword and swung the blade down forcefully, aiming for the crown of Muneyoshi's head. In a flash, the swordsman shifted his weight and blocked the hilt of the sword. Before Ieyasu had time to react to the block his sword was sent flying through the air and his wrist was pinioned in a lock. With his right hand Muneyoshi gave a controlled rap to Ieyasu's chest. He did not humiliate the great man by knocking him over but the contact was strong enough to send Ieyasu tottering backwards for several steps.

After he recovered his balance Ieyasu laughed with pleasure. He thought he had seen everything, but he had never encountered this kind of skill and timing before. "Please," he begged, "teach me the secrets of this wonderful style." Muneyoshi and the great lord entered into a close relationship that would transform the prospects of the Yagyu family. After a period of instruction, most likely somewhat abbreviated in consideration of his student's social standing, Muneyoshi handed over a document of transmission. It stated that Ieyasu was in possession of all the secrets of the Yagyu New Shadow School, secrets that he must never reveal to a living soul. Clearly flattered at receiving this special attention from such a fine swordsman Ieyasu responded with a document in which he promised to protect Muneyoshi and his family.

Before long Ieyasu proved to be as good as his word. He made Muneyoshi a splendid offer of a position as sword instructor to the Tokugawa family. Muneyoshi politely replied that he was too old to begin a new life and asked Ieyasu to instead employ his twenty-four year old son Munenori. The young man was accepted, joined the Tokugawa household, fought alongside Ieyasu at Sekigahara and then settled into a lucrative position as the senior sword instructor to the Shogun and his family. Meanwhile the father retired to spend his final years among the mountains of Nara where he could enjoy the new era of peace.

Teacher to Power
Thanks to his father's influence Munenori Yagyu was established as a distinguished member of Edo society before reaching the age of thirty. But he was not going to be a soft city samurai. Munenori's father had been happy to recommend his son to Ieyasu because he knew that the young man was both skillful and determined. Munenori was, in fact, the only son of Muneyoshi who had truly inherited his father's passion for the sword. His oldest brother had been seriously injured in battle and the other brothers, although quite willing to fight, had little interest in in the rigors of daily sword practice. It was the teenage Munenori who would climb up into the woods surrounding Yagyu village to work on his sword skills. He tied stones to twines hanging from the trees and then, after shaking the branches, tried to hit the bouncing stones with his wooden sword, perfecting his control. In the depths of the bitter mountain winters of Nara Munenori would train in thigh-deep snow, building the strong legs and hips that give a swordsman unshakeable balance. In this age of war he was like many other young samurai, dreaming that war would present him with a glorious opportunity. Both destiny and skill would help him to rise to the very top.

Munenori was fated to be more than just a sword teacher in the Tokugawa palace. He became a trusted counsellor to Ieyasu and seems to have played an important role during the preparations for the great battle at Sekigahara. Ieyasu sent Munenori to his home village to raise forces for the coming battle and did so in the knowledge that Yagyu village is very close to the famous villages of Iga and Koga. These places were ancient centers of training for the multi-skilled fighters known as shinobi, or ninja. The ninja, the special forces of their day, were experts in spying, scouting and assassination. Their stock in trade was hidden movement and sudden attack. It seems likely that Munenori visited these nearby ninja villages to recruit men for spying and sabotage missions, important work at a time when large bands of heavily armed samurai were moving around the countryside in preparation for battle. Whatever his role, it is clear that Munenori distinguished himself in the struggles that thrust Ieyasu into national power. He was rewarded for his service by being promoted to the salaried position of hatamono, an official flag-bearer for the Tokugawa family. In addition, Ieyasu restored to the Yagyu their ancient rights to rule over and raise taxes from the area around their home village.

Ieyasu soon retired from his position as Shogun to lead Japan from the shadows but Munenori was barely affected by this change as he was immediately appointed as the official sword instructor to the new

Shogun, Ieyasu's son Hidetada. In many ways Munenori was the perfect instructor for the young Hidetada who proved to be a less than enthusiastic swordsman. Munenori was sufficiently skilled to spar with wooden swords while controlling his strikes just at the point of contact. He also had enough tact to teach the rather clumsy young ruler without inflicting a major humiliation. For his part Hidetada appreciated the opportunity to practice a swordsmanship that did not involve the bruises and embarrassments that some of his other teachers handed out to him. The relationship between these two men deepened during the Battle of Osaka. Munenori was acting as the official bodyguard to Hidetada when the Toyotomi army launched a desperate break-out attack on the encircling Tokugawa forces. When a group of Toyotomi samurai attempted to smash their way into the Shogun's camp Munenori took out his sword and personally cut down seven of the attackers. He then led the grateful Hidetada away to safety.

Munenori was responsible for the entire Tokugawa family and taught sword fighting skills to all of the Shogun's descendants. Among the sons of Hidetada the most enthusiastic student was Iemitsu, the boy who would later succeed his father as the third Tokugawa Shogun. The relationship between Munenori and Iemitsu was a particularly close one and Munenori was still at the height of his powers, aged fifty three, when the twenty-one year old Iemitsu became Shogun. Unlike his father Iemitsu was a determined swordsman, so determined that on one occasion he wrote a letter of complaint to his teacher suggesting that he was not being pushed hard enough. Such demands undoubtedly caused a few sleepless nights for Munenori. There was a limit as to how much punishment he could hand out to the ruler of all Japan. And he was uncomfortably aware that no member of the ruling family would be able to put up with the long and arduous training that was required to become an expert swordsman .

Iemitsu rather enjoyed tormenting Munenori and he often tested the older man out to see if his skills were really at the level they were said to be. On one occasion, as Munenori entered his room and touched his forehead to the floor in greeting, the young Shogun grabbed a spear and thrust it at Munenori's prostrate body. Instinctively, the swordsman swept the Shogun's legs from under him. The ruler of Japan, to the dismay of his servants, was sent sprawling onto his back. But this kind of incident only served to bring the two men closer together. Iemitsu demonstrated his trust in Munenori by raising his salary to a level where his income was equivalent to that of a great regional lord. Munenori became a very important man, someone who had access to the great councils of state as an advisor. Many believe that Munenori was the creator of the network of spies that underpinned Iemitsu's centralized control of Japan.

Yagyu Munenori had connections and a polished manner that placed him on an elevated social rank far above the rough and tumble of everyday samurai rivalry. Whether or not he was truly the greatest swordsman in the land he was certainly, by this time, a great man. It would not have been seemly for Munenori to have accepted challenges from socially inferior swordsmen on the make. The inaccessibility of this top ranking swordsman was of great significance to Miyamoto Musashi, who lived in Edo for extended periods during the time when Munenori was serving as sword instructor to the Shoguns. We know that Musashi considered himself to be at least the equal of any other swordsman in the land but there is no record of the two men ever coming face to face.

The Empty Sword
Munenori attained his distinguished position at the very time when the Tokugawa government was taking decisive steps to transform the social standing of the samurai. Ieyasu had begun the process in 1615 by creating laws to govern samurai behavior. The samurai, he decreed, were an aristocratic class and should behave as such. They could continue their study of the martial arts but should balance these activities by developing an interest in subjects that were appropriate to their elevated status, such as classical literature. Munenori, who had trained in the philosophically-oriented New Shadow School, was an ideal figure to give leadership and expression to the changing role of the samurai. He played a vital part in shaping a new conception of the martial arts, helping to give them a significance that went beyond learning how to damage other human beings. Munenori encouraged the Japanese samurai to think of the martial arts as a vehicle for human transformation. Above all, he almost single-handedly created the idea, still so influential today, that Zen Buddhism and swordsmanship are two sides of a single coin (kenzen toitsu).

Zen Buddhism had been first introduced to Japan in the 12th century by the monk Eisai after a long and arduous journey to China. He brought back a tradition that quickly became popular with the warrior class. Zen requires regular practice of seated meditation, a meditation that produces a deep inner stillness that can quieten the anxieties of everyday life and even the fear of death itself. These benefits of Zen practice were welcome to samurai who were keenly aware that the span of their lives was likely to be brief. They were deeply conscious that they could meet death at any time on the battlefield. A practice that helped them make sense of the extremity of their lives, and allowed them to maintain calm in the face of present danger, was something that these men of war could appreciate. Between the thirteenth and seventeenth centuries Zen Buddhism exerted a wide influence on Japanese culture and on the Japanese approach to life and death. Only a small minority of samurai actually became serious practitioners of Zen but many more absorbed the ideas of the religion. And some serious thinkers about the warrior arts, including Miyamoto Musashi, made regular Zen meditation practice an important part of their training routine.

Yagyu Munenori had been introduced to Zen by one of the outstanding masters of the time, Takuan Soho. The two men were almost the same age and they became intimate friends over the decades before they both died as septuagenarians. Takuan was an unconventional and self-confident monk who had made a name for himself at an early age when he was placed in charge of the Daitokuji temple in Kyoto. But he was a restless figure who soon fell out with the Zen establishment and then with the government. He was banished to the extreme north of Japan.

Takuan's career seemed to have come to an end. But he was rescued by his friend Yagyu Munenori who intervened with the new Shogun Iemitsu. He persuaded the ruler of Japan to allow Takuan to return from exile and to live in Edo under the nose of the very government he had criticized. Munenori then took a further step by arranging for the recalcitrant priest to meet with the Shogun. Iemitsu could not fail to be impressed. He came to value Takuan just as highly as he did Munenori and made the priest a regular, and trusted, advisor. The two friends of the young Shogun died within three months of each other, both wrapped up in work to the end of their long lives. Takuan famously raised himself up on his deathbed to paint the character 'dream' as his final teaching. Munenori exited his life in a similar fashion, sitting up on his sickbed to whisper a few final words about swordsmanship into the ear of Iemitsu.

These two men were the first Japanese writers to make a serious attempt to integrate the ideas of Buddhism with those of the martial arts. Each was strongly influenced by the other and Munenori himself readily admitted that his own writings had been inspired by the letters he had received from Takuan. The priest, who took a close interest in all the leading swordsmen of the day, urged Munenori to integrate the Buddhist concept of non-attachment into his martial training. The secret of expert swordsmanship, he argued, lies in losing all attachment to technique, to the opponent's intention, to worrying about the next move. All of these mental activities, in fact, stop the mind. The mind must be entirely free to move in whatever direction is necessary. A free mind, and a body that has mastered technique, will be unstoppable.

> If the mind stops with the sword with which a man is going to strike you, there will be an interval, and your own action will be lost. But if in the interval between your opponent's striking sword and your own action you cannot introduce even the breadth of a hair, your opponent's sword should become your own. (9)

Expert swordsmanship, Takuan wrote, is indistinguishable from Buddhism in action. The true mind is never separate from reality but moves with reality at the speed of sparks rising from a struck stone. Beginners in the martial arts have a need to hold their mind in a strong and concentrated state but the expert is free at every point.

> The opponent is Emptiness. I am Emptiness. The hand that holds the sword, the sword itself, is Emptiness. (9)

The Mirror Mind

Munenori, in his own writing, drew on the suggestions of Takuan to create a profound and inspiring vision of the inner meaning of swordsmanship. He wrote that a swordsman who has his mind fixed on the sword is not fully in control. The true way of the martial arts is to maintain an empty, calm mind with no attachment to any single facet of battle. Like Miyamoto Musashi, Munenori wrote for a select readership of experienced swordsmen. Only decades of training could instill the subconscious of a samurai with the kind of instinctive control of technique that he advocates.

Yagyu Munenori's most important writings are found in Heiho Kadensho (Martial Legends). In this book Munenori firmly presents himself as the successor to a great martial tradition that had been founded by Kamiizumi Nobutsuna and had passed through Yagyu Muneyoshi to Munenori himself. He would, in turn, take responsibility for passing the teaching on to his children and students. He viewed himself, therefore, as an accomplished insider, the antithesis to a wandering self-taught outsider like Miyamoto Musashi. The ideas in his book fit squarely with the mood of the times. The Tokugawa rulers were determined to create a peaceful society and Munenori's book contains none of the fanatical death-lust that would disfigure some later writing on the martial arts. This battle hardened swordsman did not regard fighting and killing as glorious accomplishments but as necessary evils. At times, he writes, one must kill in order to save thousands. The sword has a positive role in society. It can be life-giving.

Like Takuan, Munenori compares the state of mind of a beginner in the martial arts with the mind of an expert. At first a beginner is free in his movements because he knows nothing and has no doubts. After a certain amount of training the complexities of the new techniques he has learned bind up his mind and slow his reactions. Only with long, hard and thorough training can this problem be overcome. For an advanced swordsman movement no longer exists in the mind but purely in the body. The mind, in fact, completely ceases to intervene between action and reaction.

> That is the ultimate end of all disciplines. The final state of any discipline is where you forget what you have learned, discard your mind, and accomplish whatever you set out to do without being aware of it yourself. You begin by learning and reach the point where learning does not exist. (9)

In keeping with the tradition of his New Shadow School Munenori is primarily concerned with the defensive, reactive aspects of swordsmanship. In a duel every strategy should be employed to try to make the opponent commit to the first attack. When the attack comes victory is guaranteed if the mind does not hover at the point of deciding on a response to the attack. Strike should follow immediately upon strike, not giving the opponent time "even to raise his face."

In another echo of Takuan, Munenori places the attachment-free and empty Mind of Zen at the heart of his writing. All human actions, he writes, have the same nature. The correct way to shoot an arrow, to hold a sword, to ride a horse or to play a musical instrument is to lose the remnants of conscious control that prevent any action from being conducted with complete freedom and naturalness. Without thought, things happen easily and smoothly.

> The mind of a man of the Way is like a mirror; because it has nothing and it is clear, it is "mindless" and is lacking in nothing. That is the mind in a natural state. (9)

This 'mindlessness' advocated by Munenori is not a state of dreamy unconsciousness. It is, in fact, quite the opposite. The empty mind is fully present and immediately and fully aware of everything in the environment. In another document Munenori cautioned swordsmen that their very lives depended on maintaining a state of radiant awareness of every detail around them. Here are some of his rules of behavior for advanced swordsmen.

- When meeting someone, place at least three meters between yourself and the host. Carefully observe the furnishings of the room and the positioning of the entrances.
- When receiving tea, pay close attention to the hands of the server.
- When walking at night, stay behind your servant and out of the light. If you meet someone unexpectedly, speak quickly to discover their intentions.
- When sleeping, place your lamp as far as possible away from your body.
- Never sleep next to the doors of your bedroom. (10)

Single Combat
The Yagyu family were the most important sword instructors at the early Tokugawa court. But the rulers of Japan were wealthy enough to keep several other martial experts in their employment. Some years before Munenori arrived in Edo Ieyasu had appointed an altogether different kind of man as sword instructor to his family. Ono Tadaaki was, like Yagyu Munenori, the son of a country samurai but he had none of the polished social skills or the ambition of Munenori. Tadaaki was not invited to Edo, he

arrived as a relative unknown in the new boom town in 1588 having just been appointed as the new master of the One Stroke school of swordsmanship. Edo was rapidly filling with young samurai who needed to practice their sword skills and Tadaaki found it easy to make a living as a teacher. He decided to stay in the rapidly growing city.

Tadaaki was soon to become a famous figure, believed by many to be the greatest swordsman in Edo, after an incident that allowed him to demonstrate his great skill and confidence. In a small village just outside the city a rogue swordsman had killed several villagers and had then been chased by the remainder of the residents until he was cornered in a house. The killer was a large and fierce swordsman who proceeded to slaughter several of the local police who attempted to arrest him. The murderer was so intimidating that no-one was willing to risk their life attempting to arrest the man and so a request was sent to Edo for a master swordsman who could handle this dangerous criminal. Tadaaki was just the man. Making his way to the house where the man was in hiding Tadaaki stood outside and called out a challenge to single combat. The criminal stepped outside happily, ready to dispatch another police officer. He took a swing at Tadaaki who blocked with his sword and then cut sideways so quickly that the criminal's arms were sliced cleanly from his body. The limbs landed in the dirt several meters away. Pausing to receive permission from the local police, Tadaaki raised his sword one more time and severed the man's head.

Word of this highly competent swordsman reached the ears of Ieyasu and before long he had appointed Tadaaki as sword instructor to his family, with the special task of providing training for the future Shogun Hidetaka. But Tadaaki was a rough diamond and he showed little interest in adapting his teaching methods, which could be harsh, to accommodate the young prince. Hidetaka had no liking for this severe teacher and the young Shogun never rewarded Tadaaki with the salary raises and social honors that he would lavish on the more politic Yagyu Munenori. The older teacher would remain a minor figure in the history of the Tokugawa court. But Ono Tadaaki proved to be a person of major importance in the development of Japanese sword fighting. His students and descendants eventually founded Japan's most important line of swordsmanship, a line that would be dominant among the sword schools of the nineteenth and twentieth centuries.

One Stroke
Ono Tadaaki learned about fighting from the great Ito Ittosai, founder of the One Stroke (Itto Ryu) school of swordsmanship. Ittosai was a truly self-made man who had emerged from a childhood of desperate poverty. He was born on a remote island and is said to have been washed up on a beach on the Japanese mainland at the age of fourteen after floating across the sea on a piece of driftwood. The villagers who found the half drowned teenager kept him alive by feeding him occasionally and allowing

him to sleep under the floorboards of the village shrine. The kindness shown to this orphan boy was rewarded as he grew into a young man who was a natural sword fighter. Ittosai repaid his debt to the villagers by helping them to handle aggressive traveling samurai and by chasing off marauding bandits. In gratitude for his help and bravery the village collected enough money to enable the young man to set out on a pilgrimage in search of the secrets of swordsmanship.

Ittosai made his way to Kamakura. He was well used to sleeping outdoors and spent a week living in the grounds of an important shrine where he trained with his sword and slept under the stars. On the seventh night he was resting in the dark when he sensed a hostile presence approaching from behind. Without thinking, Ittosai turned and sliced at the shadow in one flashing movement. A dead man lay at his feet. Shocked and disturbed by this strange event Ittosai hurried away from Kamakura before he could be arrested for murder. But although he was shaken he realized that in a moment of danger he had drawn and swung his sword perfectly. He would spend years trying to reproduce that instinctive speed at will.

Ittosai travelled far and wide meeting teachers and assessing their technique. He finally found a sword teacher he could respect in Kanemaki Jisai, the same man who had been the teacher of Miyamoto Musashi's great rival Sasaki Kojiro. Ittosai was gifted and he quickly became the best student in Kanemaki's sword school. But after less than five years of study with Kanemaki the student announced that his training was finished. Kanemaki was furious, he regarded Ittosai as a rank beginner in the lifelong struggle to penetrate the mysteries of the sword. The younger man was unrepentant. "If you don't believe me," he said, "put me to the test." The two men faced off with wooden swords, fighting three matches. Each time they came together Ittosai defeated his teacher easily and Kanemaki was left with no choice but to publicly recognize the mastery of his student. He handed a scroll containing all of the secrets of his school to Ittosai who left to continue his pilgrimage.

Ittosai now felt confident enough to develop his own style and he took the name of the style as his own. Itto Ryu, was the One Sword, or One Stroke school. It was a school that was noted for rapid, single strikes from a high position that could both block an attack and deliver a decisive blow in one forceful, uninterrupted movement. The One Stroke school had no place for the philosophical speculations of sword styles like the Shadow school and there was not a trace of sentimentality in its training methods. The sword, according to Ittosai, was not a vehicle for personal improvement. It was a tool for killing enemies.

The story of Ittosai's search for a successor, and his discovery of Ono Tadaaki, begins with the great swordsman hitching a ride on a ferryboat across a wide river. As his reputation spread, Ittosai had grown used to the questions of inquisitive strangers but few persisted like this boatman. The man, who was clearly not a samurai, began pestering Ittosai to demonstrate his skills. The sword master was in a rather grumpy mood and tried to ignore the chatter. But the obstinate ferryman pulled his boat onto a bank and announced that he wanted to fight. Ittosai was tempted to laugh, especially when the boatman raised an oar as his weapon. Finally accepting that this man really was angry and determined to test his skill, Ittosai drew his sword.

It soon became obvious that this was no mere drunken ferryman. Ittosai could see that his opponent had a good knowledge of swordsmanship and would have to be disarmed quickly before someone got badly hurt. He ran forward and slashed the blunt edge of his sword across the boatman's body. At once the boatman, who was experienced enough to know when he had met his match, fell to his knees. His name was Zenki, he said, and he had long dreamed of becoming a samurai. He made a habit of picking a fight with any of his customers who looked like they were strong enough to offer him some sword practice. But Ittosai was the first real expert he had met. In the face of the man's obvious sincerity Ittosai accepted Zenki as a student. The boatman was uncultured but had great determination. Ittosai taught him rigorously and eventually shaped him into the most skilled of all the students of the One Stroke School.

By the time Ittosai turned fifty he had traveled the length and breadth of Japan and had fought in thirty-three duels. He had never been defeated and only Zenki the boatman could come close to the master. It was said that the student had become good enough to win one out of three times in the regular practice matches he fought with his teacher. But Zenki had grown impatient over the years of hard training he had endured with Ittosai. He was convinced that he had attained a high enough level of skill to become a teacher himself. "Give me the scroll," he demanded of Ittosai, "give me the scroll that proves you recognize me as a fully-trained sword master. That marks me out as your chosen successor." Ittosai demurred; he was still strong, still traveling the country facing all challenges. He did not feel like retiring just yet.

Around the time Zenki was being ordered to wait for his teaching license, Ittosai discovered another excellent student. On a journey he crossed paths with Ono Tadaaki, an unknown and ambitious young samurai. In the way of the times the two men soon arranged a match. When the young man drew his sword Ittosai casually reached into a nearby woodpile and took a short branch as his weapon. Before Tadaaki could even attempt to attack Ittosai stepped in, seized the other man's sword and flung it onto the woodpile like a piece of trash. This was humiliating treatment but Tadaaki was no quitter. They faced off again and again with Tadaaki losing easily each time. Ittosai could see that there was something fine in the young man's persistence and decided to accept him as a student. He treated this apprentice just as roughly as he had Zenki but Tadaaki made such rapid progress that it soon became impossible to judge which of the two students was more highly skilled.

One evening in 1588 Ittosai called Zenki and Tadaaki to share his evening meal. "I have decided to retire," he announced after they finished eating. "Tomorrow morning I will give the scroll of succession to one of you. You must fight to decide who will be the new master. Choose the rules yourselves." Zenki and Tadaaki gazed at their master, and then at each other, in utter astonishment. This was not the way these things were supposed to proceed. In most cases, a sword master would pass the leadership of the style on to his oldest son. If a suitable son did not appear then the senior student would be appointed. Zenki had been absolutely sure for a long time that he was the natural candidate to succeed Ittosai. But now there was nothing he could do except accede to his master's strange order. The two students talked together and then announced, to the obvious approval of Ittosai, that they would settle their rivalry with real swords. The morning would decide everything. One would become the master and the other faced humiliation, or even death. Ittosai told them that he would leave his school after their duel. No one was to follow him.

The showdown the following morning between Zenki and Ono Tadaaki did not go quite the way Ittosai had expected. Rising before the sun, the three men met in a field as the first rays of light warmed the spring morning. Ittosai spread a large fan on the grass and, on top of the fan, placed one of his most precious swords and the priceless scroll containing the secrets of the One Stroke school. The two contenders took up ready stances, drew their swords, and waited. And waited. Ittosai had trained them never to make a first attack. Like the Shadow school, the One Stroke school taught swordsmen to make an instant response to their opponent's first attack. The two men circled on the grass, waiting, watching each other's breath with intense concentration. The tension between them rose higher and higher. Then, all of a sudden, Zenki ran toward the fan spread on the ground, grabbed the scroll that they had been fighting over, and sprinted into the distance as fast as his legs could carry him. Tadaaki and Ittosai looked at each other, wondering whether it was appropriate to laugh. They gave chase and the younger Tadaaki finally cornered Zenki. Holding the precious scroll between his teeth Zenki lifted a heavy branch and whirled around to attack his pursuer. Tadaaki brought his sword down. It sliced through the air, through the branch and through the body of the angry, disappointed, and soon to be dead ferryman.

Ono Tadaaki was now the leader of the One Stroke school. He made his way to Edo where he soon proved to be one of the outstanding sword teachers in the city. He was a rough and uncompromising teacher, just as Ittosai had been. In classes Tadaaki liked to use an iron practice sword that would leave heavy bruises on the arms and torsos of any students who made the mistake of leaving him an opening. Many who had seen Tadaaki in action believed that he was the very best swordsman in Edo, better even than Yagyu Munenori. It was said that Munenori's son, Mitsuyoshi had attempted to spar with Tadaaki on one occasion but had been hopelessly outclassed.

The tough sword teacher was, however, a clumsy exponent of the sophisticated manners that had become a requirement of life in the court of the Shogun. As a result, the career of Ono Tadaaki was overshadowed by that of Yagyu Munenori but his influence on the martial arts would prove to be the larger. Of the two dominant sword schools in seventeenth century Edo it was the style created by Ittosai and Ono Tadaaki that produced the leading swordsmen of the nineteenth century, men like Chiba Shusaku and Yamaoka Tesshu. And later, in the twentieth century, it was largely the followers of Ittosai and Ono Tadaaki who would give shape to modern kendo.

The Flowering Sword
Edo was a curious place in the seventeenth and eighteenth centuries. It was a large, vibrant city where technology, culture and the social classes were frozen in aspic. The samurai, who made up around ten percent of the population of the city, were easily distinguished by their swords and hairstyles. Every man of the samurai class carried two sharp swords at his side outside the house and wore his hair in the requisite chonmage style, shaved on top and tied up at the back. Very few of these samurai were employed as soldiers but they all, to one extent or another, regarded themselves as warriors in waiting. By the middle of the seventeenth century they had been waiting for a long time. Men like Yagyu Munenori and Ono Tadaaki had seen regular combat and had taken part in duels. But after 1650 the number of samurai who had any real battlefield experience declined sharply. Dueling was strongly discouraged by the government and men who had any experience of drawing a real sword in a real fight were few and far between.

In this new and peaceful world the hundreds of sword schools in Edo multiplied and adapted. Early in the seventeenth century holding a position as a sword teacher had been a dangerous and challenging profession. These teachers were required to act as the officers of the army of their local lord at short notice. Even in periods of peace a sword teacher must be prepared to receive challenges from young samurai on the make.

But by the end of the seventeenth century the samurai had been barred from changing their town of residence. In addition, fencing matches between rival schools (taryu jiai) were made illegal. These changes made the life of a sword instructor much easier and much safer. It was no longer very likely that a young upstart like Miyamoto Musashi could wander into any sword dojo to challenge the teacher and destroy a carefully developed reputation.

There was no longer any real way, in fact, of effectively comparing one sword school with another. For the first time, the profession of instructor in the martial arts became a career to which samurai could aspire without putting their lives or their reputations at risk. Anyone could create their own sword school and many did. Styles proliferated and, at the same time, skills deteriorated. Teachers found that they were able to make a comfortable living by charging fees to stable groups of students. At the same time the behavior of students changed. Under the influence of Confucianism, society became highly stratified. Complete respect and submission to those in authority gradually became the norm. In the fluid social mix of the sixteenth century teachers had been judged on their actual leadership skills and combat abilities. By the eighteenth century the sword teachers of Edo could expect to have their every instruction followed without question.

In the increasingly refined world of upper-class Edo society pastimes such as the tea ceremony, flower arranging and calligraphy became leisure pursuits that were governed by increasingly complex rules. In the same way the world of swordsmanship was reshaped by a move to codify and refine training practices. By the eighteenth century, swordsmen could no longer be found in the countryside, toughening their wrists by repeatedly slicing their blades into tree trunks. Swordsmanship was now regarded as a pursuit that young gentlemen should follow. They met in a dojo, a training hall dedicated to sword practice. Students would pair up for training that was dominated by repetitions of kata, the training method where two swordsmen would face each other and swing their swords together in prearranged patterns. Kata was not a new element in sword training, it had always been an important way of repeatedly practicing attacking and defensive moves. But now kata became the central feature of training. On entering a sword school in Edo a young samurai might not be allowed to do anything else but practice a limited number of kata for several years. Some schools required three years of kata training before any more realistic method of practice could be considered. In other schools seven years of pure kata practice was the rule.

The samurai who lived in Edo were generally of a somewhat different type from the samurai of small country towns. Many city samurai were employed as public officials or educators. They formed an intellectual class that preferred an aesthetically pleasing sword practice in which the moves of a kata resembled a kind of martial ballet. In general, kata became more 'external' and began to shed any sense of real combat danger. New kata were designed that included many graceful and impressive movements. These were showier and more extravagant than the kata of more conservative and more practical schools. Such changes did not go unremarked. Many samurai were deeply unhappy about the way things were going. By the end of the seventeenth century it had become common to hear samurai complain about the decline in fighting skills and the emergence of 'flowery' sword styles. One particularly vitriolic critic of the time wrote that the martial arts had become a game and that sword teachers were no better than geisha - more entertaining than they were deadly.

The martial arts had become rather too refined and a reaction was inevitable. It came with the appearance of schools that allowed their students to hit each other. For decades sparring with swords, or even with wooden practice swords, had been considered impossible. It was just too dangerous. The swordsmen of pre-Tokugawa times had controlled their attacks just at the point of impact. But this kind of sparring was frustratingly unrealistic. Swordsmen could not feel the strength of their techniques, and if they did fail to control attacks perfectly they could inflict serious injury on their training partner.

The problems associated with sword training were clear to all and many sword masters experimented in a search for solutions. One possibility lay in the bamboo swords first used by Kamiizumi Nobutsuna. Simple bamboo swords, known as shinai, allowed students to attack each other with full speed and power. But while bamboo swords were certainly safer than wooden swords they were still dangerous. So many cuts and bruises resulted from the unrestrained use of shinai that teachers began to experiment with protective armor. Lightweight shields, also made of bamboo, were first designed to protect the eyes. Later the protection was extended to headgear, wrist guards and finally body armor.

Nakanishi Chuzo Tsugutake, the leader of a branch of the One Stroke School, pioneered the use of both bamboo swords and full body armor in his Edo sword schools in the middle of the eighteenth century. His innovations were popular as they allowed swordsmen to be aggressive in perfect safety. This kind of training was exciting, it was fun and it was easy to learn. The schools that had introduced free sparring enjoyed a boom in membership and many new schools were opened. These new schools expanded rapidly and were able to accommodate many more students than the old style schools. Now that there was a greater focus on sparring and less time given to developing perfect technique, it was no longer so important for teachers to personally participate in, or supervise, training.

Backstreet Swordsman

By the outset of the nineteenth century the sword arts had become safer and consequently much more popular. But samurai still walked on the streets with two swords at their side and even in this relatively peaceful time there was plenty of trouble to be found. This much is made clear in the autobiography of Katsu Kokichi, a rare description of the life of a young samurai in nineteenth century Edo. Kokichi was born into a respectable, middle ranking samurai family but he grew to be a rather wild young man who would spend most of his life scraping for pennies. In his middle years Kokichi was so poor that he was reduced to selling the ceiling boards from his home to buy rice for his children.

Samurai boys, even the urban children of Edo, were expected to be tough. As a boy Kokichi once bloodied the lip of a friend. His infuriated father punished Kokichi by tying him to a post outside the house and hammering his head with a wooden shoe, leaving a lifelong scar. On another occasion his father decided to entertain the children by organizing an outdoor session of ghost stories. When the stories had been told, and the children suitably terrified, his father ordered them to walk alone, one at a time, into the middle of a pitch-dark field to pin their name on a scarecrow that lurked in the night. Like all samurai boys the Katsu sons were expected to learn warrior skills. Kokichi was enrolled for jujutsu lessons at the age of nine and for horse riding lessons at the age of ten. At eleven he began taking sword lessons and from twelve he was required to study classical Chinese literature.

Kokichi freely roamed the streets of Edo with his teenage friends. Samurai boys were allowed to carry short, blunt swords from a very early age and the friends often found themselves in scrapes that would begin with punches and sometimes escalated into confrontations with drawn swords. Somehow the boys usually managed to escape from these fights with nothing more than bruises and minor cuts. As a teenager Kokichi took sword lessons from experts who had trained in the One Stroke and the Pure Heart Shadow schools. He represented his teachers at inter-school fencing matches that were real rough and tumble affairs, a long way from the codified etiquette of modern kendo. Although the young men used bamboo swords and protective equipment they did their best to inflict the maximum possible pain and humiliation on their opponents. Anyone who fell to the floor during a match was in danger of receiving a sound thrashing.

These teenagers would not restrict their fighting to the dojos but would issue challenges to each other on the street. The boys would don their protective gear and draw bamboo swords but no other rules applied. A street match drew a crowd of fellow students and curious onlookers and could easily degenerate into a violent brawl with the competitors ripping off each other's face masks in order to be able to land solid blows to the face. For a teenage swordsman who had been humiliated in this way one option for revenge was to launch a surprise attack on the streets with a real sword. The Edo police were kept busy breaking up fights between angry boys and preventing sword duels from taking place.

Kokichi's autobiography is most vivid in describing his youthful adventures. As an adult he largely stayed out of trouble but, however settled his life became, he continued to think of himself as a swordsman first and foremost. He lived in a time of renewed enthusiasm for the sword arts and Kokichi helped to referee inter-school matches that were roared on by hundreds of spectators. He was able to supplement his income by buying and selling swords in the lively market for used weapons. If he had a particularly fine sword he might test it out by exercising his right to practice his technique on the corpses of executed prisoners at the Edo gaol.

The New Way

Kokichi took part in a revival of interest in the sword arts that swept through Edo in the early nineteenth century and eventually spread throughout the entire country. The general introduction of bamboo swords and protectors dramatically changed the atmosphere surrounding sword training and in the wake of these changes several important reformers emerged. Perhaps the most successful of the new teachers was Chiba Shusaku, an early nineteenth century sword master who had 3,500 students training under his direct supervision in a huge dojo in downtown Edo. This building, the Genbukan, was the largest dojo in Edo city and Shusaku the capital's most highly respected swordsman.

Shusaku was not from a samurai family. He had been born into one of those farming families who were wealthy enough to dream of their sons rising into the samurai class. His father managed to win unusual permission for his sons to enroll in the Nakanishi branch of the One Stroke School, the very same school that had pioneered free-fighting with bamboo swords and body armor. Many samurai continued to be highly suspicious of the modern innovations in sword training and even within the Nakanishi School there were some who refused to accept the new approach.

As a young man Shusaku witnessed a confrontation in his school between an enthusiastic young advocate of free fighting and an older samurai, named Terada, who had refused to change his training methods. In front of the entire school Terada stepped forward without body armor and took up a fighting posture with his wooden sword. The younger man attacked with all his might but could not find a way past Terada's sword. The spectators, including young Shusaku, were deeply impressed by this display. Clearly, he realized, there was something more to swordsmanship than the thrills of free-fighting practice. Shusaku began to study traditional kata alongside free-fighting techniques and sought out some of the greatest teachers of the time to learn their secrets. He became so close to one famous teacher, Asari Gimei, that he married the expert's daughter and was adopted into the family.

As he matured Shusaku engaged in a top to bottom reform of the traditional teaching methods of the Edo sword schools. The old ways, developed in the sixteenth and seventeenth centuries, were hard and unexciting and required endless repetition of techniques. The influence of the eighteenth century also lingered in some overly graceful movements and in the impenetrable philosophical mystique that surrounded explanations of the techniques. Shusaku was a new kind of teacher. He took time to speak with each student and to explain techniques in rational terms. He greatly simplified the curriculum of the One Stroke School, reducing the number of qualification levels from eight to three. Students who had been paying hefty fees to take promotion tests were delighted. Shusaku also simplified the sword techniques themselves, removing unnecessarily decorative moves and creating a sharp focus on defensive and attacking techniques that were both practical and effective. He strongly emphasized free-sparring in his dojos and created a new curriculum of sixty eight techniques that had been designed specifically for sparring with bamboo swords.

In many ways Chiba Shusaku was the most important forerunner of modern kendo. His sixty eight techniques were actually a great simplification of the secret and overly complex curricula of the old schools. With some later revisions Shusaku's list provided the basis for the set of techniques taught in modern kendo. Shusaku also reformed the way in which sword competitions were run. He was a highly physical man who loved to compete in amateur sumo matches where he made use of his knowledge of jujutsu to throw much larger wrestlers. Drawing on his experience of sumo Shusaku created a refereeing system and a points scoring method for sword competition. These important developments played a vital role in the creation of modern sport kendo.

Competitions between schools from different sword traditions had been strongly discouraged by the Tokugawa government before the nineteenth century. But the new, non-lethal style of fighting made inter-school competition socially acceptable once again. Meetings between different schools were extremely exciting affairs with students and family members roaring on the competitors. Shusaku was as competitive as any other teacher in Edo and would do anything to win a tournament. He was not above attempting to gain an advantage through the ploy of lengthening the bamboo swords of his students so they could strike their opponents from a distance. When other schools arrived for competitions with five-foot-long shinai, Shusaku would provide his students with six-foot-long swords. These swords were so long, in fact, that they could be used to sweep an opponent's legs out from under him. They were poles that were twice as long as the swords that the samurai of Edo actually carried. But they did produce victories in these all-important tournaments.

Shusaku was popular with his students who appreciated his direct teaching style and his personality. He was a warm man with an endearing sense of humor. An example of his approach to life came in a visit that he paid to one of the many new sword schools that had sprung up in Edo. The great swordsman took up a position at the back of the dojo, pretending to be a simple peasant with no idea of how to behave in a sword school. He tied his armor inside out and put his gloves on the wrong hands. As the other students laughed at his incompetence, Shusaku quietly waited until the brash young teacher condescended to give him a few pointers. "I don't really know anything about swords," Shusaku bluffed, "I just have to hit you with this, right?" "Go ahead," replied the teacher who was still smiling, "hit me any way you want." At this, Shusaku suddenly struck hard at both of the teacher's wrists. "Is that right?" asked Shusaku. Before the teacher could finish his "Yeeess..." Shusaku launched a blindingly fast attack, striking the teacher hard on the head and easily blocking his counterattacks. "That was fun," Shusaku remarked to the openmouthed teacher, "I wish I had tried it before." At which point he walked out and returned, chuckling, to the Genbukan.

Shusaku, the farmer's son, largely ignored social class and invited all of the citizens of Edo to train at his dojo. He himself was a living example of how the old limitations of sword training were rapidly breaking down in the nineteenth century as the shift to competitive sparring aroused the enthusiasm of young men from every social group. Most of the flood of new recruits to the Edo sword schools were not, in fact, samurai but farmers, tradesmen and merchants who were attracted by the sporting and democratic atmosphere of the new schools. One study of sword competitions in the middle of the nineteenth century found that 80% of the participants were commoners.

Splitting a Steel Helmet

While new-style sword fighting was incredibly popular it did not completely replace the old style schools. Up to the end of the nineteenth century and beyond many samurai continued to conduct rigorous kata training with great seriousness and intensity. Even in some of the new style schools there still remained plenty of the atmosphere of the old, warlike days. Sakakibara Kenkichi was one of the greatest sword teachers at the very end of the samurai period and one of the very few who was able to retain his fame as the samurai class disappeared and interest in sword fighting once again plummeted.

He was a teacher who pushed his students to the limit. A German professor who spent time in the kenjutsu dojo of Sakakibara reported that the powerful instructor used his bamboo sword with such aggression that it was common for several unconscious bodies to be scattered across the floor of the dojo as training went on around them. The students of this intimidating figure would bang their heads on the dojo pillars in order to toughen their skulls in preparation for Sakakibara's overwhelming attacks.

Sakakibara was one of those sword teachers who found the transition to a post-samurai world almost impossible to contemplate. He had been born in a farming family and the collapse of interest in sword training left him with almost no students and no income to fall back on. Sakakibara responded with great imagination to this crisis. In 1873 he organized the first sword-fight entertainment event (gekken kogyo) in the centre of the city that had now been renamed as Tokyo. These sword events were open to the public, for a fee, and featured rather sensational bouts between former samurai. Professional sword fighting events proved to be immensely popular, spreading throughout the country and encouraging a partial revival of interest in the martial arts. Many penniless swordsmen were able, for a while, to make a living by participating in these events. But professional sword fighting was heavily criticized by those who viewed it as a tawdry desecration of the noble history of the samurai. In the end the government, who were intent on restricting the use of weapons to the professional army, banned the events.

Sakakibara was one of the last of his kind. For three hundred years the great city of Edo had been home to thousands of samurai who had dominated the streets with swords at their sides. Almost overnight the samurai were gone. Sakakibara held out for as long as possible but even he was obliged in the end to abandon his swords and cut off his topknot. In the last twenty years of the nineteenth century handling swords, and fighting with swords, became minority interests and would remain so until well into the twentieth century. But for those who could still tell the difference, a swordsman like Sakakibara was something to admire. In 1887 in front of a selected audience of sword experts and aristocrats he achieved the almost impossible feat of slicing through a steel helmet with his sword. The powerful, razor-sharp Japanese sword was an irresistible weapon. It had played a remarkable role in Japanese history but its time had come to an end.

6. The Last Days of the Samurai

The Frozen Land

If Miyamoto Musashi had been able to travel forward in time to the Edo of 1850 he would have found himself in an entirely familiar city. It had certainly grown, but in most ways Edo was almost identical to the place where Musashi had lived two hundred and thirty years earlier. It was a large, bustling society that remained untouched by the technological revolution that had so transformed European and American cities. When the Shogun Tokugawa Iemitsu closed Japan to the outside world in 1635 he wanted to protect his islands from the dangerous world outside. He believed that isolation would allow the Tokugawa family to rule forever. But his actions had made the country a backwater, a land that had firmly averted its gaze from the dramatic changes that were taking place in the world beyond its shores.

By 1850 only a handful of Japanese people had ever laid eyes on a train line, a steam powered ship or a telegraph system. There was no way for them to do so because the simple act of traveling to the industrial cities of Europe or America was a capital crime. It was forbidden, on pain of death, for any Japanese person to leave the country. Trade with the capitalist world was confined to one tiny island near the southern city of Nagasaki where a trickle of Dutch merchants plied their wares. These businessmen and their books were the only window on the modern world that was open to the entire leadership and intellectual community of Japan. Mere crumbs of knowledge filtered through. A few academics struggled to learn the difficult Dutch language in order to understand what was going on beyond Japanese shores. Their arcane knowledge was known to outsiders as 'Dutch Learning'.

The streets of Edo still looked much as they had done in the 1600s. The buildings, constructed of pine, cedar and zelkova wood and divided internally with sliding paper screens were beautiful fire hazards. Like all Japanese cities Edo regularly suffered from uncontrolled blazes. The risk from fires was so high that watchmen toured the streets every night calling out warnings to householders. Outwardly the people also looked much the same as their seventeenth century predecessors. Most citizens wore kimono made of either cotton or silk and shod themselves in straw sandals. Among Edo's bustling crowds of merchants, laborers and craftsmen strode the samurai, for centuries the masters of all they surveyed. These samurai men still shaved the fronts of their heads, tied up their long hair at the back and carried two sharpened swords at their sides. No member of any other class was allowed to possess a weapon.

With their fixed position at the top of society, the samurai were certainly a privileged class. But not all samurai were wealthy and among their lower ranks there were many who were living on the breadline.

Some were forced to make ends meet by pawning their swords and selling off treasured books. There were even cases of infanticide among impoverished samurai who could not feed their families. But although there was a huge social gulf between the highest and lowest ranks of the samurai, they were as a whole a conservative class. Almost all samurai were proud of their social position and resistant to change. There had not yet been any sign in Japan of the social revolutions and reform movements that had so invigorated the European nations.

But change did come. The end of the long history of the unique warrior class of Japan is a story of self-extinction. When they found that their fighting traditions could not hope to compete with the modern weapons of the outside world, or even stop that world from barging its way into Japan, the samurai quickly sacrificed the system that had kept them at the top of Japanese society for centuries.

The tale of the end of the samurai is both tragic and exhilarating. Just as in the sixteenth century, when turmoil allowed talented individuals to rise from the lower classes to the very top, the nineteenth century was a period of enabling chaos in Japan. Many of the men who led the transformation of Japan in the second half of the nineteenth century were born in remote regions and into humble families. Among the ranks of the revolutionary samurai were three outstanding individuals, three names that are well known to every Japanese person in the modern age – Katsu Kaishu, Saigo Takamori and Sakamoto Ryoma. All three were born into obscure, low-ranking families. All three would rise to shake Japan out of its long slumber.

Beloved Son

Katsu Kaishu, the oldest of these three great contemporaries, was a child of Edo. He was born into one of the capital's least promising families as the son of the wild, impoverished samurai/author Katsu Kokichi. The boy grew up in an unstable household where his spendthrift, party-loving father often had to pawn household possessions in order to put food on the table. But there was no question about the deep affection that the father felt for his son. Kokichi's autobiography includes a description of how he anxiously nurtured his son back to recovery after a nasty dog bite to the testicles. He trusted his son enough to hand over leadership of the family to him when he was fifteen.

As a samurai youth Katsu was sent to study both swordsmanship and Zen Buddhism. But his outstanding quality was his shining intelligence. The young Katsu was bright enough to come to the notice of one of the many regional lords who kept a home in Edo and the lord adopted the brilliant boy into his family. It was a remarkable stroke of luck for Katsu as he was now given access to the best teachers and the best information. He did not waste his opportunity. The young Katsu became an enthusiastic student of 'Dutch Learning', the very limited scraps of knowledge about the outside world that made their way through the tight cordon that protected the Japanese islands. He learned to read the Dutch language and forced himself into the small circle of samurai who were regarded as experts on the world beyond. When strange and threatening American ships appeared off the shores of Edo in 1853 Katsu was one of those experts who were recruited by the government to provide advice on what could be done with the unwelcome foreigners.

Satsuma Boy
Saigo Takamori was born in Satsuma, the prefecture known today as Kagoshima, a place that lies at the very southern tip of the main Japanese islands. Satsuma was a thousand miles distant from Edo and consequently had been able to maintain a good deal of independence during the long autocratic rule of the Tokugawa family. The Shogun's government had operated a spy network throughout Japan but most of the spies it sent to Satsuma were discovered and executed.

The Satsuma samurai had a fierce reputation and a stronger social position than samurai in any other part of Japan. Almost one third of the entire population of Satsuma were from the warrior class, 170,000 out of the total population of 650,000. In Kagoshima, the largest town, seventy percent of the residents were samurai. This ratio of samurai to commoner was five times higher than it was in most other regions. As a result, many of the Satsuma samurai were not town dwellers but lived in the countryside and farmed for a living.

There were ten social ranks among the Satsuma samurai and the Takamori family belonged to the bottom rank. Saigo's father worked in the regional tax office and, with his meagre salary, provided for an extended household of sixteen children and relatives. Their home was a shabby one. In the short Satsuma winters all of the children had to huddle together for warmth under a single blanket. To make ends meet the family bought a small parcel of land and grew their own rice and vegetables. It was a modest start in life and Saigo would always be a farm boy at heart. In his adult years he would live among the wealthiest citizens of the nation but he never lost his taste for simple, outdoor activities. To the end of his life he showed no interest in accumulating wealth.

Satsuma had created the toughest system in Japan for the education of samurai boys. During the invasion of Korea at the end of the sixteenth century the region had been drained of mature samurai men and thousands of boys were left to run wild. In order to prevent a repeat of that chaos a school system was created that placed samurai boys in charge of maintaining their own order and providing their own training. The teenage boys in each region of Satsuma were responsible for teaching the basic arts of warrior life to the younger boys. This warrior training started early. At the age of six a boy would be presented with his first, rather blunt, short sword and taken to register at the local training centre.

The Satsuma boys were under a strict curfew at night that lasted from six in the evening until six in the morning. At sunrise they would walk to the home of a teacher, usually an older boy, for rote memorization of classic Chinese texts. From eight to ten in the morning they took part in rough physical exercise that included sumo and outdoor races and competitions. After further study of Chinese texts they would gather again at four in the afternoon for two hours of formal martial arts training. Even the younger boys made no use of the bamboo swords and body armor that had become popular in other parts of the country. They practiced with wooden swords and learned an aggressive style of swordsmanship that taught no other technique but straight ahead attacking slashes.

At nine years old these samurai boys began to teach the younger boys and at thirteen they were recognized as adults. They went through a coming of age ceremony that involved shaving their heads and putting on adult clothing for the first time. Even as adults, however, their training continued and expanded to include study of moral dilemmas. What should they do, the teenage boys were asked, if they cornered their father's murderer in a situation where only the murderer could save their life? The correct answer, their instructors taught them, was to first be rescued, to politely thank the rescuer, and then to immediately kill him. It was a fierce education. At the end of the year the boys were marched to the regional prison to observe executions. As the executioner raised the severed head of a prisoner the custom was for the boys to run forward and struggle to be the first to bite an ear or a finger from the corpse. The winner of this grisly competition was then allowed to practice his sword work on the still warm human flesh.

Saigo was not destined to become a great martial artist. At the age of twelve he became mixed up in a sword fight on the street and received a serious arm injury that would hamper him for the rest of his life. He became an unusual teenager, toughened by his rigorous upbringing but driven by his injury towards an inner life that was unusually rich for a boy of his class. He read deeply in the Confucian classics, absorbing their emphasis on loyalty, honor, bravery and direct action. He also studied Zen Buddhism and acquired an impressive stillness and directness that at times made him an intimidating figure to those who did not know him well. He grew into a burly six-footer, a young man of few words who, when he did speak, liked to cut straight to the heart of the matter.

When the time came to enter employment Saigo became, like his father, a clerk in the local tax office. The Takamori family were low ranking samurai and Saigo could have hoped for little better than a career as a mid-level clerk. But the dramatic times and a miraculous series of events conspired to lift him into the very heart of Japanese politics.

In 1854 Saigo was appointed to a position that involved traveling to Edo with the new lord of Satsuma on his compulsory regular visits to the capital of the Shogun. Nariakira took the slow route to Edo, as his father and his father's father had done, traveling overland with a large contingent of samurai guards, servants and concubines. Near the back of this procession was Saigo who walked all of the nine hundred miles between the two capitals. Just as the Satsuma contingent drew close to Edo they began to hear strange rumors of foreign gunboats that had appeared off the Japanese coastline. On the last, weary stretch of road before he finally entered the capital Saigo looked out to sea and, with his own eyes, saw the dark threatening shapes of the American ships.

I Will Cut Off A Foreign Head
The youngest of these three great reformers was Sakamoto Ryoma. He was born in 1835 in Tosa, one of the remotest places in Japan. It was the distant, southern region of the backwater island of Shikoku; a land so surrounded by seas and mountains that it was practically inaccessible from the rest of Japan, never mind the outside world. It was rare for any resident of Tosa to be given permission to travel to other regions, and even with permission such a journey was a major undertaking. The rough roads were irregularly maintained and the crossing points to other domains were strictly guarded.

The Sakamoto family were at the very bottom of samurai society. They were country samurai who had previously been sake merchants. Only two generations before Ryoma came into the world the family had gathered enough cash to buy their way into the ruling class. Because of their low status and their life in the countryside the Sakamoto family were keenly aware of just how much discontent was rumbling through the farming villages over high taxation. The peasants were angry, but even the rural samurai strongly resented urban samurai who only showed their faces when they wanted to collect taxes. These upper crust town-dwelling samurai were conservative types of limited ability whose main preoccupation seemed to be preserving the system that supported their comfortable lifestyle.

Like many boys from the lower ranks of the samurai, the young Ryoma was an enthusiastic sword fighter. There was a feeling in the air that war with the foreigners was approaching. For a young man like Ryoma this was a thrilling prospect that gave him a fevered interest in sword practice. The local samurai aristocrats would undoubtedly become the generals of any new army. But war would be the first chance in centuries for the young, lower ranking samurai to prove their bravery and skill.

As in other parts of Japan the sword schools of Tosa became the key meeting place for the most daring young men. They practiced together and drank sake together after training. In these sword clubs radical ideas for dealing with foreigners were generated and could easily spread. Ideas moved quickly through the network of sword clubs as students regularly came together for training and competition. In a land where travel and social mobility were highly restricted the sword schools became the fulcrum of political agitation.

Ryoma was an outstanding young sword fighter. By the age of eighteen he was so skilled that his parents decided to send him to Edo to receive the best sword training available. As soon as he arrived in the capital Ryoma registered with the sword school of Chiba Sadakichi, the younger brother of the great Chiba Shusaku. But he was not destined to enjoy a peaceful life in the capital for long. Almost before Ryoma could unpack his bags the American ships made their first appearance.

There was uproar throughout the city. All of the samurai of Edo were ordered to defend the coastline and even the young sword students from the private academies were told to make their way to the sea. In the end the foreigners sailed away but when the American fleet returned one year later Ryoma was again sent to the coastal defenses. As he gazed out at the alien ships in Japanese waters the teenager was filled with excitement. He itched to put his sword skills to the test in a real battle. "I think there will be a war soon," he wrote to his father. "If it comes to that you can be sure I will cut off a foreign head before coming home." [11]

The Black Ships
Katsu Kaishu, Saigo Takamori and Sakamoto Ryoma all witnessed the threatening presence of American ships in Edo Bay with their own eyes. It was an event so profoundly shocking that it threw Japanese society into utter chaos for fifteen years. In reality the small exploratory American fleet that first approached Japan consisted of only two steamboats towing two sailing boats behind them. But to Japanese eyes these ships were huge and menacing, bristling with cannon. The local officials sent out small boats to warn the foreigners that they were approaching forbidden territory but the Japanese boats could not keep up with the churning pace of the steamboats. On July 8, 1853 the fleet that would soon be familiar to every Japanese person as 'the black ships' arrived in Edo Bay and struck anchor. The foreigners were within a day's march of the government of Japan.

In Edo City there was panic at the prospect of invasion by these aliens. A handful of the city intellectuals had studied 'Dutch Learning' and had some idea of what the outside world was really like but the vast majority of the local citizens had only the vaguest notion of what a 'foreigner' actually was. Frightened residents rushed here and there hiding their valuables and packing women and children off to the safety of the countryside. The samurai had kept their swords in good condition but almost all of their battle weapons had been unused for generations. Ancient armor was dragged out of store cupboards to be hastily repaired; rusty spears were sharpened, bows restrung. Seventeen thousand samurai spread out along the shores of Edo Bay and with their hearts beating wildly they made preparations for a desperate battle, the first of their lives. Long sheets of canvas were stretched along the beaches to disguise the horde of gathering samurai and their gun positions.

The American ships lined up in battle formation with cannons loaded and guns prepared to repel any attack. From shore large numbers of Japanese boats departed and sailed directly toward the American ships. As they drew close the thirty samurai on each boat did their best to board the foreign fleet. But the American sailors found that it was easy to cut the ropes the Japanese threw over their sides. They simply battered any samurai who managed to climb on board and threw them back into the water. Rebuffed, the Japanese tried another tactic. From one boat they unfurled a sign that, to the bemusement of the American sailors, had been written in French. It said 'GO AWAY!'

Watching the futile efforts of the Japanese defenders through a telescope was Commodore Perry, the commander of the small American fleet. Perry was an experienced sea captain who had fought in the Mexican War and chased down pirates. He was a tough, intelligent leader, a strong advocate of sea power and of converting the American Navy to steam. In his cabin was a letter from President Fillmore to the Japanese Emperor. It demanded that the Japanese open their country to trade with the outside world and provide bases for the American whaling fleet to resupply.

It was simply a matter of chance that an American fleet had first breached the isolation of Japan. All of the rich Western nations with their booming economies and modern military equipment were competing with each other as they pushed their way into Asia to create trading bases and build client states. Japan was the last place in the East to maintain its independence from Western colonial power and Perry was determined to be the man to bring an end to this stubborn isolation.

Perry had read every book he could find about Japan but there were still large gaps in his knowledge. When the first Japanese officials came to visit his ship he told them that he had landed in Edo Bay with the plan of delivering a letter to the Emperor of Japan. Clearly he was unaware that the Emperor lived in Kyoto and that the real power in Japan lay with the Shogun. But Perry was almost infinitely better informed and certainly more confident in his purpose than were the leadership of Japan. The Emperor was a peripheral figure who lived 'above the clouds', while the Shogun Ieyoshi was probably the weakest of his entire dynasty of Tokugawa family rulers. His response to the arrival in his waters of the Black Ships was to take to bed with a severe case of depression. With the Emperor and the Shogun both incapable of providing any leadership to Japan the decisions were being made by an informal coalition of lords who controlled the provinces closest to Edo and who had long historic links to the Tokugawa rulers. This was the true conservative force in Japan, a group of lords who were willing to do whatever was necessary to keep the Tokugawa family, and thereby themselves, in power.

But the ruling coalition had no idea about what to do with these huge, speedy ships that had resisted all efforts at boarding. In the end they decided to allow Perry to present his letter from the American President in the hope that he would then sail away, never to return. Many samurai begged their lords to let them launch a more serious attack on the ships but permission was refused. It was just as well for the samurai. The Americans, with their nineteenth century technology, were deeply unimpressed by the wooden fortifications they could see on shore and by the tiny Japanese cannons that were relics of the sixteenth century. One American sailor suggested that the Japanese guns could be loaded into the huge cannons of the American ships and fired right back at the Japanese.

Unhappily, the Japanese officials prepared an elaborate ceremony to mark the reception of the most unwelcome letter from the American President. On July 14, two hundred American sailors and marines, armed to the teeth, assembled onshore in full dress uniform. They were surrounded by thousands of samurai carrying swords, bows and spears. It was a tense encounter and one that could easily have ended in a bloodbath. In a specially built audience hall the American officers came face to face with local officials who inaccurately presented themselves as representatives of the Japanese government. Under the floor of the meeting room ten seasoned samurai fighters had been hidden and there they waited for a signal to emerge and slaughter the barbarians. Perry handed his letter over amid a frosty silence that surprised the Americans but was understandable in a land where even the act of speaking with a foreigner was illegal. "I will soon leave," Perry announced to the delight of his audience. But his next words were the last thing they wanted to hear. "I will return next year, with a bigger fleet."

As the American ships sailed off into the Pacific, trailing clouds of black smoke, the leaders of Japan wondered what to do next. Ieyasu Tokugawa and his descendants had created a tightly organized, rule bound society that had been designed to continue forever. This shocking intrusion from the outside world threatened everything. The Japanese elite were convinced that all foreigners were dangerous and greedy. They knew that only a few years earlier the British had enslaved millions of Chinese through the opium trade, had bombed and invaded Chinese ports to crush any opposition to that trade and had seized the richest port of all, Hong Kong, as British property. The Americans could not be allowed to do the same thing to Japan.

As they were unable to come up with any concrete plan to end the crisis the ruling coalition broke with all precedent and decided to distribute a copy of President Fillmore's letter to every lord in the land. Knowledge of this insulting threat from the outside world created a surge of patriotic feeling. One lord was so moved that he had all of the temple bells in his province collected, melted down, and cast into cannons that could be used to defend Edo.

Even the powerless Emperor was consulted. Perhaps, it was suggested, he could intervene with the gods to take action on behalf of Japan. The Emperor read the President's letter and immediately declared that the barbarians must never be allowed to set foot on the sacred land of Japan again. He prayed for another kamikaze, a divine wind like the typhoon that had scattered the Mongolian fleet in the thirteenth century. The Shogun, however, was unable to help. He had never recovered from the shock and depression caused by Perry's arrival and died just ten days after the Americans sailed away. In this moment of dire need Japan found itself without a leader.

Painful Medicine

The respite provided by the departure of the Black Ships was brief. In February of the following year Perry cruised back into Edo Bay at the head of an enlarged fleet of nine ships and sixteen hundred men. Once again the Japanese sent minor officials onboard to conduct meaningless talks but this time Perry was determined to play hardball. He hid in his cabin, refusing to speak to anyone but the Emperor himself. He would, he threatened, march on the Imperial Palace and, if resistance was offered, could summon one hundred warships from America. He had his ships issue twenty one gun salutes, the cannons emitting huge, frightening roars that echoed around the bay and caused the watching samurai to tremble.

Under this kind of pressure the Japanese finally agreed that the Americans could make anchor in the harbor of Yokohama, one day's march to the south of Edo. The Americans would be allowed to build jetties for their boats and the Japanese side would erect buildings where the two sides could hold onshore negotiations. On March 8 five hundred Americans, carrying every weapon they could muster, landed at Yokohama. Determined to match their bluster with charm the Americans also landed a large consignment of gifts for the Emperor, presents that had been carefully chosen to demonstrate the overwhelming superiority of American technology. One was a telegraph system that was strung for several hundred meters along Yokohama Bay. Samurai would dictate messages and then run as fast as their legs would carry them from one end of the telegraph line to the other, only to find that their words had somehow outraced them. Even more astonishing was a fully working one quarter scale railroad system. A short circular track was built and samurai took it in turns to hurtle around the track at the amazing speed of twenty miles per hour, gasping and hooting with pleasure and fear. Samurai were encouraged to visit the American ships at anchor where they were directed to poke their heads into the mouths of the huge cannons and were lined up to watch the marines conducting on-board drills.

While this somewhat comic series of intercultural encounters was taking place in Yokohama the rest of Japan was in uproar. All over the nation samurai were pleading to be allowed to travel to Yokohama to slice the barbarians to pieces. The small American landing party was actually in great danger but they remained blissfully unaware of just how precarious their situation was. Talks began and after several weeks a treaty was signed, the first important breach in the wall that had sealed Japan off from the outside world. The treaty recognized the right of American ships to make free use of two Japanese ports for trade and resupply. The two chosen ports were far away from the large urban centers of Edo, Osaka and Kyoto, but even this minor concession caused extreme pain to the rulers of the nation and provoked fury throughout the country.

Commodore Perry was delighted with his achievement. He was so happy, in fact, that he decided to sail right up to the inlet where Edo City met the sea and to let off a celebratory salute of cannon fire. The Japanese interpreters who were still on Perry's ship became terrified. They would be disgraced, and quite probably executed, if such an insult to Japanese national pride was to take place. One interpreter announced that the moment a cannon's gunpowder was lit he would prevent the firing by throwing himself into the mouth of the great gun. Another interpreter knelt and made preparations to ritually kill himself when anchor was dropped in Edo Bay. Perry, who was enjoying his birthday that day and was in no mood for suicides, gave up on his plan to stop off at Edo. He did sail close enough, however, to estimate that the city could be "destroyed by a few steamers of very light draft, and carrying guns of the heaviest caliber." (12)

Agreeing to the American demands had been painful for the ruling lords of Japan but that, they sincerely hoped, would be an end to the problem. Their plans for limiting the foreign intrusions to resupply visits to two remote ports were soon to be disappointed. Two years after Perry's second visit another American, Townsend Harris, arrived in Shimoda and introduced himself as the first American Consul General to Japan. Harris was a resilient and intelligent individual who turned a deaf ear to the many appeals for him to leave the country. Making use of a carrot to match Perry's stick he suggested to the rulers of Japan that America was a more benign option as a trading partner than the violent European powers who had already crushed Chinese resistance. Within a year Harris was granted an audience with the new Shogun. He was able to negotiate a new and improved treaty that conceded much freer trading rights to the Americans. In Kyoto this development provoked anger. The Emperor Komei condemned the new treaty in the strongest language. It would mean, he said, the end of Japan. For the first time in centuries a rift began to open between the imperial court and the government of the Shogun.

Once again the Japanese government was riven by debate. All of the greatest men of the land - lords, generals and scientific experts - were asked for their views on how to deal with the foreign menace. From the beginning, three basic approaches to the crisis took shape. The top layers of the Tokugawa government took a conservative view. The foreigners were simply too strong to be fought, they believed, and so treaties must be signed and the country gradually opened to trade. This conservative group aimed to preserve the existing political system at all costs. A second group pushed for the rapid modernization of Japanese institutions and an opening of trade relations with the world so that Japan could quickly become a nation strong enough to resist outside demands. Finally, a third group, supported by most of the younger samurai, demanded an immediate all-out war against the foreigners.

A Japanese Navy
Katsu Kaishu quickly joined the middle group, the party that wanted to rapidly strengthen Japan by implementing urgent reform. He was still a young man in his early thirties when the Americans appeared and, as one of the very few Japanese people who could read Dutch, knew as much about the outside world as anyone in the country. Katsu was young enough to be thrilled when the government asked for his opinions and quickly drew up a list of radical plans. They included the creation of strong coastal defenses, the building of a modern navy, and a plan for public service to be opened to all young men of high ability, even those who came from non-samurai backgrounds.

The government was not yet ready to invite commoners into positions of power but it did want a navy. In 1855 Katsu was sent to Nagasaki as one of a group of samurai who were to be trained in naval science by Dutch experts. The samurai embarked on an exhaustive and exhausting program of study that included lessons in mathematics, navigation and mechanics. All of their studies were conducted entirely in the Dutch language. Katsu was the leading student in his group and when the course came to an end he was asked to stay on in Nagasaki to help with the training of further groups of students. He found himself in a rather strange position. He was now directly employed by the government, and was delighted to be a person of value to the nation. But in his heart of hearts Katsu believed that Japan badly needed a new and more efficient system. He was convinced that the days of the Tokugawa were numbered. But he was still too young, and too low in rank, to be able to make a difference. He kept his ideas to himself.

By 1859 the government had come to the conclusion that it needed to know more about the outside world and decided to send the first ever Japanese delegation to visit the United States. Katsu was placed in charge of the ship that carried a group of scholars and samurai across the Pacific. He spent two months in California, touring the shipyards and munition factories, making notes and plans. Katsu was both awed and charmed by the New World and the visit transformed his thinking. It was now clear to him that Japan could not dream of competing with this thriving and energetic industrial nation until it made fundamental changes to its feudal system of government and economy. He realized that however hard Japan struggled to defend its borders it was doomed to defeat. The only way forward was to open the borders of Japan completely and to build a rich country that could find a place as the equal of the

Western nations. Katsu gathered plenty of evidence that the American barbarians were a people to be feared. But he also found much to admire and enjoy in America – this strange place where men and women held hands in the street.

The Prisoner
In the years when Katsu Kaishu was launching his career in the fledgling Japanese navy Saigo Takamori was finding his feet as a young political operative in Edo. He had arrived in the capital at the height of the turmoil that followed the arrival of the Black Ships. As a political representative of his lord, Saigo was soon involved in the debate over what to do with the foreigners.

Before long Saigo had fallen under the influence of the Mito samurai and their proto-nationalist brand of devotion to the Emperor. The leaders of the Mito region, just north of Edo, argued that the Emperor should be regarded as the true leader of Japan and the Shogun as his servant. This was a radical challenge to the well established status quo. It was the Mito samurai who were leading the calls for an immediate war to be launched against the foreigners. A war was needed, they believed, to reanimate the Japanese spirit and to restore true samurai values. The foreign enemy were dangerous, they admitted, but in a mainland war the samurai would be fighting to protect their families and home towns. The ancient spirit of Yamato would be able to overcome the industrial might of any invader. This was sweet music to the ears of Saigo who was still a passionate young man in his twenties. He prayed that his lord would accept the Mito ideas and would let him join the battle against the Americans.

Saigo became part of an underground movement that was working to launch a samurai uprising that would restore the Emperor as the leader of the nation. The young samurai in particular were baying for a fight and were disgusted with the weakness shown by the national government in the face of the foreigners. For a time it seemed that a nationwide revolution was imminent. But, just when the weak and directionless government seemed to be on the point of collapse, it suddenly found a sense of purpose. Ii Naosuke emerged from the ruling coalition to firmly take the reins of power and to lead a dramatic clampdown on the revolutionary young samurai. This powerful lord appointed himself as Regent to the weakling Shogun and took decisive steps to jail, expel and persecute supporters of the Mito led conspiracy.

Just at this critical turning point the lord of Kagoshima died. Saigo was devastated at the loss of the admirable lord who had promoted him and had taken him to Edo. He felt, he wrote at the time, like a man who has lost his ship and is stranded on an island. The mood in Edo was now hostile to the radicals and so Saigo fled to Satsuma with a fellow revolutionary, a monk named Gessho. But when he arrived in his home town Saigo was shocked to find that the new leaders of Satsuma were equally opposed to Mito ideas and would not even offer shelter to his friend the monk.

Saigo felt that he could bear no more. With his friend Gessho he took a boat out onto the open sea. Gessho was a Buddhist monk and had taken a vow not to commit suicide so Saigo wrapped his arms tightly around his comrade. He threw himself into the sea and both men sank beneath the waves. The startled boat crew reversed course and hauled the two men, still locked in each other's arms, from the cold water. After some time Saigo revived but for the monk it was too late. Gessho was dead.

All over Japan young imperial loyalists were being hunted down and arrested by the government. In this harsh political climate the rulers of Satsuma decided that Saigo, who had recovered from his suicide attempt, was more dangerous to them as a political radical than he was worth as a public servant. In order to place him at a safe distance they sent him in exile to a small island far to the south of the Japanese mainland. It was an isolated and primitive place where Saigo spent three frustrating years, unable to make any contribution to the struggle other than to send letters urging his friends not to waste their strength on hopeless attacks. Saigo's huge body and daily sword practice made him a strange and somewhat terrifying figure for the inhabitants of his southern island home. But he was, at heart, a warm and simple man who discovered that he could take great pleasure in teaching the island children. He made friends, married a local woman, became a householder and fathered two children of his own.

Men of High Purpose
Meanwhile in Edo the government clampdown had failed to crush the enthusiasm of young samurai for political change. The ineffective Shogun and his unimaginative and conservative officials were uninspiring leaders. They had lost the respect of the young men of Japan who were even beginning to question the bonds of local loyalty that had traditionally tied them to their regional lords. More and more, they saw loyalty to the Emperor, and through the Emperor loyalty to the nation, as taking precedence over their relationship with unsatisfactory local leaders. In the sword schools of Edo young men from all over Japan were sharing ideas and hatching plots.

As the political world of Japan became increasingly unstable at the outset of the 1860s the young samurai of Edo were drawn into action. They called themselves shishi, or men of strong will. While the shishi had various views about what was was needed to restore Japan they were united by their emotional outlook and by their lifestyle. These were fanatical and aggressive young men who believed in simple solutions and were eager to risk their lives in order to implement those solutions. They regarded themselves as being devoted to the highest possible duty, to the Emperor and to the people as a whole. As a result they felt that they were entitled to ignore conventional morality and the more parochial duties of responsibility to their family and their home province.

The shishi had a romantic vision of themselves as warriors in the ancient tradition of the samurai. In imitation, they believed, of old samurai values they disdained worldly possessions. They shared money with each other freely and borrowed wherever they could without thought of repayment. Drinking hard and chasing beautiful women in the entertainment quarters was all part of the exciting game of being a young revolutionary. Many political plots were hatched in late night drinking spots and brothels. The rebellious ways of the shishi extended even to their appearance. Like twentieth century teenagers they wore thin clothing in winter, grew their hair long and, with a disdain for convention that was particularly shocking to the meticulous Japanese, avoided regular bathing.

As loyalist supporters of the Emperor the young shishi were unanimously in favor of an all-out war to throw the foreigners out of Japan. They believed that the Emperor, not the Shogun, should take full control of the nation and they summed up their ideas in the slogan sonnojoi, 'expel the barbarians, revere the Emperor'. While the shishi did expend a great deal of energy on late night discussions they firmly believed that action should take precedence over considered plans. They did not have the numbers or the organization to overthrow the state so they focussed their efforts on terrorist actions that were both logistically possible and emotionally satisfying. Many of their plots revolved around the assassination of an official whom they had come to regard as a supporter of the conservative forces in the government. The plans laid during drinking sessions often evaporated with the morning but some were carried to fruition. One murderous attack against an official named Yoshida Toyo was described by a young loyalist in a letter to his father.

> We made up our minds to strike on the first day of the fourth moon and thereafter we met every night. We made a pledge together to take his head and expose it at the execution grounds. There were just ten of us, carrying parcels and waiting around at the fourth bridge. Just before midnight Yoshida returned from the castle, and we were waiting for him. I was all set to strike him from the rear and take his head, and expected to do it with one blow, but my sword struck his umbrella and was deflected. Then the men with him drew their swords and we had to do a little parrying. But soon I had a chance and took his head. First I stopped to wash my sword and the head in the ditch by the roadside, and then I wrapped up the head in a cloth I had brought for the purpose. I rushed to the west and along the way the dogs barked wildly at me; and as they were snapping at the head I wasn't sure what to do. Finally, though, I was able to hand the head over to my friends. Now it was peaceful again, and I could pack for my trip. (11)

The shishi movement was fueled by a heady mixture of boyish enthusiasm and ugly violence that the government struggled to contain. The most ambitious and daring strike by the radicals was aimed at the very top leadership of the Shogun's government. Ii Naosuke was the true leader of Japan. Acting as Regent he, more than any other official, had led the repression against the loyalists and as a result he was the number one hate figure for young revolutionary samurai.

On a snowy March morning Naosuke was being carried the short distance from his residence to Edo Castle when a group of Mito samurai surrounded and attacked his guard in broad daylight. Fighting their way past the defenders the young shishi shot Naosuke, hacked off his head and fled the scene. As they made their escape one of the group snatched up Naosuke's head and ran with his trophy to the home of a member of the ruling council. He placed the head at the front gate and then, as if more blood was needed, proceeded to disembowel himself.

As word of this attack spread Edo was thrown into uproar. It was a truly shocking triumph for the revolutionaries that had, quite literally, beheaded the government. Naosuke had been the only individual with the self confidence and determination to lead an open campaign against the loyalists. Without his powerful presence the Shogun's government returned once again to an anxious and bewildered search for political compromise.

Heavenly Punishment

As politics in Edo entered a period of confusion the real struggle for power shifted to the ancient capital, the site of the Emperor's court. Kyoto in 1862 was rapidly approaching boiling point. Samurai from every province and unattached ronin drifted into the city where they could be seen wandering the streets and gathering in tea houses and drinking dens in heated political discussion. Young members of the court who supported the ideas of the radical samurai moved away from the sidelines and began to form their own armed groups. The radicals soon gained the upper hand in Kyoto and the city became their fortress, an open centre of opposition to the regime.

Many of the young samurai who found a safe haven in Kyoto had been on the run during the rule of Ii Naosuke. Now they were anxious to take revenge for the harassment they had endured. They hung placards on the walls of Kyoto streets that were painted with the threatening slogan 'Heavenly Punishment'. A wave of attacks broke out on Kyoto officials who had supported the government. Some of these men were assassinated and their heads placed in public thoroughfares with notices listing their crimes. Public order was in a state of collapse. Even the merchants became terrified and began to hand over 'protection' payments to the radicals. The young samurai did as they liked in Kyoto, they had been freed from every restraint. They even chopped the heads from public statues to indicate what was in store for the present rulers of Japan.

Things had gone too far. The government realized that they could not afford to allow such chaos to continue in the capital. So the Shogun's officials decided to fight fire with fire. They began to organize groups of Edo swordsmen who were ordered to travel to Kyoto. Their mission was to spy on and, where possible, to directly confront the radicals. Essentially the government assembled a series of small private armies under the command of some of Edo's toughest sword instructors. As these bands of pro-government samurai arrived in Kyoto they set about creating their own terror. Their aim was to eclipse the terror of the loyalists by following, torturing and even executing members of the opposition.

Of all the pro-government groups that travelled from Edo to Kyoto the most notorious was the Shinsengumi, a band of around three hundred swordsmen who dressed in distinctive colorful outfits. They were fanatically drilled and, remarkably for the times, included in their ranks men from outside the samurai class. Farmers, priests, doctors, merchants and craftsmen joined the Shinsengumi with great enthusiasm. It was a rare chance for men from those backgrounds to wear swords and to become the greatest of all things, a warrior.

While the Shinsengumi mostly specialized in tracking and assassinating individual loyalists they were capable of large scale attacks. On one occasion they used brutal torture methods to discover the location of a loyalist meeting. Having cornered a young samurai they hung him head downwards from a ceiling, drilled five centimeter holes in his heels and filled the holes with hot candle wax. Quite understandably the unfortunate young samurai was persuaded by this treatment to tell his interrogators that the radicals could be found at the Ikedaya Inn. Shortly afterwards thirty members of the Shinsengumi surrounded the inn and trapped an equal number of provincial loyalists inside. The government forces fought their way up the narrow stairs, killing seven loyalists and forcing the remainder to surrender. In Edo this was regarded as a huge victory for the government forces and the Shinsengumi were lionized. They were reported, falsely, to have saved the Emperor from being kidnapped by radicals.

Man in a Cage
The government in Edo was making great efforts to slow the progress of the radicals in Kyoto but it was too weak to exert much control over the rest of Japan. Freed from government censure the Satsuma leaders decided to take the risk of releasing Saigo Takamori from his island captivity. Satsuma had taken a middle path in the controversy that was splitting the nation and the leaders of that region now decided that they would not align themselves with either the sonno joi radicals or the Tokugawa conservatives. The Satsuma samurai proposed that Japan should be run by a coalition of senior lords under the ultimate rule of the Emperor. They agreed that it had become unavoidable for Japan to sign treaties with foreign powers but they wanted the nation to build up its strength and to develop its own military forces as quickly as possible. The rulers of Satsuma wanted to have a national role and wanted to be involved in

the reform of Japan. To argue their cause at the highest levels they decided to send the single most respected Satsuma reformist to Kyoto as their representative. And so, in a stunning reversal of fortune, Saigo found that he would not only be released from exile but was now expected to give voice to the hopes and ideas of Satsuma. After years of raising crops and teaching children on a small island he was suddenly thrown into the spotlight as a senior political figure.

As he made his way north to Kyoto Saigo found, to his surprise, that he had become a hero to all of the radical samurai of Japan. His obvious suffering and the nobility of his attempted suicide and exile had recast him as the nation's leading symbol of resistance to the hated government of the Shogun. Saigo could clearly see that most of the young men who now flocked to his side were naïve. They simply wanted to take action and were heedless of the consequences. But Saigo was a man who trusted the human spirit more than he valued intellect. These young samurai made it clear to him that they were willing to sacrifice their lives at any moment for the imperial cause and he could not help admiring such passion and sincerity.

Once again, perhaps against his better judgement, Saigo became drawn into the circles that were promoting not reform but revolution. It soon became clear that he had little interest in promoting the careful program of moderate change that the rulers of Satsuma had ordered him to pursue in Kyoto. The Satsuma lords once again changed their minds about Saigo. He was just too dangerous a man to be free. After only a few short months of liberty the symbol of Satsuma was once again arrested and sent into exile.

This time the punishment of Saigo was much harsher. He was sent to an even more remote southern island and was placed in a cage under the stars. For two months this famous public figure lived like a zoo animal, unable to bathe or exercise, in a nine foot square enclosure. Somehow Saigo accepted his humiliating situation with resolve and good humor, spending much of his time in the cage sitting in zen meditation. When he was finally released to house arrest he once again quickly settled into making the best of island life, studying and teaching the local children. But Saigo's equanimity had limits. When the news filtered through that English warships had bombarded his home town of Kagoshima, setting five hundred houses ablaze and killing five citizens, he became a terrifying apparition of rage.

The Greatest Man in Japan
While Saigo watched events helplessly from his distant southern prison Katsu Kaishu was rising to the top levels of the shogunal government in Edo. In 1862 he had been appointed to create and lead a new Japanese navy, the military organization that was intended to be the regime's most important response to the threat of outside interference. As a government official Katsu was closely watched by the young

radical samurai in Edo who considered him be be a tempting target for assassination. Katsu himself claimed that there had been twenty attempts on his life over the years and that he carried several scars as a result. As a samurai man he had naturally been trained in swordsmanship but he did not want a confrontation with any of the passionate loyalist youth. He entirely sympathized with their ideas, if not with their tactics. Katsu made it a practice to keep his sword tightly fastened at his side so that he could not draw it too quickly if radicals attempted to attack him. To the loyalists who were studying him Katsu was a puzzle. He was a proud member of the hated government but made little secret of his support for political change.

One of the young samurai who had been observing Katsu was Sakamoto Ryoma. He was in Edo, staying with his old sword master Chiba, when he made the fateful decision to assassinate a leading official. Like many of the radical samurai Ryoma wanted to send a message to the government that opening the country to foreigners was unacceptable. He decided to target Katsu Kaishu, a man who was a strong proponent of opening the nation's borders. Ryoma viewed his decision to kill Katsu as a suicide mission. He knew that if he succeeded he would almost certainly be arrested and executed.

Ryoma managed to gain an introduction to Katsu and went to his house with the intention of drawing his sword and attacking at any moment. As he entered the building Katsu asked him, "Have you come to kill me? If you have, let's talk first." This was such an unexpected comment that Ryoma found himself sitting opposite Katsu engaging in a wide ranging political discussion. Before long his thoughts of murder disappeared. For the first time Ryoma had encountered someone who was not just blindly angry about Japan's situation but who actually had a sweeping plan to bring about real change and national revival. Ryoma saw that Katsu was just as eager to stand up to the outside world as any of the young samurai. But unlike most of the radicals he had a concrete plan to do so. In the course of an hour Ryoma had his thoughts turned around 180 degrees and was converted into an enthusiastic follower of Katsu. He later described their meeting as one of the luckiest events of his life.

> Some fellows have such bad luck that they bang their privates on getting out of a bath and die. Here I was on the point of death, and I didn't die. I really thought I was going to, and instead I am to live. Now I have become the disciple of the greatest man in Japan, and every day I can spend on things that I've dreamed about. (11)

Katsu's great project at the time was the building and staffing of a new naval headquarters at Hyogo, on the coast near Kobe. Ryoma became one of Katsu's most important and trusted helpers. He kept track of the loyalist samurai who were targeting Katsu and even convinced many of these anti-government types to join the embryonic national navy. By the end of 1863 Katsu had installed Ryoma as the head of training for the naval academy. It was an enjoyable and satisfying job but these were revolutionary times and Ryoma kept half an eye on bigger things.

Although he was still only in his twenties Ryoma was already becoming an important political figure in his own right. The once rigid stratification of the samurai class was losing significance and Ryoma was able to take part in discussions with some of the most important regional lords. He told them all that he intended to 'clean up Japan'. Ryoma sensed that something big was now very close at hand. "I don't expect I'm the sort that's going to be around very long," he wrote to his sister, "but I don't expect to die like an average man either." (11) He was right on both counts. Ryoma was an extraordinary young man, a person who combined all of the passion and directness of the sonnojoi samurai with a rapidly developing political brain.

The Choshu Revolution
For more than ten years Japan had struggled through one convulsion after another as it tried to respond to the forced opening of its borders. Now the final act in this long political drama began with the release of Saigo Takamori from his second period of exile. Once again his return to public life was a dramatic reversal of fortune as he was immediately put in charge of the Satsuma army in Kyoto. Saigo arrived in the city at a time when Japan seemed to have no solution in sight to the prevailing political impasse. A group of regional lords and officials from the Imperial house had tried to set up a government in Kyoto but the experiment had failed. These imperial courtiers were highly trained in the arts of poetry and the tea ceremony but they were beginners at politics. The aristocratic aesthetes proved to be completely incapable of harnessing the energies of the unruly and ambitious regional lords who were gathering in Kyoto. Japan seemed to be adrift. It was a nation that was waiting for some person or some force that would be strong enough to hold it together.

In Choshu, the most southern region of the main island of Japan, samurai radicals had taken control. They were revolutionaries whose extreme Emperor worship made them natural allies of the elements in the imperial house who wanted to give the Emperor dictatorial powers. With their backing at court the Choshu representatives became, for a time, the most powerful of all the squabbling regional groups who had gathered in Kyoto. They used their influence to push the Emperor into making a dangerous proclamation that called for the immediate expulsion of all foreigners.

Saigo's region, Satsuma, had steered a careful course between the demands of the revolutionaries and those of the conservatives. And now Satsuma was the only force that had enough strength to prevent the Choshu samurai from taking complete control of the capital. The Choshu fighters saw the Satsuma group as their rivals and attempted to have all Satsuma samurai banned from the court. In response the

Satsuma group in Kyoto formed an alliance of convenience with several of the more conservative regions and staged a putsch. Overnight the Choshu faction was thrown out of national power and the Satsuma samurai took centre stage. But these political maneuvers resolved nothing at all. The atmosphere in the capital continued to be both poisonous and dangerous. Every lord in the land was keeping his own private army stationed in the vicinity of Kyoto and they all waited for an opportunity to fight for the scraps of power. Into the middle of this mess came Saigo.

Saigo Takamori was now, thanks to his shining reputation and his position at the head of the Satsuma army, one of the most powerful people in Japan. But he was given little time to enjoy his newfound influence. In July 1864 the Choshu radicals rushed back into Kyoto and launched an attack on the Imperial Palace itself. Up to this point Saigo had been sympathetic to the ideas of the Choshu samurai but their assault on the sacred palace shocked him to the core. He became a determined enemy of Choshu. For the first time in centuries a huge pitched battle broke out on the streets of the ancient capital. Samurai fought with cannon, musket and sword and much of the city was destroyed as hundreds of homes burned to the ground. Saigo led a coalition of the regions to successfully block the Choshu invasion and to drive the radicals out of Kyoto.

As conflict and confusion swirled around Kyoto the paths of the three great men at the centre of this story crossed when Sakamoto Ryoma organized a first meeting between Saigo and Katsu Kaishu. Both leaders arrived for the meeting with low expectations but both came away having been highly impressed by the other. Saigo understood clearly for the first time that some members of the government, including the head of the Japanese navy, were strong supporters of reform. Katsu, he could see, had no personal stake in keeping the Tokugawa family in power and wanted nothing more than a restoration of national pride. "I first went intending to set him straight but I wound up bowing my head. It seems to me that he is smarter than anyone I know,"(13) Saigo commented after their meeting. Katsu, for his part, was not lacking in self-belief and was unused to praising others. But he admitted to feeling that the passionate, energetic Saigo might just prove to be the strong leader that Japan so desperately needed.

After the clashes in Kyoto there was a general feeling throughout Japan that the Choshu revolutionaries had gone too far and that they should be held in disgrace. An army was raised by the government to punish the Choshu region and Saigo was appointed as its commanding officer. Just eight months after being freed from his island exile Saigo found himself at the head of Japan's national army. Far from being overwhelmed by his dizzy rise he set about leading the army in his own direct and courageous style. Saigo was just as determined as anyone in the government to humiliate Choshu but he was also a passionate believer in the samurai code and he knew how important it was for the Choshu samurai to be able to preserve their honor.

Taking his life in his hands, Saigo, accompanied by just a few trusted friends, travelled deep into enemy territory to conduct negotiations. The radicals who had failed to seize control of Kyoto had since lost even their power in Choshu. Saigo negotiated an agreement with the new rulers that promised that the leaders of the attack on the Imperial Palace would be executed and their heads submitted for inspection. With this deal having being struck Saigo felt that he had done his duty to the nation. He released all prisoners and returned to Kyoto.

Saigo's bold and honorable behavior during the punitive expedition to Choshu was a turning point. Although he had led an army of invasion into their lands, the Choshu samurai recognized in Saigo a man who shared many of their values and a samurai whom they could trust. Slowly the two southern regions, Satsuma and Choshu, began to move away from enmity and toward forming an alliance that would transform Japan. The creation of this partnership, an alternative centre of power that could rival the strength of Edo, would prove to be the most important work of Sakamoto Ryoma's short life.

Ryoma on the Run
Ryoma was no longer working for the government. He had, in fact, become an outlaw, hunted by the officials of his own province who regarded him as a dangerous political radical. True to his exuberant nature, Ryoma relished life on the run and threw himself into preparations for war against the government in Edo. Satsuma had been importing modern British guns for years and Ryoma talked Saigo into persuading his foreign arms suppliers to also provide weapons to Choshu. Thanks to the intervention of these two men Choshu built up a stock of thousands of rifles and even purchased a steam-powered warship.

While the government was floundering in Edo the two radical regions had set about modernizing and reequipping their armies. They had also established militias that were, for the first time, open to all classes. This change inspired mass enthusiasm from farmers and craftsmen who threw themselves with loyalist fervor into militia training. But the new military structures were a hard pill for the samurai of Choshu and Satsuma to swallow. The faceless ranks of a modern army offered few of the opportunities for individual glory that had existed in the days of samurai warfare. Worse still, the samurai who did join these militias had their bows and arrows confiscated and were required to carry guns, a humble task that had historically been assigned to the lowest ranks.

Early in 1866 Ryoma made the impossible happen when he persuaded the once bitter enemy states of Satsuma and Choshu to open talks in Kyoto. Getting these regions to talk about military cooperation was a delicate task but the youth and humble rank of Ryoma made him an acceptable go between to all sides. These two proud samurai nations had a long history of rivalry and many found the idea of cooperation hard to swallow. One of the Choshu samurai disliked the old enemy so much that he had written 'Satsuma Bandits' on the soles of his shoes so that he could trample them into the dirt with every step he took. But the negotiators overcame their scruples and created a pact between their two provinces. The deal represented a remarkable transformation of the balance of power in Japan. Just a year earlier Satsuma had been at the head of government forces invading Choshu. Now Satsuma had promised to defend Choshu against any further attack from the government.

As Ryoma worked to build a coalition that would be strong enough to seize power he was being closely watched by the Shinsengumi who had now marked him out as a dangerous radical who deserved to die. His life in these days was a dramatic one, full of intrigue and adventure. When he came to Kyoto he would stay in an inn close to the city that was near the official residence of his Satsuma friends. The owners of this inn, the Teradaya, were strong supporters of the loyalist cause and did what they could to shelter Ryoma. In the midst of his political work Ryoma fell in love with a maid who worked at the Teradaya. Oryo was beautiful young woman from an impoverished family who charmed Ryoma as much by her strength of character as by her beauty. She was a courageous girl who had physically faced down a band of gangsters to rescue her younger sister from being sold into prostitution. Her bravery would prove vital to Ryoma one March evening in 1866.

Ryoma was preparing to lie down for the night in the Teradaya Inn when Oryo, who had been taking a bath, came running into his room. She was naked. "Look out!" she whispered into the ear of the startled Ryoma. "Men with spears are coming up the stairs." Ryoma and one other loyalist friend quickly picked up their swords and he reached for his pistol. Looking through the paper screens into the next room Ryoma could see twenty government soldiers moving towards him with spears and wooden staves. He raised his gun to hold the gang of attackers at bay but one soldier was able to hack at his hand with a sword, slicing the left index finger to the bone.

By now Ryoma had fired all of his bullets and, as he tried to reload, the pain in his damaged finger made him drop the gun. The two desperate samurai looked into each other's eyes. "Let's rush into the middle of these guys and fight to the end," said his friend. But Ryoma still hoped to live a little longer. He suggested that they could escape by dropping out of the window at the rear of the building. The two men jumped from the window and landed in a narrow space between two buildings. With no other escape route possible the friends broke through the shutters that sealed the window of the adjoining house. They found themselves in a bedroom where they were surrounded by sleepy and angry people. But their pursuers were at their heels so the two samurai desperately used their swords and limbs to kick, cut and batter their way through the thin walls and screens of the house to reach the street on the opposite side. There they ran, barefoot, until they came to a warehouse where they hid though the remainder of the night, the blood from their wounds flowing, until they could find help the following morning.

Recognizing how important Ryoma had become, and how much danger he was in, Saigo Takamori gave him protection in the official Satsuma residence on the outskirts of Kyoto. While staying there Ryoma took advantage of the respite to marry Oryo, his beautiful savior. The couple travelled to Kagoshima with Saigo and were in the audience when he announced the treaty between Satsuma and Choshu that Ryoma had done so much to bring about. The newlyweds spent several weeks getting to know the beauty spots of Satsuma, hiking in the hills and visiting shrines and hot springs. Their holiday is often described as the first honeymoon in Japanese history.

The pact that Ryoma had helped to forge between Satsuma and Choshu was a huge threat to the government in Edo. But many conservative hardliners still believed that the loyalists could be defeated. In a final, doomed attempt to prove that the government was in control these reactionary elements decided to launch an attack on what, they assumed, would be an easy target. Choshu, they complained, had not been punished enough. Another government army would be sent to invade Choshu and to humiliate its rebels. But this decision to begin another war proved to be the final straw for the regime. There was no support left in Japan for such an attack and Saigo Takamori was personally adamant that he would take no part. The samurai of Choshu were now his friends. It was Edo that he regarded as the enemy.

After some time the government managed to assemble an army to attack Choshu but it was an unenthusiastic force that set out to invade the rebel territory and the defenders were determined. Fighting broke out in the vital sea channel between Kyushu and Honshu, a confrontation in which Ryoma took part. It would be his only experience of battle. He greatly enjoyed the fighting, telling his brother that it was the most interesting and exciting experience of his life. He was particularly impressed by the way in which the Choshu commander provided his troops with a stiff shot of sake before sending them into battle. Whether or not they were fortified by alcohol the Choshu troops seemed to be full of warrior spirit. They fought with reckless commitment and died in great numbers. In one unit of the Choshu army one hundred out of the total of one hundred and forty soldiers were killed or wounded.

The two sides eventually fought each other to a stalemate and the invading army was finally withdrawn. This was a great humiliation for the government; the army of the entire nation had been held at bay by the samurai of a single province. And the government's troubles were compounded when the Shogun died. Now at last it was clear to everyone that the old system was also in its death throes. In fact the country was in such a mess that there was no one left who really wanted to be the Shogun. After a good deal of persuasion Hitotsubashi Keiki assumed the leadership of the great house of Tokugawa. He was an excellent young man, by far the most intelligent and capable leader Japan had found in decades. But even he could not prolong the rule of his family.

The End of the House of Tokugawa
Saigo Takamori, expecting the final struggle for power to begin soon, returned to Satsuma to reorganize the local army. For years samurai in Edo had been demanding reform of the national army but not a great deal had been done. Satsuma, however, had quietly set about modernizing its forces. The province had studied Western technology and had established a modern arms industry with a munitions factory that was capable of manufacturing cannons and repairing steam engines. But the Satsuma army itself was still a samurai army and Saigo took on the challenge of sorting out the complex layers of samurai into battle groups that more closely resembled the regiments of European armies. These new units were equipped with thousands of rifles that had been imported from Britain.

At the end of 1866 the Emperor died and was succeeded by his fifteen year old son, the boy who would soon become famous as the great Meiji Emperor. The father, for all his public bluster calling for foreigners to be expelled from Japan, had generally been a supporter of the status quo. Without his support for the government the pace of change accelerated. Kyoto once again began to fill up with groups of aggressive samurai from all over Japan.

Now that dramatic political change seemed to be imminent the focus of the radicals shifted to the future of Japan. Ryoma Sakamoto played a key role in outlining the ideas that would become the blueprint for the coming revolution. His plan called for ultimate power to rest with the Emperor and for the monarch to be supported by two chambers of political representatives. The samurai would no longer monopolize power - politics and official positions would be open to all classes. The office of Shogun would be abolished and all treaties made with foreign powers would be renegotiated.

The fundamental aim of Ryoma's plan was the creation of a new nation, one that the Japanese people would not be ashamed to belong to. He was embarrassed by the ineffective and outdated feudal structures of his nation. It was a feeling of shame that produced the emotional energy for the increasingly rapid modernization of Japan over the coming decades. And it was this sense of shame that brought about the end of the samurai. The greatest pain for the Japanese samurai came when they saw what a weakling their nation actually was in comparison to the great world powers. In order to remedy this wrong the samurai class itself would have to disappear.

The end of the long rule of the Shoguns came quickly. By October 1867 Saigo Takamori had arrived in Kyoto at the head of ten thousand Satsuma troops. Ryoma turned up in November, bringing one thousand more rifles for the loyalist forces that were in complete control of the ancient capital. The imperial court was also enjoying the absence of any threat from government soldiers and felt confident enough to issue a decree calling for the overthrow of the Shogun and his system. On January 3rd the young Meiji Emperor announced that the Tokugawa state was finished. In Edo the government did its best to ignore this proclamation but to the loyalist samurai the Emperor's statement was a glorious vindication of all they had worked for.

Many of Ryoma's dreams were about to come true but he would not to live long enough to see the changes that he had worked for. This young provincial samurai had taken a place among the top layer of the revolutionary forces and, had he lived, would undoubtedly have played a leading role in the Meiji Revolution. His thinking had continued to develop. He now openly viewed the lords of Japan and the senior samurai as a corrupt and incompetent class. After a transitional period, he had come to believe, the aristocratic ranks would be swept away and political leaders freely elected by all of the people of Japan. It was a great tragedy for Japan that this free-thinking young samurai would lose his life on the very eve of the revolution.

At the end of 1867 Ryoma was a prime target for the government employed thugs who still roamed the streets of Kyoto and who still hoped to stop the revolution in its tracks by assassinating its leaders. Many believed that this important revolutionary had a small army of several hundred samurai at his command but Ryoma was, in fact, at the head of no force other than a few loyal friends. He was aware of the threat to his life and had taken the precaution of sleeping in a building with multiple exits so that he could easily escape from a surprise attack. But in early December he fell ill and temporarily moved to warmer and more comfortable quarters.

On the evening of the tenth three men bluffed their way into his building and ran upstairs drawing their swords. Ryoma had no chance to defend himself. He was hacked by the attacker's blades several times and died on the floor in a pool of his own blood. He was thirty two years old and had never held an official leadership position. But history has been kind to the memory of Ryoma Sakamoto. His early death and his separation from the compromises that were to follow the revolution have preserved him in the Japanese imagination as a truly great man, perhaps the greatest of them all. Ryoma was a new type in Japanese history, an individualist who saw his own destiny and the destiny of his nation as two strands intertwined in one exciting adventure. Without him, the revolution lost a good deal of its heart.

But even the death of Sakamoto Ryoma was quickly forgotten in the face of the great wave of change that now swept across Japan. At the end of 1867 the gathering pressures boiled to the surface. The young Emperor issued orders for the creation of a new government composed of aristocrats and samurai lords. The loyalist samurai ceased to think of themselves as rebels, they were now fighting for the government. It was the Shogun and his troops who had become renegades.

Early in the New Year fighting broke out to the south of Kyoto. On one side were Tokugawa troops, much fewer in number than the huge armies of the sixteenth century but still heavily outnumbering the loyalist forces that were led by Saigo Takamori. The Tokugawa army had finally received some training from French military experts and had many brave samurai in its ranks but the real passion and conviction lay with the other side. After three days of fighting the government army was routed.

Saigo, who had just turned forty, had been forbidden by the other revolutionary leaders to play any part in the fighting. He was much too important now, they told him, to allow himself to be killed by a sword or bullet. Nonetheless, he sneaked into the front lines when he could. "I long to be free of leading this army," he wrote to a friend, "so that I can die in battle and see you in hell." (13)

The Tokugawa army fell back to its stronghold in Edo and the Shogun surrendered the leadership of his army to Katsu Kaishu. With nothing to hinder them the loyalists pressed northward at speed, halting at only a single day's march from Edo. The revolutionaries were ready to raze the great city and to slaughter the Tokugawa samurai. And Saigo himself was implacable. He was determined to burn the city to the ground and to force the Shogun to commit suicide. At this critical point Katsu decided to send his trusted friend, the great swordsman Yamaoka Tesshu, to have a face to face meeting with Saigo. The message that Tesshu brought from Katsu was that the war was a fight between samurai brothers. Rather than slaughter each other the two sides should find a way to strike a deal. The defenders would peacefully surrender Edo if the invaders allowed the Tokugawa family to step down with honor.

On March 13th Saigo, as oblivious as ever to his own safety, personally travelled into the city and through the ranks of the enemy army to meet directly with Katsu. Saigo agreed to postpone the attack and to consider a more compassionate treatment of the Tokugawa family. Katsu then announced that the gates of Edo would be opened to the imperial forces. Between them, these two great men saved Japan from a calamitous civil war. Some small groups of Tokugawa samurai did fight on in Edo and in sporadic battles further to the north of Japan but their resistance soon crumbled. Saigo and his troops quelled the remaining opposition with bravery and with great compassion for their defeated enemies.

Bewildering Days

The government of the Shogun was now gone, but what would replace it? As often happens in the wake of revolutions the overturning of all that had once been familiar created a mood of contempt for the old ways. Young, lower-ranking samurai pressed hard for an end to the rule of the samurai lords and their families throughout Japan. Any man of ability, they argued, should be able to freely rise to a position of influence. Just one year after the fall of the old government in Edo the samurai lords of Japan began to resign from their positions. Most of these lords were reappointed as governors of their regions by the Emperor and they were able to continue living in their castles. But the principle of hereditary rule was out of favor. Among the samurai class the distinctions of rank were gradually abolished and wealth became more evenly distributed.

At the end of 1870 Saigo Takamori, who had little interest in administration, was persuaded to join the government. He was one of a small handful of samurai who had stepped forward to run the country and he took responsibility for reorganizing the national army. Saigo was party to the decision to finally and officially strip the samurai rulers of their power. The Emperor, speaking to an astonished audience of lords, announced that they would all be replaced by publicly appointed governors who would raise taxes and administer the provinces. Saigo supported this move, it fitted the logic of the times. But his heart was heavy. He was a passionate traditionalist and it hurt him to see the Satsuma family that he had risked his life for being stripped of their nobility and of the positions they had held for hundreds of years.

The next logical step for the government was to deal with the samurai caste itself. The warrior class was simply too expensive for a modern nation to support. Almost half of the entire tax revenue of Japan was being used to pay the fixed allowances that were allocated to each samurai and that were passed down from father to son. There were almost two million samurai in Japan and no other reforms could be afforded until the huge cost of maintaining this privileged class was reduced. Beginning in 1876 samurai income was taxed for the first time. Later it would be replaced entirely by government bonds.

An even more dramatic change came in 1872 with the introduction of military conscription. Every able-bodied man aged twenty one was required to submit to military service. For the first time in centuries commoners and peasants were allowed to carry arms. Samurai were ordered to cut off the topknot hairstyles that had distinguished them from other classes and to wear their hair in 'western' styles. From 1876 the samurai were even forbidden to carry swords or any kind of weapon on the street. This was a bitter pill for the Japanese samurai to swallow. It seemed that their identity and their honor were being stripped away with bewildering speed.

As the pace of reform quickened Saigo cut a restless figure at the heart of the government. His brain told him that change was inevitable but, in his heart, he had little taste for this painful dismantling of the samurai heritage. He had no taste either for politics. No one in the government had greater prestige than Saigo and he could easily have become the nation's leader if he had been so inclined but he preferred to spend time hunting or walking his dogs than to sit through interminable meetings. In 1873 an international crisis gave Saigo an opportunity to return to the kind of life he liked best, a life of passionate and direct action. The government of Korea had refused to pay tribute to the Meiji Emperor and had poured scorn on the radical changes taking part in Japan. For the first time since Hideyoshi's failed invasions, the government of Japan began to consider an attack on its closest neighbor.

Saigo volunteered to travel as an emissary to Korea. Only by looking directly into the eyes of the Koreans, he argued, could he understand their true intentions. If they insulted the Emperor and killed his messenger then the decision to invade Korea would be an easy one to make. Saigo was no imperialist and he had little interest in a war of conquest. What did motivate him was the need to protect the honor of the Emperor and that of the nation. At first the Tokyo government leaned towards sending Saigo on this dangerous mission but, at the end of 1873, there was a sudden shift in the balance of power. Radical modernizers took control of the ruling council and Saigo's mission was abruptly cancelled. Angry and disappointed he resigned from the council and left Edo. He was never to return.

The Final Battle
Saigo returned to Satsuma with some trepidation. He had signed his name, after all, to the orders that had dismantled the samurai lifestyle and in Satsuma the dispossessed samurai were furious. But when he actually met with these local samurai he found to his surprise that they regarded him as a symbol of resistance. His resignation from the government had made him a hero to the angry young samurai and whatever hopes they had of keeping the warrior flame alive they now entrusted to Saigo.

Several hundred Satsuma samurai had pulled out of Edo in support of Saigo and they were now unemployed. To give these young men a sense of direction private schools known as Shigakko were set up throughout Satsuma. They were similar to the samurai schools Saigo had attended as a boy, providing military training, practice of the martial arts and discussion on the political situation. The Hollywood movie The Last Samurai presents a rather romanticized portrait of this period but Saigo did not entirely devote his energies to preserving the good old days of Japanese culture. He had, in fact, made a long journey away from the outright xenophobia that had marked the early days of the sonnojoi movement. He encouraged the shigakko schools to hire foreign instructors and even to send outstanding students for study periods in Europe.

Saigo, the passionate traditionalist, had come to the conclusion that samurai values were not unique to Japan. The chief purpose of government, he began to argue, is the "cultivation of loyalty, filial piety, benevolence and love." These were values that he now regarded as being universal, principles that existed as much in the West as in the East. Conquering and subjugating entire peoples for profit was a betrayal of these fundamental civilizing values. European nations, he believed, were ignoring their own values when they took advantage of Asian countries. Japan, if it wanted to build a truly great future as a nation, should learn the important lessons from the history of the West. It should not be distracted by the lure of imperialism and material 'toys' such as train systems.

Satsuma had been the last region of Japan to accept the reforms of the class system. But a crisis erupted in 1876 when the Edo government replaced all samurai allowances with government bonds. In one stroke samurai income was halved and their hereditary status ended. At the same time all men, except for police and army officers, were forbidden to carry swords. All over Japan many samurai found these reforms too painful to bear and rebellions broke out in several parts of the country. But these samurai rebel bands preferred to fight with their swords and, despite their fury, they were easily defeated by government troops supplied with modern weaponry.

Saigo's heart was torn as he watched these futile uprisings. He knew that Japan could never return to the feudal ages. But these young fighting samurai represented everything he truly admired – purity of heart and direct, self-sacrificing action. In Satsuma the samurai were boiling with anger and clearly on the point of rebellion. To prevent them from launching an uprising, the government sent a ship to seize the Satsuma armory. As word of the arrival of government troops spread the students of the Shigakko schools broke into the arms dumps and carried the stored guns and cannons off to hiding places.

Suddenly Satsuma was in open revolt and Saigo, whatever he thought of the situation, was left with little choice. By default he found himself at the head of a new Satsuma rebel army of twelve thousand men who were armed with modern rifles and field guns. It is probable that Saigo had no real idea of what he wanted to do with this army but he felt it was his duty to provide leadership to the proud young samurai of Satsuma. When asked about his intentions he announced, ominously, that he would 'hold discussions' with the government.

The rebel army of Satsuma had no manifesto to fight for. The one thing that gave them hope and direction was their desire to help Saigo travel to Edo so that he could deal with the government in his own way. They were full of courage and enthusiasm but they were setting themselves up for a fight against the army of the entire nation. The Japanese army was not only bigger and better equipped; it could draw on the resources of the whole country for resupply. Saigo had committed himself to a hopeless and quixotic war.

The rebels travelled north to Kumamoto where they attempted to storm one of the largest castles in the land. Their fierce sword charges were driven off by concentrated gunfire and the rebels withdrew to settle in for a long siege. In March 1877, just ten years after Saigo had led his forces into Edo, the forces of the Japanese government landed in Kagoshima and occupied his city. A large detachment of government troops was then sent north to deal with the rebels in Kumamoto. For the next seventeen days the rebels held out on a hilltop with cannon, guns and, when their bullets ran out, their samurai swords. It was a vicious battle. Four thousand men on each side had died before Saigo finally gave up control of the hill and ordered his forces to scatter into the hills and forests of Kyushu.

Saigo fought a guerrilla war for several months before he finally found his way back to Shiroyama mountain on the outskirts of his hometown. By this time his proud army had been reduced to three hundred bedraggled and exhausted men. They had almost no food or ammunition left and were surrounded by a government army composed of thousands of conscripted commoners who were armed with modern weapons. Saigo told his men that this would be the final battle and asked those who were not prepared to die to leave the camp. That night the remaining samurai sat in the moonlight on a hilltop singing songs and drinking sake.

Before dawn the government forces began to pound the rebels with artillery fire. As the first light rose Saigo and his few remaining friends and supporters drew their swords and charged downhill into the guns of the enemy. Saigo fell wounded. At his own request, his head was removed by a flashing sword stroke from a close friend. He met his death in the way he had lived, a servant of instinct and passion rather than thought. With Saigo Takamori went the last flicker of the long and glorious reign of the Japanese samurai. Their day was over.

7. Yamaoka Tesshu

How Do You Deal With Such A Man?
Japan went through so much in the middle years of the nineteenth century. The flame of revolution gave the young samurai a thrilling cause to live for. And then, almost overnight, they were told that the warrior class was to be disbanded. They were angry at first, and then depressed. In the years that followed the Meiji Restoration the martial arts fell into a deep slump. Martial artists were no longer admired and lost most of their social standing. There did not seem to be any purpose in keeping the medieval fighting systems alive. Like everything else in Japan the old martial ways seemed shamefully obsolescent when compared to the steam ships and cannons of the Western nations.

The huge events that shook Japan in the nineteenth century did produce a turning away from the nation's fighting arts. But there were a few experts who maintained a happy disregard for the march of history. Among them was Yamaoka Tesshu, perhaps the greatest of all the martial artists of his era. He was little more than a bit player in the political upheavals of his century. But the leading men of Japan, Saigo Takamori and Katsu Kaishu among them, regarded Tesshu to be one of the finest and most important of the samurai. This intelligent and cultivated swordsman seemed to personify the very best of the spirit of his class. As the flame of the martial ways burned low Tesshu kept his own vision brilliantly alive.

In his own lifetime and in the years that followed Yamaoka Tesshu was widely thought to be the greatest sword expert who had lived since Miyamoto Musashi. The two men had a good deal in common. Both lived lives that were filled with intense introspection and personal challenge. And they both transcended the simple physicality of the martial ways to engage in society as important artists and thinkers. Neither man had much interest in the trappings of wealth and both men were derided for their unkempt appearance.

Yet the lives of these swordsmen, lived at opposite ends of the Edo period, were very different. Yamaoka Tesshu never killed another man. His deepest desire was not fixed on becoming the strongest swordsman in Japan. Instead he committed himself to mining the spiritual dimension of swordsmanship to its very depths. Tesshu was undoubtedly a man of his times but he seemed to exist on another plane from his contemporaries, winning their admiration and respect. As Saigo Takamori ruefully complained, "He has no need for fame or money or position, or even life itself. How do you deal with such a man?" (14)

Mountain Boy

Tesshu was born in 1836 into the family of a middle-ranking samurai. His father, Ono Asaemon, was employed as a manager of the Shogun's rice stores, a respectable occupation that kept the family in reasonable comfort. Asaemon was a vigorous man who was sixty three by the time Tesshu was born. He had already fathered several children both in and out of wedlock and, after Tesshu's arrival, would go on to father five more boys. Tesshu was the fourth son of Asaemon but was immediately recognized as the official heir to his father. It happened that he was the first son produced by the marriage of the energetic sexagenarian samurai and his twenty-six year old 'official' wife. Tesshu's mother, Iso, was a tall, dark beauty with a fiery temper.

Tesshu's early childhood was spent among the hurly-burly of downtown Edo but when he was ten years old his father was posted to Takayama, a town high in the Japanese Alps. In the nineteenth century Takayama was already the uncommon place it remains today, a town hidden from the world by a circle of three thousand meter high mountains that are snow capped for much of the year. Despite its isolation, nineteenth century Takayama was home to a thriving community of wealthy samurai. The town was an important producer of timber for the huge Edo market and was famous as the home of the elite carpenters who had built the Imperial Palace in Kyoto. It was a mountain community that was rich in history, tradition and culture.

Tesshu had been born into the Ono family and was distantly related to the great seventeenth century sword master Ono Tadaaki. By the age of nine Tesshu was already taking sword lessons. After the move to Takayama he began to study with a teacher from his family's own sword style, the Ono Branch of the One Stroke School (Ono ha Itto Ryu). Tesshu would eventually become the Headmaster of this school and, as part of the transmission of leadership, received a famous sword that had once belonged to the teacher of Ono Tadaaki, the legendary Ittosai. The sword was known as the 'pot-cleaving' sword. Ittosai was said to have used it on a bandit who had been hiding in a large earthenware vessel. One mighty swing of his sword had sliced the pot, and the bandit, in two.

Takayama was also the setting for Tesshu's introduction to one of the greatest passions of his life – Japanese calligraphy. This kind of handwriting, known as shodo, is actually a sophisticated art form with its own variety of schools and masters. The Chinese characters that are used in writing the Japanese language allow meaning to be conveyed in just a few dramatic washes of black ink. Later in life Tesshu would become one of the greatest and most prolific shodo masters, by some accounts the greatest of the modern age.

Tesshu took his first lessons in calligraphy with Iwasa Ittei, an outstanding teacher who was also an expert swordsman. Iwasa had been a determined young student of shodo himself. He had begun his studies by spending three years practicing nothing else but the simplest possible character, the single brush stroke that means 'one' (ichi). Iwasa was a demanding teacher and refused to accept new students until they had produced a satisfactory copy of a long classical text that contained one thousand characters. At the age of eleven Tesshu sat in an unbroken two hour long sitting to produce an exemplary copy of Iwasa's own transcription of the thousand characters. The teacher could see that the boy's writing was remarkably mature and confident. They worked together for four years until, at the age of only fifteen, Tesshu received a certificate of mastery from his teacher. Tesshu eventually succeeded Iwasa as the headmaster of this school of shodo and went on to produce many of the finest works of nineteenth century calligraphy.

The Ono family had enjoyed a comfortable, middle class way of life in Takayama but in 1851 this happy stability crashed to pieces. Tesshu's mother suddenly dropped dead at the age of forty one, the victim of a stroke. Her husband, who by nineteenth century standards was a very old man of seventy nine, could not take care of the six sons his wife had left behind. One of the children was a new-born baby. Tesshu was only fifteen years old but he immediately took charge of the family. He fed and clothed his siblings, cared for his father and arranged for a wet nurse to feed the abandoned baby. Tesshu had loved his mother deeply and he grieved for her. Every evening after the family had eaten and he had settled the younger children in bed he would visit his mother's grave to make offerings and chant sutras. Right through the forty nine days it takes a Japanese soul to make its way to the afterlife the boy watched over the spirit of his mother.

But the family crisis was not yet at an end. Six months later Asaemon followed his wife into the grave and the children were orphaned. They were not completely destitute, however, as Asaemon had left behind a substantial hoard of more than three thousand gold coins. As he handled his father's will Tesshu demonstrated the indifference to material wealth that would mark his entire life. He distributed the money freely among his brothers and other relatives, keeping only one hundred gold coins for himself. The teenager arranged for all of his siblings to be taken in by other family members and then, having discharged his duty, set off to make the long walk through the mountains to Edo.

The Ogre
Tesshu arrived in Edo in 1853, at the height of the political ferment caused by the arrival of ships from America. But as Tesshu made his way through this huge labyrinth of wooden and paper buildings politics were far from his mind. With a population of more than one million souls Edo was more densely populated than the Manhattan of today. It was an intoxicating place for a young man, a city full of great samurai, fantastic entertainers, beautiful women and ideas of every kind.

Tesshu was seventeen when he arrived in Edo and even in this seething, urban mass he stood out from the very beginning. He had already grown to over 1.8 meters in height and had a powerful build – later in life he would weigh more than 100 kilograms. The average male height in Edo was below 1.6 meters so this teenager towered over most of the men around him. He was a handsome youth with a broad, open face, a strong jaw and a high forehead. It was the kind of face that inspired trust and admiration.

One of Tesshu's first actions in Edo was to register with the central martial arts institute, the Kobukan. It was a natural step for a young man who had already reached an expert level of swordsmanship through years of training in the sword style of his family. As he resumed daily sword practice his new teachers discovered that Tesshu was tremendously strong. Although most of the sparring at the Kobukan was being conducted with safe and flexible bamboo swords Tesshu was ordered not to strike at his opponent's arms. His teachers worried that he would break the bones of less solidly built students.

Among the style-conscious youth of the city Tesshu stood out. He was a young man who was crazy about sword training but completely uninterested in most other things, including personal grooming. Before long his fellow students gave him nicknames that were based on his childhood name of Tetsutaro and would stick to him for the rest of his life. One was borotetsu (scruffy Tetsu). Another, inspired by the intimidating figure he cut in the sword school, was onitetsu (Tetsu the ogre).

Tesshu's great love for the martial arts led him to visit many of the fighting schools in Edo and brought him in touch with one of the greatest teachers of the time, Yamaoka Seizan. This master of a school of spear fighting was an intense and passionate teacher who made a deep impression on the young Tesshu. Seizan had a rigorous and uncompromising personal training regime that he followed on a daily basis whatever the weather. Every morning he would practice thousands of spear thrusts. He was said to have become an enlightened master of the spear after an momentous training session in which he defended himself without pause against fresh opponents for twenty four hours.

Seizan scorned any kind of material comfort. He wore thin cotton clothing throughout the winter and lived on a simple diet. He told his students that nothing was more important than humility and family and that character was more important than technique. "No enemy can defeat a man of superior virtue," he would say, "attempting to win through exclusive reliance on technique will lead you nowhere." (14) Tesshu never forgot the way Seizan would talk about the inner life of a warrior. In later years he would take these ideas to their ultimate conclusion as he developed his own way of the sword.

But Tesshu was once again to be left behind by a person he loved. Not long after he had begun to study in Seizan's dojo his teacher collapsed and died while defending a friend in a brawl. Tesshu visited his teacher's grave with the same mournful care he had displayed in the weeks that followed his mother's death. On one dark and stormy night he was spotted making his way to Seizan's tomb where he wrapped his overcoat around the gravestone and muttered consoling words. Seizan, an otherwise fearless man, had been terrified of thunderstorms.

Seizan's death led to a crisis in his family. The prevailing tradition in the martial arts schools was for a father to pass on the leadership to his most able son. But Seizan had been unmarried and there were no relatives with enough skill to take his place as a teacher. In the way of the times the hopes of the family turned to Seizan's much younger sister, Fusako. If she could be steered into the right kind of marriage the name and the reputation of the family would be preserved. But the attractive sixteen-year-old Fusako had definite opinions on the matter. Tesshu was the only man that she had any interest in and she protested that her life would not be worth living if she could not marry him. Her family did not share her enthusiasm for this poverty stricken and distinctly odd young man. But it was clear that Fusako was determined and so the family grudgingly accepted the situation and allowed the pair to be married in 1855. It was common practice in Edo for the name of an important family to be continued through the female line and so Tesshu took his wife's name, becoming Yamaoka Tesshu. He did not inherit the leadership of Seizan's school but would become his teacher's true inheritor in matters of the spirit.

The marriage between Tesshu and Fusako was a love match that survived his free-spirited ways to last until his death and produced five children. Tesshu found a great contentment in married life and he relished the friendship that he shared with his young wife. In one of the scrolls he painted in later life he depicts an aged couple sitting comfortably together and accompanies the painting with the words, "You'll reach one hundred/ I'll reach ninety-nine/ As our hair turns white together." (14)

At first the young couple had almost no income and lived a life of grinding poverty. They had no money for nightclothes and when his wife was pregnant with their first child Tesshu gave her his kimono to sleep in while he slept naked by her side. Regularly they were forced to sell off furniture and cooking utensils to raise enough money to eat. On one occasion Tesshu even sold the tatami mats that floored their home. At times these desperate measures did not suffice to put food on the table and when money was really tight Tesshu only allowed himself to eat on alternate days. Debt collectors were regular visitors to his home but he rarely allowed their depressing demands to take away his zest for life. Once, after a friend had treated him to a reviving bottle of sake, he composed the following poem.

> When I drink sake,
> I feel spring
> In my heart.
> Even you debt collectors
> Sound like the nightingales. (15)

Later in life Tesshu had a substantial income. He was appointed to important government positions and could count some of the most powerful people in the nation as his friends and supporters. But his complete lack of interest in material possessions never disappeared and he never quite lived down the nickname of 'scruffy Tetsu'. Rather than new clothes he preferred to spend his money on helping poor relatives and acquaintances. He opened his home to anyone who needed a place to live and even extended his sympathy to the stray animals who slept close to the building because they knew that he would feed them.

One of the very few things that really mattered to 'the ogre' was sword training. As a young man he toured the sword schools of Edo looking for matches with anyone who was willing to take him on. He was so powerful that he scorned the normal practice of taking a breather between bouts. In most schools the use of bamboo swords and armor had become standard but sword training was still very different from the refined practices that would emerge with modern kendo. This was, after all, a city where samurai still carried two swords on public display as they walked through the streets. And sword fights, although officially forbidden, were still a common way of settling disputes. There was a real edge to training in the sword schools as young samurai knew they might have to put their swords to practical use some day. Tesshu, with his powerful body and irrepressible spirit, was the hardest competitor of them all. He was an intimidating sight for the hundreds of opponents he crossed swords with each year.

Tesshu was strong enough to thrash most of his fellow students but, at the age of twenty eight, he finally met his match. Asari Gimei was a famous master of the One Stroke School and was the adoptive father of the great sword teacher Chiba Shusaku. On hearing that Asari was in Edo Tesshu decided to pay a visit to his dojo and to issue a challenge. Asari was a much smaller man than Tesshu and, after an extended tussle, Tesshu used his superior height and weight to force Asari to the floor. As the older man rose to his feet he asked Tesshu for his views on their fight. He politely replied that it had been a tough and instructive exchange but that he was glad to have been fortunate enough to win. Then Asari asked Tesshu to take a look at his own chest protector. When he glanced downward he found to his surprise that three bamboo strips were broken. Asari had struck first. In a real sword fight the victory would have gone to Asari and Tesshu would have suffered severe wounds, if not death.

Embarrassed and angry at this rare defeat Tesshu brushed off the incident. But later at home he reviewed what had happened in his mind and decided to return to Asari to apologize and to become his student. When the two men sparred with more dangerous wooden swords Tesshu realized that Asari was an overpowering fighter who repeatedly threw him back against the dojo walls. On one occasion Asari even ended a bout by chasing Tesshu out onto the street where he knocked him down and contemptuously slammed the door in his face. This was something new for Tesshu, the greatest skill he had encountered in his life. He said that he had never met a swordsman like Asari, someone who was soft on the outside but completely hard on the inside. The smaller man's aura was so powerful that Tesshu could see no way to overcome it. He was tormented with self-doubt as he tried to perceive the secret of Asari's brilliance. It became a riddle that he wrestled with for seventeen years, suffering endless defeats. Tesshu would have to move his swordsmanship to another level altogether before he could understand the source of Asari's power.

A Man of Will

As a young samurai swordsman in Edo during the 1850s Tesshu was quite naturally drawn into the ranks of the sonno-joi movement as it swept through the city. The young men who adopted the slogan 'expel the barbarians, revere the Emperor' were united by their frustration at the weakness of Japan in the face of the outside world. They hated the foreign intruders and longed for the Emperor to take control of the nation. Tesshu greatly enjoyed the drama and excitement of this period – it was one of those rare times in history when youths in their teens and twenties feel that they are responsible for reshaping the world. Tesshu and his friends held their political discussions in drinking dens where their high minded talk often dissolved into exuberant parties.

Tesshu was, in fact, an enthusiastic drinker all of his life and had a capacity for alcohol that was unusual for a Japanese man. Competitive to the core he would take part in drinking competitions in which the last man capable of walking would be judged the winner. Tesshu would accept almost any challenge, happily attempting to eat a record number of boiled eggs or demonstrating that he could walk to a point forty-five miles distant and return in a single day. On one occasion Tesshu was astounded to hear of a horse that had proved too wild for anyone to mount. He demanded to be taken immediately to the beast. Walking directly toward the wide-eyed animal Tesshu suddenly grabbed it by the tail and began to drag the astonished horse around its stall. Before long, the chastened beast was quietly allowing him to lead it on the end of a rope. When asked how he had known what to do Tesshu responded, "Animals confronted with determination greater than their own immediately submit. And," he admitted, "I was pretty drunk." (14)

Tesshu did not spend all of his evenings in the company of other young samurai. Far from it. He loved women and loved sex. Even by the relaxed moral standards of Edo Period Japan he seems to have been an outstanding libertine. Later in life Tesshu claimed that during his twenties and thirties he had slept with thousands of women. Most of these amorous adventures took place in the Yoshiwara quarter of Edo, a place that was largely unchanged from the days when Miyamoto Musashi would go there to relax. Samurai checked their swords at the gate of the quarter and entered a world where the classes and sexes mixed freely. Tesshu, who was tall and handsome, was popular with the women of Yoshiwara. He was so poor that the professional entertainers often took him to their beds without insisting on payment. But some of these prostitutes found themselves at a loss when Tesshu would break off from a love-making session to sit upright on their floor in meditation. The pursuit of women, like everything else in his life, had become a philosophical puzzle. He liked to ponder over the mysterious essential difference between men and women. And his relentless enjoyment of sex was, he suggested, an attempt to cross over the gulf that separated man from woman and the self from the other.

Tesshu's wife was unimpressed by her husband's high-minded explanations for his night time adventures. Her family encouraged her to divorce him and, after years of putting up with his behavior, she finally cracked. One evening, receiving her husband home from what had obviously been another romantic encounter, she produced a knife and threatened to kill herself and the children. In the end, Tesshu did stop running around and began to demonstrate the great respect and affection he had always felt for his long-suffering wife.

While Tesshu may not have been a perfect spouse he was an outstanding young swordsman and his skills soon attracted the attention of the powers in control of Edo. In 1856, just three years after arriving in the city, Tesshu was appointed as a senior instructor at the most important martial arts academy in Edo, the Kobukan. Seven years later he was one of a group of senior sword instructors that was assembled by the government. Their mission was to travel to Kyoto where they would serve as the officer corps for dozens of samurai fighters from Edo. The government hoped that this small army could counterbalance the unruly imperial loyalists. Tesshu made his way to the old capital at the head of a group of ronin known as the Roshigumi. But as soon as they arrived in Kyoto the deeply confused allegiances of these young samurai bubbled to the surface. Many of them made it clear that, although they had been appointed by the government of the Shogun, their true loyalty lay with the Emperor. They refused to take a salary from the government and refused to take part in spying on the revolutionary samurai of Kyoto.

Tesshu made no secret of his support for those who refused to do dirty work for the government but somehow he managed to return from Kyoto with an undamaged reputation as a trustworthy and honorable samurai. In 1867, at the age of 31, he was appointed to the personal guard of the ruler of Japan, the Shogun Yoshinobu. This was an important promotion for Tesshu but accepting the post must have caused him some pain. He was, after all, a loyalist at heart who owed his allegiance to those who wanted to transfer power from the Shogun to the Emperor.

Just a few months later the final struggle for control of Japan was underway and Saigo Takamori had marched his army to the gates of Edo. In March 1868, with an attack on the city by the loyalist army imminent, the Shogun and his senior advisors were forced to choose between surrender or putting up a desperate resistance. In the end it was Katsu Kaishu who took the lead. He argued that change had become inevitable and that the only choice for the government was to negotiate the best possible terms for the handover of the city. He ordered Tesshu to travel to the enemy camp to conduct direct negotiations with Saigo Takamori.

This was a dangerous and critical mission. Failure to strike a deal was certain to result in a terrible civil war. With this great weight on his shoulders Tesshu casually bade farewell to his wife. He omitted to tell her where he was going but indicated that he would be home soon. And then he set out on foot with only one other samurai at his side, walking for hours directly into and through the ranks of the army that was preparing to burn Edo to the ground. Arriving at Saigo Takamori's headquarters he was greeted with some surprise but was admitted to a private meeting with the great general.

Tesshu announced that the Shogun pledged his total allegiance to the Emperor and was willing to take any action necessary to end the bloody war. Saigo was unimpressed. He told Tesshu that a promise of obedience would not be enough to halt his march on Edo. Such promises had been made before. Tesshu looked the general in the eye and responded quietly but firmly, "I wish to comment with the utmost respect on behalf of my lord Yoshinobu that if you do not accept the Shogun's peaceful intentions, death is my only option." He continued, "in that case, all 80,000 warriors of Tokugawa will fight to the end without fear of death. The entire nation will be plunged into war." (16)

Tesshu was not making an idle threat. There were thousands of samurai in Edo who were eager to die in battle rather than surrender to the rebels. But Tesshu's full-hearted and honorable statement of purpose was exactly the kind of spirit that Saigo respected. With all of the force of his personality Tesshu convinced the general to reconsider his plans to raze Edo. After some further discussion Saigo accepted the Shogun's offer of obedience and set out a series of harsh conditions for the surrender of Edo and the exile of the Shogun. Once again Tesshu dug in his heels. He accepted most of the terms but refused to sign an agreement that would make the Shogun a humiliated prisoner of the imperial forces.

Saigo was one of the greatest men in the land and Tesshu was of much lower status. But he spoke as an equal and with quiet determination faced down the general's angry insistence that his terms be accepted without question. Eventually Saigo conceded more favorable conditions for the retirement of the Shogun and Tesshu was satisfied. Later, as the two great men shared a drink, Saigo asked Tesshu how he had been able to safely journey to his camp from the enemy headquarters in Edo. Tesshu replied that he had simply walked directly along the main road. He added that he had greatly admired the organization and polish of the imperial forces that he had been able to observe. Saigo, laughing with disbelief, was convinced that he had discovered someone who was truly out of the ordinary. In later years he would be an important supporter and admirer of Tesshu.

Friend of the Emperor
The civil war had lasted for years and had taken three thousand lives. Now, in its wake, the city of Edo was renamed as Tokyo and the young Emperor Meiji became the focus of national power. Saigo Takamori used his influence to ensure that samurai who had been honorable fighters in the army of the Shogun would be forgiven and even employed by the new regime. Tesshu was one of those who personally benefitted from this generous policy. He was quickly rehabilitated and in 1869 was appointed as a government official for the Shizuoka region. Three years later, on the direct recommendation of Saigo, he was appointed to a key position as an advisor and aide to the Emperor.

The young ruler of Japan had been born just a year before the arrival of the Black Ships from America had thrown his country into turmoil. At the age of fourteen the death of his father made the teenager the 122nd Emperor of Japan. He would be the most powerful Emperor for several hundred years but he had no experience of government. He would need the wisest and most loyal of men around him to support him as he matured. A search went out for men of unimpeachable character and among the men chosen to stand behind the throne was Tesshu.

The Emperor was a privileged and cosseted youth who was already enjoying relations with an equally young wife and her five 'ladies-in-waiting'. He enjoyed holding late night drinking parties with his aides and advisors, most of whom were fawning acolytes. It was not a promising recipe for the development of an outstanding national leader. Tesshu was one of the few people in the young Emperor's circle who refused to flatter the ruler. One evening the boy became enraged by Tesshu's bluntness and challenged him to a bout of sumo wrestling. When Tesshu refused to assist His Majesty in doing anything so undignified the Emperor forced the issue by launching an attack. His wrestling moves had little effect on the much larger samurai so the Emperor threw a haymaker at his opponent's face. Instinctively, Tesshu shifted position and, as the startled young man flew past him, turned and pinned him to the floor. The other aides in the room were shocked by this display of lesse-majeste and dragged Tesshu from the room, begging him to apologize. "No", replied Tesshu.

> I have pledged my life to his service and would never do anything to hurt him but he must learn not to lose his temper when he drinks and not to bully others. When he comes to, tell him what I said. If he orders me to commit suicide I will do it on the spot. (14)

The Emperor did not require Tesshu to commit suicide. It was, in fact, becoming clear to him that this advisor was one of the few people he could really respect and trust. No one was more loyal than Tesshu. One evening this was confirmed when a group of army officers, frustrated by their conditions, started a violent skirmish close to the Imperial Palace. Startled awake by gunfire and shouts Tesshu grabbed his swords and ran straight toward the imperial bed chamber. As he crashed into the room he found that the Emperor, who was alone, was relieved to have an armed samurai with him. Only at that point did Tesshu sheepishly become aware that he was standing guard over the Emperor of Japan while dressed in his bedclothes. After some time the security staff and aides of the Emperor began to appear. All were impeccably dressed in their official clothing. The grateful Emperor asked Tesshu to leave his sword behind as a memento of his loyalty.

Tesshu had promised to spend ten years in the service of the Emperor and he kept his promise. As an imperial advisor he was a very important person and could have easily launched a career as a senior politician or government official. But Tesshu was completely uninterested in power and, despite his high-ranking position, he continued to be known behind his back as borotetsu, the scruffy samurai. A story still told in Japan today has the Emperor giving Tesshu money for a new set of clothes. The following day Tesshu appeared in the same ragged outfit he always wore. "What happened to the money I gave you yesterday?" inquired the Emperor. Replied Tesshu, "I used it to provide clothes for the children of your majesty." He was, in fact, looking after a number of poverty-stricken members of his own family and other vagrants. One building on his compound was kept aside for these dependents and he ensured that they were well fed.

Two Flashing Swords
Tesshu had little interest in material wealth but he was fascinated by human potential. As a young man Teshhu had been defeated by the sword master Asari and he subsequently spent many years studying under Asari in an attempt to understand just what it was that made this man different from all the other fighters he had encountered. In his youth Tesshu had been introduced to Zen Buddhism and when introspection consumed him as an adult he naturally returned to this practice. During his years in the service of the Emperor Tesshu was a student of Seijo, the master of Ryutakuji temple in the province of

Shizuoka. This monastery had been established in 1761 by the Buddhist monk Hakuin, a religious giant who had breathed new life into Japanese Zen. The temple was home to dozens of monks who followed the Rinzai Zen practice of koan training.

In koan practice a monk is given a Zen question and must present an answer to the question when he meets the temple master in a private encounter. The monk struggles to prepare his answer as he sits for hours every day in the silence of zen meditation. In the dim light of the meditation hall the monk allows the question to sink deeply through his conscious and unconscious mind until an answer spontaneously emerges. But meetings with the master take place on a fixed schedule and when the time comes to present his answer the monk may have little idea of what to say. His desperate attempts to speak are often received with only a shout, a blow, or a muttered dismissal. It is a frustrating process that finally drives a monk into the mental and emotional spaces that lie beyond everyday patterns of thought.

Tesshu lived a very long way from his master and a single visit to the Ryutakuji monastery required him to make a two day round trip. On the occasions when he had a free day Tesshu would finish his evening meal in Tokyo and would then set out to walk through moonlit rice fields and along mountain trails to the distant countryside temple. On arrival the following morning at Ryutakuji he would be admitted to the master's room and would present his answer to the koan he had been mulling over. On many occasions Seijo, seemingly unaware of the arduous journey his student had just made, would dismiss Tesshu's answer abruptly. After a meeting that had lasted only a few seconds Tesshu would be forced to begin his long walk home to Tokyo.

But Tesshu was nothing if he was not determined. After three years of this long-distance study program Seijo informed Tesshu that his understanding was satisfactory and his training was finished. The student had experienced no feeling of enlightenment and he was rather puzzled by the approval of this tough master. In a dark and gloomy frame of mind Tesshu was once again beginning the long trudge towards home when all of a sudden the huge bulk of Mount Fuji emerged from the clouds. Tesshu stopped in his tracks. Right now everything was clear. He gave a shout of appreciation and ran back to the temple to thank his master. Later he composed this poem to express the understanding that had come.

> Fine on a clear day
> Fine on a cloudy day
> The original shape of Mount Fuji
> Never changes. (15)

The taste of awakening had been sweet. But after some time Tesshu began to feel that he was still not satisfied. Some doubts about the nature of life and death remained. He decided to study with another teacher named Tekisui who was master of the great Zen temple Tenryuji in western Kyoto. Tekisui was a tough, straightforward teacher who was able to pay occasional visits to Tesshu's home in Tokyo to provide instruction. He gave Tesshu little room to be satisfied with his own accomplishments, responding to his answers with blows, shouts and slaps. For this particular student it was the best teaching method. Tesshu wanted to be pushed to the limit, he wanted to find the deepest truth. Finally he was given a koan that he simply could not find an answer to.

> When two flashing swords meet, there is no place to escape. (14)

For three years Tesshu sat in zazen for long hours every evening, wrestling for an answer that would break the impenetrable barrier. Gradually the koan became an inseparable part of his psyche. He would leap out of bed at night and, thrusting a sword into his wife's sleepy hands, would force her to play the role of 'opponent' as he tried out a solution. Finally, early in the morning of March 30th, 1880, while seated in deep meditation, Tesshu took hold of the inner meaning of the koan. This time he was sure that he was experiencing a complete breakthrough and there was no need to check his understanding with Tekisui. In his excitement these words came to him.

> The walls surrounding me suddenly crumbled,
> Like pure dew reflecting the world in crystal clarity,
> Total awakening has now come. (14)

Tesshu had at last been able to directly perceive his own nature. As the ecstasy of the moment subsided one of his first actions was to present himself at the dojo of his old nemesis, Asari. Now, Tesshu felt sure, he would be able to demonstrate the answer to his koan in practice. He would show Asari just what happens when two flashing swords meet. Asari accepted the sudden challenge from his student and the two men crossed swords. As their eyes met Asari recognized the change in Tesshu. He took a step back and lowered his sword. "You have got it," he announced.

Tesshu had a similar reception when he visited his Zen master Tekisui. The monk took one look at Tesshu and, rather than listening to his answer to the koan, ordered a case of beer in celebration. Tesshu quickly and with great pleasure knocked back twelve bottles. "This is the best thing I have ever tasted", he exulted. Tekisui later gave inka to Tesshu, the formal recognition that he had fully completed his studies.

What was the insight that had so transformed Tesshu? In his own writing he attempted to put this realization into words. He noted that as a youth he had practiced freely with his sword but on becoming a young man, although he was immeasurably stronger, he had been fixated with trying to understand the actions of his opponents. He became stuck. It was a frustrating time but he had been carried onwards by a determination to proceed to the very end. He would continue to practice even if swordsmanship disappeared and there were no opponents left to fight. In the end, at the age of forty five, he realized that everything that had troubled him for so long had been nothing but the creation of his own mind.

> If there is self, there is an enemy; if there is no self, there is no enemy. If we are enlightened to the truth of this principle, skill-ineptitude, weakness-strength, child-adult and so on are no longer seen as two separate entities. This is: "lovely snowflakes falling one by one nowhere else" - a marvelous place. (14)

No Sword

After this great religious breakthrough Tesshu felt completely free to follow his own path. One of his first acts was to establish a sword school that he named the No Sword School (Muto Ryu). It was a name that had obviously been inspired by his religious beliefs but in practice the style of the school was very similar to that of the One Stroke School that Tesshu had studied in as a young man. The One Stroke School put little emphasis on the subtleties of defensive swordsmanship but instead pushed its students to develop a determined and overwhelming attack. Tesshu took this approach to the extreme. He had new students spend their first three years in his school practicing nothing but direct blows to the top of an opponent's head. They were trained to never flinch under pressure, to never step backwards but simply to press on to total victory. Students complained about the endless repetitions of basic techniques and many gave up on this exhausting and rather boring school. Like his contemporaries in Okinawan karate circles, Tesshu dismissed the importance of new students being able to acquire a wide range of techniques. He wanted them to go after something more important; they needed to have a strong abdominal centre (hara) and an indomitable power of both mind and spirit.

By 1882 Tesshu had completed his vow to serve the Emperor for ten years. With his substantial retirement payments he built a new training hall for the No Sword School. Tesshu named this new dojo The Hall of the Spring Wind (Shunpukan) in tribute to the great Chinese Zen master, Bukko, who had travelled to Japan to teach Zen Buddhism in the thirteenth century. Bukko is most often remembered for a famous incident in China when Mongol soldiers suddenly rushed into his quarters as he was sitting in meditation. The soldiers brandished their swords in the air but were astonished to see that Bukko remained calmly seated. Clearly expecting to die he spoke these words to mark the occasion of his death.

> Not one place to hide throughout heaven and earth,
> True joy lies in knowing that man and all things are completely non-existent.
> The Mongolian longsword is magnificent -
> A lightning flash cuts the spring wind!

Instead of removing his head the Mongol soldiers are said to have returned their swords to their sheaths in the face of this impressive display of fearlessness. To find a courage that goes beyond courage was, for Tesshu, the ultimate aim of swordsmanship.

> Our true secret is complete fearlessness, but it has to be complete. Some are brave in the face of enemies with swords but are easily defeated by greed or fame. Our secret is to be fearless in the face of both our outer enemies and our inner enemies. (14)

Tesshu expected new recruits to his sword school to be able to show courage from the start. If a prospective student visited the dojo he would tell the young man to stand still and would pound a staff repeatedly into his body. After this painful welcome there were few who wanted to return the following day but those who did were accepted as students. The recruits were told that the purpose of their training was to reach enlightenment and they they must be willing to risk their lives to achieve it. Tesshu would test new students further by ordering them to attack him over and over again. Each time he would knock them to the floor. They would only learn something from this school, he told them, if they showed unwavering determination.

Training at the Hall of the Spring Wind took place between six and nine in the morning. Every morning. Between seventy and eighty swordsmen would gather to practice kata with wooden swords. They would then dress in body armor and pick up their bamboo swords for extended sparring sessions. Tesshu expected total commitment from his students and that commitment involved a promise to attend training every day without fail. Few risked taking a morning off. Tesshu had been known to march to the house of a sick student and to drag the feeble absentee to the dojo to take part in training.

This uncompromising atmosphere produced many outstanding students and even in the years after the Meiji Restoration when interest in the martial arts collapsed the unshakeable self-belief of Tesshu helped to keep his students committed and his dojo active. After the master's death several of his students became leaders in the revival of sword fighting toward the end of the century. They were also instrumental in the creation of modern kendo. Perhaps the outstanding student of the Shunpukan was Kagawa Zenjiro, a man who would later become head instructor of swordsmanship at the National Police Academy and who would create his own powerful tradition of tough and fervent training.

In order to push his best students beyond their comfort zones Tesshu created a monumental challenge that he named Vow to Practice (seigan-geiko). Kagawa was the first of the Shunpukan students to undergo this test. Before even attempting the final challenge of the seigan-geiko students were required to complete one thousand training days without missing a single day. On the final day of the thousand the candidate would spend the entire day facing two hundred opponents in continuous sword matches. One hundred fights would be held in the morning and one hundred in the afternoon. During these fighting periods the candidate would stand without a break as his opponents lined up to take him on. For those wishing to experience an even more grueling test of self-discipline it was possible to continue the challenge for three, or even for seven days.

Kagawa fought on and on through his first day of the Vow to Practice. He felt strong and in control of his sword. On the second day he continued from six in the morning until six in the evening feeling pain and exhaustion gradually suffuse his entire body. At the end of the day his legs were badly swollen and he had difficulty in making the journey home. Even using the toilet was an ordeal, his urine stained red. D. T. Suzuki, in Zen and Japanese Culture, gives us Kagawa's own account of what happened next.

> On the third day of these strenuous exercises I could hardly lift myself from bed and had to ask my wife's help. When she tried to lift me she felt as if raising a lifeless corpse and unconsciously withdrew her hands which she had placed underneath my back. And then I felt her tears on my face. Hardening myself to the utmost I admonished her not to be so weak-hearted. Somehow I succeeded with her help in raising the upper part of my body.
>
> I had to use a cane to walk up to the training hall. I had also to be helped to put on my protecting equipment. As soon as I took my position, the contestants began to crowd in. After a while I noticed one member come in and approach the master to ask his permission to take part in the exercises. The master permitted him right away. I looked at him and at once realized that he was a rascal and an unfair fighter. When I saw him coming up to me, I made up my mind that this would be my last combat, for I might not survive the contest. With this determination I felt within myself the surging up of a new energy. I was quite a different person. My sword returned to its proper position. Lifting the sword over my head I was ready to strike him down with one blow. At this moment came the master's emphatic command to stop, and I dropped my sword.
> (17)

On the following morning Kagawa somehow dragged himself out of bed. It was raining outside but he found that he did not have the strength to hold an umbrella over his head so his wife draped a blanket around his shoulders. He felt that this was going to be his last day on earth. But he was resolved to die rather than fail to complete the test. Tesshu was waiting for him in the dojo. "Are you ready to fight?" the master asked sternly. In the strongest voice he could muster Kagawa replied "Yes, I am!" At that point Tesshu let a gentle smile break over his face and brought the test to an end. Kagawa had become the sword of no-sword. He had passed through the great death of the ego-self that is the beginning and the end of Zen Buddhist practice.

The Vow to Training that Tesshu created was clearly not primarily designed to improve the technique of his students, or perhaps even their fighting skill. But it was designed to take them to the very end of their strength and then beyond, far beyond the limitations imposed by their conscious mind. It was not a test to be undertaken by the average student. In all, eight of Tesshu's direct students completed a one day, two hundred match challenge while three students, including Kagawa, completed a three day challenge. The ultimate test of spirit, a seven day ordeal involving one thousand four hundred contests was completed by two students, one as a tribute to Tesshu following his death.

Tesshu led the No Sword School for eight years, personally teaching more than four hundred students. He was, he believed, at the height of his powers at this time and liked to say that he would be able to defeat even Miyamoto Musashi if the great swordsman came back from the afterworld to challenge him. Such supreme self-confidence in what was now a middle-aged body aroused some skepticism among the other swordsmen of Tokyo. One who wondered if Tesshu was really as strong as he claimed was Nakajo Kinnosuke, a man who had known Tesshu, and had been his senior, when they were both young samurai. Nakajo challenged Tesshu to a match and, although he was overwhelmed by the younger man's power, refused to submit. In the end Tesshu had no choice but to attack so hard that Nakajo was knocked unconscious. Some hours later the defeated man woke up in his own bed and, rousing himself, walked to the home of Tesshu where he opened the door and shouted "You win!"

Another of Tesshu's former seniors, Ogusa Takijiro, was infuriated that this 'young man' had the gall to form his own school of swordsmanship. When they met Ogusa, screaming "How dare you!", began to pummel Tesshu on the face and head. Tesshu meekly submitted to the pounding, perhaps unwilling to strike back at a senior. At any rate, he later told his students, the incident had been good training. He had defeated Ogusa as he had been able to take punishment for longer than Ogusa had been able to dish it out.

Tesshu held many matches with the leading swordsmen of his day and was never defeated. He was held to a draw, however, by his only rival for consideration as the leading swordsman of the late nineteenth century, Sakakibara Kenkichi. When they met, the two outstanding masters drew their swords and held them aloft, gazing into each other's eyes. Their bodies began to pour with sweat but neither man moved a muscle. After forty minutes of this stand-off, with no weaknesses making themselves apparent in either man, they lowered their swords and bowed to end the match.

The No Sword School had followed the decision of most nineteenth century sword schools to adopt the use of bamboo swords. But Tesshu had serious reservations about this practice. The great swordsmen of history had fought their matches with steel swords or with heavy wooden practice swords. They had faced a real risk of death or serious injury in their contests. Tesshu believed that there was nothing worthwhile to be gained from studying swordsmanship unless students were ready to risk their lives. He told his advanced students that he would sanction them to accept challenges from other schools. But any such matches were to be conducted with wooden swords and without armor.

One Page at a Time
Later in life Tesshu began to devote more and more of his time to art. He had been a student of Japanese calligraphy since childhood and, following his enlightenment at the age of forty-five, had become a great master of shodo. As he aged his work lost the careful control of his younger years and became astonishingly free and expressive. Even in his own day he was recognized as a genius with the brush but he showed little interest in using this talent to enrich himself. Once he realized that his art could be sold to raise money to help others he began to spend several hours each day producing everything from copies of classic Chinese scripts to huge screens for temple doors.

Tesshu became a veritable one-man production line of high quality calligraphy. He is said to have produced the extraordinary number of more than one million pieces during his lifetime. Working with a team of assistants who prepared his materials he could turn out one thousand sheets of calligraphy in a single day. His assistants would be exhausted at the end of such a day but Tesshu never seemed to grow weary. "Bringing the entire universe into this brush, there is no room to be tired," he chided them. (14)

Tesshu painted to raise money for temple restorations, to help the victims of disasters and to pay off his many creditors. He did not charge a fee for his works but gladly accepted donations that he kept to hand and would often simply hand over to beggars. Toward the end of his life Tesshu announced that he planned to make a copy of the entire canon of Buddhist scriptures. A concerned friend, who had estimated that it would take one man a hundred years to undertake such a task, suggested that Tesshu was overextending himself. "Not at all", Tesshu replied, "I will only copy one page at a time." (14)

In 1888, at the age of 53, this huge, indomitable man was finally felled by stomach cancer. Tesshu was a keen traditionalist and was determined to maintain the best form, even in the face of his own death. Two days before the end he asked his wife to help him bathe, and then to dress him in a white robe. On the following morning two hundred of his followers gathered at his house. For centuries Zen masters had been producing verses to mark the approach of death and one of Tesshu's students asked him if he had a verse to give them. He immediately recited a haiku he had composed on the spot.

> Swollen stomach.
> In the midst of pain,
> The morning crows. (15)

He then sat up, in a formal meditation posture, holding a fan in his right hand to cool himself in the intense summer heat. Sitting erect and surrounded by friends he died quietly, passing into Nirvana. Tesshu is believed to have been the only person of his era to die in this formal, composed way. As he sat in death the master was sketched by one of his students. The drawing, which still exists, is blurred here and there by the freely flowing tears of the artist.

Yamaoka Tesshu lived through some of the most exciting times in Japanese history and in his own lifetime witnessed earth shattering changes. Like those around him he was caught up in the passions and quarrels of Japanese society as it hurtled at great speed from feudalism into the modern age. Tesshu was not a man who strove to live in the past – one of his paintings approvingly depicts a great iron steam boat billowing black clouds of smoke. But he gave himself to something that seemed even more important than the excitement of the turning world, to a search for the essential nature of humankind. Martial training, he insisted, can be a path that leads to a deeper understanding of life. Many martial artists who followed him would come to the same conclusion.

8. Bushido

Even during the confusing upheavals of the late nineteenth century there were many like Yamaoka Tesshu who viewed the Way of the martial arts as the inner core of their lives. They believed that there was an essence, a code of behavior, an essential approach to life that had prevailed among the samurai and that continued to be relevant in the modern age. The value system that Tesshu followed is often described as bushido, or "the way of the warrior".

Bushido is a modern term and a modern concept. It first appeared in the Japanese language in the fifteenth century but was used only sporadically to refer to the inner world of the samurai. It was not until the end of the nineteenth century, as Japan rushed into the modern era, that bushido finally became a word in common use. Today it is everywhere in Japanese discourse, used to explain history and also used to describe a set of human values that are generally regarded as both profound and admirable. And yet the term itself is rather slippery. Used and abused in a very wide range of settings, bushido is dismissed by some writers as an empty concept that resembles other abstract ideas like chivalry, or patriotism; a word that can mean almost anything to the user. But, however vague the concept, bushido does seem to represent something that is both real and important for the modern Japanese, something that captures their distinctive feeling about the inner meaning of the martial arts. It is an idea that brings modern Japanese people closer to the richness of their own history, an idea that can only be fully understood by examining the many strands of meaning that it contains.

Proud Warriors
One thousand years ago the samurai first appeared as a group of fighters who were regarded as rough and unsophisticated by the aristocrats who ruled Japan. These warriors shaped a confident identity for themselves by taking pride in their professional fighting skill and by making their prowess clearly visible to society at large. The key element in their sense of self was, therefore, honor – they were marked out from the rest of society by the pride, both private and public, that they took in their own fighting skill.

To a samurai warrior his name was everything. If a leader was recognized as a courageous man he could attract other fighters to serve alongside him. Recognition of courage also ensured that lower ranking fighters would receive the best rewards for their bravery. In this way honor became a crucial factor in military success. If a samurai was regarded as a coward he found it hard to attract allies and impossible to win battles. The honor of the lower ranking samurai was essentially an individual sense of dignity and was not necessarily linked to the strength of the lords that led them into battle. Close master-follower relationships certainly existed but hierarchical relationships among the samurai were not at first as important as they would become in later centuries. The samurai were, above all, a community of honorable individuals.

The role of honor as the core identity of the samurai helped to shape the nature of warfare in Japan. Battles in the Heian Period were highly ritualistic. Large groups of warriors lined up to confront each other but they would usually withdraw from the field after a relatively small number of deaths. Around the twelfth century the emergence of a more developed code of personal honor and the strengthening of honor bonds between samurai made it much more difficult for a warrior to leave the battlefield. Wars were now more likely to be bloody struggles to the very end because the battlefield was the one place where, by risking and facing death, a samurai could create his personal honor.

Most samurai lived as farmers in the countryside. When they went into battle they rode their own horses and brought their own followers and servants along with them. These small bands of closely connected men took their place in an army and served as compact units that were only loosely associated to the other groups around them. The samurai on horseback were primarily interested in gaining recognition for their own bravery and so they tended to fight as individuals. They strongly disliked massed movements where individual bravery would not be visible.

Battles began with both armies listening to official declarations of the names of important samurai in their ranks and time was set aside for these men to make personal expressions of courage. The Heike Monogatari, an epic account of the struggle for power in late 12th century Japan, provides a colorful, if somewhat romanticized, description of how the samurai of that time behaved in battle.

One adrenaline-fueled warrior is said to have announced his entry into a battle by charging his horse in among the ranks of the enemy. In the middle of a host of opponents he stood high on his horse and shouted.

> Listen to my voice if you are far away, and come closer to see me if you are nearby. This is the very man, Imai Shiro Kanahira ... age thirty-three. Even the lord Kamakura knows me; knows that there is such a warrior. Kill me and show him my head! [18]

These aggressive mounted samurai dressed to emphasize their individuality. It was unusual for samurai to attempt to coordinate their clothing. Instead each man wore his own colorful armor and distinctive helmet. When fighting began the chief aim of a warrior was to seek out important samurai among the enemy lines and to take their heads. Medieval battles in Japan typically ended with the display of dozens, sometimes hundreds, of severed heads to the victorious general.

Samurai women took charge of the grim task of cleaning up the heads for this official presentation. They would comb the hair of their trophies and might even dye the teeth black in the fashionable style. To have one's head exhibited in such a fashion was a potential humiliation for any warrior and samurai would go to great lengths to avoid this kind of disgrace. If a battle was going badly and a warrior faced the shame of having his head taken he might beg his friends to cut off his head and to bury it in a secret place where the enemy could not find it.

Honor and Death
Honor and death were two sides of a single coin for these warriors. Although individual samurai may not have relished the idea of dying on the battlefield, it was conventional for them to cheerfully discuss the possibility of losing their life in combat. A violent death was thought to be a good one. If the humiliation of defeat was drawing close a samurai could avoid shame by committing suicide on the battlefield.

The Heike Monogatari contains several descriptions of honor-preserving suicides. One despairing warrior stabs himself with his own sword and then flings himself from his horse so that the weight of his body can drive the sword deeper into his body. Another defeated samurai on horseback shouts to draw attention to himself, places his sword in his mouth, and throws himself from his horse so that the sword can pierce his brain. Even entire armies would take steps to preserve their honor in horrific mass suicides. In 1333 a struggle for power left an army from Kamakura fighting against overwhelming odds until only five hundred men were left. Realizing that defeat was imminent, their general cut his belly open. The Taiheiki records what happened to the rest of his samurai.

> Four hundred thirty two samurai simultaneously cut their bellies. Their blood smeared their bodies and ran as if it was the stream of the Yellow River. Their corpses filled the yard, like corpses in a slaughterhouse. (18)

By the sixteenth century the notion of suicide as an noble means of preserving personal honor had spread beyond the battlefield. It became a recognized practice for samurai who faced any kind of disgrace to be given time and space to kill themselves. This kind of suicide, known as seppuku, was a privilege of the samurai and was not encouraged for the lower classes. Warriors were given the right to take their own lives rather than face the disgrace of a brutal execution or, even worse, the disgrace of living with the shame of defeat.

Detailed rules were created for the performance of a ritual suicide. The doomed samurai was expected to first purify his body, to dress in white clothing and to seat himself on clean tatami mats that had been covered in white cloth. When the moment came the condemned man would take a razor sharp dagger and thrust it into his own belly. If his courage held, he would then pull the knife across his midriff in a horizontal line so that it sliced through his inner organs. Behind the agonized samurai a friend or follower waited with a drawn sword for the appropriate moment to cut off the head of the dying man and bring an end to his pain.

During the endless wars of the sixteenth century this kind of suicide was most likely to happen at the end of a pitched battle. In many cases the victims were overwhelmed by the frustration of defeat and their resulting suicides could be both emotional and dramatic. Some of these samurai made heroic expressions of bravery and anger, even dragging out their own intestines through the cut they had made in their belly.

In later centuries ritual suicide became less of a personal drama and more of a social custom as it was codified into a respectable means of execution for upper class samurai. The outer form of a suicide remained roughly the same but the inner emotion changed. The victim was often provided with a wooden dagger, or even a fan, that served to symbolize the old style of seppuku. As soon as the hand of the victim moved toward the substitute for a knife the executioner would cut away his head.

A rare non-Japanese witness to a ritual suicide was the British Ambassador to Japan, Algernon Mitford, who found himself among a group of foreign representatives that had been assembled to witness one of the very last suicide ceremonies. The event took place in 1868, the final year of the Edo period.

> Bowing once more, the speaker allowed his upper garments to slip down to his girdle, and remained naked to the waist. Carefully, according to custom, he tucked his sleeves under his knees to prevent himself from falling backwards; for a noble Japanese gentleman should die falling forwards. Deliberately, with a steady hand, he took the dirk that lay before him; he looked at it wistfully, almost affectionately; for a moment he seemed to collect his thoughts for the last time, and then stabbing himself deeply below the waist on the left-hand side, he drew the dirk slowly across to the right side, and, turning it in the wound, gave a slight cut upwards. During this sickeningly painful operation he never moved a muscle of his face. When he drew out the dirk, he leaned forward and stretched out his neck; an expression of pain for the first time crossed his face, but he uttered no sound. At that moment the kaishaku, who, still crouching by his side, had been keenly watching his every movement, sprang to his feet, poised his sword for a second in the air; there was a flash, a heavy, ugly thud, a crashing fall; with one blow the head had been severed from the body. A dead silence followed, broken only by the hideous noise of the blood throbbing out of the inert heap before us, which but a moment before had been a brave and chivalrous

man. It was horrible. The kaishaku made a low bow, wiped his sword with a piece of rice paper which he had ready for the purpose, and retired from the raised floor; (19)

A Changing Code
The forms of samurai honor were reshaped by the constant warfare of the sixteenth century. Armies were becoming larger, needed more generals and made greater use of massed attacks. Groups of foot soldiers carrying bows and spears began to dominate the fighting. In the end, however, it was the arrival of guns from Europe that really changed things. From that point onward even the lowest ranking foot soldier was capable of shooting down the greatest samurai warrior from a distance. In this new style of warfare it was much more difficult for individual samurai to stand out and to distinguish themselves. As a result, the emotional focus of individual samurai began to shift away from self-glorification and towards preserving the honor of their region and their lord. Personal bravery on the battlefield grew less important and was even, in the end, discouraged. Tokugawa Ieyasu sternly ordered that any samurai who to tried to rush into battle early in an attempt to distinguish himself should be executed.

But the samurai did not completely lose their sense of personal honor. They just found different ways to express it. These warriors were often mettlesome and hot-headed men in private because they were allowed few opportunities to demonstrate their confidence and bravery. Arguments among these proud men, who were always armed outside the home, could quickly escalate into violent quarrels and even killings.

Before the sixteenth century duels had been generally regarded as a fine and natural expression of manhood. But in the sixteenth century the need to maintain military discipline became paramount and duels and vendettas came to be seen as a dangerous distraction. To put an end to duels a harsh ordinance was introduced that made all parties equally responsible in the eyes of the law. New regulations, known as kenkaryoseihai, required lords and military authorities to ignore both the circumstances of a private fight and the actual outcome of the fight. All participants were to be punished equally and the punishments were usually extremely harsh – it was common for both samurai involved in a public quarrel to be required to commit suicide. One, even harsher, punishment was occasionally enforced. Some samurai were punished for their part in a quarrel by being deprived of the right to carry swords for life. This was an unbearable disgrace for a proud warrior. One samurai successfully appealed against his sentence and was shown the mercy of being allowed to commit suicide instead.

As opportunities to take part in war and even the memory of war began to disappear in the seventeenth century many samurai became frustrated with their lot. They were, they complained, warriors who had almost no way of demonstrating their courage or of protecting their honor. In the first half of the seventeenth century this feeling was particularly strong. Older samurai who could remember the good old days of the sixteenth century liked to bewail the easy life and the softness of younger samurai who had never fought in a battle. They hated the law of kenkaryoseihai as it forced samurai to suppress their natural aggression and rewarded them for being calm and reasonable. Without violence, after all, what did it mean to be a samurai? One writer griped that the warrior class, even though they wore swords, were nothing more than farmers in fancy dress.

By the middle of the seventeenth century the Japanese samurai were faced with a rather confusing variety of messages about their role in life, a confusion that produced strongly repressed emotions. These passions were released in a number of strange ways, one of which was the practice of junshi, a ritual suicide following the death of a lord. Battlefield suicides had been common enough in earlier centuries but this kind of suicide, deliberately killing oneself in the days after a master succumbed to illness or old age, was a new thing.

At first junshi was regarded as a brave and respectable practice and the families of the dead samurai were often handsomely compensated. But junshi became something of a fashion in the middle of the seventeenth century and its popularity troubled the government. In 1657 the death of the lord of Saga was followed by the unusually high number of twenty six suicides among his followers. Shortly afterwards the government made the practice of junshi illegal and enforced the prohibition ruthlessly. The sons of samurai who committed junshi were executed and their family lands were confiscated. Unsurprisingly, the custom soon died out.

Samurai were strictly forbidden from engaging in quarrels and duels with each other but they were still allowed to carry swords in public at all times. To prevent the samurai from feeling that their swords were useless symbols the law did allow three exceptions to the outright ban on drawing a sword in anger. The first exception came into play if a samurai was insulted by a member of a lower class. In such a case the samurai had, in theory, the right to dispense instant justice by cutting up the disrespectful person.

The second exception protected the rights of any samurai who discovered his wife in the act of adultery. In this case the betrayed husband had the right to use his sword to slice his wife and her lover into four parts. But although this rather frightening dispensation existed it was rarely put in practice by a jilted samurai. Anyone who found it necessary to cut up his wife would be an obvious cuckold. It was often easier to simply turn a blind eye to such behavior.

A final exception to the ban on violence was possible if a family member had been murdered. In this case a samurai was allowed to petition the authorities for permission to seek revenge. A document providing official sanction would be issued and then the sons and brothers of the dead man could register their names as a legally registered posse that had been formed to hunt down and dispatch the killer of their loved one. The government had no wish to encourage feuds and so counter-revenge was strictly forbidden. It was impossible for samurai to strike back against those who had carried out these sanctioned killings.

Although these men could be proud and aggressive, the peaceful atmosphere of seventeenth century Japan gradually undermined the importance of honor in samurai psychology. In the place of honor, loyalty to one's local lord became the central moral axis of the warrior class. Under the rule of the Tokugawa Shoguns there was a demand for social order and this, combined with the growing weight of Confucian philosophy, made hierarchy and obedience to those in power even more important. Loyalty had become such a dominant feature of Japanese life by the nineteenth century that Lafcadio Hearn was moved to describe it as the religion of Japan.

But loyalty had often been a somewhat uncertain quality in earlier periods of Japanese history when the samurai were marked as much by their disloyalty as by their loyalty. Centuries of armed combat between warlords made those rulers anxious to recruit the most experienced and effective fighters. The competition to persuade professional warriors to fight for a certain side could be intense. Even in the middle of battles, as the balance of power shifted, samurai might be convinced to switch loyalties with relative impunity. It was common for generals to calculate the odds before they decided on which side to fight. Tokugawa Ieyasu worked his way to the very top of Japanese society by employing a finely tuned instinct that helped him direct his loyalty to the right people. And generals often turned on their lords in shocking betrayals – the death of Nobunaga is only one example. At the key battle of Sekigahara many of the participants travelled to the battle, and even waited for the fighting to begin, before they made up their minds about which side they were going to support.

So there had been less room for romantic notions of loyalty in the sixteenth century. It was a commodity that was generally believed to be for sale. As a result, taking the family members of leading samurai as hostages became common practice. In the end this hostage taking system was so widespread that it became an institutionalized process. Throughout the Tokugawa period regional lords were required to keep their families in Edo and to spend every second year in the city. It was a great irony that the governing system of Japan, which preached the fundamental importance of loyalty, was itself based on a belief that no one could really be trusted.

I Would Give My Life Seven Times

Despite all of the deceit and betrayals of samurai warfare there were many examples of extraordinary devotion and self-sacrifice in the name of loyalty. For the Japanese people the greatest historical paragon of faithfulness is Kusonoki Masashige, a subject of the Emperor who was so loyal that seven hundred years after he died his memory served as a stirring symbol for Japanese troops as they went into battle in the Second World War.

Kusunoki was a samurai who decided to take up arms in support of the Emperor Go-Daigo as he vainly attempted to establish an imperial dictatorship in the fourteenth century. Kusunoki was a determined fighter who learned to use daring guerrilla tactics to hold his own against overwhelming opposition. In doing so he changed the shape of samurai warfare by making creative use of quickly built rough forts that allowed him to control the strong points of a region. But it was his heroic struggles in the face of almost certain defeat that made him such an important icon. His name was invoked by Japanese troops as they found themselves fighting terrible defensive island battles against American forces during the Second World War.

In 1331 Go-Daigo was competing for power with the government of the Shogun in Kamakura. Most of the army of the Emperor had been routed by the Kamakura troops but Kusunogi decided to prolong the struggle by holding onto a hilltop in Akasaka. He hastily constructed a wooden fort on the hilltop, placed two hundred of his men inside the fort and hid another three hundred samurai on a neighboring hillside. An overpoweringly strong army from Kamakura arrived and surrounded the fort but it was driven back by showers of arrows. As the attackers regrouped Kusonoki sent his hidden soldiers down from the hillside and released his samurai from the fort. The attackers were confused and scattered but their superior numbers allowed them to regroup and to once again surround the fort.

Kusonoki continued to use unconventional tactics to fight this impossible battle. From his high point he had rocks and boiling water dumped onto the heads of the attackers and lowered huge tree trunks to block the approaches to his fort. When the attacking samurai tried to clamber over these logs, the supporting ropes were cut and the invaders were crushed far below in the valley.

Eventually, however, there were just too many enemy soldiers to hold back and Kusunoki ordered his men to sneak away under cover of dark. He built a mound with the bodies of his dead fighters and left one living samurai behind. As the attackers finally entered the Akasaka fort the one remaining defender set fire to the bodies and began to weep, he told the attackers, for the death of an entire army. The intruders relaxed, thinking that the battle was over. But just as they began to celebrate their victory Kusunoki attacked and retook the fort. The infuriated Kamakura forces cut off the water supply and forced Kusonoki into making his final retreat. He somehow survived by leading his men away through the midnight forests.

The courageous and resourceful defense of Akasaka made Kusunoki a hero for samurai throughout the country and many travelled to join his army. But he was still heavily outnumbered by the Kamakura forces and so once again he decided to fight a defensive battle. This time he based himself in an even more impregnable hilltop fortress at Chihaya, a peak that is surrounded by steep ravines. Learning from his previous mistakes Kusonoki ensured that the fortress had its own spring so that the defenders would not be driven out by thirst. Once again the attackers made futile charges up the steep slopes and died in their hundreds. In desperation they brought five hundred carpenters from Kyoto to build a bridge across the ravine. Kusonoki simply waited until the bridge was packed with soldiers and then set it alight, pouring oil onto the heads of the attackers so they were engulfed in flames.

As the fighting continued Kusonoki had a contingent of straw men dressed in battle armor and placed outside the fort during the night. When dawn rose a few living samurai made their way among the dummies and began to fire arrows down at the enemy. The attackers thought that the defenders had finally come out to fight and hurried up the slopes but, just as they did, the few actual samurai above them raced back into their fort. Gazing upwards in horror the attackers realized that boulders were crashing down on their heads. Three hundred of them were killed in the bombardment. The Battle of Chihaya is remembered as the most brilliant defense in Japanese history. So many of the attacking soldiers were killed that twelve officials had to be employed full time just to keep a record of the dead.

Kusonoki's outstanding tactics made him one of the leading generals in the Emperor's army and he was at the Emperor's side when the imperial army was betrayed by Ashikaga Takauji who had decided to seize power in Kyoto for himself. Kusonoki advised the Emperor to retreat into the mountains near Kyoto but the ruler refused to fight a guerrilla war. Putting loyalty above personal survival Kusunoki remained with the Emperor. On the open ground his forces were hopelessly outnumbered and it soon became clear that there was no possibility of escape. Kusonoki told his eleven-year-old son that he was happy to die for the Emperor and urged the boy to carry on the fight. When the enemy began their final attack Kusonoki decided to commit ritual suicide with his brother. His last words were, "I would give my life seven times for the country."

Kusunoki would never be forgotten. He lived on in Japanese folk memory as a shining example of self-sacrificing loyalty. But it was not until the nineteenth century that his particular loyalty to the Emperor became significant. For the young revolutionary samurai who wanted to seize power on behalf of the Meiji Emperor he was the perfect symbol of allegiance to the throne. Later his status would climb even higher. As Emperor worship was made official state policy in the years before the Second World War Kusunoki became a semi-divine figure, the story of his exploits read to children in every Japanese classroom.

While the abstract loyalty that impelled Kusunoki to protect his Emperor was remarkable it was also atypical. The bonds between samurai were generally much more concrete. These young men were loyal to their comrades, and to their lord, because they had all grown up together in a closely knit friendship group. The intense loyalty and devotion that many samurai felt for their masters was the result of years of shared experience and of a clan loyalty that had been bred into them since childhood.

The bonds between samurai who had been friends from an early age were often passionately felt and could be romantic. Young samurai lived in almost exclusively male societies and it was rare for them to have much contact with women during puberty and their teenage years. It was therefore natural that many of these samurai developed homosexual attachments, attachments that were generally accepted by society. Love between samurai men was, in fact, celebrated by the literature of the time and was so common that several samurai writers took it upon themselves to suggest guidelines for this kind of relationship.

The socially approved form of homosexual love was a relationship between a teenage boy, who had not yet passed through the ritual shaving of the head that marked the transition to adulthood, and an older samurai man. The younger man was expected to be completely devoted to the man who acted as his protector until he himself came of age. At that point he was free to take other lovers. Most samurai formed attachments with women as they reached adulthood but many of these men still continued to have homosexual affairs.

Romantic attachments were a hidden undercurrent in samurai society, one that could be the cause of violent confrontations between two men who had designs on the same lover. Senior samurai could take their pick of the young men and the suicides of younger samurai who killed themselves after the death of their lord were at times the outcome of mental anguish caused by the death of a lover.

Simply Become Insane
The samurai had a strong sense that they belonged to a social class that was governed by rules, codes of behavior and moral standards. But this inner world of the samurai was rather poorly defined and so over the centuries several writers attempted to formulate just what the proper samurai approach to life actually should be. By some distance the most interesting attempt by a samurai to explain his worldview can be found in the fascinating collection of writings known as the Hagakure, or Hidden Leaves. This

almost random gathering of thoughts, stories and nuggets of advice provides modern readers with a startlingly intimate insight into the mind of a single samurai who lived at the beginning of the eighteenth century.

The book is a written transcription of a series of meetings between a retired samurai and a younger man who copied down the other man's thoughts. For almost two hundred years the Hagakure survived as a secret text that was unknown to anyone outside a small circle of samurai in the Kumamoto region. The book only became widely read in Japan at the end of the nineteenth century and in the twentieth century it soared in popularity after it was promoted by extreme nationalists. As a result, the Hagakure is viewed with some reserve by modern Japanese. But it does provide an unrivaled glimpse into the emotions of a real samurai who had realized that he could never prove himself in battle and reluctantly made a living with his pen.

The Hagakure is a collection of the thoughts of a samurai named Tsunetomo. As a boy he was given a strict samurai education by a grandfather who had been actively involved in the wars of the sixteenth century and by a father who had seen fighting in the last Tokugawa battles at Osaka and the suppression of the Shimabara rebellion. But Tsunetomo, who was born in the early years of the great Tokugawa peace, was no warrior. He served the lord of Saga as a secretary and compiler of documents and was a low-ranking participant in the bureaucratic reforms that swept the nation as Tokugawa rule became permanent.

When Tsunetomo's lord died in the year 1700 the secretary decided to retire from public life. His preferred option would have been suicide but that step was, he grumbled, forbidden to him by the new laws. He shaved his head, taking the common step for a retired samurai of adopting a religious path, and spent the remainder of his life in a secluded hermitage. Ten years after the death of his lord Tsunetomo made the highly unusual decision to have his thoughts recorded and for the next sixteen years he had a series of meetings with a younger samurai who carefully transcribed his monologues. The scribe, possibly disturbed by the older man's uninhibited and rather unconventional views, tried to have the book burned after Tsunetomo's death. Fortunately it survived as an underground document for the following two hundred years.

Tsunetomo idealized the lord he had served most of his life, Nabeshima Mitsushige. He had good reason to. When Tsunetomo was born his father had been seventy one years old and completely uninterested in raising another son. He tried to give his child away to a salt salesman. Eventually the sickly and unwanted boy was adopted and at the age of nine was employed as a page by the lord of Saga. Given the rejection he had felt from his own father it is unsurprising that Tsunetomo reserved his deepest feelings of love and admiration for his employer. He certainly became a servant who aimed to please. At one point, after hearing that his lord found his face to be too intelligent, Tsunetomo spent a year struggling to change his facial expression. He matured into a rather complicated and conflicted man and the Hagakure is a work full of pain, frustration and love. The book provides us with a gripping insight into the mind of this unusual samurai. In many ways, however, it is not entirely representative of the outlook of the entire samurai class.

The sixteenth century, when Tsunetomo's grandfather had been active, was a time of great danger and samurai knew that death was never far away. To be afraid in the face of death was a clear professional disadvantage for a warrior as personal honor had its roots in displays of unshakeable courage. Samurai had to fight in terrifying battles and they needed strategies to help them overcome the fears that naturally arose. Tsunetomo lived close to those dangerous times but he had never taken place in large scale combat and his views on how members of the samurai class should prepare for death were rather distorted and extreme. Like many before him he suggested that a samurai should steel himself for extinction. But Tsunetomo's description of how a warrior should face the prospect of death is remarkably violent.

> Meditation on inevitable death should be performed daily. Every day, when one's mind and body are at peace, one should meditate upon being ripped apart by arrows, rifles, spears and swords, being carried away by surging waves, being thrown in the midst of a great fire, being struck by lightning, being shaken to death by a great earthquake, falling from thousand-foot cliffs, dying of disease or committing seppuku at the death of one's master. And every day without fail one should consider himself as dead. [20]

Tsunetomo, in fact, went far beyond advocating preparation for death. He suggested that samurai should become obsessed with death, and hungry for it. At a time when most samurai were dying in their beds he developed a strange nostalgia for the years when an early death was just around the corner.

> The Way of the Samurai is found in death. When it comes to either or, there is only the quick choice of death. It is not particularly difficult. Be determined and advance.
>
> The fact that a useless person often becomes a matchless warrior is because he has already given up his life.
>
> The Way of the Samurai is in desperateness. Ten men or more cannot kill such a man. Common sense will not accomplish great things. Simply become insane and desperate. [20]

As well as longing to die, samurai men must be capable of killing. Tsunetomo was a strong advocate of young men being taught how to kill, something he approvingly noted to have been part of the education of his own lord. As a boy Nabeshima was taken to the execution grounds and presented with a line of ten condemned criminals. The boy worked his way down the line decapitating head after head but when he reached the last man he realized that he was facing a mere youth. With great humanity, he spared the last in the line.

Death lust is the best known feature of the Hagakure. And it is certainly a violent book. But the overall tone is one of disappointment. Frequently we encounter rather peevish complaints about the way things have become. Tsunetomo, like middle-aged men in every country and age, found the young men of his day to be deeply unimpressive.

> In the last fifty years men's pulse has become the same as women's. I knew that men's spirit had weakened and that they had become the same as women, and the end of the world had come. That there are few men who are able to cut well in beheadings is further proof that men's courage has waned.
>
> When young samurai gather together, if there is not just talk about money matters, loss and gain, secrets, clothing styles or matters of sex, there is no reason to gather together at all. Customs are going to pieces.
>
> Everyone, by the time they were fourteen or fifteen, was ordered to do a beheading without fail. Today even the children of the lower classes perform no executions. [20]

Tsunetomo roundly scolded the youth of his day for their lack of martial spirit and their love of trivial pursuits. But he does not seem to have been completely free from a certain insecurity about his own lack of combat experience. It troubled him deeply that he had never fought in a battle. Fortunately, he cheerfully remarks, he had been able to find a good way to sharpen his skills.

> Last year I went to the Kase Execution Grounds to try my hand at beheading, and I found it to be an extremely good feeling. [20]

The Hagakure is a deeply nostalgic book. The time he would have preferred to live in, Tsunetomo made clear, was the blood soaked turmoil of the sixteenth century. In the eighteenth century there was no need to go to war any more but his book is nonetheless scattered with nuggets of advice that seem to have been perfectly preserved from an earlier age.

> Every morning the samurai of fifty or sixty years ago would bathe, shave their foreheads, put lotion on their hair, cut their fingernails and toenails, and without fail pay attention to their personal appearance. It goes without saying that their armor was dusted, shined and arranged.
>
> If you are slain in battle you should be resolved to have your corpse facing the enemy.
>
> If ones sword is broken he will strike with his hands. If his hands are cut off, he will press the enemy down with his shoulders. If his shoulders are cut away, he will bite through ten or fifteen enemy necks with his teeth. Courage is such a thing.
>
> When one departs for the front ... his underwear should be made from the skin of a badger. This way he will not have lice. [20]

The bulk of the Hagakure consists of a series of fascinating accounts of samurai behavior. Tsunetomo recorded stories that were of great relevance to the central dilemma, as he saw it, of eighteenth century samurai. Repeatedly he describes the actions of men who were forced to choose between the law and their own personal honor. Tsunetomo made it clear that he stood on the side of honor. In an age without battles the aggressive spirit of the warriors could only find release in personal quarrels. A samurai, he insisted, should take violent action to preserve his honor, whatever the consequences.

> The way of revenge lies in simply forcing ones way into a place and being cut down. By considering things like how many men the enemy has, time piles up; in the end you will give up. No matter if the enemy has thousands of men, there is fulfillment in being determined to cut them all down, starting from one end.
>
> Even if it seems certain that you will lose, retaliate. Neither wisdom nor technique has a place in this. A real man does not think of victory or defeat. He plunges recklessly towards an irrational death. [20]

Tsunetomo, the armchair warrior, was infuriated by new rules that had outlawed violent quarrels. A fight, he repeatedly insisted, should be fought to the finish. In one of his tales two samurai fall into a brawl that involves a good deal of punching and kicking and are finally dragged apart by their friends. He approvingly noted that the two fighters were later crucified for their unmanly failure to resort to swords, while the friends who stopped the two men from fighting were banished.

In Tsunetomo's moral system violence was an integral part of personal honor. He described a samurai who had received a severe cut to the leg in a quarrel over a board game. The samurai hid his wound and pretended to be appeased until his attacker had relaxed sufficiently to offer him a drink. At that point the wounded samurai drew his sword and severed his attacker's head.

The Hagakure is a book that treasures violence but the greatest praise in the book is reserved for those samurai who display great loyalty and devotion to their lord. Tsunetomo, thinking of his own dead lord, expressed his feelings with a startling intensity. He had no need for an afterlife in heaven, he insisted. His dream was to be reborn many times so that he could continue to serve the family of his lord.

> A man is a good retainer to the extent that he earnestly places importance in his master ... Having only wisdom and talent is the lowest tier of usefulness. (20)

The good samurai, Tsunetomo believed, was so committed to the welfare of his lord that no detail was too small to be overlooked. Medieval lords had high expectations of their servants and they would often, according to Tsunetomo, create absurdly difficult tests for their samurai. He related the example of a a lord who was engaged in clipping his fingernails. As he passed the shreds of cut nail to a subordinate samurai, the lord asked him to dispose of them. Then he noticed a puzzled expression on the retainer's face. When the lord asked what the problem was the attentive samurai replied, "Ah, there is one piece missing". At that point the contented lord handed over the hidden nail clipping to the faithful servant.

A good samurai was able to endure any kind of pain and discomfort for the sake of his lord. Tsunetomo told of a Shogun who tested one of his servants by secretly heating the tongs in the fire. The loyal young samurai picked up the tongs but did not make any display of pain until the satisfied master relieved him of his agonizing burden. In an even more striking story Tsunetomo spoke of a lord who, on a hunting expedition, became angry with one of his attendant samurai and began to beat him with a sword. In the excitement of the exercise the lord lost his grip on the sword and it flew off into a nearby ravine. The chastised samurai immediately threw himself into the ravine where he retrieved the sword and climbed out to return it to the owner.

These are bizarre tales of a loyalty that is so extreme that it defies common sense. Perhaps the strangest story in the Hagakure is of a retainer who was with his lord when the mansion containing the family treasure caught fire. When he heard that his lord's most valued possession was the scroll containing the family history the samurai raced desperately into the flames. Later, when his scorched body was dragged from the ruins, the rescuers found that the samurai had slit open his own belly and inserted the scroll inside his body so that it would be saved from the flames by his blood. These disturbing accounts of slavish devotion make it clear just how strongly the cult of service, a morality that clearly benefitted the lords of Japan rather more than it did their subject samurai, had penetrated the psyche of that time.

But amid the blood and thunder of the Hagakure, the invocations of death and the approbation of violence, something else is lurking. That something is civilization, the peaceful civilization that was becoming the norm for Japan despite the begrudgings of men like Tsunetomo. Scattered among his tales of samurai feuds are suggestions that would not be out of place in a customer service manual today. Tsunetomo advised samurai to show compassion, to avoid harsh treatment of commoners and not to pretend to know more than they do. Children should not be scolded too severely. Yawning in front of others is to be avoided and hands should be kept out of pockets.

Despite himself, and to his great regret, Tsunetomo was a man of his times. All around him Japan was busily remaking itself into a nation under the rule of law. The samurai of olden times, he wistfully admitted at one point, were a rough bunch. Tsunetomo may have longed to be one of these uncouth warriors and to experience the violence and simple passions of the sixteenth century; but there was to be no going back.

Forty Seven Angry Men
Tsunetomo was an extreme case, but the changes in Japanese society that troubled him so deeply were equally confusing for many of his contemporaries. During the eighteenth century there was a long national debate over the shift from a society based on personal honor to one based on the rule of law. The divisions between those who welcomed the changes and those who opposed them were exposed by a dramatic incident that took place in Edo just as Tsunetomo was dictating his book.

In 1703 a government official was murdered by forty seven samurai who were then arrested and forced to take their own lives. The men who died had not been common criminals but a group of intensely loyal samurai who claimed to have been motivated by their warrior values. It was a real-life revenge drama that shocked the nation and provoked an intense discussion over the role of the samurai in the Tokugawa state. The forty seven dead men were compelling figures in their day and they were not quickly forgotten. The thrilling story of their deeds has continued to fascinate Japanese audiences for more than three hundred years, spawning endless recreations in fiction, on stage and on film.

The series of events that led to the deaths of these men began in a simple quarrel between two senior samurai. Asano was the lord of a small province in western Japan. Visiting Edo, as he was required to do on regular occasions, he came into contact with officials at the palace of the Shogun. One of these officials, a man named Kira, treated the visiting lords with disdain. Kira may have been a relatively low-ranking samurai but he was a senior court employee and this position enabled him to issue brusque instructions to the lords and even to demand bribes.

A grudge developed between Asano and Kira, a simmering anger that finally burst to the surface at the worst possible time. Early in 1701 the Emperor was making a visit to Edo. This was an extremely important occasion and the ceremony of the court, for which Kira was responsible, was raised to its highest possible pitch. Kira was busily marshaling the minor lords, scolding them with his usual arrogance when Asano suddenly drew a dagger in one of the palace corridors and took a swing at the official. He fluffed the attack, merely managing to cut Kira in the face with his first strike. Asano missed completely with a second attempt and was then dragged away.

When the Shogun heard about the scuffle that had taken place in his palace he was outraged. On this day, of all days, Asano had broken the strict injunction against drawing any kind of blade within the palace grounds. He was ordered to commit suicide before the day was over. To make it perfectly clear just how angry the Shogun was, Asano's family were stripped of the leadership of their province. His wife, children and retainers were thrown out of their castle. Every one of the three hundred samurai who had been in service to Asano found themselves out of work. Overnight they had become ronin, samurai without a master.

Shortly after the death of Asano forty seven of these newly unemployed ronin met in secret. They were indignant and swore to each other that they would revenge the death of their lord by killing Kira. But this would not be an easy task. Kira, who had been fortunate not to be executed himself, was fully expecting these samurai to launch a revenge attack. He turned his mansion into a fortress that was strongly defended by night and day. The ronin decided to bide their time until they could catch Kira off his guard.

In a remarkably disciplined campaign of deception the group went their separate ways. Many of the forty seven even cut off their samurai topknots and became priests or merchants. Oishi, the leader of the group, moved to Kyoto where he appeared to have given up his samurai lifestyle and become a libertine who spent evenings drinking and carousing with geisha. Even today Japanese writers puzzle over the year that Oishi spent in Kyoto. He divorced his wife and sent his family away. It certainly looked as though he had really given up the idea of avenging his master. But if Oishi was deliberately staging a deception to put Kira off his scent, the plan worked. After a year there seemed to be no organization left among the former samurai of Lord Asano.

They waited for a long time, so long that the original incident was almost forgotten. On the second anniversary of Asano's death his former retainers came together in Edo. On a freezing, snowy morning they silently surrounded Kira's mansion in the dark. At the arranged time Oishi and his comrades unsheathed their swords and charged towards the front gate. Their assault was held back with difficulty by the samurai inside the compound. But there was a simultaneous attack on the rear entrance led by Oishi's son and this group soon broke through and entered the compound. The shocked defenders sent out messengers to the Shogun's palace asking for reinforcements. Oishi, who had anticipated such a move, had posted archers along the road to the palace and they easily shot down the messengers.

A violent hand to hand confrontation was now being fought inside the walls of the compound and sixteen of the samurai loyal to Kira were killed. When the attackers had taken control of the inner courtyard they found Kira cowering in a storehouse. They dragged him in front of Oishi. The leader of the ronin respectfully kneeled in front of the enemy and requested that he take his own life. Kira was too frightened to give a reply so Oishi produced the same dagger that his master Asano had used to commit suicide and with it he cut off Kira's head.

With their mission accomplished the triumphant ronin marched to the tomb of their dead master. They washed Kira's head in a well and then placed it in front of the gravestone of Asano. On their master's grave they also left a letter explaining their actions. "We could not face you in paradise," they wrote, "until we had finished the work you had begun."

The sun had been rising as the gang of ronin carried the head of their victim through the snowy streets of Edo. Wondering at the noise, bleary-eyed householders came out of their houses to gape at these proud samurai and their grisly trophy. Word quickly spread of what had happened and more people crowded onto the streets to cheer the ronin and to offer them refreshments. Within days the events of that morning had become well known to the general public and most people expressed full support for their actions. Even before the attack there had been widespread anger over the harsh treatment of Asano and his family, an anger that was shared by some of the highest government officials. For the common citizens of Edo there was nothing to fault in the actions of these honorable men. The ronin had set out on a suicide mission. They fully expected to be executed and made no attempt to hide themselves once they had killed Kira. Instead they handed all of their remaining cash over to the priest who witnessed their presentation of Kira's head to their dead master. The cash was intended to pay for their funerals.

The ronin were indeed detained but they were not immediately executed. Instead they were confined to house arrest as a huge public debate broke out over what should be done with them. From a legal point of view they had outrageously breached the peace and had defied the rule of the Shogun. To the Confucian intellectuals these men were pure criminals. But for the majority of the samurai, including some advisors to the Shogun, their behavior seemed to have been entirely honorable and appropriate to the situation. Their supporters believed that there was no higher value than the code of loyalty that bound samurai to their lords – it was the very basis of the feudal system. Caught between two irreconcilable points of view the Shogun and his government fretted for two months over a suitable punishment.

In the end it was decided that the ronin should not be humiliated by a public execution. Instead, they were offered the more honorable option of a ritual suicide. The forty six remaining ronin, one had left Edo after the attack, were prepared for death. They were dressed in white clothing and led out one by one to a yard that had been draped in white cloth. It had already become common practice to place a symbolic fan rather than a knife in front of a condemned man but the Shogun ordered that these men be given knives. Many of the ronin died with great courage, cutting their bellies deeply and then expressing thanks to the executioner before he made his final swing of the sword.

The forty six dead ronin lived on as popular heroes. Within weeks a kabuki play had been produced that strongly hinted at recent events in a story that showed samurai taking revenge for the death of their lord. The play was a smash hit and was cheered to the rafters by the townspeople of Edo. Startled by the unusual public criticism of its actions the government quickly banned the production. But it was not possible to outlaw public debate. Every thinker in the land took up a position either for or against the actions of the ronin. The author of the Hagakure, who represented one extreme pole of public opinion, actually criticized the ronin for taking so long to plan their attack. They should have gone after Kira immediately, Tsunemoto grumbled, however hopeless their plan.

The nobility of the forty seven ronin proved to have a lasting effect. Their refusal to let their lord be forgotten was a model of behavior that would once again find admirers in the nineteenth and twentieth centuries. They had demonstrated, it was said, that honor is more important than position, that action is more important than the law, and that loyalty is more important than life itself.

The Chinese Way
A time for passionate, unthinking action would come. But in eighteenth century Japan these kind of opinions were outside the mainstream. The fierce code of honor and the emotional bonds of loyalty that had been key to samurai identity for centuries were compulsions that were too unruly for the Great Tokugawa Peace. As a counterpoint to the old preference for instinctive action, Confucian and Neo-Confucian ideas gradually took hold. These Chinese philosophies had been part of the cultural background of Japanese life for centuries and were highly esteemed. The upper layers of the samurai class had inherited from the aristocracy a deep respect for China as the home of true civilization – the place where philosophy, religion, art, and even language itself had been born. And the moral ideas of Neo-Confucian philosophy were in many ways a natural fit for the emerging society of Tokugawa Japan.

They included belief in a well defined social hierarchy, in citizens displaying loyalty to their leaders, and in sternly enforced public discipline.

But there were some difficulties in applying this kind of Chinese model to the very different circumstances of life in Japan. In China Neo-Confucian thinking had produced an educated elite, a group of experts who were selected on the basis of academic merit and who dedicated themselves to running society in as efficient a manner as possible. A meritocratic system was, however, entirely unacceptable to the upper layers of the Japanese samurai. These were men who had fought their way to the top and who had no intention of relinquishing their position. And there were many, like Tsunetomo, who found the very idea of samurai becoming philosophers and administrators a revolting distortion of true warrior nature.

Gradually, a more Japanese brand of Neo-Confucianism emerged. The samurai were encouraged to think of themselves as both warriors and as sophisticated intellectuals. As Japan moved into the eighteenth century and memories of the old warrior ways faded many samurai did begin to throw their energies into administration, paying only lip service to their official status as fighters. The creation of special schools for the sons of samurai helped to entrench Confucian ideas among their class. Just as the boys of England were obliged to pore over Greek and Roman classics the samurai youth were trained in the classic texts of Chinese Confucian thought, texts that they learned to recite by heart.

The popularity of Neo-Confucian studies in Japan led to the first serious attempt to define the 'Way' of the warrior. Yamaga Soko was a leading seventeenth century expert in both philosophy and military strategy. For Yamaga, morality was not an abstract concept but something that had to be embodied in action. The role of the samurai, he suggested, was to provide living examples of morality to the rest of society. The best qualities of the samurai – fearlessness, complete loyalty, and self-discipline – could provide a model for the other classes to follow. The true samurai, according to Yamaga, was a sober individual who maintained perfect control over his actions and his words.

Yamaga did not use the word bushido to describe his 'Way of the Warrior'. The term had not yet entered common use and Yamaga's chosen expression was shido, the 'way of a gentleman'. But his views did have great influence on subsequent explanations of bushido. The energy that had produced the violence of war, he argued, could now be converted into an inner strength and self-control that would be devoted to the leadership of society. Change was also needed in the relationship between a samurai and his lord. Yamaga argued that this relationship was becoming outdated and that samurai should centre their loyalty and love on the nation as a whole.

Neo-Confucianism became the official state philosophy of Japan in 1790. But its message proved to be rather difficult for many of the samurai to fully accept. They were told repeatedly that self-control and dutiful service to society were the modern way of life. But these ideas were hard to reconcile with the stories that every samurai boy had been raised on, tales about the wild and violent exploits of their ancestors. For those who preferred a more emotional approach to life there was an alternative to the rather worthy strictures of mainstream Neo-Confucian, a philosophy that had originated within Confucianism itself.

Another Confucian school had long existed in China, a school that clearly belonged to Neo-Confucian thought but that was significantly different in tone. The Wang Yangming school taught that morality and virtue were not subjects of learning but qualities that are inherent in human nature. A true man is born with the ability to take action that is directed by a natural, intuitive awareness of the right thing to do. This branch of Neo-Confucianism was highly attractive to samurai who longed for a life of action and were more inclined to follow their feelings rather than their intellect. In the nineteenth century, when taking action once again seemed to have become more important than accepting the social order, it was possible for samurai like Saigo Takamori, who was deeply influenced by the ideas of Wang Yangming, to play a prominent role.

Despite the efforts of senior Japanese Confucian scholars no single philosophy that described the inner life the samurai was ever completely accepted. The 'way of the warrior' was, in fact, a rather confusing notion for many. The idea that a samurai needed to be brave was uncontroversial, but most samurai in the eighteenth century lived lives that were marked by the absence of danger. Loyalty, everyone agreed, was an important samurai quality. But who should they be loyal to? Should a samurai be loyal to his local lord, to the Emperor, to the nation, or to his own moral creed? It was a matter of common sense that frugality and simplicity were admirable samurai qualities but most Tokugawa samurai did their best to accumulate as much wealth as possible. Even the suggestion of thinkers like Yamaga Soko that the samurai could become moral exemplars for society was very well and good but the history books told another story. There were just as many stories of treachery, cruelty and betrayal in the history of the samurai as there were examples of heroism, loyalty and generosity. The samurai were a proud class but they were a class that always struggled to clearly define the purpose of their lives.

Fleshly Tablets of the Heart
By the end of the nineteenth century the samurai had disappeared and Japan was running away from its own history as fast as it could. The Japanese ruling classes became obsessed with imitating the Western powers and, for a while, no one cared very much for tradition. The future was good, the old ways were deeply unfashionable. But this hectic rush into the future could not last forever. Eventually there was a

movement to rediscover and reinvigorate 'traditional Japan' and Japanese intellectuals began to attempt to describe just what it was that made their nation 'Japanese'. They aimed to rebuild national pride and also to explain their nation to a curious outside world.

One of the most important Japanese writers to take on the challenge of explaining Japan to the world was Nitobe Inazo. In his book Bushido, he made the first modern attempt to define the core values of the samurai and to argue for their relevance to the modern age. In 1900, when Bushido was first published, Nitobe was swimming against the stream. As far back as the eighteenth century writers like Ogyu Sorai had dismissed the values of wartime samurai as embarrassing feudal relics. And by the beginning of the twentieth century most Japanese people agreed. They had come to the conclusion that their samurai heritage was a rather foolish and shameful memory that was best forgotten. Nitobe helped to turn the tide. Appearing half way between the first modern war that Japan had been involved in, a successful war with China, and the victory over Russia in 1905, the publication of his book coincided with an upsurge in Japanese patriotism. The Japanese had reached a point where they were ready to listen to someone who told them that their nation was special. Nitobe's book was timely and was enthusiastically received.

And yet Nitobe did not even write his book for the Japanese. He was, in fact, a most unlikely choice for a person who would make his reputation as an interpreter of the Japanese warrior code. After a childhood in the distant and rural north of Japan he was sent by his wealthy family to study in an English school in Tokyo. He continued his studies with foreign professors of English at a Hokkaido university and finally followed his love of the English language to make a new life in the United States. Nitobe was one of the first Japanese to take up residence in North America and he quickly adapted to the new environment, marrying an American woman and adopting the Quaker faith. He was, perhaps, the single most Westernized Japanese person of his generation. It was this life overseas, the need to constantly answer questions about his mysterious homeland, that forced Nitobe to consider just what it meant to be Japanese.

Nitobe's Bushido was written in California and was written in English. The author had a burning desire to become a "bridge across the Pacific" and he would fulfill this ambition, going on to build a career as an important internationalist. He was a senior official of the League of Nations, helped to create the organization that was the forerunner of UNESCO, campaigned for the worldwide adoption of Esperanto and became a leading Japanese politician who represented his nation at many international conferences. Nitobe was a liberal humanist and an outspoken opponent of military expansionism. It is one of the great tragedies of his life that the ideas he espoused in Bushido would be exploited as nationalistic propaganda during the war years.

When he was writing his book Nitobe believed that he had coined the term bushido. To his surprise, he later found that the word had been in use throughout the Edo period and even earlier. But it had never been a commonly used word and Nitobe was certainly the first Japanese writer to give the word the prominence it still has today. His book has great importance as one of the very first Japanese attempts to suggest that the values of the samurai have relevance to people in the modern world.

From a modern perspective it is tempting to dismiss Nitobe's work as a romantic and inaccurate portrayal of the world of the samurai but such criticisms are, perhaps, missing the point. For a Japanese thinker of his time Nitobe had an unusual confidence in the moral code of his own society and he was happy to state that it was the equal of anything that existed in the West. Bushido, he told his Western readers, is not a relic of the past but "a living object of power and beauty among us." It is an unwritten code that is "written on the fleshly tablets of the heart." (21) These were questionable assertions but they did carry a psychological truth. With his bold statements Nitobe made it possible for Japanese martial artists in the twentieth century to feel that they belonged to a moral and ethical tradition that had solid roots in the samurai past.

The enormous impact of Nitobe's book on the Japanese was not something that Nitobe had himself expected. He wrote for a foreign audience and strove to make the spirit of the Japanese people comprehensible. In doing so he drew parallels with Greek history, medieval chivalry, Christian morality and German philosophy. The essential elements of Bushido, he suggested in his book, are rectitude, courage, benevolence, politeness, veracity, honor, loyalty and self-control. None of these qualities, he readily admitted, were unique to the Japanese. What was unique, according to Nitobe, was the combination of qualities that stemmed from the unwritten samurai code and had subsequently filtered into the national character.

Much of Nitobe's book reads more like a cultural tract on the Japanese than a description of the samurai. Many of the characteristics he drew attention to were fresh observations for overseas readers at that time and have since become common features of descriptions of Japanese life. Nitobe explained the importance of shame in Japan, the precedence given to group loyalty over individual freedom, the unwillingness to be direct in situations where it can cause offense and the close attention given to ceremony and tradition.

At a time when Japanese culture was largely a mystery to the outside world, Nitobe was an important interpreter. He explained the significance of tea culture: "it is poetry, with articulate gestures for rhythms." (21) He outlined the importance to the emotional Japanese of being able to control their expression of emotion, approvingly describing the father of a sick child who spends a night listening to his child's troubled breathing from behind a screen, unwilling to display his concern openly.

Above all, he argued, at a time when Western views of the Japanese were colonialist at best and frankly racist at worst, that the Japanese were the equal of other nations in the richness and depth of their culture. This richness stemmed from the samurai, he wrote. They were "not only the flower of the nation, but its root as well." (21) The spirit of the samurai had filtered down to the entire people of the nation, becoming the Soul of Japan (Yamato Damashii). Bushido was alive and was relevant, he told the world, because it was "the animating spirit, the motor force of our country." (21)

The book was an immediate success. In 1905, just five years after the book's first publication, Nitobe wrote an introduction to the tenth English edition and remarked that nine editions had already been published in Japanese. The book had also been translated into several other languages. President Teddy Roosevelt was an enthusiastic early reader who bought thirty copies to give to his friends. Another early reader was Baden-Powell, the founder of the Scouting movement who incorporated some of the book's ideas into the moral code of Scouting.

Nitobe never personally translated Bushido into his mother tongue but it was in Japanese that the book had its greatest impact. It was a clear and optimistic account of the value of Japanese history to the modern Japanese way of life that was so perfectly suited to the times that it quickly became part of the national subconscious. The many Japanese translations of Bushido have been reprinted more than one hundred times, selling millions of copies.

While his book was a huge success Nitobe's life ended in failure. He wanted the world to regard the core values of the Japanese as a kind of noble humanism. For a few years in the 1920s, it seemed that Japan would become the modern, democratic country that he dreamed of. But the economic depression of 1929 created a despairing national mood that made it possible for right wing military officers to work towards a seizure of power from the elected government. These officers draped themselves in the colors of bushido, and claimed that democracy and liberalism ran counter to the spirit of the samurai. Nitobe was doomed to spend the last years of his life engaged in futile protests as his beloved Japan drifted towards the violent embrace of the right wing factions.

If You Only Spoke
A very different interpretation of samurai history from that of Nitobe lay behind the activities of the ultranationalist groups as they weaved an underground network of plots to overthrow the government and establish a dictatorship. On May 15th 1932, eleven twenty year old naval officers assassinated the

Prime Minister. Immediately after their attack the officers claimed that they were the heirs of the shishi, the young samurai who had struggled against the Shogun's government in the nineteenth century. The last words of the Prime Minister as he died were: "If you only spoke, I could understand". "Words are useless," one of the rebels coldly replied. When they were put on trial the young murderers were supported by no less than 350,000 people who signed their names in blood to a petition calling for their release. Eleven young men went as far as to cut off a finger which they sent to the court as down payments for the lives of their heroes. They wanted, they wrote, to be executed in the place of the eleven officers. Nitobe's vision of a proud and gentle Japanese nation was being washed away.

As Japan was overrun by military fanatics, the traditions and legends of the samurai were revived in the service of the nationalist dictatorship. The heroism of Kusonoki Masashige in the fourteenth century was promoted as a model for the absolute and unthinking loyalty to the Emperor, and therefore to the state, that the military leaders of Japan required. The Hagakure, with its thrilling invocations of death, was distributed widely and was carried into the skies by Kamikaze pilots. Sadao Araki, like many Japanese generals, ordered his troops to commit suicide rather than surrender. He told them that this was a samurai tradition. The Japanese soldier must expect death, he wrote. "Our lives, from the very beginning, are given up for His Majesty!"

While the Japanese army fought with great bravery during the Second World War the cruelty and occasional outright bestiality displayed by army units had little in common with the traditions of the samurai. Samurai wars had been fought over land and for the right to rule and tax the peasantry of a certain area. There were few examples in Japanese history of the population of conquered lands being put to the sword. Samurai battles were certainly brutal but they did not usually end in hopeless sacrificial fights to the last man. Japanese warriors, especially those of the sixteenth century, had regarded retreat, surrender and even switching sides as the natural coda of a battle. Their honor had been bound up with their loyalty to their local lord and clan. Before the middle of the nineteenth century there was almost no tradition of samurai who longed to die for their Emperor.

The Japanese Army exploited and twisted the ideas and the history of the samurai. By the end of the war the notion of a Warrior's Way had become hopelessly entangled with the right-wing fanaticism that had consumed Japan. The American occupiers outlawed references to bushido and martial culture because they had been so important to the military expansionists. In the years after the war the great majority of Japan's exhausted and depleted population viewed bushido as an ugly and dangerous idea. They wanted nothing more to do with it.

Tough Guy

But the warping of the ideals of bushido in the cause of right-wing ultranationalism was to have one final day in the spotlight. On November 25th, 1970 Yukio Mishima, perhaps the greatest of the post-war generation of Japanese novelists, led a group of four young men into the office of the Commander of the Japanese army. Mishima tied the Commander to a chair and threatened to kill him unless he assembled all of the troops at his disposal to listen to a speech. At noon Mishima stepped out onto a balcony overlooking the parade ground where several hundred soldiers were waiting to hear what he had to say.

Mishima's growing fascination with bushido in the 1960s made him a very unusual Japanese intellectual and the path he had taken was a startlingly strange one for a member of Japan's liberal post-war literary elite. Three years before the attack on the military headquarters Mishima had published a guide to the Hagakure. In his bestselling interpretation he relished that book's fascination with death and its calls for direct and unthinking action. Mishima had not been a physically impressive youth and he had avoided conscription into the wartime military by faking illness. But by the time he reached his thirties something had changed. He took up bodybuilding, built a muscular physique and began studying kendo and karate in order to develop his strength and martial spirit. By 1970 he had gathered a small private army of confused young men and was lost in a private fantasy that with one dramatic action he could provoke a nationalist revolution. On the day he arrived at the army headquarters he was determined to shake the Japanese people out of their pacifist slumber.

Mishima, dressed in a military uniform, began to read out the text of his revolutionary manifesto to the soldiers on the parade ground below. He called on them to rise up, to overthrow the government and to establish a new state under the direct control of the Emperor. The soldiers responded with boos and catcalls. After five minutes of fruitless dialogue with the unwelcoming troops Mishima gave up and returned to the office. He took off his shirt and knelt on the carpet. Then he shoved a dagger into his belly. Behind him Morita, a young member of the private army, was holding Mishima's seventeenth century samurai sword. "Don't let me suffer too long," Mishima said as he fell forward. But the suicide was as incompetent as the attempted putsch had been. Morita swung the sword twice, missing Mishima's neck and only cutting into his body. After a horrifying pause another young member of the group took the sword from Morita and sliced off his leader's head. It had been the first case of ritual suicide in Japan since the war.

Throughout the country there was very little sympathy for Mishima. The Prime Minister called him a crazy man and few people outside the tiny extreme right-wing groups disagreed with that assessment. Rather than spark the revolution he had been dreaming of, Mishima had simply revealed how little support there was in Japanese society for a return to militarism. Thanks to his strange death bushido once again became a word that the Japanese linked to the shameful mistakes of the past.

Several decades have now passed since Mishima's suicide and Japan has become a wealthy and stable society. Today the people of Japan have little time for those who argue for a return to right wing militarism but they do readily value the samurai traditions of their nation. Bushido in modern Japan has lost the aura of dangerous association with fanatical right wingers. Instead it is a term that has largely been appropriated by mainstream conservative politicians who regard bushido as one of the key elements of Japan's glorious past. Yasuhiro Nakasone, one of the nation's most influential politicians and a former Prime Minister, has specifically called for a revival of bushido.

> European countries have Christianity but Japan has no such philosophical or ideological footing ... Since the war, Japan's traditional disciplines have been lost: disciplines such as the five virtues of Confucianism and Neo-Confucianism; the sense of shame; and the code of the samurai or Bushido. (22)

For conservatives like Nakasone invocations of bushido reflect their nostalgia for a social order where rule from the top was meekly accepted, women knew their place and young people were seen but not heard. But among the Japanese martial arts community bushido has a somewhat different meaning. It is not regarded as a social ethos so much as a personal sense of purpose, a decision to live one's life with the commitment, discipline and selflessness of the ancient warriors. Many today would agree with the words that were chosen by Yamaoka Tesshu to describe bushido.

> We must look after each other without regard to our own welfare, kill selfish desires, bravely face all enemies, and keep a stainless mind - this is Bushido. (14)

Images attributed to Miyamoto Musashi

Below: Self Portrait
Right: Image of Daruma
Lower Right: Shrike

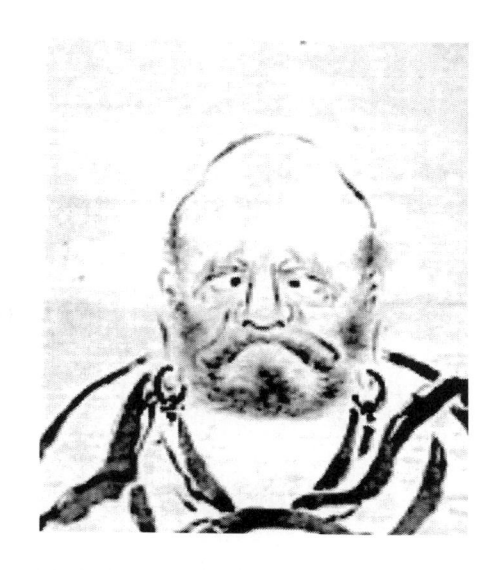

Yamaoka Tesshu

Jigoro Kano

Top left: Morihei Ueshiba
Top right: Ueshiba later in life

Bottom left: Gichin Funakoshi
Bottom right: His son Yoshitaka

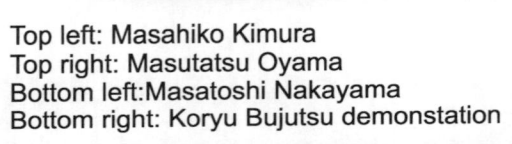

Top left: Masahiko Kimura
Top right: Masutatsu Oyama
Bottom left: Masatoshi Nakayama
Bottom right: Koryu Bujutsu demonstation

9. The Birth of Judo

A World Upside Down

It had only been yesterday, but by the end of the nineteenth century the idea of samurai carrying swords in the street already seemed to belong to a different universe. Japan embraced change as it raced into the future. The young Meiji Emperor in Tokyo ordered his government to take aggressive steps to catch up with the West and, after centuries of isolation, Japan threw its doors wide open to the outside world. Thousands of foreign experts from every conceivable field were shipped in to work as government advisors and university professors. Their knowledge was hungrily consumed and immediately applied.

In the thirty years that followed the Meiji Restoration coal, steel and iron production rocketed. Thousands of miles of train lines snaked across a nation that had previously relied on rough footpaths for transport. There was a fad for new brick buildings, sensations in a land where everything was made of wood. Culture was turned upside down. European music, art, philosophy and fashion became all the rage. Even dress styles changed. Men were no longer allowed to wear their hair in topknots and among the kimono and hakama one could see women walking in Western skirts and men wearing caps.

This enthusiasm for the new was mirrored in a violent rejection of everything that was old. The jewels of Japanese culture, great paintings and sculptures among them, came to be seen as worthless and shameful relics. Many artworks that would be considered priceless today were simply dumped in the trash. In the 1870s, at the height of the fever for change, Japanese people turned sharply away from the traditions of their own culture. They felt a disinterest bordering on distaste for the old ways and the warrior arts were one of those ridiculous old ways. The samurai had, after all, vanished into history. What possible reason could there be for wasting time on martial arts in this new world? Fighting could be left to the professional military and the modernized police.

Bare Hands

Sword fighting, the most important of all the martial arts, went through a serious decline during the 1870s. Other fighting systems faced extinction. For the weaponless fighting styles it was a shocking reversal. Just twenty years earlier, in the middle of the nineteenth century, unarmed combat had been hugely popular. There had been more than seven hundred different schools of fighting that described themselves in names such as kumiuchi, taijutsu, yawara and torite. But the most popular name for bare handed fighting was jujutsu. Some of the jujutsu schools were hundreds of years old and had their origins in the days when samurai trained for hand to hand fighting on the battlefield. One of the oldest and most powerful styles, the Takenouchi Ryu, had been founded in 1532.

In the seventeenth and eighteenth centuries the samurai largely gave up practicing unarmed fighting in armor. It was more important to be ready to handle attacks on the street than it was to prepare for battlefield combat. Those centuries saw the creation of many new and more fluid forms of jujutsu. But the teachers who created these new styles were highly secretive and guarded their repertoire of techniques closely. As a result, jujutsu had become an overly complex and esoteric art. Every school had its own secret syllabus and its own set of secret techniques. Some masters claimed that they knew of more than three thousand. The veil of mystery behind which they hid their knowledge was one way of keeping the paying customers interested. Jujutsu trainees needed to train for years, or even decades, before they were allowed to study the most secret and dangerous techniques.

In Edo the situation had been a little more open. So many jujutsu schools existed close together in the city that they had taken to challenging each other in inter-school matches (taryujiai). In imitation of the sword schools of Edo the jujutsu schools became fierce competitors, desperate to beat each other. These inter-school matches were the only forum for the best fighters to meet and the only way for the public to decide which style was most effective. Open competitions brought together fighters who had mastered many dangerous techniques such as strikes to vital points, joint locks, hard throws and strangulation. As a result, the inter-school fights, with no set rules, could be bloody affairs.

The violent jujutsu tournaments were extremely popular with the public. The prospect of dramatic defeats made it easy to sell tickets and crowds gathered to cheer on their favorite fighters. But the reputation of jujutsu suffered as public matches became common in the middle of the nineteenth century and the art acquired a rather unwholesome reputation. When the Meiji Era arrived and students flooded out of the martial arts clubs it was the unarmed fighting schools that suffered most. Most jujutsu teachers found that they had no students left to teach and they were forced to find other ways of making a living. Even the most popular teachers could count on only handfuls of committed followers.

The Brilliant Boy
At this time of utter disinterest in the old martial ways a reformer was badly needed. The person who emerged to save jujutsu was Jigoro Kano, undoubtedly the most important individual in the creation of the modern martial arts of Japan. Kano's birth into a merchant family in 1860 came at just the right time. Had he been born twenty years earlier the young Kano would have been trapped in the mercantile class. But he arrived into a new world where it was possible for even a boy who was not a samurai to have big ambitions.

After his mother's untimely death when he was only nine years old Kano was taken to Tokyo by his father. He arrived just in time to see the last of the samurai walking along the streets of the capital with swords at their side. His father was a leading progressive and he wanted his son to be able to take advantage of Japan's new connections with the outside world. He enrolled his son in a school where all Japanese was banned in the classroom and all of the lessons were taught in either English or German. Kano thrived as a student. He became a brilliant linguist, so proficient in English that he would write his diary in that language for the rest of his life.

But Kano did not thrive physically. He was so bright that he was placed in a class with older boys and those older boys liked to bully him. Kano was small for his age, he never grew taller than 158 centimeters, and he did not yet have the muscles that he would acquire later in life. The older boys forced him to confront them in sumo bouts where they threw him around like a rag doll. It was a frustrating and humiliating time.

Kano was desperate to find a way to defend himself. One day a former samurai who was visiting Kano's father told the boy about jujutsu. He was immediately fascinated to hear of an art that allowed a defender to throw an attacker to the ground. Jujutsu, the visitor told him, was a good way for small people to deal with enemies who were bigger and stronger. Kano was thrilled, this was just what he had been looking for. He pestered the ex-samurai to show him some moves and, when the man obliged, Kano begged for regular lessons. But to the boy's dismay the visitor poured cold water on his enthusiasm. Jujutsu was interesting, he told Kano, but it was a relic of the past. A smart boy like him should concentrate on his studies.

Kano could not accept this advice. He was being bullied too often to forget that wonderful image of a small man defeating a bigger man. He asked two other family acquaintances to teach him but was again rebuffed. Finally, he went to his father to ask for help in finding a jujutsu teacher. But he had chosen the wrong man. Kano's father was a convinced social reformer who was deeply involved in the daily work of modernizing the nation's ports. He was the last person to allow his son to study anything as out of date as an ancient martial art. "Forget it," the father told his son, "The age of the samurai is finished. You should take up tennis or running instead."

A Grey-Haired Teacher
It was fortunate for the future of the Japanese martial arts that this outstanding boy held on to his dream. By the time he was seventeen and had registered as a university student Kano decided that he would set about looking for a jujutsu teacher himself. But finding a teacher who was still able to teach would be no easy task. Most of the old jujutsu teachers had lost all of their students when interest in the ancient arts

collapsed. These teachers still needed to make a living and their only remaining practical skill was the intimate knowledge of the human body that they had acquired over decades of treating students who had been injured by hard throws and joint attacks. Many of these former teachers were making a living in osteopathic practices where they treated customers for back pain and joint problems.

When Kano realized that a large number of the older jujutsu teachers were now osteopaths he began to make it his practice to walk into any building that was advertising osteopathic services and to strike up a conversation about jujutsu. After a long search he found someone who actually was a master of jujutsu. The man disappointed the young Kano by telling him that he had retired from the martial arts and that most of his acquaintances had also given up teaching. But he did know of one man who was still offering classes. Kano secured an introduction to this teacher, a certain Master Fukuda, and hurried to the Fukuda osteopathy clinic. To his delight he found that there were indeed jujutsu classes being held in the clinic's waiting room after business closed for the day.

The little, grey-haired osteopath who came out to meet the eager university student was actually one of the few living Japanese masters of unarmed combat. In the years before the Meiji Restoration Fukuda had been an instructor in the Kobusho, the Shogun's official military academy. He was a teacher of Divine Willow (Tenjin Shinyo Ryu) jujutsu, a style that had been the dominant brand of jujutsu in mid-nineteenth century Edo when it boasted thousands of registered students. The Divine Willow School was a relatively modern style that made use of lighter and freer techniques than those taught in older schools that were still oriented towards combat in heavy armor.

Like most other jujutsu schools Divine Willow had a deep curriculum consisting of hundreds of secret techniques made up of throws, chokes, trips, locks and strikes. Many of the techniques taught to the more senior students were highly dangerous and these were kept well hidden from outsiders. All of the skills were taught through practice of kata. A student would watch the master as he demonstrated a move and would then try to use the same move against an unresisting partner. This school did have one important difference from some other forms of jujutsu. Students were encouraged to try out the techniques they had learned in free sparring sessions known as randori.

Even an expert teacher like Master Fukuda had been deserted by most of his students. When Kano joined the Divine Willow School only seven students were practicing in Fukuda's classes and only two of this group had very much experience. Despite the small numbers the Master made few concessions to beginners. Everyone who entered his dojo had to practice the same technique at the same time as Fukuda looked on. He did not offer much in the way of instruction or explanation but preferred to simply throw his students over and over again onto the hard tatami mats that did little to cushion their falls. He expected his students to grasp the meaning of the techniques through constant repetition. Fukuda discouraged too much thought. Everything had to be instinctive.

For the teenage Kano this introduction to jujutsu training was a physical shock as he was soon covered in painful bruises. But the recent memories of his long search for a teacher helped him to put up with the discomfort. As he trained every day Kano realized that jujutsu was not going to transform him overnight into a superman. He found the students who were bigger than him almost impossible to throw. One student in particular was thirty kilograms heavier and Kano, struggle as he might in randori practice, could find no way to throw this large, experienced fighter.

At this point the intelligence and determination that would make Kano one of Japan's greatest men came to the fore. He began to pester everyone in his circle for knowledge about unarmed fighting and before long he discovered that a large man who held a humble job in the university canteen had been a sumo wrestler in his youth. He persuaded the cook to teach him some moves and for several days the two wrestled together as Kano extracted all the information he could on sumo throwing techniques. But when he returned to the jujutsu dojo he found that none of the ideas he had absorbed from sumo helped him at all.

Refusing to give up, Kano turned to the world he knew best, the world of books. He trawled the local libraries and took out every book he could find that contained descriptions of Western wrestling. As he leafed through the photographs and illustrations he spotted something that looked as if it had been designed for his small body. It was a photograph of a move that not even a much bigger man could resist. Kano practiced with a friend until he was satisfied and then returned to Fukuda's dojo to face his nemesis.

This time when his opponent pushed forward Kano did not resist the pressure but pulled the larger man towards his body. Ducking low, Kano told hold of his opponent's right leg and suddenly hoisted the startled fighter into the air and right across his shoulders. From that position it was an easy matter to keep the helpless ninety kilogram frame moving until it crashed with a satisfying thump into the mats. Kano grinned with pleasure at his convincing triumph. Although he was not yet aware of the fact, he had just invented, or adapted, a technique that would one day be taught to millions of judo students all over the world. Known today as kata guruma, it is a move that snatches away all of the advantages of weight and strength as contact with terra firma is removed and the lifted fighter flails helplessly in the air. With this innovation Kano proved to himself that he could do more than simply learn old techniques, he could also update them. It was a modest beginning for what would soon become his lifelong project - the remolding of jujutsu for the modern age.

In 1879 the recently retired president of the United States, the Civil War hero Ulysses S. Grant, paid a visit to Japan. Grant was just as eager to inspect this newly opened country as the leaders of Japan were to impress such an important politician. The government laid on many entertainments for the visitors and among them was an exhibition of the martial arts. To represent jujutsu the officials asked Master Fukuda to give a display. Perhaps the government was unaware just how few students were training in Fukuda's dojo but the master did his best to put on a good show. He personally demonstrated kata and arranged for Kano, who had by now been training in jujutsu for two years, and another student to give a demonstration of free sparring. The ex-president seemed to mightily enjoy what he saw and after the demonstration a relieved Fukuda shared a confidence with his young student. "Old men like me have been able to keep jujutsu alive," he told the twenty year old. "It is up to your generation to spread jujutsu around the world." Nine days later Master Fukuda was dead.

The Young Master
Kano had already shown flashes of independence but the sudden death of his master forced the young man to think for himself. Immediately after the funeral Fukuda's wife took Kano aside and told him that her husband had already decided that Kano would be his successor one day. She asked him to take over the teaching duties at the family dojo. Kano was shocked but he was not the type of young man to evade such a responsibility. At the raw age of twenty he took charge of teaching students and keeping the legacy of his master alive. He threw himself into this task with such energy that his training outfit grew ragged and had to be repaired regularly. Kano would be so exhausted after his long hours of daily training and teaching that he found it hard to walk home without falling asleep on his feet. At night he would dream of jujutsu and would shout, or kick down the sliding doors of his room as he relived fights in his sleep. After a few months of this relentless schedule it dawned on Kano that he could not become an expert by simply training hard. He was too young and inexperienced to be a successful teacher. He needed to learn more.

At the exhibition for the American President the role of partnering Master Fukuda in his demonstration had been taken by another expert from the Divine Willow School, Master Iso. Iso was a small man of sixty years who was more interested in teaching kata than in encouraging his students to spar with each other. He was an expert in atemi waza, the art of felling an opponent by striking a vital point of the body. Iso was so accurate with his punches that he could knock down several attackers in quick succession. After Kano finished teaching his own classes he would race to Master Iso's dojo where around thirty students were training regularly.

Kano did not confine himself to the Divine Willow School. He also made it his habit to attend any jujutsu exhibition in Tokyo and would be the first to volunteer if there was a chance to spar. He was hungry for knowledge, hungry to find a system that would match his boyhood dreams of being able to defeat any challenger. But the knowledge he wanted so badly was hard to obtain. The jujutsu schools regarded their methods as both dangerous and valuable and so maintained a high wall of secrecy around their innermost techniques. Kano decided that he would penetrate the secrecy, discover the best elements of each school and combine his discoveries to create his own integrated and revolutionary fighting style.

For all his hard work Kano had little luck with his teachers. Less than a year after the death of Master Fukuda, Master Iso also died. But by now Kano understood the jujutsu world intimately and he was able to secure an introduction to an expert he had admired for some time. Master Iikubo was very different to Kano's two previous teachers. He was relatively young, at 47 years, and was tall and powerful. Iikubo was also of interest to Kano because he belonged to a different style of jujutsu, the Rising Falling School (Kito Ryu). This school placed less emphasis on groundwork techniques such as body pins and chokes but was particularly rich in throwing techniques. Iikubo enjoyed free sparring and, although he was stronger than Kano at this point, he proved to be a perfect partner for the younger man. In his time with the Divine Willow School Kano had learned to throw in the way taught by most jujutsu schools. Attacks began with a strike to a vital point that weakened an opponent and made a throw possible if sufficient leverage and strength were applied. But as he sparred with Iikubo Kano began to perceive that there could be a more subtle, more instinctive and more effective way to throw a heavier man.

Although he was engaged in hard physical exercise for several hours every day Kano was also pushing hard to complete his university studies. In 1882 he completed a post-graduate degree and found work as a teacher at Gakushuin, a famous school that educated the children of Japan's elite. As if he did not have enough on his mind the energetic Kano decided that he could also find the time to open his own jujutsu training centre. Eishoji, a nearby Buddhist temple, had three empty rooms for rent and Kano took them all. He moved his possessions into one room, converted the largest room into a dojo and set aside the third room as a place for his students to live and sleep.

It was an unconventional headquarters for a martial arts group. As the days became filled with the regular thumping of bodies being thrown onto tatami floors and against wooden pillars Kano found himself in trouble with the temple priest. Perhaps the priest had expected judo students to train with the disciplined dignity of a sword club. Instead, it seemed as though his temple was being reduced to rubble. Kano tried to solve the problem by crawling under the floorboards to hammer in nails but it became clear that his rumbustious group of young fighters had outstayed their welcome. Kano needed money to pay for a move to a more permanent headquarters so he began to stay up late at night translating English texts into Japanese. He was determined to be the master of his own destiny.

When enough money had been gathered he set about having a small hall built on vacant land near the Eishoji temple. As the building neared completion a great weight lifted from the young teacher's shoulders. Now at last he felt free to set his own direction. When the group of students gathered in their new training hall for the first time Kano welcomed them with a formal speech. Jujutsu had acquired an extremely poor image due to its connection with commercial wrestling matches. The name of jujutsu itself had become tarnished and so he had decided that his group needed to start afresh. He announced that he would call his fighting style judo. It was to be not just a martial art but also a way of life in which technique would be subordinate to character and decency. The 'ju' of the name stood for softness and pliancy while the 'do' indicated that judo was a path of self-improvement. It would be a rational and progressive form of training where strength and willpower would be counterbalanced by civilized behavior and morality. He gave his little wooden hall a name that would later be a famous one. It would be known as Kodokan, The Place for Teaching the Way.

Kano was still only a youth at this time, a mere twenty two years of age. And he had only a handful of students. Eight young men registered as students with the Kodokan in 1883 and ten more joined the following year. But Kano was an outstanding figure, a martial artist who was marked out by his intellectual curiosity. Unlike most of his contemporaries he did not want to simply preserve the past but to create a revolutionary new way of fighting. With all the discipline and determination that had helped him become one of the best speakers of English in Japan Kano used his brain to master the martial arts. He visited the training halls of teachers all over Tokyo and supplemented his practical knowledge by reading everything he could find on fighting systems and on physiology. He experimented constantly. If a new idea came to him he would rouse one of his students from bed late at night to try the technique out. He continued to visit Master Iikubo and now Kano found that he was acquiring the subtle, instinctive sense of how to upset an opponent's balance. A fighter in a stable stance was hard to throw but if that balance could be broken then even someone as strong as Master Iikubo could be toppled easily.

By this time the shape of modern judo was emerging. Kano himself made it clear that his style had been derived mainly from the techniques of the two schools he had belonged to. From Divine Willow he took techniques for choking, for locking joints and for pinning an opponent to the floor. From the Rising Falling School he took many effective throwing techniques. Kano added to this knowledge by investigating all of the other surviving jujutsu schools. There were, he reported, only eight styles of jujutsu left in Japan that were teaching significant numbers of students. Kano's aim was to keep this precious physical culture alive by making it relevant to future generations. To the techniques he had adopted from jujutsu he added ideas of his own devising and techniques he had found in other sports such as sumo and Western wrestling.

At first Kano had only a handful of students and he was able to directly teach and spar with them all. But as enrollment at the Kodokan grew this kind of direct instruction became impractical. Kano had to find a more efficient teaching system and so he decided to adopt some of the methods of the old schools. He began to teach kata that allowed his students to formally practice their moves together under the guidance of an instructor. His earliest students had plenty of time for practice as many of them lived in the Kodokan. They rose early to clean the premises and then began a long day of study and judo exercises. In winter they observed the custom of waking particularly early for long outdoor runs and vigorous sparring sessions in the pre-dawn dark between four and seven in the morning.

Empty Jacket
Up to this point Kano had been swimming against the tide. Judo was a rather eccentric hobby for a young man in Tokyo to pursue at the outset of the 1880s. But from the middle of the decade there were signs that interest in the old fighting ways had begun to revive. Tokyo was filling up with new arrivals from the Japanese countryside and the city police were keen to investigate methods that would help them to control this growing and unruly population. However, not many people regarded judo as something new. To most outsiders it appeared to be just one of the many brands of jujutsu. Kano needed to convince the public that judo was a truly fresh and distinctive style. One opportunity for his art to prove its worth came with the revival of competitions between the Tokyo jujutsu schools. These were popular events and crowds flocked to the matches to see who would come out on top. Kano was at the peak of his powers in these days. He was so skillful, in fact, that one opponent said that sparring with the young master was like "fighting with an empty jacket." But Kano was the leader of a style and it was not appropriate for him to take part in inter-school brawls. Instead he relied on four of his earliest and best students to represent judo. These four young men, Tsunejiro Tomita, Yoshiaki Yamashita, Sakujiro Yokoyama, and Shiro Saigo would become famous as the 'Guardians of the Kodokan'.

An impressive early victory was scored for the Kodokan by Tomita who was drawn in a match against a big, tough opponent who was already employed as a jujutsu instructor by the city police. Tomita, who realized that he had no chance of outmuscling his opponent, waited for the man to make contact and then immediately fell backwards with his right foot in position against the big man's stomach. The startled opponent found himself falling forwards and then, pivoted on Tomita's foot, flying through the air to land two meters behind the judo man. Enraged, he scrambled to his feet and attacked only to find himself once again flying through the air. He was being thrown with the judo technique known today as tomoe-nage. As the crowd cheered Tomita shook the confidence out of the bigger man by throwing him for a third time in succession. When he then approached more cautiously Tomita was able to insert one foot under his opponent's knee, pull him to the floor and apply a strangle hold. Within seconds the police instructor was unconscious and the room was buzzing with talk about the Kodokan and their judo.

Judo fighters were able to win most of these competitive matches for a good reason. They had tough bodies, high levels of strength and fitness and razor sharp reactions as a result of the time they spent practicing against fully resistant training partners. This gave them a definite edge over jujutsu students who came from schools where most of the training was conducted through kata practice. One of Kano's most important innovations had been to create a safe form of sparring where any technique that was likely to cause injury was banned. As a result, his students could throw each other around with great vigor without running too high a risk of badly hurting themselves. In the confrontations organized by the Tokyo police it was Kano's students that soon emerged as the toughest and most effective fighters. Later in life Kano wrote that the time when judo began its rise to prominence was 1886 and in particular after a match the Kodokan fought against the strongest of the traditional jujutsu schools, the Totsuka. In front of an audience of police officers Kano's students easily defeated the Totsuka team, winning twelve matches out of fifteen.

By the end of the 1880s Kano's school was being recognized as Kodokan judo by those who mixed in Tokyo martial arts circles. Everyone could now see that this was something new. It was a school that concentrated on preparing its students for the rigors of free sparring. Everything learned in a class was intended to be used in sparring, rather than in a street fight. Dangerous techniques had been gradually disallowed, usually when a serious injury made it clear that a technique was especially risky. But choking attacks continued to be used as students were able to recover quickly from unconsciousness when pressure on their carotid artery was released.

Kano had rejected the haphazard teaching methods of his own instructors. Instead he was following a path similar to that of Chiba Shusaku, the teacher who had rationalized kenjutsu instruction in the middle of the nineteenth century. Kano offered his students detailed explanations of the techniques they were learning and created a curriculum that allowed them to measure their own progress through a series of clearly differentiated stages.

Kano became the first martial arts teacher to award dan grades when he gave a grade of shodan, or first dan, to Shiro Saigo and Tsunejiro Tomita in 1883. Typically, it was an idea that he had discovered outside the martial arts. Ranking the skill levels of students with dan grades had first been used for the popular board game of go in the Edo period. At first the judo fighters who received dan grades had no way of advertising their rank so, in 1886, Kano asked them to wear wide black sashes around the waists of their training kimono. Several years later, in 1907, Kano came up with the idea of a white training outfit, a judogi that was fastened to the body with a black belt in the case of senior students and with a white belt by all others. This new outfit had longer sleeves and leggings than the traditional costume. It gave more protection to the body and helped students to spar in greater safety because they could take hold of cloth rather than human flesh as they grappled.

As a free-thinking teacher Kano had made a close study of British education and he had been impressed by the way in which that country made use of tests and awards to measure progression. He began to divide the less experienced students of judo into six ranked groups, known as kyu grades, through which they could rise by taking examinations of their technique and fighting skill. All of these students wore white belts. Colored belts were not introduced into judo until Mikonosuke Kawaishi, a Kodokan instructor in Europe, began using them in 1935.

Kano also decided to rethink the philosophical connotations of the name of his style. The 'ju' of judo carries a meaning that is related to English words such as 'softness' or 'flexibility'. Because of this name, a feeling had become widespread that the secret of judo lay in first giving way to an opponent's strength and then unbalancing him. For Kano, it was clear that strength and force were often invaluable in judo and he was dissatisfied with the idea of 'softness'. Consequently, he created the concept of Seiryoku Saizen Katsuyo as a basic explanation of the inner meaning of judo. This phrase conveys the idea that judo fighters use both their body and their mind with maximum efficiency.

The old jujutsu schools were so secretive that no standardization of their complex techniques had been possible. The Divine Willow School alone contained no less than eighteen different weapons systems in its curriculum. Kano believed that such complexity prevented any jujutsu student from really mastering the most effective techniques. He decided to greatly simplify the content of the old schools and in 1895 he formalized the techniques of judo into a list that he named the Gokyo no Waza (five sets of techniques). Altogether there were forty techniques in this core curriculum, all of them throws. While many of the jujutsu throws had been designed to throw an opponent onto their face, or even their neck or the crown of their head, the Kodokan throws were only valid if the opponent landed on his back. This safety measure allowed students to throw each other with great force.

Kano was always more interested in throwing techniques. He found them to be more elegant than wrestling on the floor and his preferences were reflected in this original set of techniques. But his students also studied techniques for holding down opponents and, when they had sufficient experience, were taught the application of joint locks, chokes and striking techniques. It seemed to be a rounded curriculum. In 1900, however, Kano's fighters experienced a shocking defeat at the hands of the Fusen school of jujutsu. These fighters won their matches by refusing to engage with the Kodokan students in the standing-up sparring at which they excelled. Instead, they simply fell onto their backs when contact was made. They were much better at ground fighting than the Kodokan fighters and soon wrestled them into submission.

Kano responded to this crisis of confidence in his usual pragmatic fashion. He brought the masters of the Fusen school to the Kodokan to teach his own students more effective ground fighting techniques and the judo fighters soon became second to none in applying the floor moves they called ne waza. But Kano was rather discouraged by the shift to ground fighting. More and more competitors began to spend all their time wrestling on the mats and throws became rare. Finally, in 1925, Kano had competition rules changed so that fighters who fell to the floor deliberately would be penalized.

From the outset judo matches had been fought without time limits and fighters would simply continue sparring until one of them had taken two points. Kano used a best of three points system (sanbon shobu) because he disliked the sudden death atmosphere of traditional martial arts competitions. The old method attempted to recreate the dangerous feeling of real combat by awarding victory to the first person to clearly apply a technique. Kano's system encouraged more relaxed and open fighting but it could be exhausting. Matches often went on for forty minutes, or even longer, until one of the competitors was too tired to put up any kind of defense. Later, in the intensely military atmosphere of the 1930s, ippon-shobu or sudden-death matches were thought to be more in keeping with the samurai spirit of the times and judo competition rules were changed.

Early judo matches, in fact, had very few rules. Matches frequently resulted in injury and these injuries could be serious. Kano used his experience of supervising competitions to gradually refine the rules and to ban techniques that were causing injuries. Early on it was agreed that breaking bones would not be acceptable in a judo competition. Later strikes and kicks of all kinds were prohibited and locks became restricted to attacks on the elbow joint.

At the outset of the twentieth century judo was growing rapidly. By the year 1900 the Kodokan had expanded from its first, cramped ten-mat training room to a luxurious 300 mat hall in Tokyo. There were several Kodokan branches in the capital and a total of 212 black belts had been awarded. In that year 6000 students were registered with the Kodokan and it had become the most popular martial art in the capital after sword fighting. People began to take notice of this judo phenomenon and famous and distinguished visitors started to appear at the Kodokan hall to see what all the fuss was about. Among them was the elderly Katsu Kaishu who, after watching a demonstration of judo, inscribed the following words on a scroll that was displayed in the Kodokan for many years.

> With no self, discover the mystery of Nature;
> With no intention, master the secret of Change.

National Judo

The almost desperate longing of the Japanese people for their nation to become more like the outside world was fading and many were left to wonder just what it meant to be Japanese in this modern age. In the first war that Japan had fought with a modern army China had been easily defeated and tensions with Russia were rising. The surge in patriotism around these foreign wars created a natural opening for Japan's discarded martial traditions to once again find a place at the centre of Japanese life. In 1895 the martial arts were given their first official recognition for many years when the Great Japanese Martial Association (Dai Nippon Butokukai) was created with the support of the Emperor himself. Although it was officially a private organization, the Butokukai had been created and was supported by very highly placed people in government, military and industrial circles. It was an attempt to bring some order and planning to the Japanese martial arts and to preserve their historical legacy. Many of the most powerful people in the land now had an uneasy feeling that the decimation of the samurai class had been a mistake that had robbed the nation of its life force.

The Butokukai was headquartered in Kyoto where it opened offices and a large training hall. This new organization set about establishing, for the first time, a truly national approach to the martial arts. The plan was to bring the leaders of each fighting art together to agree standardized rules for training methods, kata and competitions. At this time Japan had a bewildering variety of mostly very small martial arts organizations and so one of the first tasks facing the Butokukai was to produce a system that would make it possible for these smaller groups to meet in broadly-based national competitions that were both fair and safe.

The Butokukai at first spent some time creating rules for the sword fighting schools and then turned its attention to jujutsu. In 1899 a meeting was called of the most important jujutsu instructors from all over Japan. Even among this group of mostly older masters the highly educated and well connected Kano stood out. After a vigorous discussion it was decided that the competition rules and safety measures of judo should be accepted as the model for all jujutsu practice. Following this conference many jujutsu teachers did gravitate towards Kano's organization and his reformed teaching curriculum. Others continued to teach a more traditional curriculum but these groups were very small in comparison to Kodokan judo.

Kano had built a national organization and had created a new kind of martial sport. Remarkably, he had done all of this in his spare time while simultaneously building a stellar career as an educator. In 1893 he reached the pinnacle of Japanese education with his appointment as the headmaster of the Tokyo Teachers' Training College. It was a position that gave him enormous influence over the development of modern education in Japan. He fought for better conditions for teachers, promoted overseas study visits, created opportunities for Chinese teachers to study in Japan and upgraded the status of the teacher training colleges.

Kano's greatest ambition as an educator was to make his nation aware of the importance of sport. He required all trainee teachers at his college to take part in sport education sessions and fought for the inclusion of sport in the school curriculum. One of his greatest successes came in 1908 when it was decided that all junior high school students would be required to study either kendo or judo at school. In fact Kano's drive to promote sport education was so powerful that it strongly influenced the direction that judo was taking. Kano pushed judo towards becoming part of the world of competitive sport because he believed that competition was a vital means of developing healthy bodies and strong minds. In later life he did have some doubts about the distance he had gone to shift judo away from its martial origins. As he grew older his own practice became increasingly refined and he grew more interested in the aesthetics of his sport. He was inclined to scold young competition fighters for relying on brute strength rather than on elegant technique.

As he aged Kano became the most famous and respected member of the Japanese martial arts community and one of the best known people in the nation. He continued to be a liberal intellectual and a convinced internationalist at a time when Japan was beginning its tragic drift towards ultra-nationalism. With his superb language skills he greatly enjoyed the regular trips he made around the world to promote judo. These were the days of travel by ship and the aging Kano liked to astonish his fellow passengers by giving impromptu demonstrations of judo using tough young crewmen as his partners.

In 1909 Kano became the first Japanese member of the International Olympic Committee. He threw himself into the task with all the enthusiasm of his younger days, developing elite training groups and building an Olympic team. A wonderful photograph from the Berlin Olympics of 1936 shows Kano sitting quietly in the background as the great Jesse Owens stands on the gold medal podium beside a defeated German runner who is giving a Nazi salute. Kano worked assiduously to secure a promise that the 1940 Olympic Games would be held in Japan. His dream was realized and the Games were promised to an Asian country for the first time. But by that time the entire world would be consumed in the flames of war and Kano would be dead.

Crossing the Ocean

Kano thought on a global scale and one of the great joys of his life was to watch the spread of judo around the world. The story of how judo became a major international sport can be traced back to the very beginning of the twentieth century and the presence of a wealthy American businessman at a demonstration of judo in Tokyo. The American was impressed by what he had seen and decided that this was just the kind of physical training that his undisciplined son needed. He asked that a judo teacher be sent to America and promised to cover all of the costs. This unexpected request threw the leaders of the Kodokan into some confusion. It was obvious that foreigners had no understanding of the cultural rules that lay behind judo practice. If they were going to send one of their own to teach in America that person would need to be strong enough to handle the foreigners and intelligent enough to help them understand the intricacies of judo.

After a lot of thought Kano chose one of his most outstanding students to represent judo overseas. Yoshiaki Yamashita had been the nineteenth ever member of the Kodokan and now, in his thirties, held a 6th degree black belt. He was a certainly a dignified and urbane man who could speak excellent English, but Yamashita was more than a mere diplomat. As one of the four 'Guardians of the Kodokan' he had fought for the honor of judo in innumerable rough matches against the strongest members of other jujutsu clubs. In addition, unlike the younger members of the Kodokan who had only trained for competition judo, Yamashita had extensive experience of traditional jujutsu. He knew how to knock an aggressive attacker out.

Yamashita's fighting skill had proved invaluable on one occasion when he had been attacked in a Tokyo restaurant by a gang of seventeen laborers. Along with a friend from the Kodokan he had cooly disposed of the aggressors. As one of the two judo experts knocked a laborer senseless, the other heaved the unconscious body through the door until a heap of bodies lay in the street outside. On another occasion Yamashita had been dining in an upstairs restaurant when a drunken ruffian suddenly attacked him. Yamashita threw the man down the stairs and had already forgotten about the incident when his attacker returned with fourteen friends. Yamashita dealt with the gang by simply standing at the top of the stairs and tossing his attackers one after another back to the bottom as they ran at him. His throws were merciless, several of the men were badly injured and one suffered a broken neck. Yamashita was charged with assault over this incident. He was acquitted in court but was not treated so leniently by Kano who strongly disapproved of any kind of violent behavior outside the judo hall. He suspended

Yamashita from the Kodokan for a period but the incident had been long forgotten by the time Kano decided to send this streetwise, intelligent man to teach the Americans.

In the autumn of 1903 the thirty eight year old Yamashita, his wife, and a nineteen year old assistant sailed to Seattle. Sam Hill, the businessman who had issued the invitation, wanted to show this wonderful fighting art to America and so he quickly arranged for Yamashita and his assistant to give a demonstration in front of an invited audience of journalists and curious onlookers. At first it went badly. Few in the crowd understood the purpose of judo kata and they were deeply unimpressed by the prearranged moves. Some in the audience began to mutter that judo looked more like gymnastics than fighting. Hill decided to try to change the mood in the hall by calling a British boxer up onto the stage to spar with Yamashita. The boxer, who weighed almost one hundred kilograms, did his best to knock out the judo man but he had the worse of the encounter.

> I confess I have never been up against such a slippery customer as the little Jap. To land him fairly on the head or body was impossible. He avoided punishment by falling backwards or forwards, and once even passed between my legs, almost throwing me as he did so, and recovering his feet behind me in time to avoid a vicious back-hand swing ... Once he had come to close quarters a certain fall for me was the result. After taking three or four heavy tosses, I had had enough of it. (23)

The Fighting President

After his stay in Seattle Yamashita travelled onwards to Washington and was there introduced to the naval attaché at the new Japanese embassy, Lieutenant Commander Isamu Takeshita. Takeshita would later become one of the most important members of the martial arts world in Tokyo but for now his biggest ambition was to impress the Americans. After meeting Yamashita he decided to arrange a demonstration of judo at the White House for the President himself. The rambunctious and physically fearless Theodore Roosevelt had been an enthusiastic reader of Nitobe's Bushido and he was eager to see how a real Japanese fighter performed.

Roosevelt arranged that his friend Grant, the middleweight wrestling champion of America, would be in attendance and would stage a demonstration bout with the judo fighter. Yamashita was realizing that his American hosts expected him to grapple with their largest and most determined men. On the evening after the demonstration Roosevelt described what he had seen in a letter to his son.

> It was very interesting, but of course jiu jitsu and our wrestling are so far apart that it is difficult to make any comparison between them. Wrestling is simply a sport with rules almost as conventional as those of tennis, while jiu jitsu is really meant for practice in killing or disabling our adversary. In

consequence, Grant did not know what to do except to put Yamashita on his back, and Yamashita was perfectly content to be on his back. Inside of a minute Yamashita had choked Grant, and inside of two minutes more he got an elbow hold on him that would have enabled him to break his arm; so that there is no question but that he could have put Grant out. (23)

Roosevelt was impressed and attracted by what he had seen of judo and came to the conclusion that he wanted to master the art. The burly politician had a room in the White House converted into a judo dojo and for two months he made it his practice to invite any of his visitors who were in sound physical condition to visit the judo room where he would enthusiastically throw them around. Yamashita gave lessons to the President for a while but he must have been delighted when Roosevelt's interest in judo finally waned. The heavy and determined Roosevelt liked to attack with vigor and Yamashita was forced to exert great care to control the President without causing serious injury to the man and thereby damaging Japan's diplomatic relations with America.

With his duties at the White House now completed Yamashita was, at Roosevelt's insistence, given a teaching position at the US Naval Academy. He gave judo lessons to the cadets for eighteen months but the young soldiers were never entirely convinced by the strange Asian art. The moral instruction and the subtle techniques of judo largely went over the heads of the students and most of them were highly skeptical that anything they learned would be effective in a real fight. With his adventure at an end Yamashita returned to Japan to become one of judo's senior statesmen. He left no students behind in America other than a small group of Japanese immigrant farmers in Seattle who quietly continued to practice judo among themselves. But the Japanese Embassy regarded the visit of Yamashita as a public relations triumph. They sent messages to the Kodokan urgently requesting that more judo experts be sent to America.

Count Koma

To their surprise, the Embassy found that another judo expert was already in the United States. While Yamashita had been teaching judo to the naval cadets another member of the 'Four Guardians of the Kodokan' decided to make a journey to see modern America for himself. Tsunejiro Tomita had been Kano's very first registered student and was the first judo fighter to receive a black belt from Kano. He arrived in New York early in 1905 hoping to somehow establish himself as a judo instructor in that great city. Tomita was thirty nine years old when he arrived and, like Yamashita, brought a younger assistant along with him to help give demonstrations. This young man, Mitsuyo Maeda, would prove to be the greatest judo traveller of the pre-war years. Maeda was twenty six years old and already held a fourth dan in judo. He was a tough and skillful fighter who had defeated many jujutsu fighters in open competition.

In the judo hierarchy Tomita easily outranked Maeda but it was the younger man who would prove to be the more influential of the two.

Almost immediately after they arrived in America Tomita and Maeda set about putting on demonstrations for large crowds at Columbia University and at Princeton. They needed all of their confidence and courage in giving these demonstrations as the students would inevitably call for the largest and toughest among them to be given a chance to spar with the Japanese. At Princeton a football player and the gymnastics instructor were chosen and were soundly defeated. But things did not go so well for the judo missionaries at the West Point military academy. After impatiently watching a demonstration of judo throws the cadets nominated one of their own to fight the Japanese. Maeda, whom Tomita had brought along for exactly this kind of encounter, easily won his fight. But the crowd demanded that they wanted to see Tomita fighting. He was, after all, the higher ranked of the two Japanese. This time the cadets nominated a huge football player who began his attack on Tomita by rushing into a headlong football tackle. Tomita attempted a tomoe nage throw by falling onto his back so that he could pivot the attacker through the air. But the football player was so heavy that Tomita's leg crumpled under the weight and he and was pinned helplessly under the student's bulky body. It was a very public disgrace for the Japanese. They continued to tour universities but once again opinions were mixed as to how effective this oriental fighting art really was.

The two men returned to New York where they opened the city's first judo club. Tomita stayed to spend five years in New York as a judo coach before returning to Japan in 1910. But Maeda soon drifted away from his senior. He was young, energetic and thrilled by what he had seen of the world outside Japan. And he soon found, to his great surprise, that there was money to be made by fighting. In 1905 professional fights were a major source of entertainment for the American public. Many of these contests were like primitive versions of the mixed martial arts competitions of today. Wrestlers, boxers and occasionally characters who claimed to be jiu jitsu experts competed for cash prizes. Very often these matches were fixed but the pattern varied. At times they could be grueling tests of strength and endurance with the fighters sparring round after round until one of them collapsed in exhaustion. A fighter needed great strength, confidence and showmanship to make a successful living in this world.

Breaking away from the New York judo club Maeda began to travel from tournament to tournament through the southern United States and then made his way via Cuba to Europe. He fought in a bewildering variety of matches, winning more often than he lost. While in Spain he somehow acquired the stage name of Count Koma, or Count Trouble, a name that may have been a reference to Maeda's perpetual money worries between fights. When he returned to North America Maeda teamed up with Soishiro Satake, one of his old friends from the Kodokan, and the two men collaborated to put on a number of dramatic confrontations. In Mexico City they announced that they would fight each other for the "World Jujutsu Championship". They roundly abused each other in the press and eventually fought each other twice, the two 'enemies' each winning one fight. Maeda seems to have supplemented his income during his stay in Mexico by offering to fight any willing member of the public. He promised a reward of one hundred pesos to any challenger he was unable to throw and five hundred pesos to anyone who could throw him.

In 1914 Maeda arrived in Brazil, the country where he would spend the greater part of his remaining life. He quickly made himself famous throughout the nation in a series of impressive demonstrations and sensational fights. In one of these matches he faced a much larger exponent of the native Brazilian fighting art of capoeira. His opponent was allowed to wield a knife but Maeda was able to overcome the armed man. The Japanese fighter decided to settle in Brazil where he established the nation's first judo club and became heavily involved in helping the crowds of Japanese immigrants who were traveling to Brazil at this time to establish farming communities in the countryside.

Maeda is believed to have taken part in more than two thousand public matches during his life. He was victorious in most of these matches, regularly defeating much larger opponents and he was never defeated in a match where both men followed judo rules. This adventurer never returned to Japan and buried his bones in Brazil. He had been one of the first Japanese martial artists in the twentieth century to make a living by fighting commercially. As a result the Kodokan hierarchy regarded him with some distaste. But after his death they did reevaluate his life and recognized the role that Maeda had played in pioneering the overseas spread of judo. The Kodokan awarded Maeda with a posthumous 7th dan in 1941.

Maeda is a particularly important figure in martial arts history for the role he played in helping to create a distinctively Brazilian form of judo, Brazilian jiu jitsu. One of Maeda's many Brazilian students was Carlos Gracie and he, in turn, passed on his knowledge of judo to his younger and more gifted brother Helio. Helio Gracie is regarded as the founder of a Brazilian form of grappling that would become internationally popular in the 1990s and would play a key role in the development of mixed martial arts competitions. Brazilian jiu jitsu places great emphasis on grappling in a prone position and it has been speculated that this can be linked to the date of Maeda's departure from Japan, a time when Kodokan judo was itself dominated by fighters who preferred using locks and chokes over throws. The Gracie family has acknowledged the vital role that Maeda played in shaping their style. His experience of fighting public bouts in many countries, they suggest, made him a uniquely pragmatic and effective fighter.

While Maeda was approaching the end of his life his teacher Jigoro Kano died at sea. The year was 1938 and Kano had been returning to Japan from the scene of one of his greatest triumphs, the Olympic committee meeting that approved the award of the 1940 Olympic Games to Tokyo. After Kano's death his students created a unique honor for the founder of judo by awarding him a posthumous grade of 12th dan. Martial arts grades in Japan normally rise no higher than 10th dan so Kano's grade was a one off. Kano deserved this special recognition for the crucial role he had played in reshaping the Japanese martial arts for the modern age.

Jigoro Kano lived to see his own brand of judo become one of the leading sports of Japan. Judo clubs existed in every school, town and university and millions were training in judo halls every day. He died as a famous and respected statesman and yet there must have been a good deal of sadness in his final years. Kano had been an advocate for peace, a liberal voice in a nation that was now in the hands of hardline militarists. Even his beloved judo had grown so large that he had no longer been able to personally shape its direction. As competitive judo began to overshadow all other aspects of the sport Kano had often reflected on the idealistic speech he had given at the opening of his first, tiny Kodokan training hall. Judo, he had promised, would be dedicated to creating healthy, moral and progressive human beings. In his later years Kano wondered if that aspiration had slipped out of his grasp.

The Moment Before
Kano's idealistic vision for judo did survive. That it did so is largely due to the influence of Kano's greatest student, Kyuzo Mifune. Mifune was a wraith of a man who never weighed more than fifty kilograms. But he had an almost supernatural timing and a sense of balance that allowed him to easily defeat much larger opponents. The dignified, calm, gifted presence of Mifune in the Kodokan during the years before and after the Second World War was a physical reminder of Kano's boyhood dream that technique and skill could overcome the greatest strength.

Mifune joined the Kodokan in 1903 at a time when Kano was still presiding over every detail of the organization. Just signing up for training had been a far from simple matter. Mifune was forced to pester one of the Kodokan's senior instructors in order to secure an introduction to Kano. He then had to endure an interview with the great man himself and sign his name in blood to the Kodokan rules.

Mifune was a brilliant student. He was never defeated in a Kodokan tournament and by the age of thirty he had already been promoted to 6th dan. Despite his small size he was more than capable of taking care of himself in the world outside the dojo. On one occasion he and another judo expert were attacked in a Tokyo restaurant by a gang of thirteen thieves. The judo men knocked the entire gang senseless within three minutes. At the age of forty Mifune was still competing and he was able to defeat a sumo wrestler twice his size in a challenge match. He was awarded the highest possible grade, tenth dan, in 1945.

Kano had opened his first school and launched judo as a new fighting style on the basis of his realization of the importance of breaking the balance of an opponent before applying a throw. Mifune was the ultimate exponent of Kano's thinking in this area. Like the great masters of sword fighting he was able to read his opponent's intention in advance and apply a devastating counterattack at the very instant his opponent moved forward.

> It is quite natural that you should apply a technique the moment when the opponent reveals a broken form, but it is more important to read the opponent's intention quickly and apply a technique the moment just before his broken form is revealed. (24)

In the years after the war it was the memorable sight of Mifune, a tiny white-haired man in his seventies, confidently throwing large young men around the Kodokan dojo that convinced many foreign visitors that his art deserved further investigation.

Tree Feller

If the effortless ability of a great teacher like Mifune was one expression of Kano's legacy, another was represented in the explosive fighting power of Masahiko Kimura. Kimura has been described as the greatest judo fighter of the Showa Era (1926-1989) and in the years around the Second World War he was certainly the strongest fighter in Japan. Whereas Mifune could rely on perfect timing to throw opponents, Kimura's success stemmed from a fantastic physical strength that made his throws devastatingly powerful. He fought before the time when weight categories were introduced to judo competition but Kimura, who was only 170 centimeters tall, made the most of his size. At his peak his body was sculpted from eighty five kilograms of solid muscle.

Kimura was born with a fighter's spirit. His introduction to the world of judo came at elementary school when he found out that a teacher who had been punishing him happened to be a black belt in judo. The young Kimura decided to become a second dan in judo so that he could throw his teacher around. As a junior high school student he became obsessed with the sport and began to train with his club before classes began in the morning and again after school ended. Even as a schoolboy he would often work out for five hours in a day and regularly did three hundred push ups. Before long he was throwing the other boys in his school around with ease. At the age of fifteen he travelled to the Butokukai headquarters in Kyoto to take the nationally recognized grading exam. He was awarded a third dan in judo and in the following year, at the unprecedentedly early age of sixteen, he became a fourth dan.

This teenage fighter was invincible. Other boys did their best to avoid having to tussle with him in the dojo and were polite to him outside school. It was only when he entered Takushoku University, a place notorious for the toughness of its martial arts clubs, that Kimura finally reached his limits. He decided to make an attempt on the test for fifth dan but it was a truly grueling examination. Kimura was required to fight over and over again against other fourth dan students. Although he was the youngest student taking the test he managed to defeat eight opponents in a row. But by the ninth fight his strength had run out and he succumbed to defeat. Kimura refused to be downcast. He had, after all, won almost all of his fights. Quite naturally he went to a bar to celebrate his promotion to fifth dan. This was the 1930s, however, and the atmosphere in Japanese martial arts clubs was intense. When one of his teachers heard that Kimura had been defeated in a single bout he pulled him aside and slapped him repeatedly in the face.

> A judo match is like a real fight to the death between samurai. Throwing your opponent is like killing him. Being thrown is like being killed. You killed eight opponents and were killed by the ninth. Remember, if you want to make judo your life you have to throw all of your opponents, no matter how many dozens of them come at you. Understand? (25)

Kimura faced his hardest test in 1935. For the first time in years he experienced four defeats including a fight with a tough police officer who threw him so hard onto his head that he was knocked out. But after he turned twenty Kimura would never again be defeated in a judo competition. He trained like a demon and took every opportunity to practice. At the end of 1935 he paid a visit to the judo club of another university and found that his growing fame had preceded him. Fifty black belts were waiting to spar with Kimura. He took on all fifty, sparring continuously for four hours without a break. At the end of the night he was exhausted but felt that he could achieve anything.

Two years later Kimura won his first All-Japan championship. The tournament was fought without weight categories and in the final Kimura was matched against a much bigger opponent. They struggled over two exhausting rounds of fifteen minutes each, often crashing off the raised platform into the spectators. After thirty minutes neither fighter had gained an advantage and as they kneeled to prepare for the extension period Kimura found that he was so tired that he could hardly untie his judo belt to straighten his jacket. Desperately, he looked over at his opponent and saw that the other man was rubbing his calves. He had been hurt. As the fight restarted Kimura immediately began to sweep at the other man's legs. After some time the opponent crumbled and Kimura was able to throw him. The fight had lasted for forty grueling minutes, but he was now the champion of Japan.

After this famous victory Kimura began to wonder how he could stay at the top. He had been able to defeat opponents with greater experience and size simply because he had trained with such intensity. Most serious judo competitors trained for around three hours per day. Kimura had been outmatching his rivals by doing six hours of training per day but now, he believed, some would redouble their effort. He decided that he would make a triple effort. He would stay ahead of the pack by training for nine hours every day.

Kimura began to rise at 5.30 in the morning and, after cleaning his room, commenced physical conditioning. He had spent some time studying karate and knew that karate men had a powerful grip. Kimura emulated their methods by striking a makiwara post one thousand times each morning and by thrusting his fingers repeatedly into a sandbox. He would do more than one thousand consecutive push-ups and would bunny hop for more than a kilometer. This was just the beginning of his day. After breakfast Kimura would spar for two hours at the dojo of the Tokyo Metropolitan Police. Then he would spend two hours in the afternoon with his own university club before riding the train to practice at the Kodokan for an hour. In the evening he would relax by sparring at a local judo club for one final hour. Here the competition was not so fierce and he could concentrate on perfecting his technique.

It was a grueling routine and Kimura had a huge appetite. While the average Japanese salaryman might eat two bowls of rice with his dinner, Kimura would wolf down fourteen. At midnight he sometimes made his way to a local forest. He would pull tree trunks towards his body and try to fell them with a leg sweep. Usually he went to bed at one or two in the morning. This fierce training routine made Kimura so powerful that the other judo students began to avoid him in the practice hall. Many of them had received concussions from his irresistible throws that began with devastating leg sweeps. He felt at that time, he later wrote, like a modern day samurai. If he had lived in the days of Miyamoto Musashi he knew that he would have been swinging a sword.

Kimura went on to dominate the all-Japan championships for the following two years. In 1940, as war fever and Emperor worship mounted, Kimura won a special tournament of the top judo fighters that was staged for His Divine Majesty. After the war years Kimura once again became the dominant force in Japanese judo and won the first all-Japan championship to be held after the war in 1949. But like millions of other Japanese people at that time Kimura was broke and unemployed. In 1950 with his wife in hospital and bills to be paid he decided to join a new professional judo organization. He quickly proved to be the strongest of that group of fighters but the experiment with professional judo was stillborn and Kimura had to look for another way of paying the medical bills. He accepted an invitation to tour Hawaii, giving demonstrations of sparring in front of large crowds. Kimura took on anyone who was willing to face him and found, as he later admitted, that it was a great joy to be able to toss Americans around. Back at home the occupiers would never have allowed a Japanese person to treat them in such a way.

A Moral Victory

Kimura's next overseas adventure took him to Brazil where he was one of three Japanese judo experts who toured the country to demonstrate and explain their art. Kimura did not know when he arrived that he was about to fight his most famous match, the legendary battle with Helio Gracie. Helio had grown up as a sickly child and had spent years quietly watching from the sidelines as his older brother Carlos studied judo with Mitsuyo Maeda. When he took up the martial arts Helio adapted the judo techniques of Maeda to better suit his own slight build. He became an expert at ground fighting. He would pull an opponent to the floor and then use one of a wide repertoire of chokes and arm locks to gain a submission. This fighting style was given the name of Brazilian Jiu-Jitsu and Helio turned out to be a brilliant publicist for his art. Before the three Japanese judo fighters arrived in Brazil in 1951 he had already staged a series of dramatic public bouts with fighters from a range of martial disciplines. As soon as the Japanese team arrived in Brazil Helio issued a challenge.

The prospect of a showdown between the local hero and these visitors from Asia became a sensation in the Brazilian press. After some discussion a series of rules was agreed for the matches. To the great disadvantage of the Japanese it was agreed that no points would be awarded for throws or immobilizations. Forcing the opponent into submission with a lock or a choke, or knocking them unconscious would be the only route to victory. Even with this advantage, Helio still worried about the throwing ability of the Japanese. He arranged for the floor of the ring to be softened so that however hard they threw him his injuries would be limited.

Shockingly, the first Japanese contender, a man named Kato, was defeated. The Brazilian students of Gracie carried a coffin through the streets of Rio de Janeiro. "Japanese judo," they shouted, "is dead." Until this point the Japanese visitors had been lionized by the Brazilian press and had drawn large crowds to their exhibition tour. But now that it had been demonstrated that they were not invincible the crowds began to melt away. Kimura felt that it was up to him to rescue the reputation of judo and so he offered to fight Gracie himself. He was confident that he was the stronger man of the two but he also knew that Gracie had enough skill and determination to stay in a match until a draw had been secured. It would be a huge moral victory for the Brazilian champion if he could remain undefeated by the strongest fighter from Japanese judo.

The fight took place in front of a baying crowd of twenty thousand spectators that included the President and Vice-President of Brazil. When he arrived Kimura found, to his amusement, that the

Brazilian fans had placed a coffin at ringside to carry his corpse away at the end of the match. The crowd pelted him with raw eggs. As the fight began Kimura was able to release his tension by throwing Gracie around the ring but, just as in the match with Kato, Gracie shrugged off these throws and no points were awarded. Kimura began to throw Gracie onto his head, trying to knock him out but the soft surface of the ring made this almost impossible. Finally, Kimura pinned his taller, thinner rival and applied a chokehold. He waited for his opponent to tap the mat in submission but a tap never came. Puzzled by this Kimura assumed that he had failed to apply the chokehold correctly and released Gracie. Later in life Gracie admitted that he had, in fact, passed out while he was wondering whether to submit or not. Helio had promised his older brother that he would give up if he got into trouble but he had also been aware that the President was in the audience and he did have a reputation to protect.

Once again Kimura searched for a way to end the fight. He took Gracie in a painful shoulder lock and once again the incredibly tough and determined Brazilian refused to submit. As the packed stadium suddenly hushed Kimura tightened the lock further. There was a cracking sound. Gracie clearly had an astonishingly high pain threshold as, even now with his elbow broken, he did not submit. Kimura applied the lock again and once more a crack rang out over the quiet crowd. Carlos Gracie, Helio's older brother, threw in the towel. The following day one Brazilian newspaper carried this huge headline: VICTORY TO HELIO GRACIE. Above the headline, in small letters, the word 'moral' was appended.

Duel of the Century

After this famous victory in Brazil had been rapturously received by the Japanese press Kimura was drawn further and further into the seedy underworld of Japanese professional wrestling and fixed matches. He had been awarded a seventh dan by the Kodokan at the age of thirty but the inheritors of Kano's legacy strongly disapproved of these kind of commercial adventures and they never allowed Kimura to attain a higher grade.

In 1954 Kimura took part in a truly sensational bout with Rikidozan, the undoubted superstar of Japanese professional wrestling at that time. Rikidozan had been a sumo fighter. He was a huge, powerful figure whose gimmick of felling his opponents with 'karate chops' had made him famous. The match between the two was hyped to the skies, with newspapers pronouncing it to be the 'Duel of the Century'. But Kimura did not take the circus too seriously and described their meeting as 'show-business'. Amicably, the two men agreed on a set of prearranged moves that would result in a draw in the first match, allowing them to hold two further, and profitable, rematches.

The first meeting in the ring between Kimura and Rikidozan turned out to be very different from all expectations. For fifteen minutes the two men circled each other slowly and cautiously as they applied rather lame professional wrestling techniques. Then, perhaps infuriated by an accidental kick to the testicles from Kimura, Rikidozan suddenly lost his cool. What followed was a dramatic demonstration of the daylight that exists between a real fight and 'wrestling'. Rikidozan began to pound a bemused Kimura around the head and, with the judo man looking to the referee for some protection from this unexpected assault, Rikidozan slapped him to the ground and began to kick him in the face. Finally, a powerful strike to Kimura's neck knocked him out cold.

Kimura had a wide circle of friends that included several Yakuza members and Mas Oyama, the founder of Kyokushin karate. They were in horror at this betrayal of the code of professional 'fighting' and angered by the humiliation of their friend who had been given no chance to defend himself. They would, they promised, have Rikidozan killed. Oyama even went as far as to make direct threats to Rikidozan in a nightclub but the huge wrestler does not seem to have been particularly intimidated. Rikidozan did have a bad end, many years later, when he succumbed to the wounds he received in a stabbing by a minor member of the Yakuza.

Kimura left the shady world of the professional fighting circuit behind and returned to judo as an instructor. When he applied his own fierce training methods to developing students he was able to develop a third career as an elite coach who produced several superb international fighters. Kimura died in 1993 and was mourned as perhaps the greatest judo fighter of them all. He had lived long enough to see the dawn of modern judo. As it became part of the Olympic movement judo moved in a direction that took it very far away from the temptations of professional spectacles. Networks of clubs in schools, universities and companies allowed the best fighters of the modern age to live and train as full-time competitors without financial worries. In the end judo was saved as a healthy, competitive sport. And the leaders of judo continued to promote their art as a path to developing a strong mind and a strong body. Jigoro Kano could rest easily in his grave.

10. Okinawa

In the Garden

Gichin Funakoshi had a secret. As darkness fell over the rice fields around his house the young Okinawan schoolmaster lit an oil lamp and changed out of his teacher's suit into loose, traditional clothing. Outside the night was pitch-black and moonless. Funakoshi needed the oil lamp to find his way along the rough path that led him to the house of Master Azato. As he arrived at the courtyard behind the house he noticed that two young men were already practicing the secret movements of tode. Standing alone they punched and kicked at the empty air with great force. Their eyes glared as if they were staring at an onrushing enemy and, in the warmth of the evening, sweat beaded on their foreheads.

Just a few years earlier these men would have been at risk of arrest by the island police for practicing a fighting art. Even now, in 1890, the old ways of training at night and in complete secrecy were still being followed. Master Azato sat on the veranda of his large house watching Funakoshi as he stretched and warmed up in preparation for practice. Azato said little to the students as he watched them and, if he made a comment, it would be terse and devoid of praise. Most often he would say nothing more than "again", or "harder this time."

Before the end of his life the young schoolteacher would become famous as the father of Japanese karate. Thanks to the efforts of Gichin Funakoshi this secret fighting art would spread beyond Okinawa to sweep the world, winning tens of millions of passionate adherents. But for now, in his twenties, Funakoshi was nothing more than a student who trained every night with his friends. He came to this courtyard to practice kata, an arranged series of moves that were performed as if in a fight against imaginary opponents. Each kata had fifty or more movements that included punches, kicks, blocks, evasions and attacks on vital points. Funakoshi had been repeating these kata over and over again for years. Training with great power and intensity he had acquired perfect balance and had learned to focus the muscles of his entire body into one, powerful strike.

Master Azato repeatedly told his students that they should think of their arms and legs as swords. He wanted them to be able to hit and kick with so much power that their blows would kill if they struck a vulnerable part of the body. The atmosphere in his garden courtyard was informal but Azato was a more serious teacher than he may have seemed to an outsider. His students knew that he expected them to give their all to training. The teacher had mastered many different kata but a new student would be assigned only one kata to practice. Every night, perhaps for as long as three years, the student would repeat the same kata over and over in front of the intent gaze of the Master. At some point after midnight Azato would at last allow his exhausted students to rest. They would gather around him, drinking water and tea to quench their thirst as they listened to him talk about the history of Okinawa and its fighting arts. When just a few hours remained before sunrise they would thank the Master, light their lamps, and begin the long, dark trudge back to home and bed.

Island Boy
Funakoshi was born in 1868, the same year that the Shogun was overthrown in Edo. His birthplace was a truly remote backwater; a most unlikely starting point for an international movement. Okinawa (the name means 'sea rope') is a long and thin island that is less than ten kilometers wide. It is the largest island of the Ryukyu group, a string of thirty two populated islands that stretch across the Pacific from the southern shores of Japan all the way to Taiwan and mainland China.

In 1890 Okinawa was an isolated and unimportant place with a population of around two hundred thousand people. The recent arrival of steamboats had made travel much easier but the island was still so cut off at this time that it felt like an independent kingdom, a place with its own customs and its own language. Although Okinawa certainly had a strong identity it had never been a strong state. For hundreds of years the islanders had been dominated by the great, distant empire of China and the fierce samurai of Satsuma, in southern Japan.

Funakoshi was a premature baby and a weakling of a child. He had been born into the upper class of Okinawan society, the shizoku. But, like many other members of the shizoku class that formed almost one-third of the population, the Funakoshi family was actually very poor. The poverty was made worse by his father's alcoholism. It was a dysfunctional family and the infant Funakoshi was sent to live with his grandparents. However, a turning point in the highly unpromising life of this boy arrived on the day that he found a teacher of tode, the old unarmed fighting art of the island.

Becoming a student of tode was no easy matter as there were no professional teachers and those who did practice the fighting art were under orders to never discuss their training with outsiders. Funakoshi just happened to be in the same elementary school class as the son of Master Azato. Making use of this connection he became a student of Azato at the age of eleven and began a daily practice of the martial arts that he would continue for the rest of his long life. He continued to be small, never surpassing 150 centimeters in height, but the tode training gradually transformed his frail body into one that was tough and muscled. From the age of eleven to the end of his life Funakoshi had a ruddy complexion that glowed with rude health. As an old man he liked to boast that he had never needed medicine or received an injection.

Master Azato must have been an overwhelming figure for the eleven year old Funakoshi. He was tall and powerful, a skilled horseman and archer and an expert swordsman who, most unusually for an Okinawan man, had actual experience of sword duels. Azato was also a scholar, he was well read in the Chinese classics and had a passion for Okinawan history. At first Funakoshi found that he was the only student of Azato and for a while he was able to enjoy the undivided attention of one of the few Okinawan fighting experts who also had a good knowledge of both the Chinese and the Japanese martial arts.

Azato's home looked like a training camp for warriors. There were fixed and hanging posts for striking, a variety of swords and clubs, stone weights and iron balls for strength conditioning, and a wooden man for speed training. Such a teacher and such a place to train were rare on Okinawa. Funakoshi knew that he was lucky and he responded to Azato's teaching with an enthusiasm that carried him through years of repetitive and grueling practice. In old age Funakoshi remembered that he would often have to lie face down on the ground of Azato's courtyard, exhausted after performing dozens of kata at full intensity.

Although the new Meiji government in Tokyo had launched a nationwide reform program, the changes took some time to make their way to Okinawa. When they did arrive there was uproar. The most shocking announcement for the Okinawan upper class was that men would be expected to have their heads shaved. This was an outrage to the aristocratic islanders who were even more attached to their topknots than the mainland Japanese. Okinawa was swept with angry debate between those who agreed with the modernization program and those who wished to resist it to the end. Funakoshi's relatives were strongly opposed to the demeaning orders from Tokyo but Master Azato was in the progressive camp. He advised Funakoshi that if he wanted to make his mark in the world he would have to move with the times. With great reluctance Funakoshi had his own head shaved, took the qualifying exam for teachers and, at the age of 21, applied for work as an elementary school teacher.

He found it surprisingly easy to secure a job. Many of the teenage boys on Okinawa were furiously opposed to having their heads shaved and the schools, which were responsible for carrying out the actual shaving, were eager to employ teachers who were physically confident enough to control the unruly boys. He became a teacher, but a teacher at the very bottom of the island's school system. Funakoshi found that his salary was exceedingly small and that he was now expected to act as the breadwinner for an extended family of ten. It was a humble family that could not make ends meet without growing their own rice and vegetables but it would have been a public disgrace for a schoolmaster to be spotted working in the fields like a peasant. Funakoshi wore a large hat on the occasions when he helped his wife pull up the vegetables. Somehow he also found time to continue training with Master Azato and other tode experts. The official disapproval of martial arts on Okinawa was disappearing as the modernization reforms took hold and Funakoshi found that he could even allow some of the local boys to gather around his house in the daylight to practice kata.

Two Masters

At this time Japanese government officials were taking steps to absorb the culture of Okinawa into the mainstream of mainland life. But the Tokyo bureaucrats had to come to terms with a society that was distinctively different from their own, a place with its own ancient history and culture. The string of Ryukyu islands have been inhabited since prehistoric times. It was only at some point in the seventh century that traders and explorers began to make long and perilous sea journeys between China and Japan. Okinawa, situated half-way between those two growing nations, was a convenient stopping off point.

For many centuries it was China that dominated these islands. By the fourteenth century China was a magnificent civilization ruled by the Ming emperors who were willing to trade with outlying states and to grant recognition to their kings and princes on the condition that proper tribute was paid and protocol observed. It was in this light that official representatives of the Okinawan kingdom were first brought to China and escorted to the huge, elaborate palace in the capital city of Nanking. On arrival they were encouraged to offer gifts and to kowtow (from the Chinese k'o-t'ou), a ritual procedure that involved a series of prostrations and bows in the direction of the emperor. With courtesies having been observed, Okinawa then became, in the minds of the Chinese government, a distant part of the Chinese empire. It was the start of a relationship that would continue for five hundred years, almost into modern times. A Chinese settlement was established in the port of Naha in southern Okinawa and Chinese culture began to flow freely into Okinawan life. Permanent Chinese residents in Naha raised their families and lived in much the same way as people did on mainland China. The presence of these settlers was supplemented by visits of imperial legations, often numbering in the hundreds, from the Chinese court.

It is believed that the native fighting traditions of Okinawa predate even the arrival of the Chinese but there is no doubt that they were greatly influenced by the introduction of weaponless fighting systems that arrived with the Chinese settlers. The Japanese name for the unarmed Chinese martial arts is kenpo, a word that means 'law of the fist'. Kenpo had already evolved over many centuries in China before it first arrived in Okinawa. Some accounts of the origins of kenpo trace the art as far back as the arrival of the great monk Bodidharma, who travelled to China from India in around 550 A.D.

Bodidharma is the legendary figure who introduced Buddhism to East Asia and established Zen Buddhism in China. When he first arrived in Henan Province Bodidharma, according to the legend, spent nine years sitting in meditation in a cave. One day he fell asleep in the middle of his meditation. Waking, he was so disgusted by his own slackness that he cut off his eyelids where, dropping to the floor of the cave, they flowered into the first tea plants.

On emerging from this long seclusion Bodidharma settled in the nearby Shaolin Monastery. He found that the monks there did not have enough strength to engage in long periods of meditation and were defenseless against attack from bandits. He decided to teach the monks a series of exercises that were the basis for a form of weaponless self-defense.

These, at any rate, are the founding legends of the Shaolin Monastery which did become an important centre for the practice of unarmed martial arts in China at a time when only aristocrats were allowed to possess weapons. Modern kenpo can be traced to the sixteenth century and to a Shaolin monk named Zhue Yuen who reorganized the fighting systems of his monastery and categorized training methods and techniques into five groups that he named after animals: tiger, crane, leopard, dragon and snake. In the seventeenth century the Shaolin temples were destroyed by government troops and the monks scattered across China. They took with them the fighting styles that would become modern Chinese kenpo.

On Okinawa the popularity of unarmed fighting systems is believed to date back to the fifteenth century. After a long civil war Sho Hashi became the king of a newly unified Okinawa island and one of his first decisions was to impose a ban on the possession of all weapons. His grandson Sho Shin reinforced the ban. He ordered that the swords of even the aristocrats should be collected and held in a central storehouse. Despite these bans, Okinawa never became an entirely peaceful island and the unarmed people took a natural interest in effective methods of self-defense. Hand fighting arts became prominent, as did weapons systems that made use of everyday objects such as walking staffs and rice sickles.

The Okinawan kings came to regret their ban on weapons. In the years after the Battle of Sekigahara in 1600 the Satsuma samurai from southern Kyushu, who had fought on the losing side in the great war for control of all Japan, found that they were hemmed in. Under the stern rule of Tokugawa Ieyasu they could no longer risk wars of expansion with their northern neighbors. The only remaining outlet for their ambitions was the southern islands, a place so far away that no one in Edo thought it to be worth very much attention.

In February 1609 a fleet of ships carrying three thousand samurai from Satsuma set sail for Okinawa. The island defenders were hastily equipped with unfamiliar weapons from government stores and the Okinawan army put up the bravest resistance they could. But they were no match for the battle-hardened samurai from Kyushu. By April the samurai had occupied all of Okinawa. They ransacked the castle at

Shuri and forced the Okinawan king to sail to Kyushu. He was made to sign a humiliating 'treaty' in which he apologized for his crimes and acknowledged the right of the Shimazu family to rule Okinawa.

This demeaning treatment of the Okinawan king is still remembered on the island today. At the signing ceremony one of the king's officials, a man named Rizan, refused to sign the surrender documents and was immediately put to death. One popular version of the story of Rizan's death relates that he was sentenced to be boiled alive in oil. He was a master of an early form of karate and asked his captors to allow him to practice his exercises one last time before his execution. He was released from his chains and began to perform his kata. Just as the guards moved in to take him to his death Rizan suddenly took hold of two of the guards. With his powerful grip he dragged them behind him into the vat of boiling oil where all three men perished. This dramatic final act of revenge was commemorated for centuries on the flag of the Okinawan kingdom. The bodies of the three dead men spinning on the surface of the oil formed a distinctive pattern that may have been the origin of the symbolic shape, the hidari gomon, that can still be seen everywhere in Okinawa today.

Life under the rule of the Shimazu was hard for the people of Okinawa. Taxes equivalent to more than one fifth of the entire national output of the islands were imposed. The Shimazu family held complete control over the islands but they encouraged the Okinawans to continue trading with China and even to maintain the fiction that Okinawa was still part of the Chinese empire. The Japanese occupiers wanted a lively trade with the Asian mainland as this produced great profits for the Shimazu. The Japanese rulers renewed and further tightened the ban on weapons of any kind, making it illegal for any Okinawan person to possess or import swords.

Chinese Hand
These unique conditions on the small island of Okinawa - the military occupation, the weapons ban and the cultural influence of both China and Japan - gave shape to the underground fighting styles that would later evolve into modern karate. All over the island, but particularly in the capital of Shuri, the nearby port town of Naha and the village of Tomari, groups of men began to meet in secret to practice unarmed fighting. Some of their techniques dated back to the indigenous fighting arts of the island but a greater number of the techniques were of Chinese origin. Fighting systems had arrived with the community of Chinese settlers and others were brought back from China by Okinawans who had lived there. Less importantly, there was a certain influence on Okinawan fighting styles from the samurai culture of Japan and the jujutsu of the Satsuma samurai. The illegality of weapons encouraged the Okinawans to train extensively in ways of using hardened parts of the body to inflict injury. Among the Okinawans their fighting system was commonly known by the simple name of te (手 is pronounced as 'ti' in the Okinawan dialect and means 'hand'). In the nineteenth century the term tode 唐手, meaning

'Chinese hand', came into use and by the end of the nineteenth century an alternative reading of the same characters, karate 唐手, began to appear.

Most of the karate practiced in Japan today can be traced back to the central strand of Okinawan karate Shorin Ryu. The name comes from Shorinji, the Japanese name for the Shaolin monastery. The origins of this style on Okinawa are somewhat obscure but can certainly be traced to the early nineteenth century and the birth of a great teacher named Sokon Matsumura. Matsumura was already a strong fighter by a young age and was appointed as a bodyguard to the king of Okinawa. He went on to serve three kings over a span of fifty years as a bodyguard and a chief military officer. His important position at the court enabled him to take part in diplomatic missions to both China and Japan and he is believed to have used these trips to develop his fighting skills. Matsumura also took fighting lessons in Okinawa from a local expert named Sakugawa. Sakugawa had studied White Crane kenpo and had created a kata named Kushanku in honor of his own Chinese teacher.

Matsumura was a fierce man with a penetrating gaze but he was also a free thinker who set about reshaping the unarmed fighting style of his native island. Chinese kenpo makes a far greater use of circular movements than the direct, powerful karate of Okinawa and Matsumura is believed to be the person who brought about the shift to a more linear style. He introduced several important Chinese kata such as naihanchi and seishan to the Okinawan training circles and personally created some kata including bassai and chinto. That, at least, is the view of Matsumura held by most scholars. In reality, the secrecy that surrounded the martial arts on Okinawa during the eighteenth and nineteenth centuries meant that almost no written records were kept. The pre-history of Okinawan karate is largely an oral history, a history that may have been exaggerated or distorted by loyal students.

Matsumura's technique is said to have been fast and penetrating. He believed that regular training would enable a karate student to develop "the spirit of a ferocious tiger and the speed of a flying swift" (25). He lived to a great old age and was still alive when Funakoshi began to study karate. The younger man was even able to take some lessons from this master. But it was the direct students of Matsumura who were the teachers of Funakoshi and who passed on the ideas of their teacher. This generation of experts were the true creators of a karate for the modern age.

The greatest of these teachers was Anko Itosu, an individual whom Matsumura himself described as the strongest karate man of his time. Itosu was a close friend of Master Azato and later became the second of Funakoshi's beloved teachers. Like so many other karate legends he was small and frail as a child and was sent to Matsumura to build up strength. Matsumura liked to make his students harden their hands on a makiwara, a straw pad attached to a wooden post that has been driven into the ground. His students would strike the pad hundreds of times every day, toughening their knuckles and making their wrists thick enough to absorb the impact of a powerful punch. The young Itosu was keen enough to want to continue his practice at home and so he tied a leather sandal to a garden wall as a target for his punches. When the stone behind the sandal began to crumble the boy shifted his footwear to another spot. In the end the entire wall collapsed.

As a man Itosu had incredible strength and a punch that was like the kick of a bull. In later years Funakoshi described an incident from Itosu's life that demonstrated his strength and self-confidence. He had been just about to enter a restaurant one evening when a mugger punched him sharply in the side. Without breaking stride the karate man absorbed the blow, took hold of his attacker's wrist and continued his progress into the restaurant. Taking a seat Itosu proceeded to order food and drink. Then, using his free hand, Itosu raised his drink and with his other hand dragged the terrified attacker into his view for the first time. Smiling, he remarked, "I don't know what your problem is, but let's have a drink together."

Itosu was close to the Okinawan royal family and served as a secretary to the last king. He had a high-minded view of karate, an outlook on the martial arts that deeply influenced his student Funakoshi. He saw karate as a potentially deadly form of fighting that should never be used except to defend life. Karate was not for brawling in the street but for the cultivation of a healthy body and a settled mind. On the surface this seemed to be paradoxical but Itosu firmly believed that a man who knew how to fight should devote his life to creating a peaceful society.

- In order to protect one's parents or one's master, it is proper to attack a foe regardless of one's own life. Never attack a lone adversary. If one meets a villain or a ruffian one should not use tode but simply parry and step aside.

- The purpose of tode is to make the body hard like stones and iron; hands and feet should be used like the points of arrows; hearts should be strong and brave.

- Tode cannot be learned quickly. Like a slow moving bull, that eventually walks a thousand miles, if one studies seriously every day, in three or four years one will understand what tode is about. The very shape of one's bones will change.

- During practice you should imagine you are on the battlefield. When blocking and striking make the eyes glare, drop the shoulders and harden the body. Now block the enemy's punch and strike! Always practice with this spirit so that, when on the real battlefield, you will naturally be prepared. (26)

Itosu wrote these words in 1908 at a time when he was attempting to usher karate out from the shadows. They form part of a letter in which he urged the introduction of tode instruction to all Okinawan schools as a prelude to its introduction throughout Japan. Itosu argued that the physical toughening and character building produced by Okinawan karate were just what Japanese society needed if it wanted to develop as a modern imperial nation.

The thinking of many progressive Okinawan leaders was undergoing a remarkable transformation. Okinawa had been persecuted by the Japanese and Itosu, who had been close to the Okinawan royal family, must have been involved in the elaborate measures that were taken to conceal karate from the Japanese rulers. But like many of the Okinawan people Itosu came to change his mind about Japan. Difficult circumstances had transformed his view of the mainland Japanese as unwelcome invaders. Now he saw full integration in the Japanese nation as the only possible future for his island.

Darkness Prevails
During Itosu's childhood Okinawa had been an island in the grip of a terrible poverty. Typhoons, diseases, earthquakes and droughts were regular afflictions and these miseries were made even more painful by the tyrannical and punitive rule of the samurai from Satsuma. The king of Okinawa expressed the bitter feelings of his entire people in the 1820s.

> Darkness prevails; nobody awakens ... both the ruler and the people are hard pressed, and are robbed by those among them whose storehouses are filled with spoils. (27)

The Okinawans were forced to pay taxes they could ill afford to the Japanese and at the same time they had to maintain the elaborate deception that they were still a loyal part of the Chinese empire. Okinawan trade was enormously profitable for the Satsuma lords. It was one of the very few ways that Chinese goods could reach the world lay lay beyond the Chinese empire and also one of the only ways for Japanese goods to pass beyond that nation's strictly controlled borders. The Okinawans strongly resented the way they were being squeezed between these two great Asian nations. But still worse was to come in the middle of the nineteenth century when Western powers including Russia, America, Britain and France began to turn their avaricious eyes towards Okinawa, considering the island as an interesting location for their own trading ambitions.

A truly disturbing event for the almost unarmed people of Okinawa came with the arrival of Commodore Perry in 1853 as he sailed towards his epochal encounter with the Japanese mainland. By the time he arrived Perry had already decided to establish a base on Okinawa from which to conduct relations with the Japanese government and he treated the local officials with a calculated rudeness. Perry informed those islanders who met with him that he wished to speak with the king of Okinawa and, whatever their objections, that he was determined to visit the palace at Shuri Castle.

On June 6th Perry, accompanied by two hundred heavily armed marines, set off to pay his most unwelcome respects. He found that the gates of the palace were closed and that a delegation of Okinawan officials was waiting to beg the Americans to instead attend a reception in another building. Perry responded by having two of his huge ship cannons pointed directly at the palace gates. After some time the gates swung open and the marines marched in to the sound of their band playing Hail Columbia. A frosty encounter then took place in one of the palace halls.

The humiliated Okinawan nobles were, naturally, unarmed during this meeting. Quietly standing among their ranks, however, were some of the island's greatest masters of unarmed combat - Matsumura, Itosu and Azato. These men, who could easily kill with their bare hands, would have been ready to fight to the death to protect their king. But in the end the tense reception finished peaceably enough. The Americans, again ignoring all protests, commandeered a building on the beach that they planned to use as a storehouse and settled in for a pleasant stay on the island. The sailors, delighted to be on shore on a tropical island, began to make expeditions to make purchases and to drink the local liquor. In general they were treated with the gentle patience that the islanders normally displayed to outsiders. But there was no forgiveness for one American sailor who broke into a home and raped a girl. He was pursued and stoned by an angry crowd until he fell into the harbor and drowned.

The shocking and rather frightening behavior of their Western visitors drove many Okinawans to conclude that they were too weak a people to protect themselves and that their destiny lay with their Japanese cousins to the north. And as they turned their eyes to Tokyo the turbulent events of the Meiji Restoration brought a resolution to many of the island's problems. Once more Okinawa became an irrelevance to the rest of the world. With ports being opened in every corner of Japan no country had any need to forcibly conscript this ocean bound island for use as a trading centre.

The reforms sweeping throughout Japan at the end of the nineteenth century were so radical and violent that they reached Okinawa almost as an afterthought. In 1879 the Japanese government announced that Okinawa was now a constituent prefecture of Japan. The king was stripped of his position and was required to live in Tokyo while Japanese troops occupied the palace at Shuri. As the island came under direct rule from the Japanese capital the local officials were instructed to implement the same reforms that had transformed the mainland. Men were required to shave their heads and children to learn Japanese. Among the Okinawan people there was an intense debate over whether these reforms should be resisted or wholeheartedly supported.

The Birth of Karate

Anko Itosu was fully in favor of the reforms. Above all, he wanted to bring the fighting arts he loved into the open and make them part of the modern educational system that was being created. In 1901 Itosu began to teach karate at an elementary school in Shuri. As he considered how he could best introduce his art to Okinawan children he set about making changes that would have a major influence on the future of karate. In the secretive nighttime classes overseen by Itosu his students were learning how to strike with every part of their body. Itosu taught more than one hundred different ways of inflicting injury. His kata were largely composed of techniques that were designed to break bones, to gouge eyes and testicles and to knock an opponent unconscious.

Clearly these violent elements of the karate curriculum were not suitable for the pre-teen students of an Okinawan elementary school. Itosu set about creating a form of karate that was safe for young children to practice. He simplified the techniques, concentrating on fist punches and low kicks, and removed many of the most dangerous moves. To help children learn the basic elements of karate he created a series of introductory katas known as the Pinan katas (Heian in some karate styles). Okinawan school classes were large and it would not be possible to teach so many students in the old, informal manner. Itosu decided to line the children up in rows and trained them to perform their kata in unison as he counted out the moves. Without knowing it, Itsou had created a template for the future of karate instruction.

Itosu worked for a long time to have karate incorporated into the educational system and in 1909 his efforts had a spectacular payoff when karate was adopted as part of the official curriculum of all Okinawan schools. Suddenly every school needed a karate teacher. Itosu, who was now in his seventies, and his senior students decided to target their efforts towards training recruits to the new teacher training college. In their classes at this institution the karate instructors passed on a simple, modern and safe brand of karate that the young graduates of the college then took to their new schools in every corner of Okinawa.

Prominent among the small group of senior students who helped Itosu to spread the karate gospel was Gichin Funakoshi. He was now his early forties and was an established expert in his own right but Funakoshi continued to train with Itosu and the other old masters of Okinawa. He was not, perhaps, the strongest karate fighter on the island but he was a dignified and disciplined individual who had been training in karate with great intensity for thirty years. In his autobiography Funakoshi describes how he would make use of the typhoons that regularly sweep through Okinawa by climbing onto the roof of his house to practice karate stances as the powerful winds buffeted his small body.

Unlike other Okinawan karate experts Funakoshi never became a street fighter. The island was a rough enough place at the beginning of the twentieth century and many of the older karate masters had opportunities to test their skills in encounters with bandits and street toughs. Itosu, however, had held the view that karate was something that should only be used in a life threatening emergency and Funakoshi strongly supported the moral stance of his teacher. He was frequently out after dark and could not completely avoid trouble but he usually talked his way out of tight spots or simply blocked the punches of attackers without hurting his assailants in any way.

Hard Soft

Shuri, where both Itosu and Funakoshi lived and worked, was the ancient capital of Okinawa. It was a town with a population in the nineteenth century of around thirty thousand people. Just a few kilometers away, in the port town of Naha, a very different type of karate was beginning to emerge. The fighting style that would in later years be known to the world as Goju Ryu karate was created by a young man named Kanryo Higaonna. As a teenager he had often fallen into conversation with the Chinese traders in his port town and had been fascinated by their amazing stories of the kenpo masters of mainland China. Many people in Naha practiced the Chinese katas but Higaonna had never seen anyone with the almost supernatural powers that the traders talked about.

Higaonna decided that he would travel to China to see real kenpo for himself. He sailed to Fuzhou, a coastal town that is close to modern Taiwan, but on arrival he found that he could not communicate in the local language and he struggled to make enough money to survive. After great difficulties he found the master of Chinese fighting that he had been searching for. Ryu Ryu Ko was a tall and powerful man who had trained in one of the southern Shaolin monasteries and had been a bodyguard of the king of Fukien before civil war had broken up the old kingdoms. He was a master of White Crane kenpo. When Higaonna arrived in Fuzhou Ryu Ryu Ko had fallen on hard times and was teaching only a handful of students. But Higaonna soon recognized that this was a truly skillful master and he became a passionate student. He is believed to have stayed for ten years in Fuzhou, undergoing tough daily body conditioning and practicing kata that had been designed to build great inner power. He trained for so many hours each day that he would often pass blood in his urine.

Higaonna returned to Okinawa at the end of the nineteenth century. He was now a master in his own right and was eager to teach his fellow islanders everything that he had learned. To his dismay he found that Okinawa had succumbed to a frenzy for all things Japanese and there was no one who wanted to listen to him talking about the old Chinese arts. It was years before Higaonna could attract a few students to train with him in the courtyard of the house belonging to his parents. His classes were tough and repetitive. The students lifted weights, hardened their hands and feet and practiced the kata Sanchin endlessly. Many of them gave up on this strange karate, deciding that it was simply too boring. But for those who stayed the benefits were profound. Hiagonna's long term students developed enormous strength and an unshakeable central force that made them almost impervious to kicks and blows.

One of the youths who joined Higaonna's courtyard class was Chojun Miyagi. He began training with the master at the age of fourteen and remained as his student for more than fifteen years. As Miyagi approached the age of thirty he decided that the time was right to follow in his master's footsteps by traveling to Fuzhou. He stayed there for a year, investigating the source of the techniques he had learned from Higaonna. But when he returned to Okinawa he found that the master had died and that he was just in time to attend the funeral. Miyagi was obliged to step into the shoes of his teacher.

Miyagi had around ten students who met in the garden behind his house three times a week. They would train for long periods of around five hours, hours that were filled with sessions of lifting heavy stones and iron weights to strengthen the muscles, exercises to harden the hands and feet and endless repetitions of kata. Miyagi is believed to be the teacher who first introduced the explosive, hissing breathing patterns to the practice of Sanchin kata that are a distinctive feature of Goju Ryu karate. He would push his students to harden their inner muscles as they practiced and the strange breathing patterns were an outward expression of this hardening.

Miyagi would make his students practice bare chested and would strike their chests and backs as they moved to check that they were maintaining the appropriate tension. He told his followers that they should become like a willow tree that can let its branches blow freely in the wind while the trunk remains upright and unmoved. One further difference with the Shorin Ryu schools lay in his attitude to sparring. Itosu had banned his students from fighting because he thought that it was just too dangerous for karate men to hit each other. But Miyagi experimented with free fighting and designed protective equipment to make this safer.

The Miyagi branch of Okinawan karate had no formal name of its own until 1937. A demonstration was given in that year at the headquarters of the Dai Nippon Butokukai in Kyoto and the kata were so distinctive that the Kyoto officials asked what this intense brand of karate was called. After some thought, Miyagi turned to a phrase from the Bubishi, a seventeenth century collection of Chinese martial philosophy. The phrase he chose in Japanese reads, ho wa goju no donto su, or "exhalation and inhalation are both hard and soft". The choice of Goju as a name pointed to the feature that is so immediately distinctive about its training methods, the extraordinary muscle tension and loud breathing sounds produced by exponents as they perform kata.

The Outside World
The powerful and secretive fighting art of Okinawa was practically unknown on the mainland of Japan until the early years of the twentieth century. Things changed when public demonstrations of karate

became possible on Okinawa, events that were observed by visiting Japanese officials and naval officers. They had noticed that young Okinawan karate students who joined the Japanese army were in extraordinary physical condition. With war against Russia in the offing the army was looking for new ways to train its recruits and officers began to travel to Okinawa to learn karate. Word of the once secret art was slowly leaking out.

Anko Itosu, the father figure of Okinawan karate, died in 1916 at the age of eighty five. After his funeral the leaders of Okinawan karate discussed the question of who among them should attempt to fulfill Itosu's dream of spreading karate to the Japanese mainland. An answer began to emerge in 1917 when Funakoshi travelled to Kyoto to give an exhibition at the headquarters of the Japanese martial arts, the Butokuden. This was probably the first demonstration of karate outside Okinawa but it seems to have had little impact in Japan itself. The importance of the event lay in the choice of Funakoshi as a representative for Okinawan karate. He was now a dignified man of fifty and the president of the Okinawa Shobukai, a grouping of many of the most important karate teachers on the island. Of equal importance, perhaps, was the fact that Funakoshi was a highly educated man who spoke impeccable Japanese. If anyone could represent karate without disgracing the island it would be him.

It took several more years, however, for the Japanese public to become fascinated by karate. The great breakthrough came in 1921 when the Crown Prince Hirohito visited Okinawa as he returned by ship to Tokyo after a visit to Europe. This was the first time that a Japanese crown prince had ever made an overseas tour and his movements were reported breathlessly by the Japanese press. At Shuri Castle the young prince viewed with obvious pleasure a demonstration of karate kata that was given by Funakoshi and some of his students. His words of praise for karate after the event had great importance. The commendation of such a prominent member of the imperial family was widely reported throughout Japan and made it much easier for the conservative aristocrats who dominated the Japanese martial arts to give a welcome to this fighting style from the southern islands.

Cock Fighter
Not everyone in Okinawan karate circles was equally committed to the collective effort to make karate more respectable. As Funakoshi was performing for the Crown Prince some other karate experts on Okinawa were carrying on with the ancient process of making themselves as tough and dangerous as possible. One person who seemed to have zero interest in the destiny of karate was Chotoku Kyan. He was a close contemporary of Funakoshi and the two men would have often trained side by side in the secret training sessions run by Masters Azato and Itosu.

Kyan was born into a family that had been badly affected by the ending of the island's independence. His father had been the king's chief of staff and had been forced into exile in Tokyo when the king had all of his powers stripped away by the Japanese government. Chotoku, small and thin, was left in the care of a series of karate masters who were given instructions to toughen him up. He became a superb fighter who was the antithesis of the saintly Funakoshi, a man with a relish for drinking parties, visits to brothels and midnight gambling sessions. Kyan's students liked to tell a story of an occasion when their master was attacked by a violent gang on his way home from a cock fight. Kyan, who was holding his fighting bird under one arm, proceeded to knock the entire gang down without releasing the startled cockerel from his grasp.

Kyan was an old-school Okinawan karate fighter. He specialized in eye gouges, attacks to the testicles and punches to the throat. His approach to fighting can be judged from the reports of a match he fought in 1930 during a visit to Taiwan. A young local judo instructor challenged the sixty year old Kyan to demonstrate his skills. After circling his opponent for some time Kyan suddenly stepped close, gripped the judoka's cheek in a fierce pinch and kicked hard at his knee. As the Taiwanese man fell to the ground Kyan kneeled over him and delivered a powerful punch to the face that he stopped just at the point of contact. The local man quickly conceded defeat.

Kyan was clearly a dangerous man. He was rumored to have once killed an opponent by waiting in hiding in the branches of a tree until the man passed by. At that point Kyan leapt from the tree, wrapped the other man's head between his legs and snapped his neck. Kyan was not just a violent fighter, he was also an innovative and interesting teacher who attracted many students. He encouraged his protégées to train in the dark to improve their balance and liked to add to the degree of difficulty for sparring students by throwing water at the ground under their feet. He trained them to block and duck their way out of attacks but to use a decisive knockdown strike when they had no more room to escape. "There is nothing more frightening than karate", he told them, "so try not to fight." (26)

Kyan lived long enough to witness the greatest disaster in the long history of Okinawa, the terrible battle of 1945. The Japanese army, in full retreat after its calamitous failure to conquer Asia, formed a defensive line across the narrow waist of Okinawa and tried to hold the southern part of the island. America planes attacked in waves, destroying ninety percent of the largest town Naha. The precious castle at Shuri, the spiritual home of Okinawan culture, was blasted to smithereens. The Japanese defenders fought desperately but the Americans had overwhelming advantages and they finally broke through the defensive line and pressed south. The attackers poured fire into the mouths of caves with little way of knowing whether they contained dangerous squads of Japanese soldiers or huddled groups of terrified civilians. In this dreadful battle thousands of the Okinawan people were conscripted to fight against the Americans. But the majority of the islanders were helpless victims of the brutality and violence that rained down on them from all sides.

The Okinawan government believes that close to one hundred thousand Okinawans died in the carnage of 1945 from bombing raids and from starvation. Men, women and children died making desperate leaps off the southern cliffs at the urging of the Japanese military. Buried among the ruins of Naha and Shuri were the bones of most of the old karate masters. The decimation of the ancient culture of karate was one of the tragedies hidden among the chaos of war. Like many other islanders Chotoku Kyan died of malnutrition in the months after the battle ended. Chojun Miyagi lost three of his children, many of his best students and all of his research on the origins of karate. As the surviving islanders picked through the rubble and began to lay their dead to rest few of them gave any thought to karate. It had been buried, it seemed, together with hope itself.

11. Karate Becomes Japanese

I Swear to the Heavens

A tiny, middle-aged Okinawan man stepped down from the gangway of his ship onto the wharves of Tokyo Harbor and disappeared into the teeming crowds. This insignificant and unassuming figure dressed in kimono and wooden sandals was Gichin Funakoshi. The date was May 1922. Within twenty years Funakoshi would make his obscure Okinawan fighting art familiar to almost every Japanese person. The remainder of his life would be devoted to spreading the gospel of karate. And it would cost him dearly. Funakoshi would never see his native island again.

He was in Tokyo at the request of the Okinawan Department of Education who had asked Funakoshi to give a presentation of karate at an important sports festival. He had promised his wife and children that he would return to Okinawa within a month. At the back of his mind, however, Funakoshi was keenly aware that his master Itosu had died with an unfulfilled hope that Okinawan karate could be accepted throughout Japan. Funakoshi knew almost no one in the capital and he had little enough money in his pocket. But he dared to dream. On the long ferry ride from Okinawa he poured his excited emotions into his notebook.

> The fighting arts of Southern China are in a pitiful state
> And my tears flow when I consider their decline
> Who can revive this authentic tradition?
> With all of my heart I swear to the heavens that I will play my part

Funakoshi arrived in Tokyo at a time when the Japanese political world was beginning a slow lurch towards extreme nationalism. Foreigners were objects of suspicion and natives of Okinawa, who had only recently begun to think of themselves as Japanese, were not treated much better. The islanders were regarded by most Japanese people as curiosities. They were scorned for their incomprehensible dialect, their uneducated ways, their strange clothing and even for their penchant for eating pork.

The refined and dignified Funakoshi had been chosen as a person who would be acceptable to Tokyo society. At the sports festival he was the sole representative of Okinawan karate. It was his second visit to Japan and, although his previous visit to the mainland had been largely ignored, this time his demonstration was noticed and it was noticed by the right people. Jigoro Kano, the most important member of the martial arts community in Tokyo, attended the exhibition and he later invited Funakoshi to visit the headquarters of judo at the Kodokan to give a talk and demonstration.

When the time came Funakoshi made his way to the famous judo building with some trepidation. His apprehension must have deepened when he realized that, instead of the small reception committee he had been expecting, two hundred judo experts had gathered to see him in action. In front of this knowledgeable crowd Funakoshi demonstrated kata, explained the history of karate and showed the audience how some of his kata moves could be applied in actual combat.

Jigoro Kano was always on the lookout for new ideas that could be integrated into judo. He questioned Funakoshi closely after his demonstration and arranged to take private lessons from him. A friendship was struck up between the two men but undoubtedly it was Funakoshi who gained the most from their relationship. In the time he spent with Kano he learned a great deal about the running of a modern martial arts organization and he soon adopted several of Kano's innovations including the use of white suits and colored belts. Most of all Funakoshi benefitted from the patronage of a respected figure like Kano. This connection was an important first step towards his ambition of having karate accepted by Japanese society. Funakoshi never forgot the kindness of Kano and until the end of his life he was deeply reverential to the memory of the judo man who had helped him to find his feet.

Leaf Sweeper
With the encouragement he had received from the leaders of judo Funakoshi decided that he would stay in Tokyo and do his best to build a base for karate in Japan. To make it clear that he was not acting out of selfish interests he wrote to his fellow karate masters in Okinawa seeking their blessing. Whether or not he also sought the approval of his wife and family has not been recorded.

By the standards of urban Tokyo Funakoshi was a poor man. He lived in a dormitory for Okinawan students where he had one tiny, dark room to himself. But even this humble accommodation was rather expensive for his tight budget so Funakoshi worked as a janitor for the dormitory in exchange for a reduction in rent. He taught karate to the dormitory cook and was able to eat cheaply. Despite these economies he continued to live in such poverty during his first year in Tokyo that he regularly had to take items of clothing to the pawn shop.

Funakoshi was a truly unassuming man and he never complained about the biting hardship of his early years in Tokyo. One day a journalist arrived to conduct an interview with the Okinawan karate master. He approached a small figure who was sweeping leaves in the garden and asked where Funakoshi could be found. "One moment sir," the servant replied before disappearing upstairs. Funakoshi then changed out of his janitorial clothing and into a formal kimono whence he descended to greet the astonished newspaperman. This humility was a trait that would stay with the karate master even as he became a famous figure and his life somewhat more comfortable.

Funakoshi was given permission to use a lecture hall that was attached to the dormitory as a base for his karate teaching. Word about this unusual Okinawan art was spreading slowly and at first only a handful of curious young men turned up to the classes that Funakoshi offered each afternoon. These students would arrive in their everyday clothes, remove their jackets and begin the repetitive and tiring routines of kata training. For onlookers it was not the most impressive of sights. It seemed unlikely that this provincial art could win popularity in a city that was already packed with famous kendo, judo and jujutsu schools.

But karate represented something entirely new for the Japanese martial arts. On the surface it was just another form of jujutsu, a system of unarmed combat. There was, however, a great difference. Experienced karate men could punch and kick with an astonishing power. Stories about this punching kicking art filtered into the universities of Tokyo and an increasing number of young men made their way to study with Funakoshi or to invite him to teach at their colleges. Within a year he found that he had gathered enough students to be able to retire from sweeping leaves. He wrote to his family to ask them to join him in Tokyo and his three sons did eventually make their way north. But his wife refused to leave Okinawa. She wrote that she could not leave the family graves to gather dust unattended.

Just as Funakoshi was beginning to settle in Tokyo the world collapsed around him. On the first day of September 1923 a huge earthquake rocked the capital. Thousands of houses collapsed, instantly burying the people inside. But the worst was still to come. It was lunchtime and all over the city the residents had been cooking over open fires. Blazes spread in an uncontrollable fury through densely packed residential neighborhoods that were constructed of little more than wood and paper. In panic more than thirty thousand people crammed together onto one patch of open ground as they scrambled to escape the omnipresent flames. That huge crowd was surrounded by the inferno and incinerated on the spot as the very air caught fire. Nobody could stop the burning. The earthquake had fractured most of the capital's water lines and it was a full two days before work could even begin to quench the terrible flames. Altogether one hundred thousand people died in the chaos that followed the earthquake and two million were left homeless.

Even when the flames in Tokyo finally flickered out the panic continued to spread. There were false rumors in the capital that most of Japan had been destroyed. Newspapers printed outrageous and mostly untrue stories that gangs of foreigners, especially Koreans, were profiteering amid the chaos. One newspaper even suggested that Koreans were poisoning the water supply. Gangs of vigilantes began to wander the streets attacking and sometimes killing foreigners on sight. Okinawans were not entirely safe from this xenophobic rage but cautiously Funakoshi and the few students he could contact emerged to help with the rescue work. He found that many of his young students were dead and many more had simply disappeared amidst the confusion. Karate was forgotten for a while as Funakoshi, his sons and his students cleared rubble, buried the dead and did what they could to help the desperate crowds of homeless people.

Monkey Motobu
After some time the capital began to shake off the trauma of the great disaster and Funakoshi returned to teaching. But he soon found that he had lost his status as the only Okinawan teacher of karate in Japan. There was now a rival karate man, a powerful fighter of around the same age as Funakoshi who was named Choki Motobu. Motobu was a very different man from his counterpart. He had none of the refined social skills of Funakoshi, his Japanese was poor and he was not particularly interested in polite behavior. What Motobu did possess was an aura of great toughness and directness - for Japanese students he made an interesting contrast to the elegant Funakoshi.

Back on Okinawa Motobu had been so fast and agile as a teenager that his friends had named him 'monkey Motobu'. At that time his dream was to become the strongest fighter in Okinawa and he did all he could to make it a reality. He took lessons from a range of tode masters, including Itosu, lifted stone weights every day and began a daily practice of hitting the makiwara post one thousand times.

Itosu wanted more than anything else to make karate a respectable and publicly accepted pastime. He strongly discouraged his students from taking part in street brawls. But Motobu ignored those strictures. He liked nothing better than a street fight and would hang around in Naha's entertainment quarter hoping to get involved in a punch up. After several years Motobu matured into one of those rare karate experts who had actually experienced a lot of street fighting and his experiences had altered the nature of his karate. He liked to use direct and violent techniques such as knuckle strikes, open-handed thrusts to the face and testicle kicks. He even used his defensive moves in a way that would hurt his opponents, using maximum force as he blocked high on their arms or legs.

Motobu probably came to the Japanese mainland as an economic migrant and he did earn a living for a while by working as a security guard in Osaka. But he made a return to karate in 1924 when he attended a boxing tournament in nearby Kyoto. The boxers were advertised as being willing to take on all comers for cash prizes and Motobu arrived at the ringside in time to see a young and powerful foreign boxer making short work of several judo fighters. The foreigner taunted the crowd, daring anyone in the audience to try their luck against him. The fifty two year old Motobu donned a borrowed judo outfit and climbed into the ring. After dodging the boxer's punches for a couple of rounds Motobu jumped into the air and with one strike knocked his opponent out, probably using a strike to the temple.

Later, in his first book, Motobu described the approach he had taken. "In a real fight," he wrote, "strike to the head first ... punch the face as if you are punching a hole in the head." (27) In those days karate was still regarded as a rather mysterious art by the Japanese public and his victory over the foreign boxer became a minor sensation. But Tokyo journalists had no idea what Motobu looked like and there were no photographs of the event. To his horror, when the first magazine article celebrating his victory was published the story was accompanied by drawings of the better known Funakoshi striking a kata pose over a fallen opponent.

In 1927 Motobu moved to Tokyo and the two Okinawan men became rivals for recognition as Japan's leading karate instructor. Their relationship was an uneasy one. Motobu's tough and aggressive instincts were completely at odds with the aspiration of Funakoshi to present karate as a dignified and spiritual path. Mobobu was no great shakes as a speaker or writer but he was enough of a teacher to tempt several of Funakoshi's students to secretly take lessons with him. There are a number of stories that suggest the rivalry between the two masters even descended into a physical confrontation, with Funakoshi coming off worse. Whatever the truth of these rumors, Motobu did not create much of a legacy. He continued teaching karate in Tokyo until the war years but left no lasting organization behind. It was to be the comparatively gentle Funakoshi who would become the "father of karate."

One other Okinawan expert who arrived in Japan to teach karate in the 1920s had a more successful relationship with Funakoshi and a more lasting impact on karate history. Kenwa Mabuni was an unusual figure in the rather cloistered world of Okinawan karate who had attempted to fuse the techniques of the two dominant schools, the so-called Naha-te and Shuri-te branches, into one unified karate curriculum.

Mabuni was yet another frail child who had taken up karate at an early age as a means of developing physical strength. His parents initially sent him to Itosu's training circle and he later spent some time training under the founding father of Naha-te, Kanryo Higaonna. Mabuni became such an expert in the kata of both systems that he was eventually recognized as the preeminent kata expert on Okinawa. He was a sociable man with a wide range of friendships and was one of the few islanders who could claim to have trained and studied with both Gichin Funakoshi and Chojun Miyagi.

Even on Okinawa there were many who felt that it was rather ridiculous for the karate schools of Naha and those of Shuri to regard each other as rivals. It was, after all, possible to walk from one town to another in less than an hour. In the early 1920s Kenwa Mabuni and Chojun Miyagi took an initiative to bring the two main branches of karate closer together when they created the Okinawan Karate-do Club. It was a club that was open to students from any brand of karate. The two young masters encouraged their students to try out the techniques they had learned in their own styles as they faced the masters in sparring sessions.

When Jigoro Kano paid a visit to Okinawa he attended a training session at this club and encouraged Mabuni to travel to mainland Japan. On arrival in Tokyo Mabuni received a good deal of help from Funakoshi but found it difficult to build up enough interest among the public to start his own club. Later, in 1929, he opened a karate dojo in Osaka and named his brand of karate the Half-Hard Style (Hanko Ryu). This was a rather unfortunate choice of name and Mabuni eventually changed the name of his style to Shito Ryu, a name that paid homage to the style's diverse roots by combining characters from the names of Mabuni's own teachers, Itosu and Higaonna.

Empty Hand
Towards the end of the 1920s expatriate Okinawan men like Funakoshi, Motobu and Mabuni found themselves living in a nation that was increasingly nationalistic and expansionist in outlook. A serious problem for these karate teachers as they tried to fit into Japanese society was that the name of their art, karate, was written with characters (唐手) that essentially meant 'Chinese Hand'. This was a name that made perfect sense to karate men from Okinawa. They were all closely acquainted with, and relaxed about, the Chinese origins of their art. But the Japanese military establishment was engaged in attempts to conquer northern China and jingoistic campaigns in the press insisted on the right of the Japanese to rule over the 'inferior' peoples of China. Contempt for the Chinese was normal practice in the 1930s. It was an atmosphere that brought inevitable pressure to change the name of karate so that the art would be more acceptable to the Japanese people as a whole.

The suggestion that the word karate could be written as 空手, or 'empty hand', had been circulated on Okinawa as far back as 1905. As karate began to win popularity in Japan both Okinawans and mainlanders debated the idea of changing the name permanently. Predictably, the Butokukai, the body that controlled the Japanese martial arts, was strongly in favor of such a change and in 1933 the head of that organization visited Okinawa to put the suggestion directly to the island's karate officials.

Gichin Funakoshi did not invent the new name for karate but he was the person who did most to create the rationale for a change. In his book Karate Kyohan, published in 1935, he used the new characters for the first time and gave a lengthy explanation of the reasons for the modification. First of all, he wrote, it is wrong to think of karate as a Chinese martial art, it is essentially Okinawan. Secondly, the new reading of 'empty hand' more accurately reflects the fact that karate is an unarmed combat system. Finally, Funakoshi suggested, the emptiness of the first character in the new name has a philosophical significance. Although he was not a particularly religious person Funakoshi did have some experience of Zen Buddhist practice. His suggestion that there was a connection between the name of karate and the Buddhist conception of emptiness was a smart tactical move that was guaranteed to appeal to the sentiments of Japanese martial artists. The promotion of the new name by Funakoshi was pivotal. In 1936 a meeting of karate masters on Okinawa decided, with some reluctance, that the name change was a price worth paying to ensure wider acceptance for karate.

A further concession to Japanese sensibilities came when Funakoshi decided to change the names of several kata that had been passed down to him by Itosu and Azato. Many of these kata had Chinese names that were difficult for Japanese readers to make any sense of. The basic Pinan katas that had been developed by Itosu for schoolchildren were further simplified by Funakoshi and renamed as the Heian katas. Kushanku, a kata named after its Chinese creator, became Kanku; Naihanchi became Tekki; Wansu became Empi; Seisan became Hangetsu; and so on. Funakoshi introduced several other changes to make karate more 'Japanese'. Towards the end of the 1920s Funakoshi began to describe his art as Karate Do, rather than Karate Jutsu. This was in line with the mood of the times in Japan. The leaders of the Butokukai were encouraging all of the martial arts to rename themselves as 'ways' (do), rather than 'arts' (jutsu). Karate therefore followed other martial arts such as kendo which had replaced kenjutsu as the official name for sword practice in 1920.

The Japanese Way
In 1924 Funakoshi adopted the judo practice of using white training suits and colored belts to indicate rank. In the same year he created seven shodans, the first people in Japan to wear a karate black belt. Outstanding among these early black belts was Hironori Otsuka, a young man who had been born into a family with samurai roots and had as a child received training in jujutsu from his father and from a great-uncle. At the age of thirteen Otsuka began to train under the Grand Master of New Willow (Shindo Yoshin Ryu) jujutsu. He stuck to those studies and learned how to use a broad range of throws, joint locks and holds. Otsuka also learned how to strike to vital points and even how to attack with kicking techniques. In 1921, at the age of twenty nine, he was already a fully qualified jujutsu teacher.

Otsuka was an ambitious young martial artist and, when news of karate began to filter into mainland Japan, he decided to make a journey to Okinawa to see this fighting art for himself. But just when he was planning his trip to the heartland of karate he discovered to his surprise that lessons in karate were already being offered in Tokyo. Otsuka attended Funakoshi's very first demonstration of karate in the capital and he was one of those who came away deeply impressed. This, he quickly decided, was something new. The techniques were explosively powerful and the art seemed to have more coherence than the almost random collection of techniques that made up the jujutsu curriculum. Otsuka decided to find out more about karate. He was from a middle class background and worked as a bank employee so when he visited Funakoshi at his dormitory he was rather startled by the poverty of this teacher's living conditions. But he found the man himself to be charming. Funakoshi was open, honest and welcoming and Otsuka quickly became one of his first students.

After years of jujutsu training Otsuka was in outstanding physical condition. He made rapid progress in his karate lessons and was awarded a black belt within only two years. As the number of karate students grew the master needed assistant teachers and Otsuka was a natural choice as Funakoshi's right hand man. He became one of the first mainland Japanese people to teach the Okinawan art. With his intimate knowledge of the Japanese martial arts community Otsuka would play a key role in the development of Japanese karate.

The training in Funakoshi's dojo was rigorous but simple. Beginners would receive some basic instruction in how to make a fist and how to punch. Otherwise almost all of their training would consist of endless repetitions of kata that they performed alone. This was very different from the kendo and jujutsu clubs of Tokyo where training was based around pre-arranged sequences of attack and defense that were practiced by two fighters acting in concert. The teaching methods of these arts offered obvious ways for karate to improve its training system. At some point in the middle of the 1920s Funakoshi, with Otsuka's assistance, introduced a series of prearranged (yakusoku) pair fighting techniques. One partner would attack with a strike or a kick and the other would respond with a move or two from one of the katas. This innovation brought a new degree of realism to karate training and was so obviously effective that it would later spread to all styles of karate and even to the karate schools of Okinawa.

Otsuka could not be content for long with a background role as assistant to Funakoshi. As he led classes he began to introduce more and more ideas from his own jujutsu experience. He brought weapons to practice and would teach students how to throw each other and how to use locks and hold down moves. This was all too much for Funakoshi and he took to scolding Otsuka in front of the students, warning him that karate and jujutsu could not be mixed. Eventually Otsuka's position as the number one assistant to Funakoshi came under threat from the master's youngest son, a youth in his early twenties who was becoming a karate prodigy in his own right.

Otsuka trained with Funakoshi until 1932 but his final years with the master were restless ones and he often took lessons with the other Okinawan teachers in Tokyo. With Choki Motobu he practiced free fighting techniques and absorbed the prearranged sparring methods that Motobu had developed independently. With Kenwa Mabuni he drew on that teacher's unrivaled knowledge of Okinawan kata and was influenced by Mabuni's enthusiasm for sparring in the dojo, an idea that Funakoshi strongly opposed. Otsuka decided that he wanted to be free to find a way to blend the best of karate with the best of jujutsu. He wanted to imitate the success of judo and kendo by allowing his students to develop their skills in regular sparring sessions. It was time for him to break away.

In 1934 Otsuka formed his own organization, the Great Japanese Karate Promotion Club. This was not just a new karate group, it marked the introduction of a completely new style of karate. Otsuka took the power of Okinawan karate but applied those techniques from a more natural, upright stance with an emphasis on body shifts to avoid attacks and simultaneous counterattacks. In his system solo kata practice was supplemented by a wide range of pre-arranged sparring methods. Weapons training not been encouraged by Funakoshi but Otsuka introduced a series of exercises that involved unarmed defense against attacks by knife or by sword. Above all, he encouraged competitive sparring and looked for ways to emulate the competitions that had made judo and kendo so popular.

At this point karate was still regarded as a purely Okinawan fighting art. But by 1938 Otsuka felt confident enough to place himself in the spotlight as the first non-Okinawan leader of a karate style. He marked the shift in consciousness by renaming his group as Wado-Kai. 'Wado' (和道) is commonly translated today in unthreatening phrases such as 'the way of peace' or 'the path of harmony'. But the character 和 also carries the connotation of 'Japanese'. In the ultranationalist atmosphere of 1938 Otsuka was surely making a point in choosing such a name. His move proved highly popular with the conservative figures who ran the Butokukai. In 1940 they recognized Otsuka as the leader of an officially registered style of karate, Wado Ryu, and in 1944 they named him as the chief karate instructor for all Japan. The Japanese student had finally outranked his Okinawan master. Funakoshi's feelings about this development are unrecorded.

The Tough One
One final transmission of Okinawan karate to the Japanese mainland was to take place in the years before the war. Chojun Miyagi visited Japan on several occasions to lead seminars and meet students but his life was on Okinawa. In his place a young man named Gogen Yamaguchi emerged as the pioneer of a uniquely Japanese brand of Goju Ryu karate. He was a southerner from Kagoshima, a town at the very bottom of the Japanese mainland. There, at the age of fourteen, Yamaguchi began to learn karate from

an Okinawan teacher named Takeo Maruta who had learned karate from Chojun Miyagi in Okinawa. Yamaguchi was an enthusiastic student but his teacher was no expert and Yamaguchi picked up a rough and ready style of karate that he would only polish later in life when the opportunity came to study with more experienced teachers.

In the late 1920s Yamaguchi's large, middle-class family moved to Kyoto and he soon became a student at Ritsumeikan University, an institution that was playing a key role in training leaders for Japan's colonization of Manchuria. In 1930 Yamaguchi opened a karate club in the university. It was a club that would play a major role in the development of Japanese Goju Ryu and today still takes pride in its position as the first Naha-te university club in Japan.

Yamaguchi's personality at this time was as rough as his karate. He liked to fight and he and his fellow club members would pick fights with the other martial arts groups and left-wing organizations that they ran across on their campus. In 1931 Yamaguchi met Chojun Miyagi for the first time and this encounter had a profound effect on the young man. He realized that karate was part of a rich and sophisticated tradition and that he had a role to play as a founding teacher of Goju karate in Japan. Miyagi was by far the most skillful karate man that Yamaguchi had met and the Okinawan teacher was also impressed by the student. It was Miyagi, in fact, who came up with the nickname Gogen, which means 'tough', for Yamaguchi.

The powerful student began to develop an interest in the spiritual side of his karate. He started to spend time at Mount Kurama in the hills north of Kyoto where he would meditate under waterfalls and purify his body by fasting. Later he wrote that this period of his life transformed his karate. His perceptions became so sharp that he could anticipate attacks before they arrived. In 1934 Yamaguchi graduated from university with the clear ambition of building a Japanese organization to nurture the karate of Chojun Miyagi. He was just starting out on this path when the outbreak of war put all of his personal plans on hold.

Father and Son
By the 1930s it had become clear to informed Japanese martial artists that there were now several different styles of karate. But for Gichin Funakoshi this was all meaningless. For him there was only one karate and he took little interest in the new developments. In his quiet way he continued to promote karate primarily as a healthful and dignified way of life. He was certainly a dignified man, despite the poverty that he had to endure throughout his fifties and early sixties. For years he made his life in one room of the student dormitory, eating the simplest of food and giving lessons at the university karate clubs.

In 1930 things began to change. Funakoshi had been joined in Tokyo by his three sons and, while his eldest son was more interested in gambling than karate, his youngest son Yoshitaka was a karate prodigy. Funakoshi moved out of his dormitory to live with Yoshitaka and found a better venue for his karate school in the dojo of the great sword master Hakudo Nakayama. This was another friendship with a famous martial artist that turned out to be highly advantageous for Funakoshi.

Nakayama was one of the outstanding fighters in the nation. He held senior expert qualifications in kendo, in swordsmanship and in staff fighting (jodo). He was a kendo instructor with the Tokyo police, a military advisor to the army and a key reformer of the sword arts. Nakayama was the person who had coined the term iaido to describe the art of sword practice using live blades. He was the ultimate insider in the martial arts community and an invaluable source of advice for Funakoshi and his son. Undoubtedly the two men gathered many ideas about paired practice and free competition as they watched Nakayama's students train in his Yushinkan dojo.

Yoshitaka was trusted enough by his father to be allowed to teach classes and even to introduce changes to the karate curriculum. But a cloud hung over Yoshitaka. He had been diagnosed with tuberculosis at the tender age of seven and the doctors had told him that he was unlikely to live long beyond the age of twenty. Perhaps as a result of this shocking revelation in his childhood Yoshitaka lived his life with great intensity after reaching the age of twenty. Despite his suspect health he pushed his mind and body to great lengths and often hit the makiwara so hard that the supporting wooden post split in two.

Yoshitaka is believed to have been the originator of many changes in the karate that his father had brought from Okinawa. He created a five step system of paired kata (Gohon Kumite) that had been directly inspired by his experience of watching the students of Hakudo Nakayama work together in training. This innovation was followed by the introduction of several other kinds of paired training and experiments with free sparring that circumvented his father's strong distaste for karate competition.

Yoshitaka was also responsible for instigating dramatic changes to the look of karate during his short life. Back on Okinawa karate experts practiced their kata while standing in high, natural stances. They preferred to use hand strikes and if they kicked they kicked low and fast, aiming for the groin or the shins. But Yoshitaka had the insight that kata training could itself be an effective way of building body strength and so he began to push his students to take up exaggeratedly low and long stances from which they moved with powerful hip twists. He began to kick higher, even at head height, and introduced circular kicks that could swing up and over the blocking arms of an opponent.

During the 1930s Gichin Funakoshi was in his seventies and ready to gradually relinquish his teaching duties. As the old master pulled back from activity his two leading young students Yoshitaka and Hironori Otsuka competed for the leadership of Japanese karate. Both men were keenly aware of all of the changes that the other had introduced and their rivalry drove them to innovate at high speed. One matter on which they agreed was the need for karate to have some form of free sparring. By the late 1930s most of the karate groups in Japan had begun to meet each other for occasional challenge matches (kokan geiko). But in Tokyo the karate clubs had less fighting experience and they lagged behind the Goju Ryu fighters in Western Japan who had been sparring among themselves for years. On one trip to Osaka Yoshitaka had a shocking experience when his team of fighters from Tokyo were easily defeated and humiliated by the local karate men. After that setback he ignored his father's reservations and made a determined push to improve fighting skills in the capital's karate clubs.

In 1936 the father and son Funakoshi team became the proud owners of their own training space, the first purpose built karate dojo in Japan. It was a tiny hardwood floored room of five tatami mats, or approximately three square meters, in size. But it was all theirs. The second floor had living accommodation for the two teachers and the building was named Shotokan by Funakoshi's students. Shoto (wind in the pines) was Funakoshi's rather poetic pen name and Shotokan, therefore, simply meant 'the house of Shoto'. In later years Shotokan would acquire a wider meaning as the name for Funakoshi's brand of karate. But the old man himself had no use for the idea of karate 'styles' and he never wanted to describe his art as anything but karate.

Possession of his own dojo gave Funakoshi a new lease of life. He shared the emotions that the young Jigoro Kano had experienced when he first opened his Kodokan. Karate was now no longer something that had to be practiced in the temporary surroundings of a rented room. It had a home and a centre. With a new seriousness Funakoshi began to regularize training schedules, to draw up rules for students and to create standard examinations for promotion to higher grades. At almost seventy years of age he was still a lean and powerful man but the growing number of clubs in the Tokyo area had become too much work for him to handle. The father now took on the roles of philosopher and figurehead for the karate movement. It was his son who became the effective leader of the young men who turned up to learn how to fight.

You Face a Million Enemies

Gichin Funakoshi was widely admired but some in the martial arts community did criticize the old man for the limitations of his training methods and for his refusal to encourage free fighting. However, there can be no doubt about the intensity and sincerity of the Okinawan teacher's feelings about karate. Echoing his own teachers, Funakoshi described karate training as a matter of life or death.

> In every step, in every movement of your hand, you must imagine yourself facing an opponent with a drawn sword. Each and every punch must be made with the power of your entire body behind it, with the feeling of destroying your opponent with a single blow. You must believe that if your punch fails, you will forfeit your own life. Thinking this, your mind and energy will be concentrated, and your spirit will express itself to the fullest. No matter how much time you devote to practice, no matter how many months and years pass, if your practice consists of no more than moving your arms and legs, you might as well be studying dance. You will never come to know the true meaning of karate. (29)

Funakoshi is above all treasured for the role he played in convincing the Japanese people that the fighting art of Okinawa could also be regarded as a lifelong path of commitment and dignity. He was a convinced rationalist who went to great lengths in his books to dismiss beliefs that martial arts training can produce superhuman strength or mysterious skills. The true purpose of karate, he believed, was to enable its followers to live their lives with purpose and in peaceful harmony with those around them.

In 1938 Funakoshi published a list of twenty rules for karate students. Some of the maxims are reminiscent of the earlier writings of his master Itosu but it is Funakoshi's list that has continued to be widely read and often quoted. His second rule, which in Japanese reads karate ni sente nashi, is one of the few sentences in that language that is familiar to martial artists all over the world and it is the epitaph carved into his gravestone: "There is no first strike in karate."

When he explicitly argued that a life in karate should be a peaceful one Funakoshi ran the risk of alienating many. His list of rules was written at a time when Japan had begun to fight a ruthless war in Manchuria. The nation was in the hands of ultra-nationalists who were planning a wider assault on most of Asia. And these people wanted to use the martial arts for the most aggressive ends. Funakoshi had certainly become a proud Japanese citizen but he largely avoided the jingoism that infected the nation's martial arts community during the 1930s. The world is dangerous, he suggested, and we must be ready for anything. But we will never strike first.

The Twenty Rules of Gichin Funakoshi

1. Always remember that karate begins and ends in respect.
2. There is no first strike in karate.
3. Karate stands for decency.
4. You must know yourself before you can know others.
5. Spirit is more important than technique.
6. You must set your heart free.
7. Laziness is the root of all evil.
8. Don't believe that karate only belongs in the training hall.
9. Train in karate for your entire life.
10. The beauty of karate lies in applying it in everyday life.
11. Karate needs constant practice; without it, the hot water becomes cold.
12. Rather than winning, you must feel you will never lose.
13. Change according to your opponent.
14. A battle lies in controlling your opponent's strengths and weaknesses.
15. Think of your hands and feet as swords.
16. When you step into the street, you face a million enemies.
17. Exaggerated stances are for beginners; later, one can stand naturally.
18. Practice kata accurately, a real fight is another matter.
19. You must control your power, extension and speed.
20. Always keep training in your heart.

12. Aikido: The Divine Art

The Art of the Gods

A little old man with a long white beard and twinkling eyes stands quietly at the centre of a circle of much younger men. One by one they run at him, raising their arms to attack, and he shifts this way and that. His body remains erect. Beneath his flashing glance one hand thrusts at an onrushing throat as the other hand takes control of a wrist.

The figure spinning with great speed and perfect composure at the centre of a whorl of flailing bodies is Morihei Ueshiba. Something about him does not seem to belong to the modern age, or perhaps even to the human race. In his white robes he appears to be more spirit than man, a presence that has been transported to a fleshly realm where nothing can resist his magical powers.

Ueshiba is one of the most colorful and controversial figures in the long history of the Japanese martial arts. He was the creator of the fighting style known as aikido, a martial art that is often described by its adherents in language that is more emotional and romantic than might be expected when talk turns to fighting. Ueshiba himself was characterized by his students in thrilling phrases like this:

> The moment we faced each other, I felt as if I had turned into tiny seeds, and that he would inhale me into his body when he took a breath. (30)

He was worshipped by many of his followers who believed that he was in command of 'godlike techniques' (kami-waza) that were far beyond normal human ability. And yet there were skeptics who attended demonstrations where the aged Ueshiba could be seen to send bodies flying through the air with the merest of touches, or to knock grown men flat onto their backs with the sound of his voice. It seemed to them that the whole thing was a fake, a psychological con-trick in which his students were subconsciously complicit.

In his day there were plenty of powerful martial artists who doubted the reality of Ueshiba's claims and who were ready to test him. A number of those who did so found their suspicions dissolving as soon as they came into physical contact with the tiny genius. Many challengers were converted into loyal students. There was more to aikido, it seemed, than met the eye.

Ueshiba was a figure who stood outside the tide of rationalism that swept through the martial arts at the beginning of the twentieth century. Explanations of technique were of little interest to him. If someone asked a question Ueshiba would throw the questioner to the floor one more time and then ask with a smile, "Do you understand now?" Although he had thousands of students he was himself more of a lifelong student than he was a teacher, a man who lived his life engrossed in a passionate search for the secrets of existence.

The Dreamer
Ueshiba was the third great modern day reformer of the Japanese martial arts after Kano and Funakoshi and the youngest of the three. He was born in 1883 in Wakayama, a mountainous peninsula to the south of Kyoto that even today feels remote and timeless. The valleys of Wakayama shelter many temples that belong to the secretive and mystical Shingon sect of Buddhism and Shingon monks share the valleys with the ancient Shinto gods who are worshipped in thousands of shrines. Wandering between these temples and shrines are the yamabushi, mountain dwelling monks whose Shugendo religion, a mystical blend of Shinto, Buddhism and Taoism, preaches the unity of mankind with the divine. Wakayama was, and is today, a religious magnet for pilgrims from all over Japan. Ueshiba was born among a great wealth of religious ritual and ancient knowledge. The spiritual dimension of his birthplace would have a decisive influence on the way he lived his life.

He grew up in the oceanside village of Tanabe, the child of a relatively wealthy farming family that also fished the seas that lapped close by their rice fields. Ueshiba learned to spearfish at a young age, wriggling through forests of seaweed as he searched among the crystalline depths for a juicy prey. His father was a determined, hot-tempered man but he had fathered four daughters and was forty years old when Morihei, his only son, was born. It was a surprising and delightful blessing for the family and Morihei's father was, from the outset, an indulgent parent. He smiled at his son's mischief and made a habit of opening his pockets to support whatever madcap project the boy could dream up.

As he approached manhood the teenage Ueshiba was placed in a job at the local tax office. But the romantic, passionate Ueshiba was never going to make much of a public official. Before long he abandoned his desk job to become the leader of a local revolution. The Meiji government was at this time imposing dramatic changes on the nation's legal and tax systems. Among those who were suffering most from the changes were the fishermen of Tanabe. They were suddenly threatened with increased taxes and unwelcome rules that would transform their working lives. Ueshiba burst into action at the head of a protest movement that went as far as building barricades to keep out the Tokyo officials. It was an exciting start to his public life but he gave up on agitation when he found that the older fishermen could not take him seriously for very long. He was a mere youth of seventeen and only five feet tall.

At the age of eighteen Ueshiba moved to Tokyo, with his father's help, to set up a stationery business. He built up a customer base through exhausting door to door selling and eventually had enough business to employ five staff. In his spare time Ueshiba attended jujutsu classes, coming into contact for the first time with the art that would define his life. But he had overtaxed his young body and fell ill with beriberi. Displaying the decisiveness that would mark the rest of his life Ueshiba suddenly gave up on the business he had established with such pains. He handed the customers over to his remaining employees and took a train back to Wakayama. Penniless, he confessed to his father, "I went to Tokyo with one suit of clothes, and that's how I come back!" (30) His father laughed and embraced his son as they talked over what Morihei would turn his hand to next.

What the young man really wanted to do was fight. War with Russia was on the horizon and in common with many young Japanese men of his day Ueshiba imagined that war would be a wonderful adventure. Only one thing held him back. He was 155 centimeters tall and the military required their recruits to reach at least 156 centimeters. But, although he was short, Ueshiba did not lack in determination. He began to spend days strengthening his body in the hills above Tanabe where he ran, clambered up the steep mountain trails, hauled heavy logs and swung his wooden sword. Mostly he spent hours hanging from branches, willing his body to stretch just a little. His height did not increase very much but his body slowly became tough and powerful. As short as he was, Ueshiba built his weight up to seventy five kilograms and in the end he was so muscled that he seemed to be almost as wide as he was tall.

When the war with Russia finally began Ueshiba pestered his superiors to send him to the front. There, on a battleground in northern China, he found himself under fire for the first time. But he felt no fear. Instead he experienced a thrilling sense of heightened perception in the face of danger. He later reported that he could track bullets as they flew through the air. "I could see them coming from left and right, and so I could easily get out of their way." (30) Ueshiba enjoyed battle so much that he seemed to be an ideal candidate for officer training. But for unknown reasons he left the military soon after these wartime experiences and returned to Wakayama. It may be that his doting father had pulled strings to have Morihei taken out of harm's way.

At first the return to rural Wakayama felt like a mistake. Without the routine and challenge of military life Ueshiba was lost. He was still in his early twenties and, although he had married, he was deeply reluctant to settle for a quiet existence in the remote farming village. Ueshiba was spiritually and physically restless at this time. He spent days either wandering in the mountains or locking himself up in a room to pray. Some of the villagers whispered that he was becoming unstable. His worried father decided that Morihei needed a physical outlet for his energy. When a judo master visited their village the father persuaded the teacher to stay in Tanabe and to offer lessons to the local young men. With a teacher and a dojo provided by his father Ueshiba was able to study judo every day. His depression vanished and his spirits lifted as he encountered the pleasure of throwing his friends around.

The Frozen North

But Ueshiba had simply too much energy to be bottled up in his home town. What he really needed in his life was adventure. He soon found an outlet for his high spirits in Hokkaido, the great island that lies to the north of the Japanese mainland. The government was urging farmers to settle this wild frontier and the lure of unlimited land, natural riches and a fresh start proved to be highly attractive to many of the young men who had returned from the bitter war with Russia. Few of them realized just how difficult making a life in Hokkaido would actually be.

In the spring of 1910 Ueshiba set off to search for a suitable place to settle. He found himself making a terrible journey through constant snowstorms, icy mountain passes and frozen rivers that gave way underfoot. At last he found his way to a broad, fertile valley that was surrounded by forests. This valley, known as Shirataki or 'white falls', is in the far north east of Hokkaido. It has a harsh climate that is so cold that even the sea freezes over in wintertime. Ueshiba thought it to be perfect. He returned to Tanabe and enthusiastically described this extraordinary valley where a wonderful new life was waiting. Before long he had signed up eighty of the younger village residents to his party of settlers. They had almost no funds to equip and provision their expedition but once again Ueshiba's indulgent father opened his pockets.

The group of settlers left Wakayama on the last day of March 1912 in the hope that the snows would be melting in the far north by the time they arrived. The scene that met them in Hokkaido was shocking. Snow was still meters deep and falling so heavily that the paths they cleared soon disappeared again under the drifts. When they arrived at the mountains that ring the Shirataki valley the party shivered at the sight. They had brought clothes that were warm for the mild winters of Wakayama but hopelessly inadequate for this frigid world. On top of that they were carrying enough food to last them a year - huge containers of rice and other foodstuffs. How, they wondered, could they get themselves and their supplies over the high mountains? Constructing improvised sleds they fought their way up and over the high pass that was the only way into the valley. The land journey had taken them a full month but at last they arrived in Shirataki.

The first year in the valley of the white falls was incredibly tough. The settlers cut down trees, built rough huts, fished the streams and tried to raise crops. The only thing that would grow for them in that first year was potatoes. Ueshiba threw himself into the struggle to survive. He cut down hundreds of trees, chased off foraging bears and dealt with bandits. On horseback he toured the north of Hokkaido making deals to sell the meagre produce of the Shirataki collective and to secure government support.

Finally, after three years of disastrous harvests, the small community learned how to work this stubborn land and began to earn money by selling lumber from the endless forests. Slowly their rough settlement became a real village and a school was opened for the growing number of children. But just as Shirataki was beginning to find its feet Ueshiba had an encounter that would transform his life. In the winter of 1915 he set out on one of his regular business trips and stopped for the night at a roadside inn. Staying at the same inn was a master of jujutsu, a small, intense man named Sokaku Takeda.

A Crossing of Paths

An anonymous country inn located in the wild lands of northern Hokkaido was the unlikely setting for this miraculous meeting between two men who were destined to become famous martial artists. After falling into conversation in a hallway Takeda invited Ueshiba to his room and they talked and drank sake until the sun came up. Ueshiba was a powerful man who already possessed great physical self-confidence but here, he soon realized, was an expert with infinitely greater knowledge and skill than his own. As Ueshiba listened to Takeda's stories of the martial arts he became desperate to learn from this man. But how, he wondered, could it ever be possible? Their paths were not likely to cross again. Takeda, sensing the younger man's hunger for knowledge, made a suggestion. "Stay here at the inn for a while," he said, "and I will teach you everything I know." Ueshiba was a creature of impulse and he immediately accepted the offer. Business was forgotten and his responsibility for the little community of which he was the effective leader was cast off. Ueshiba became a student of Takeda for the next thirty days. The people of Shirataki thought that he had been lost forever among the snows.

Ueshiba had been willing to drop everything to spend time with this master because he had discerned that Takeda was a living treasure chest of hidden knowledge. The older man had been born into the Takeda clan, one of Japan's most prominent samurai households, and in his younger days he had studied all of the classical samurai skills. He had taken lessons in swordsmanship, spear fighting and staff fighting. From his father he learned the secret techniques of the Great Eastern School (Daito Ryu), an aggressive style of jujutsu that had been developed by the samurai of the Aizu region.

Takeda's father was a friend of Sakakibara Kenkichi, one of the greatest and toughest swordsmen of the late nineteenth century. Thanks to this connection the son became a resident student at the hell-dojo run by Sakakibara, a place where students were often knocked unconscious by their teacher's overwhelming blows. Takeda himself became a master swordsman in the final days of the samurai. It was rumored that he had been one of the last swordsmen to have fought duels with real swords and had killed opponents.

But by the end of the century all of his intense training seemed to have been for nothing. Takeda had been born at the worst possible time for someone who longed to be a great swordsman. When carrying swords became illegal and public interest in their use disappeared almost completely Takeda switched focus and began to practice and teach the secret jujutsu skills he had learned from his father.

Secluded in their little country inn the two men trained together for a month as Takeda took Ueshiba through the entire curriculum of the Great Eastern School. It was a fighting style that included many striking techniques and joint twists that were designed to cause either instant submission or broken bones. As they trained together the two men forged a bond that was so strong that Ueshiba decided to invite his new master to travel back to Shirataki with him so that he could teach jujutsu to the villagers. One can only imagine the mixed emotions of the worried residents of Shirataki when Ueshiba arrived through the snows to tell them that he was not, in fact, dead but had been holed up in a hotel studying martial arts with this little master.

Whatever the feelings of the villagers Ueshiba did his utmost to make Takeda feel welcome. He arranged his baths, organized his meals and played chess with him in the evenings. Later he built a home for Takeda and formed a group of fifteen villagers to act as his training partners. Takeda greatly enjoyed being treated as a visiting prince. Unlike the open-hearted Ueshiba he was a critical, suspicious and avaricious man. He was delighted to have Ueshiba run around on his behalf and made it his business to extract as much money as he could from the arrangement. The two men continued in this unequal partnership for two years in the frozen north as Ueshiba gradually absorbed every scrap of Takeda's knowledge.

After several years of desperate struggle the village of Shirataki was finally beginning to expand. More and more families were being attracted to the area and its farms and forests were turning a profit. Then disaster struck. In May 1916 villagers were burning stubble in their fields as they prepared for the planting season. Suddenly, out of nowhere, a great wind blew down from the mountains and whipped the small, smoky fires up into a conflagration. As huge flames swept through their village the people ran desperately to throw themselves into the river or into the nearby swamps where they rolled in the protecting mud. Ueshiba was on yet another business trip but from miles away he could see the sky fill with billowing smoke.

Ueshiba rushed home to discover a scene of devastation. The village that he and his friends had built with their bare hands had been destroyed. Eighty percent of the homes were gone and most of the farmland was scorched and useless. The villagers huddled together in a cold, hopeless despair. But Ueshiba was not the type to give in. He became a whirlwind of action, organizing the residents to build temporary shelters and clear the fields. He toured regional governments to demand emergency relief and campaigned for a train line to be built to the valley. Thanks to his vigorous leadership the village had soon not only rebuilt itself but was once again able to attract new settlers. Just as the crisis was resolved another great turning point occurred in Ueshiba's dramatic life. He had struggled for eight epic years to wrestle a civilization from these wild lands but now his time in the far north suddenly came to an end. He received word that his father was dying. Quickly he packed up a few possessions and left.

The Great Source

There was no doubt that Ueshiba dearly loved his father and he waited impatiently throughout the ten weary days it took to travel from the north of Hokkaido to Wakayama. Just as his train was pulling into Kyoto, only a few hours away from Tanabe, Ueshiba fell into conversation with a fellow passenger who told him about a new religion. It had been created, the passenger told him, by an old woman who believed that she could change the world. Instantly forgetting about his dying father Ueshiba changed trains. He had to see this new religion for himself.

He soon found himself in the small town of Ayabe, north west of Kyoto. The place looked nothing like a typical Japanese town. The streets were full of young men and women who wore their hair long and dressed in the uniform of the new religion, a religion that called itself Omoto Kyo (Great Source Faith). Ueshiba made his way to the Omoto Kyo headquarters, a startlingly beautiful complex of wooden buildings. He entered the grounds, walking through freshly fallen snow, and asked for permission to pray there for the soul of his father. He was allowed to enter and was on his knees in a prayer room when he felt a powerful presence approaching him from behind. Turning, Ueshiba saw a soft-featured middle-aged man. "There is no need to worry about your father," the man said.

The speaker was Onisaburo Deguchi and he would prove to be the greatest influence on the remainder of Ueshiba's life. Deguchi was the new leader of the Omoto Kyo religion having succeeded the founder of the religion, his mother-in-law, after her death a year earlier. That lady was a poor, illiterate housewife who had suddenly been seized by spirits that flowed through her body into a brush and onto paper. Deguchi proved to be a brilliant leader who transformed the tiny religious group. He created teams of missionaries to tour the large cities and set up newspapers to spread the ideas of his religion.

With Deguchi in charge Omoto Kyo became a large and wealthy organization that attracted the support of many intellectuals and members of the establishment. But some members of the government were deeply suspicious of this new religion. Deguchi had constructed a complex description of the spirit world, one that implied that the goddess Amaterasu, believed by most Japanese to be an ancestor of the imperial family, was a usurper. Deguchi instead encouraged his followers to accept that he himself was the descendant of a divine lineage that was more powerful than that of the Emperor. The passionate Omoto Kyo followers took him at his word. He became an object of worship and some believers would scoop up the soil that he walked on and boil it into a kind of holy tea. Deguchi's more political ideas - a rejection of all foreign influence and a call for the unification of the world as one family - were highly acceptable to ultranationalist politicians. But even the right wingers were concerned about his priorities. Did Deguchi put Japan, or his personal religion, first?

Ueshiba stayed in Ayabe for three days, drinking in the sights and sounds of the Omoto Kyo headquarters. When he finally took the ferry to his home town he found that he had arrived too late. While he had been praying, his father had died. Ueshiba was so shocked by the loss of his loving parent that he became deranged. He ran up into the mountains and wandered around swinging at the trees with his wooden sword. In the end, after three days, his family sent the police to search for him. They found him alive, but confused and half-starved. When the officers brought him down into the town his family rejoiced. Morihei was, after all, the only son. Now he could inherit the leadership of the family, take care of his father's substantial landholdings and replace his father as one of the leaders of the Tanabe community. But Ueshiba had a shock in store for everyone, including his long suffering wife. He announced that he and his family would immediately relocate to Ayabe where they would devote themselves to serving the new religion.

The Greatest Martial Artist in Japan

Ueshiba was thirty-seven years old when he arrived in Ayabe. His outdoor life in Shirataki had given him great physical power and he was highly skilled after years of training alongside Sokaku Takeda. But he did not yet have any thought in his head of creating a martial art. It was Onisaburo Deguchi who started Ueshiba on the path that would lead to the creation of aikido. In his colorful way he informed Ueshiba that he was the greatest martial artist in all Japan. The best way for him to serve the gods would be to create his own style, a new martial art that "halts violence with virtue and love." (30) Deguchi provided a building in the Omoto Kyo complex that was to serve as Ueshiba's dojo and ordered the staff and the younger members of the religion to practice there regularly. Before long fifty students were training with Ueshiba every day.

Ueshiba was determined not to disappoint his master and with his usual energy he threw himself into the challenge of creating a new fighting style. His dojo became a living testbed for techniques and the students were expected to help him create and try out new ideas. The basis of his style was undoubtedly derived from the sharp movements of the Great Eastern School jujutsu that he had learned from Sokaku Takeda but Ueshiba cast his net wide, drawing in ideas from the sword and spear fighting schools. On top of the physical knowledge he was accumulating Ueshiba was also rapidly absorbing the sweeping philosophies of Omoto Kyo. He began to develop a conception of the physical world that placed ki at the centre. Ki, he believed, is a vital force that flows through the universe and passes in and out of our bodies as we breathe.

As he became a teacher in his own right Ueshiba melded the ideas and the style of his two dominating and unconventional mentors. They were two very different men but the harsh instruction of Takeda and the unconditional encouragement of Deguchi seemed to have produced a unique self-confidence in their student.

Ueshiba did not have much time to enjoy this new and settled life. The highest levels of the government had become deeply alarmed about the Omoto Kyo religion with its predictions of imminent national upheaval and its calls for top to bottom social reform. Many influential officials came to believe that the cult was preparing a bid to seize power. Early in 1921 the government moved to suppress Omoto Kyo. Several hundred police raided all of the properties of the religion under the highly serious charge of treason against the Emperor. Many of the Omoto Kyo buildings were demolished, the assets of the religion were seized and Deguchi himself was jailed for five years.

Deguchi had dreamed that his new faith would be able to provide leadership to the Japanese nation. But this hope was crushed and in the midst of the government repression members flooded out of the organization. In the end, Deguchi was released on bail after only four months in prison. Chastened, he set aside his national ambitions and instead allowed his mind to flow in ever more fantastic directions. He took to his bed and began to dictate his masterwork, a sprawling eighty-one volume account of the universe and its religions. Around him the remaining members of Omoto Kyo struggled to grow enough food to keep themselves and their families alive.

Into Mongolia

Deguchi was far from finished. Just two years after his imprisonment he took Ueshiba along on what would prove to be the wildest and most dangerous adventure of the martial artist's life. Deguchi had decided to embark on a grand project of uniting all of the world's great religions and came to the conclusion that he needed to search for a base, somewhere in Asia, where this could begin. He planned a journey through the Manchurian region of northern China into Mongolia to locate his new headquarters.

Once again Ueshiba happily abandoned his family in search of adventure. Together with Deguchi and two other members of Omoto Kyo he was smuggled out of Japan and into northern China. As they arrived on the Asian mainland Deguchi announced to anyone who would listen that he was the reincarnated Dalai Lama and had come on a mission to unite all religions. But some of the shadowy types at the fringes of his party paid little attention to these extravagant ideas. They were more interested in building a North China army that would fight for independence from Beijing. Traveling towards the west the Japanese group began to negotiate for the allegiance of gangs of mountain bandits and slowly drew together a motley armed force that called itself the All Mongolia Independence Army.

The group travelled for four months through increasingly lawless lands facing danger at every turn. As they arrived in eastern Mongolia Deguchi was introduced to the local population as a great religious teacher. Curious people drifted in from the countryside to seek his blessing and cures for their varied ailments. Ueshiba helped Deguchi to perform rituals for these arriving masses and entertained the crowds by putting on demonstrations of jujutsu. But the Mongolians had little experience of martial arts demonstrations and they sometimes misinterpreted what they saw. On one occasion Ueshiba applied a grip too firmly and severely hurt one of the locals. The man's friends decided that Ueshiba was an evil spirit and made plans to kill him in his tent during the night. Just in time Deguchi heard of the murder plot and managed to defuse the tension by offering the angry locals his watch in compensation.

The All Mongolia Independence Army had travelled a very long way away from civilization and now began to disintegrate under the pressure of attacks from local bandit groups. Soon the four Japanese Omoto Kyo members realized that they were no longer being accompanied by a large, armed escort and would have to conduct their own self-defense. Ueshiba regarded himself as Deguchi's personal bodyguard and he took the lead when their small party came under fire. As he did so he noticed that, in the face of extreme danger, he remained calm and seemed to be possessed of a supersensory ability to deal with attacks.

> I couldn't move away, so when bullets came toward me, I would twist my upper body away to avoid being hit. As I sharpened my vision, I became able to sense clearly the direction from which bullets would come. A split second before the bullet, I would see a white flash – and if I moved away from the white flash, I could avoid the bullet. (30)

The small remnants of the expeditionary army soon found themselves surrounded by superior forces who moved in to arrest them. They were disarmed and the officers were beaten to death. The four Omoto Kyo members were in a desperate situation and they did not expect to live to see the next morning. At midnight they were woken, tied and taken to an execution ground. The group kneeled, waiting for shots to ring out. Deguchi spoke a farewell to life and then shouted 'Banzai!' three times as a final farewell to Japan. Just then a messenger ran towards the executioners. The Japanese authorities had heard of the group's plight and had sent a local to secure their release. Having stared death in the face Ueshiba found to his great surprise that he was still alive and was going to be allowed to return to Japan.

A further surprise awaited as the small, exhausted party reached Japanese shores. To their astonishment they discovered that their adventures in Manchuria and Mongolia had been covered with breathless admiration by the Japanese press and that they were now regarded as returning heroes. Omoto Kyo was no longer a dangerous cult. It had become a brave representative of the national will.

True Enlightenment
As Ueshiba returned to the martial arts his students could see that the journey through China had produced a profound change in the man. His strength and energy were as great as ever but now he had an aura of unbreakable self-confidence. He would urge his students to attack him with real swords and to cut him up if they could. Something inside the man was moving towards a breakthrough and the explosion arrived in the spring of 1925 when a naval officer who happened to be an expert in kendo visited his dojo.

The visiting officer was skeptical about this little martial artist and was irritated when Ueshiba told him to attack with a wooden sword. "Hit me as hard as you can," Ueshiba told the expert. The officer was now rather angry and began to attack with greater and greater power, aiming to hurt Ueshiba. But he found that his swings met only empty air as the jujutsu man simply slid out of each attack. Losing his temper the officer gave up on single attacks and began to swing his sword continuously. In the end, he fell over exhausted. Later Ueshiba explained how he was able to outwit the navy man so easily. He had been able to predict the paths of Mongolian bullets and now he could tell where the sword was going to strike before it even moved.

> Every time my opponent was about to attack, a white flash the size of a grain would precede the attack by just a split second ... so by avoiding that white flash I managed to evade the sword without any problem [30]

That night the spirits of the forty-one year old Ueshiba soared to a new height. After the officer had gone he walked through the garden to wash away his sweat at a well. On his way back through the garden he suddenly realized that he was frozen and had been surrounded by a golden light that was emanating from the sky. His body filled up with the same golden light and Ueshiba sensed that he was becoming one with the entire universe. This was true enlightenment, he later wrote. It was clear and unmistakeable. A new vision of a martial art where enemies did not exist rose up inside him. Combat would now cease to be a matter of humiliating opponents. Instead, it would evolve into a path that led towards victory over the self.

> This would be the victory of merging with one's opponent, of humans becoming one with God, of the universe becoming part of love's creative energy. It would surpass the mere victory or defeat of individuals. (30)

Ueshiba, already strongly inclined to mysticism, was convinced that this new vision was a religious one and that he had been shown that the martial arts are a spiritual path. He felt like a new man. In later years he would say that at this time his body seemed to be filled with the power of the universe and that his skills transcended mere physical ability. He also believed that other people, if they encountered the right kind of training, could experience the same things that he was feeling. All human beings needed to harmonize their minds and bodies with the movements of the universe. They could do so because of the flow of ki, the invisible energy that exists everywhere and is freely breathed in and out of the human body. When internal ki is merged with universal ki there is no limit, he said, to human potential.

Superhuman Power

Ueshiba had now reached a spiritual and physical peak, an aura of power surrounded the man and was apparent to anyone who met him. Despite his isolation in rural Ayabe stories began to circulate throughout the country of this little man who talked like a character out of an ancient legend. Kenji Tomiki, a young judo expert who became a student of Ueshiba at this time, remarked that although he had met many tough and powerful martial artists in his life Ueshiba was in a different category altogether. It was difficult for the admirers of this outstanding man to understand why he was hiding himself away in a religious compound. Influential people made moves to bring Ueshiba into the heart of the Japanese martial arts establishment.

Isamu Takeshita, the man who had supervised the visits of the first judo experts to the United States, had become an admiral in the Japanese navy. In Tokyo Takeshita was also an enthusiastic promoter of the martial arts. He was a close friend of the sword master Hakudo Nakayama and was intimately involved in the development of modern sumo. A major drive been launched to reorganize the armed forces and Takeshita was one of those officers who argued that the Japanese military should blend the best of samurai culture with modern fighting methods. Above all, he wanted to find an inspirational figure who could help to instill belief in the Japanese people that they belonged to a truly great warrior nation. On the suggestion of a friend Takeshita travelled to Ayabe, watched the little master in action, and was quickly convinced he had found his man. He became both a supporter and a personal student of Ueshiba.

The connection with Admiral Takeshita brought about yet another twist in Ueshiba's tumultuous life. Before long he was taken away from the simple life he had been leading in a remote religious commune. He found himself in the nation's capital giving demonstrations to the elite of Japanese society - politicians, military leaders and aristocrats. Ueshiba's first month in Tokyo was occupied with a three week long seminar for some of Japan's leading martial artists, men who were all high grade teachers from the top kendo and judo schools. If the praise and attention went to Ueshiba's head he showed little sign of it. He seemed as absorbed as ever in his inner quest for transcendence.

Among the martial artists who visited Ueshiba in Tokyo was the great Jigoro Kano. The two men had begun their martial arts careers in a similar way by investigating traditional jujutsu. From the same starting point they had taken widely diverging paths but Kano was now at a stage in his life when he was beginning to yearn for the elegance and purity that had been sacrificed in prioritizing competitive judo. The seventy year old Kano visited Ueshiba's Tokyo dojo in 1930 and he was sufficiently impressed to send two of his leading students to study with Ueshiba. One of these men, Minoru Mochizuki, never returned to judo and went on to become a famous aikido instructor. Of his first meeting with the master he later said that Ueshiba had "... superhuman power. I felt that ... he was someone who had acquired something out of the ordinary, the innermost secret." (30)

Ueshiba's stellar reputation did not guarantee automatic respect wherever he went. On a visit to the Toyama military school he was invited by a group of young cadets to try his hand at jukendo, a martial art that uses wooden bayonets. The soldiers knew that Ueshiba had little experience of bayonet fighting and lined up to fight the eminent teacher one at a time. "Don't be ridiculous," Ueshiba told them, "I am a professional martial artist. Attack me at the same time." Four of the young men took him at his word and ran at the master at once but he moved with blinding speed, leaving them all lying on their backs.

By 1931 Ueshiba was a famous man and, with the help of several wealthy backers, he was able to open a large, purpose-built dojo in downtown Tokyo. It was named Kobukan (Place for Teaching the Martial Way) and soon became home to a group of young resident students (uchi-deshi) who attended five training sessions a day while also taking care of the building and their teacher. Most of these live-in trainees had long experience of judo or kendo and they helped to create an atmosphere that was tougher and more competitive than anything that would be seen in the more refined aikido that emerged after the war. Ueshiba liked to describe his art at this time as consisting of seventy percent strikes and thirty percent throws. It was his normal practice to hit his attackers at weak points so that he could more easily set them up for throws.

The teaching methods at the Kobukan were frustrating for many of the students. Ueshiba was almost completely disinterested in providing rational explanations or in evaluating the progress of his trainees. He would normally demonstrate a technique only once and would dismiss any questions, preferring to spend his time talking about arcane religious topics. The students soon learned to wait until after class to record and discuss among themselves what had happened during a lesson. They felt that Ueshiba was too intimidating a figure for them to probe for information. He was still powerful, and had the roar of a lion. But often, at the most unexpected moments, he would burst into cackles of delighted laughter.

As the military tightened its grip on power during the 1930s Ueshiba found that he was in great demand. Many of his students had become high ranking army and navy officers and they promoted their own teacher among the military schools. Ueshiba found himself shuttling between army academies, naval bases and police training centers. He became, for a period, an instructor at the Toyama Military Academy, the elite training school for army officers, and also taught at the Nakano School where Japan's spies and intelligence operatives were being trained.

As war approached the training methods in all of these schools became tougher. Military planners wanted their students to learn the most effective methods of quickly disabling an opponent. Ueshiba needed all of his strength and self-confidence as he taught in the military academies, especially as he was not among his own well-disciplined students. Instead he had to deal with excitable recruits who fully expected to find themselves at the war front within a year or two. At one military police academy the students formed a group of the toughest among them to stage a surprise attack on the 'old man'. When Ueshiba was walking across the training ground one day thirty students jumped out and rushed at the little man swinging a collection of wooden swords and rifles. The master, according to his own account of the incident, was undisturbed.

> They attacked from every direction, but all I had to do was step off the line of attack and gently push them away. They were flying all over the place! ... when there are so many people, things become quite chaotic for the attackers. After five or six minutes, they were out of breath and lost their will to fight. (30)

The army was absorbed at this time in the creation of a puppet state in Manchuria and was planning to invade the remainder of China. Ueshiba was closely involved in the moves to establish a workable Japanese colony in northern China. He paid many visits to Manchuria, visits that allowed him to see some of the places he had travelled through a decade earlier. This time, however, he was in Manchuria as an honored guest who gave demonstrations of aikido to the rulers and top generals of the fledgling state.

At one of these demonstrations Ueshiba, perhaps conscious that his audience included many high ranking judo and kendo experts, sensed that his smooth performance of aikido throws was not entirely convincing the spectators. "Very well," he said, halting the demonstration. "Everyone here is a famous martial artist. Let's do some serious practice. Is there anyone who will volunteer to attack this old man all out?" After some discussion the crowd nominated Tenryu, a famous and powerful retired sumo wrestler, as their representative. Tenryu, according to his own account of the incident, was unprepared for what happened next.

> From appearances, he was an ordinary, friendly, little old man. When he challenged me to come at him, I had great confidence in my own martial skill and strength … I tried as hard as I could to control him, but even as I put out my full power, he took control of me instead, and without any apparent effort. Well, I was totally taken by surprise. I let out a yell! There was no purpose in going any further, so I knelt down and bowed to him, saying, "I give in." (30)

Tenryu became one of Ueshiba's many instant converts. He accompanied the master back to Tokyo and joined him for an intensive two-month long training period. Ueshiba clearly enjoyed the company of the renowned wrestler and brought him along as he toured Japan. On one occasion they visited Mount Kurama, the legendary hill to the north of Kyoto where Yoshitsune is said to have honed his fighting skills. On a moonless night, at three in the morning, Ueshiba took Tenryu on a hike to the top of the mountain. It proved to be an expectedly hard training session for the sumo wrestler as Ueshiba leaned back and told Tenryu to push him up the innumerable steps that ascend the steep path to the summit of Mount Kurama. There, on the pitch-black plateau at the top of the mountain, Ueshiba announced that they would engage in combat with swords. This highly unusual training regime was repeated night after night and the frustrated Tenryu found himself swinging wildly at an invisible opponent who could easily knock him down. In the end he learned how to sense his attacker coming at him in the dark.

Turning Away

Ueshiba had become close to the expansionist factions at the heart of the military government of Japan and he seems to have shared many of their political views. In stark contrast to the pacifist statements that would mark his post-war years he strongly argued before the war that the martial arts should apply themselves to supporting the Japanese military effort.

> … the true task of Japanese martial arts is to become the leader of all the martial arts on earth as part of the continuing process of realizing an Imperial Way for the whole world. Japan is the suzerain of the globe, the model for the earth and the will of the entire world is Greater Japan. Japan is the model form for the

perfect world. It is only after this spirit is completely understood that one can really understand the true meaning of Japanese martial arts. (31)

But becoming too close to any of the military factions in the turbulent Tokyo of the 1930s was a dangerous game as so many different currents of right-wing opinion were openly competing to take control of the nation. Early in 1935 a group of young army officers attempted to stage a coup when they assassinated several members of the government and briefly occupied central Tokyo. In the aftermath of this rebellion the shocked establishment moved, for a time, to stamp out violent radicalism.

One target of the government's anger was the Omoto Kyo religion. The authorities were keenly aware that Onisaburo Deguchi had been in close communication with the radicals. Once again the government decided to "erase the pagan religion from the face of the earth." By the end of the year Omoto Kyo had become subject to severe official repression. Members of the religion were tortured by the police and its buildings were dynamited. Ueshiba, who had never hidden his ongoing connection to Omoto Kyo, was widely expected to be a target of the crackdown. But in the end it turned out that several of the policemen responsible for questioning Ueshiba also happened to be his students. After just a day in custody, during which he explained his philosophy of life to an attentive audience, Ueshiba was released without charge.

Around this time Ueshiba purchased some farmland in Iwama, just to the north of Tokyo city. It was land on which he planned to build a retirement home for himself and his family. But as war clouds darkened over Japan Ueshiba made a typically unpredictable decision, a decision that came as a great shock to many of his friends and students. Without warning he quit his prominent position in Tokyo and relocated to Iwama. Perhaps the move was a response by the mercurial Ueshiba to the unwelcome bureaucratic interference that his martial art was attracting. Japan was rapidly becoming a society that was dedicated to total war and the martial arts organizations were expected to play their part in the effort. The Butokukai in Kyoto had taken a close interest in Ueshiba's group and had pressured him into adopting the same dan grading system that was followed by the rest of the martial arts community. It may also have been the Butokukai that pushed for Ueshiba's art to be renamed as aikido so that it would fit neatly among the judo, kendo, karate-do and kyudo organizations. Ueshiba, who was a supreme individualist, must have found all of this meddling hard to take.

But as bombs began to fall on Tokyo in April 1942 it is also likely that Ueshiba sensed that the war was beginning to turn against Japan. He had reached a position where he was the most famous martial artist in the entire nation. Now he suddenly walked away from it all. Ueshiba turned his back on the epic and disastrous struggle that his nation was waging against most of the rest of the world. For the next twenty years he would hide himself away among the rice fields and the hills of Iwama.

13. Total War, Total Defeat

The Land of the Gods

The cyclone of change that blew through Japan during the first three decades of the twentieth century swept the martial arts along with it. Old samurai fighting traditions were transformed and revitalized by reformers such as Kano, Funakoshi and Ueshiba. The Japanese martial arts were reborn. But all of this innovation and progress was cast into shadow by the clouds of war that settled over Japan in the 1930s.

At the onset of the Second World War the oldest Japanese people could still remember the days when their land had shut itself away from the outside world. By 1940, in a terrible reversal of course, the leaders of Japan took the decision to outdo the colonial powers that their grandfathers had feared most. Their nation would become a rampaging invader, a military machine dedicated to the pillage of foreign nations. It is the destiny of Japan, they said. The Land of the Gods has a right to rule over the peoples of the earth.

Anger that Japan would never be accepted as an equal by the Western powers lay behind the growth of ultranationalism. It was a movement that quickly expanded from tiny secret societies to penetrate the inner ranks of the army and government. By 1932 Japanese democracy was effectively dead and fascist Germany had replaced Britain as the model that Japanese politicians aspired to emulate. From this point nothing could slow the momentum that carried Japan towards war. The entire nation was reshaped to meet the needs of military expansion and the martial arts were no exception. All over Japan martial arts instructors became tools, often willing tools, of the military drive to produce young people who would be ready to fight in the coming war.

The Body of the Nation

By 1930 the Japanese martial arts had fully recovered from the low point that they had sunk to in the late nineteenth century. Two and a half million citizens now held a black belt or an equivalent ranking in one of the eight officially recognized martial arts. A large proportion of these black belt holders were very young. Most Japanese of the pre-war generation had begun their studies of the martial arts after 1911 when a choice of either kendo or judo became a required subject for all boys in the nation's junior high schools.

Kendo and judo were the dominant martial arts but tens of thousands more were practicing karate, aikijutsu, kyudo, jujutsu, naginatajutsu, or iaido. Many more belonged to older martial schools that had preserved fighting skills from the days of the samurai. Presiding over this thriving world was the Dainipponbutokukai, the Great Japan Martial Virtue Association, based in Kyoto. From the outset this was an organization with a mission to integrate the martial arts with the nation's military forces. Its proclaimed aims were the restoration of the samurai spirit of bushido, the promotion of the martial arts, and the creation of a strong military culture in Japan.

The Butokukai opened its own training school in Kyoto in 1911 and, as war approached, this school became the Japanese equivalent of West Point, a place where young men could study martial arts and learn military strategy. For twenty years it continued to be possible for constituent members of the Butokukai to hold relatively liberal political views but in Kyoto the organization became a cheerleader for nationalism. Branches of the Butokukai were set up throughout the country and these groups promoted the idea, so important to the coming war effort, that the life of the nation as a single body (kokutai) was of greater importance than the life of any individual.

The Butokukai school in Kyoto was closely involved in a push to change the names of individual martial arts, dispensing with titles such as karate jutsu and replacing them with names such as karate do. In 1919 the school appointed the prominent nationalist Hiromichi Nishikubo as principal. Nishikubo was not the first figure to argue for a change in the names of martial arts. Jigoro Kano had changed the name of his art to judo from jujutsu because he wanted to emphasize his vision of judo as a Way ('do' in Japanese) that leads to the development of the self and upright service to society.

But Nishikubo had a very different conception of the meaning of 'do', for him the Way of budo was a path that ended in a commitment to sacrifice one's life for the Emperor. He wrote that it was more important for young people to develop a feeling of self-abandonment to the national will than to worry about their actual martial skills. Martial arts training, in other words, was to be a path for developing self-sacrificing soldiers. When he took over the leadership of the Butokukai school in 1919 Nishikubo changed the name of the school to Budo Senmon Gakko and under his influence the Butokukai strongly promoted the use of budo, kendo, judo and kyudo as replacement names for bujutsu, gekken, jujutsu and kyujutsu.

As war approached the Butokukai moved beyond promoting militarism and became an actual instrument of the military government. No less a figure than the Prime Minister, Hideki Tojo, was appointed as the president of the organization. The government had decided that education should have military objectives in a time of total war and the Butokukai helped to organize classes in bayonet thrusting, bomb throwing and spear fighting for twelve year olds all over the nation. By March 1942 the war had truly become a total war and the Butokukai was officially ordered to make all martial arts instruction subservient to the war effort. The emphasis was to be on training young people to kill and to kill quickly.

For the Emperor

As the undeclared war with China slowly grew in scale and Japan moved towards becoming a war society the way that the martial arts were practiced underwent a profound change. Most schools became more military and more formal in their training methods. Students were expected to bow as they entered a training hall and to kneel in lines that were organized in strict order by rank. Training would begin with further bows, often to a photograph of the Emperor or to the national flag. Many dojos adopted a practice, common in nineteenth century sword schools, of requiring their students to participate in communal seated meditation. As they rose to their feet the students would move in synchronous lines, chanting in unison as they followed the orders of their instructor.

When instructions were issued the students were expected to answer in military fashion with a loud Hai! ('Yes, I understand.') In other schools the students would shout Oss! in response to commands, a practice that is believed to have originated with the students of the Butokukai school who would shout a morning greeting Ohayogozaimasu! to each other. Eventually the greeting, which was rather a mouthful, was shortened to the mutually encouraging interjection it remains today, Oss!

This militarization of the martial arts was particularly marked in karate, a fighting form that had dramatically changed since its origins in semi-informal training circles on Okinawa. The intense and collective atmosphere of karate practice in the 1930s was not entirely a new development. Synchronous group training had emerged earlier in the century thanks to the efforts of Kentsu Yabu, a chief assistant to the aging master Itosu in the introduction of karate to Okinawan schools. Yabu had been one of the first Okinawan men to serve in the Japanese army. On return to Okinawa he set about introducing several aspects of military discipline to his school classes. But the forced atmosphere of the 1930s led to Yabu's reforms being hardened and intensified. Discipline in karate dojos became rigid, the teacher a commanding officer rather than an advisor. Karate training had become parade ground training.

Although Japan's military leaders paid a good deal of lip service to the idea that the martial arts were a vital part of the training of their troops, many of them were actually quite skeptical of the value of the old fighting methods. The generals had zero interest in preserving historical techniques or in helping soldiers to absorb life enhancing philosophies. What they wanted from the martial arts dojos was an uncomplicated system of battlefield survival. Judo, from the point of view of the military, was a sport and therefore a waste of time. Kendo was little more than dancing with wooden sticks and the older martial arts were relics of the middle ages. The army wanted something much more direct. Under military pressure the conception of budo shifted sharply away from mind-body-spirit development. Budo would now be seen as a method of training the population in ways to conduct desperate hand-to-hand fighting in defense of the state and of the Emperor.

The actual fighting training that young army recruits received was largely designed by the Toyama Military School in Tokyo. Serious problems had become evident during the Russo-Japanese war when the Japanese troops proved to be inferior to their Russian counterparts in sudden close-quarter fighting. One reason for their failures had been that, in the rush to modernize everything, the army had discarded the excellent Japanese katana in favor of European style sabers.

With this experience in mind, the army decided in the 1920s to issue katana to officers and to train these officers to use their swords in samurai fashion. They appointed the leading swordsman Hakudo Nakayama to create a battlefield fighting system for the modern age. He designed a simple curriculum of techniques for close quarter fighting using sword (kenjutsu), bayonet (jukenjutsu) and knife (tantojutsu). Nakayama's ideas were adopted at first by the Toyama School and then spread throughout the military. The new approach proved effective. When fighting began in China the Japanese soldiers had a great advantage in situations where they could secretly approach the enemy and attack with terrifying speed using their guns and blades.

In Tokyo, the Nakano School was the central institution for training soldiers to act as counterintelligence and guerrilla warfare agents. This school, which turned out around two thousand five hundred elite operatives during the course of the war, was eager to find the most effective unarmed combat system for its agents. The staff of the Nakano School invited instructors from various martial arts for evaluation and in the end they settled on the directness and power of Gichin Funakoshi's brand of karate.

Shigeru Egami, one of Funakoshi's leading students, became the chief unarmed combat instructor at the spy school. He simplified the karate curriculum to very basic elements, teaching students only how to punch and kick in straight lines. It was rough training. The students wore uniforms and combat boots and learned how to injure opponents by kicking each other in the shins and testicles and by punching each other in the face. Injuries were common but the trainees were expected to continue to practice and to ignore cuts and severe bruising.

Marching Bravely
The long, unofficial war with China finally became an open war in 1937. The one million Japanese troops of the invasion force had enormous advantages in organization and technology but China was a huge

country and its population was much larger than that of Japan. The Japanese generals soon realized that a war against the entire Chinese nation could not be won quickly and that they needed to inspire their troops to endure a long period of suffering and self-sacrifice. In a search for uplifting propaganda the military increasingly turned to the nation's samurai traditions for source material. This adoption of samurai tradition was not an entirely new idea. As early as 1882 the Meiji Emperor had described bushido as a "reflection of the whole of the subjects of Japan." But by the late thirties the elitist individualism of the samurai was being recast as something completely different. It was decreed that every member of the armed forces, and the people at large, were to act as a fearless heroes, without self-interest but with the courage of a samurai fighter. Such invocations of samurai bravery were not always militarily effective. Japanese officers began to enter battles marching boldly at the head of their units with their samurai swords clinking at their sides. Only in 1941 did the army acknowledge the astonishingly high death rate among Japanese leaders on the battlefield. Officers were ordered to take up safer positions in the rear of attacks.

As the Japanese army raced across China the national press reported the exploits of troops in battle as a thrilling revival of the heroism of the samurai past. In 1937, during the battle to take control of the Chinese capital at Nanking, Japanese newspapers published breathless accounts of a 'competition to cut off one hundred heads'. Two army officers, fighting in desperate hand-to-hand combat, were said to be racing each other to the grisly target of one hundred severed heads. The officers were pictured in Japanese newspapers proudly posing with their swords in front of a running total of the number of heads they had lopped off. They looked for all the world like a couple of sportsmen boasting of their most recent baseball score. In fact, as the two admitted after the war, they had not been fighting with their swords but had simply been executing helpless prisoners. And there was nothing heroic about the subsequent destruction of Nanking and the barbaric massacre of its population. It was one of the very blackest episodes in Japanese martial history.

The war with China was a very long one, stretching over the years between the Manchurian Incident in 1931, when Japanese fanatics created a ruse to justify their occupation of Northern China, and the final defeat of 1945. One million Japanese troops were based in China throughout the war, as were millions of other Japanese nationals performing non-military tasks. It was a huge undertaking that involved Japanese martial artists at every level as fighters, administrators and educators. One of the most prominent of the martial artists who played an active role in Japan's expansion into China was Gogen Yamaguchi, the leader of Goju-Ryu karate in Japan.

Yamaguchi abandoned his leadership of Goju Ryu karate after coming under the spell of the charismatic General Ishiwara, a man who had a fevered vision of a utopian Manchurian state that could serve as a model for the rule of all China by Japan. In 1938 Yamaguchi, at the request of Ishiwara, travelled to Manchuria to act as a trouble-shooter and spy and to provide leadership to the Japanese troops who were struggling to maintain order in the wild lands of the north. Yamaguchi had many dramatic adventures in Manchuria and often had to use his karate skills to defend himself against angry crowds and armed bandits.

At the end of the war the Japanese colonial army in northern China became embroiled in desperate battles against the attacks of much larger groups of Chinese Communists who were intent on forcing them out of their country. Yamaguchi had to fight for his life during these clashes. In his autobiography he includes this hair-raising account of how he survived one attack.

> I took two revolvers and hid myself downstairs. I heard cries everywhere as many bandits invaded the city and attacked in full force, killing many of the inhabitants. Citizens were running and bullets were flying everywhere as the city was thrown into utter confusion. Bandits on horses stopped in front of our office. I took cover as I fired my revolvers through the window, until both guns were empty. Twenty bandits with guns and Chinese swords rushed our defense. Five or six bandits broke the door down with the butts of their guns and rushed into the room. With my guns empty, I resorted to Goju school of karate for my defense. I adjusted myself with breathing and was ready to fight. The room was dark and the bandits could not use their guns freely without possible injury to each other. I had trained myself to see in this amount of light and knew I would be able to withstand the onslaught of four or five people at a time. Under such a situation, I had to dispatch the enemy, one by one. I avoided the first bandit who tried to strike me with his gun, and turning quickly to the right, struck him between the thighs with a roundhouse kick. He cried and fell to the ground. Another fired his gun at me from behind, but he missed. My elbow found the pit of his stomach with great force. A bloody Chinese sword slashed at me as I struck, with my right fist, the man who was wielding this sword. The fighting was confused but the narrow room was to my advantage. They rushed at me in the close quarters, which made it easy for me to fight them. When they drew near, I knocked them out using nukite (finger strikes), hijiate (elbows), shuto (sword hand) and seiken (fists), against the guns, I used tobi-geri (jumping kicks) and yoko-geri (side kick). I was able to fight more freely than in practice because I did not have any regard for my opponent's welfare. Some of the bandits started up the stairs but were shot by my men who were protecting the women and children. I attacked the bandits, aiming at their eyes or between their thighs, moving quickly as I fought. Fighting hard, I hoped we could last until help arrived. Soon there were cries at the front door and the bandits started to scatter. It appeared that they had been ordered to retreat. My men came down the stairs, asking if I was injured. Luckily, only my left arm had been injured by the slash of a dagger. I went upstairs to obtain a better view and observed the bandits fallen back with stolen weapons, gun powder and supplies. It was now 7 o'clock in the morning ... When I discovered the bandits had gone, I suddenly lost all my strength and had to sit down. I had fought with them, hand to hand, for forty minutes. (32)

Yamaguchi survived several skirmishes with bandits but he was finally taken prisoner by the Soviet army as they entered Manchuria at the end of the war. He was transported to a prisoner camp in Mongolia, a terrible place where a great many Japanese inmates would die. Yamaguchi's tough frame and mental fortitude helped him to survive the freezing winters and harsh conditions. He improved relations with the camp guards by teaching them karate but he does not seem to have completely won them over. According to Yamaguchi's autobiography, a group of prison guards entertained themselves one day by locking him into a room where they had placed a Siberian tiger. He survived, he tells us, by striking the beast on the nose, elbowing its head and then leaping onto the tiger's back from where he could choke it to death.

Another famous martial artist who was called up as the Pacific War reached its height was Masahiko Kimura, the judo champion of all Japan. He graduated from university in 1941 and was soon drafted into an Air Defense unit in Kyushu. Kimura was a supremely fit and strong individual and basic training was never going to present him with much of a challenge. But he did have to learn some new skills. One of his classes was in jukenjutsu, a system for fighting with gun-mounted bayonets that had been developed from the the spear fighting arts of the samurai. In his autobiography Kimura described his first experience of bayonet fighting.

The jukenjutsu teacher, who happened to be one of the nation's leading experts in this school of fighting, confidently asked for volunteers to step forward. Kimura was a judo man and knew nothing about weapons but he was pushed forward by an officer. He slowly walked towards the expert, pretended to initiate an attack with his wooden practice rifle and then suddenly hurled his gun at the instructor's face. Just as the teacher blocked the flying weapon Kimura dived into a judo throw, grabbed the man around the knees and tipped him onto his back. In a flash, Kimura leapt onto his opponent's chest, ripped off his face guard, and prepared to knock the celebrity out.

Superior officers rushed to drag Kimura away but the outburst of violence probably saved his life. Kimura had already volunteered for front line service in the Pacific. When the officers realized that they had a famous martial artist in their ranks they decided to hold him back from combat duty. Kimura's comrades sailed to the Solomon Islands where every member of his platoon, with only one exception, was killed.

With so many young men being called up to serve in China the martial arts training halls of Japan were emptied of most of their students. Gichin Funakoshi, a pacifist at heart, had sombre memories of the war years. As he recalled in his autobiography, the approach of war made karate more popular than ever. His dojos were so full of young men anxiously trying to toughen up their bodies that numbers of them were forced to train outdoors. In his classes, as in those of every other martial art, training became harder and more practical. These young men who were facing the draft simply wanted to learn how to knock an opponent down quickly. Then the exodus began. Funakoshi's students would approach him one by one to kneel and announce, "Sensei, I have been drafted and I'm off to serve my country and my Emperor."

Life was desperate for these troops when they arrived in the war zones. In the first glorious months of the war the Japanese soldiers won victory after victory. But the tide eventually turned and the young men were faced with constant battles against larger and better equipped forces. Takatoshi Nishizono, a member of Otsuka's Wado Ryu karate group, was one of those martial arts instructors who experienced the desperation of that time. He was responsible for teaching karate to an elite army group in China toward the end of the war. His charges were an undercover unit that was certain to find itself mixed up in trouble and the unit commander asked Nishizono to prepare the men for deadly combat. He was given only a month to train the soldiers and so he concentrated on instruction in simple blocks, punches to the face and kicks to the testicles. The young recruits practiced these basics and then spent the remainder of their training time on hard fighting practice. Nishizono reported that if any soldier slacked off he would personally fight with that man until the recruit could no longer stand. Nishizono was a tough teacher but after a month of training he was left with nothing but pity for these men. The teacher was able to return to his job in Beijing but the young volunteer soldiers were sent into battle where they all, to a man, died.

I Felt My Heart Would Break

Morihei Ueshiba, the most respected martial artist in Japan, began the war at the centre of the military establishment. Many of the nation's generals and admirals were among his personal students and he had influential contacts throughout the government and among the forces fighting in China. Above all, Ueshiba was close to Prince Konoe, the aristocrat who had become Prime Minister of Japan in 1941. Konoe was the leader of the wing of nationalist opinion in Japan that supported expansion in Asia but wished to avoid an outright confrontation with the industrial might of the United States. But more radical voices held sway and the case against launching a war on every front was lost. Konoe resigned his position shortly before the attack on Pearl Harbor.

For a while it seemed that the radical nationalists had been entirely justified. The Japanese army and navy thrilled the nation during the final months of 1941 as they made stunning advances on every front. But behind the scenes some of the more rational Japanese leaders were horrified at the thought of fighting the huge international coalition that had now pledged itself to destroy their country. Konoe himself felt that going to war with the entire world was an hopeless task. He asked Ueshiba to travel to China to negotiate an end to the conflict in that country so that the one million Japanese troops in China could at least be transferred to other battles. Ueshiba willingly made his way to southern China with the aim of negotiating directly with Chiang Kai-shek, the President of the Chinese Republic.

Ueshiba's mission proved to be a failure and he returned to Japan without even having laid eyes on the Chinese leader. As he made his report Ueshiba must have noticed the disappointment and worry in the eyes of Konoe and the other politicians who had supported his doomed journey. Suddenly this well-connected martial artist seemed to lose interest in his high social standing and the confidence he had once felt in the outcome of the war. Ueshiba decided to move to his rural bolt hole in Iwama. It was a place where he could at least keep the legacy of aikido alive, whatever might happen in Tokyo.

Leaving his son in charge of the aikido dojo in Tokyo Ueshiba moved into a ramshackle converted barn in the countryside. It was a dilapidated building but Ueshiba now proclaimed that it to be 'the birthplace of aikido.' In a life of dramatic twists and turns this was perhaps the strangest move of his life. He had always behaved as a leader but now he chose to hide away himself away in rural seclusion while the nation around him was being whipped into the frenzy of total war. At the same time that Japanese schoolchildren were being trained to throw bombs and teenage boys were being recruited as suicide pilots Ueshiba devoted his energies to clearing fields, planting crops and building an elaborate shrine for the forty-three guardian gods of aikido. He was finished with war.

> The Way of the Warrior has been misunderstood. It is not a means to kill and destroy others. Those who seek to compete and better one another are making a terrible mistake. To smash, injure, or destroy is the worst thing a human being can do. The real Way of a Warrior is to prevent such slaughter - it is the Art of Peace, the power of love. (33)

In Tokyo the Ueshiba family had been well-off. His dojo had charged the highest fees of any martial arts organization and he had attracted all kinds of material and personal support from the elite ranks of Japanese society. Now, in Iwama as the war situation worsened, Ueshiba faced an increasingly tough situation. But he was a resilient man who had already lived through the worst that the winters of Hokkaido could throw at him.

At the end of the war the Ueshiba family was completely impoverished. Like everyone around them they grew what food they could. While others struggled to cope with the painful destruction of everything familiar, Ueshiba's solipsism carried him through. He simply plowed the fields and talked happily about the future of aikido. He practiced his martial art in the open air with anyone who made the journey to visit him.

In Tokyo it seemed very unlikely that aikido would have any kind of future. The Kobukan dojo had been one of the few buildings to survive the American bombing raids but it was soon filled by thirty families who were taking refuge from the ruins. Aikido, the most fashionable martial art of the pre-war years, was now being practiced nowhere in the world but in the fields around Ueshiba's country home. Just a handful of people throwing each other around under the ceaseless buzzing of the cicada.

For Gichin Funakoshi the war was disastrous. He had sent dozens of young men off to join the fight and so few of them had returned.

> Of course, many students died in battle, so many, alas, that I lost count of them. I felt my heart would break as I received report after report telling me of the deaths of so many promising young men. Then I would stand alone in the silent dojo and offer a prayer to the soul of the deceased, recalling the days when he had practiced his karate so diligently. (34)

As endless clouds of bombs fell on Tokyo in early 1945 Funakoshi's home and dojo, the most important place in the karate world, was demolished. The dojo, painstakingly built by his students, had been his pride and joy. To Funakoshi it was the best thing he had accomplished in his life. After one night of explosions it was gone forever.

When Japan finally surrendered Funakoshi left the bombed out wastes of the capital to be reunited with the wife he had left behind in Okinawa twenty five years earlier. The aging couple scraped a living from the land in the rural depths of Kyushu, gathering seaweed from the beach to feed their hunger. Shortly after Funakoshi left Tokyo his treasured son Yoshitaka succumbed to the tuberculosis that had troubled him since childhood. His death was a tragic loss to the family and to the subsequent history of karate. Yoshitaka had been his father's heir apparent, a man who was described by several of his contemporaries as a karate genius.

In 1947 Funakoshi's wife also died and the old man decided to make his way back to Tokyo. He took a slow train back to the capital that stopped at almost every station. The small figure clutching the precious container of his wife's ashes must have felt that his life was over. He was astonished to find that at many of the stations on the long passage to Tokyo former students were waiting on the platform to greet him and to express their condolences. "Tears," he understandably relates, "flowed down my cheeks unchecked." (34) The karate pioneer was now almost eighty years old. Despite all of the tragedies of the war he would once again be able to find a certain happiness in Tokyo. He would live to a grand old age, sharing a house with his remaining family and acting as the figurehead of karate as it slowly climbed out from the ashes.

No Longer Enemies

Japan was a simply terrifying place to be in the early months of 1945. On one side, the people were being ordered by their government to fight to the very end against a merciless enemy, to die like "one hundred million shattered jewels." From the other side came American bombers dropping their explosive charges on towns and factories by day and by night from defenseless skies. Masahiko Kimura, the judo champion, experienced the full terror of the final days of the war on his wedding night.

> I was just about to take my new wife into my arms when three hundred B29 planes attacked our town. Amid the explosions I sat up and ran down the stairs. I lifted two of the floor mats over my head and my wife and parents took shelter under the mats. It was too dangerous to stay in the house so clinging to each other we ran through the bullets and took shelter in a mulberry field. I felt that my eardrums would split open with the sound of bombs exploding all around us. My peaceful town was transformed into horror as the people raced around in panic. Children screamed in terror and the sky turned into bright midday as it filled with hundreds of tracer bullets. It was like a fireworks display in hell. (25)

On August 15 the strange high-pitched voice of the Emperor, a voice that very few had ever heard before, spoke from radios all over Japan. The aristocratic vocabulary was difficult to comprehend but the meaning soon became crystal clear. The war was over.

Japan was in such ruins that even the first Americans to enter the country were shocked to find out how smashed up it actually was. Three million citizens had been killed and tens of millions more were sick, injured, homeless or stranded overseas. The cities had largely been abandoned. Of Tokyo's seven million residents five million, including Gichin Funakoshi, had deserted the city. It was easy to see why so many had fled. Sixty-five percent of all Tokyo homes had been destroyed. In Japan's third city, Nagoya, the figure was eighty-nine percent. Nine million homeless people were sleeping in workplaces, in train stations or on the street. In the three years after the end of the war crowds of stranded Japanese made their way back from prison camps overseas. But few of those who had remained at home had any sympathy for these disorientated and completely impoverished refugees. Newspapers in Japan had begun to openly report the atrocities that had been committed by the Imperial Army overseas and many blamed the returning soldiers and their families for the disaster that had eviscerated Japan.

Among these ruins most of the population abandoned any thought of the old martial arts. Few people were able to consume sufficient calories to have the spare energy to engage in any kind of physical training. A small number of dojos continued to operate quietly but they were almost empty. At the heart of the martial arts community some of those who had been leaders before and during the war struggled to express a new philosophy that would match these strangely changed times. There were a number of strained attempts to explain that Japanese budo could actually become a vehicle for the creation of peace and amity between nations.

Hakudo Nakayama, the great sword master who had been intimately involved in creating fighting methods for the Japanese army, explicitly argued that the true spirit of bushido required the Japanese people to welcome their recent enemies.

> There is no sense in going over what is past and done. To brood over past events is the way of the weakling. In olden times, the samurai never mouthed what was finished. He fought for all he was worth against the enemy, but, once he owned defeat, the way of a true samurai was to love his enemy with greater love than before the fight ... It is the ultimate meaning of the art of fencing. We must greet the Allied Army with just such a spirit. Yesterday they were enemies but today they are no longer so. If we cannot think of them as being no longer enemies, then it cannot be said that we truly understand the spirit of bushido... If there is the least feeling of ill-will harbored in our hearts and if we cannot take a broad outlook, it is bound to show in our faces and attitude, giving reason for others to think of us as cowardly.[35]

Nakayama, who had come through the war unscathed, was one of the lucky ones. Many of the key figures in the martial arts community were dead and many more were scattered in prison camps across the Asian mainland. Among those who died one of the greatest losses was Jinan Shinzato, the karate expert who had been expected to inherit the leadership of Chojun Miyagi's Goju Ryu organization. Shinzato was killed at the mouth of an Okinawan cave as his army unit desperately sought cover from relentless American attacks.

Occupation
Under the messianic leadership of General MacArthur the American occupiers assumed total control over Japanese society. Many of their first actions were targeted at exterminating any existing remnants of militarism. This did not prove to be a difficult job. The defeated army and their arrested leaders were deeply unpopular with the Japanese people who had paid such a heavy price for the wartime adventures. The top layers of the military and of the right-wing organizations were convicted in War Crimes Tribunals that ended with nine hundred and twenty individuals being executed and several thousand more imprisoned.

At the same time the occupation forces moved to ban all activities that had been linked with the war effort. They paid particularly close attention to the schools where, towards the end of the war, 'sports' education had largely been reduced to activities such as grenade throwing, bayonet practice, radio transmission and running in military uniform while carrying sandbags. It soon became clear to the occupying forces that there had been a direct connection between martial arts classes in the schools and the Japanese war effort. The US forces summarily imposed a ban on all martial arts teaching in educational institutions. The central martial arts organization, the Butokukai, was also investigated and in the end took the decision to disband before it could be closed down.

Bushido and budo had become strongly associated with Japanese fascism in the minds of both the occupiers and the Japanese people. To make such a connection was rational enough as so many important martial artists had taken extreme nationalist positions during the war. There was, in fact, such a cloud of suspicion hanging over the martial arts that most Japanese people came to believe that a ban had been imposed on every kind of budo. In fact no martial art was completely outlawed for the general public but for some time the American forces kept a close watch on those who continued to play active roles in the kendo associations and the karate clubs. The Japanese martial arts had been in the ascendant during the war. Now they reached the lowest point in their entire history.

Among the crowds of Japanese soldiers who were slowly making their way back to the mainland from overseas prison camps was the man who would go on to head an international Goju-Ryu karate organization. Gogen Yamaguchi was finally released from captivity in Mongolia in late 1947. As he arrived in Japan he was astonished to see the change in his country; the shattered, bombed out cities and the hopeless people. There was no fighting spirit left in the country and no-one seemed to care about the martial arts anymore.

In despair Yamaguchi decided to kill himself. He dressed in a formal kimono and made his way to a shrine that was one of the few still standing among the rubble of downtown Tokyo. He placed a dagger on the ground and sat on his knees in silent prayer. Suddenly, a flash of inspiration surged through his mind and body.

> In the course of time I lost all feeling and had a sense of walking amidst the clouds, floating in the sky with no existence of my own. Such feelings are beyond my ability to describe. All past troubles were forgotten and I felt as if my soul was floating in a world of glory and peace. Then I found myself stretched out face down on the floor. How long I had been there I didn't know. Coming to my senses I found everything appeared to be shining brightly as if the whole world was living in happiness. Never will I forget my mental state at that moment. (32)

As he revived Yamaguchi realized that he had been drowning in self-pity. No more, he vowed. He had a responsibility to help the young people of Japan to pull themselves out of their depression and helplessness. Later that year he opened the first of what would come to be hundreds of Goju-Ryu karate dojos.

For the great mass of the Japanese population there was little to be done in the years after the war but humbly accept the domination of their nation by the Americans. But among the martial arts community there were several powerful individuals who found it most difficult to behave in a docile manner. Gozo Shioda, a tiny but aggressive aikido expert, on several occasions witnessed drunken GIs abusing Japanese citizens. In his autobiography he describes one such incident.

> Then, I heard the report of a gun. When I looked in the direction of the shot I found one of six black soldiers holding up his gun over his head for fun and threatening people around him. Passersby were all frightened and panicked, some of them running into a nearby shop to hide. I walked towards the man little by little. Maybe he thought I was just a child and he turned his back on me. I seized this chance and struck him in the back of the head. The instant he turned around I struck him with the side of my hand repeatedly with all my might while nearly jumping up at him. While he was disoriented, I wrestled the gun from his grasp and threw it far away. Then I applied the shihonage technique and threw him to the ground. At that time an MP jeep came with sirens wailing from afar. (36)

Mas Oyama, the powerful karate expert who would later create Kyokushin karate, had been an aviation student during the war and had begun many heartbreaking days by sharing breakfast with a group of kamikaze pilots who flew off into a sky from which they would never return. By his own admission Oyama was an angry young man after the war and he repeatedly found himself mixed up in brawls with the U.S. Military Police.

Oyama's good friend, the judo expert Masahiko Kimura, was also regularly in trouble with the Americans. On one occasion in 1946 Kimura was waiting in line for a train when he witnessed four military police making their way down the line. The Americans insulted and physically intimidated each person as they passed.

> As they made their way down the line to me I decided on the spot what I would do. As one of the men reached for my collar I struck his hand as hard as I could. The four men instantly changed color. "Let's throw this cheeky Jap in the river," they shouted as they closed in to drag me onto the bridge. I knew that this was not just a scuffle. I was fighting for the honor of judo and I had to win.
> A black man threw a fast punch at my face. I blocked with my left hand and kicked him in the crotch as hard as I could. As he crouched in pain I looked behind to see a huge white man making for me with both hands. I struck his right arm really hard with a knife hand blow and then threw him into the fast-flowing river with my favorite shoulder throw. The other two MPs were gazing at me with their

> mouths hanging open in surprise but they came at me one at a time. I head-butted the third man so hard that he fell over and then I grabbed the last MP by the testicles and twisted them. Ever since Junior High School I have been famous for my skill in twisting an opponent's testicles. I had complete confidence that this technique would work. (25)

After this showdown Kimura worried that he would be arrested and jailed, but once again he had a lucky break. On the week following this confrontation he was visited by an American Military Police officer who told him that the men he had fought with were rogue elements with a bad reputation. The army did not plan to arrest Kimura. On the contrary, they wanted him to come to their camp to teach his obviously superior fighting skills to American troops.

Kimura managed to gather up some cotton and thread and had judo suits made up for the American military police. He began to teach judo to the GIs and as he did so he found himself in an exceedingly strange position, one that was shared by many other martial arts teachers across the devastated nation. The training halls were almost empty of Japanese students but here were young, healthy Americans who had money to spend and a desire to learn about the Oriental way of unarmed self-defense. From Tokyo to Okinawa those few Japanese fighters who had managed to stay involved in the martial arts were astonished to find themselves training alongside people who, just months ago, had been the sworn enemies of their nation. It was undoubtedly strange, but somehow it had come about. Perhaps, in some new, unimagined way, the martial arts could have a future after all.

14. The Way Back

Among the Ruins

All through the winter of 1945 a cold wind blew on the towns and cities of Japan. The people were bewildered, passive and exhausted; they had given everything to the war effort. Their nation and their culture seemed to have lost all meaning. Their hearts were broken. Japan had become a nightmare, a place that felt like an evil dream in that frigid winter. Every face was shadowed with confusion, sadness, loss.

The biggest problem facing the Japanese people was hunger. In the last months of the war supplies of the nation's beloved white rice had almost disappeared. Families were instructed by the government to eat grain husks, seeds, insects and vermin. But hunger only intensified after the end of the war when the harvest failed. Thousands died of starvation before the first shipments of protein and calorie rich foodstuffs from America began to ease the crisis. The economy collapsed, so badly that a huge black market sprang up overnight. Crime and lawlessness swept through a population that had been obedient and self-disciplined for centuries. On top of all of this confusion and misery came plagues of cholera and dysentery that sickened millions and killed many.

But despite all of these horrors, the Japanese people had survived. It was an outcome that had not seemed certain in the final, terrible months of the war when military fanatics had ordered all civilians to prepare for mass suicide attacks on the American forces. The people had survived and they would now set about rebuilding their nation with growing energy and determination. All over Japan the martial artists who had lived through the war began to rebuild their training circles with the same slowly returning vigor that was emerging everywhere. Out of the ashes judo fighters, kendo players and karate experts created new organizations that would make their arts more popular and influential than ever before.

For the defeated population one clear fact of life in this new world was that the war had been a huge mistake. Everyone wanted a permanent peace. The Americans forced a new constitution on Japan that forbade the nation to possess an army, let alone go to war. But such a prohibition was hardly necessary. The people were sick of war and they were sickened by what the newspapers were telling them about the war that had been fought in their name. Military men who had once strutted at the highest levels of society were now despised and even ordinary, conscripted soldiers returning from overseas were suspected of the most awful crimes.

The effect of this new national mood on the martial arts community was profound. Morihei Ueshiba, once an intimate friend of many generals, now spoke for the majority in his criticisms of the war.

> In the old days Budo was used for destructive purposes - to attack others in order to seize more land and possessions. Japan lost the war because it followed an evil, destructive path. From now on, Budo must be used for constructive purposes. (37)

Everyone in the martial arts community, including Ueshiba, had been forced to adopt a new approach and a new language. For some this merely involved suppressing their true feelings of anger and frustration. But most martial artists genuinely wanted to reshape their language and their practices to fit this new world. The wave of pacifism that swept through Japan found its most ironic expression among the martial arts community. In word, thought and deed the leaders of the budo groups set out to represent their fighting arts as non-violent ways. This was a relatively simple task for unarmed arts like aikido or judo. But in some of the older fighting styles it was more difficult to draw a veil over their bloody history. Senior experts from these groups set about removing or disguising violent techniques that could only have been used to kill an opponent. The final thrusts of a sword into an imaginary body were quietly dropped from some of the sword kata of iaido.

The Americans had quickly banned all martial arts practice from Japanese schools and they were deeply suspicious of the idea, promoted so heavily during wartime by the budo community, of spiritual education (seishin kyoiku). But the occupiers were quite willing to see traditional sporting activities resume. Just a few months after the end of the war the first sumo tournaments were held and towards the end of 1946 American officials agreed to the creation of an All-Japan Judo Black Belt Association.

The judo community had certainly joined in with the patriotic tub thumping of the war years but judo had managed to avoid outright identification with right wing politics. Consequently the judo clubs bore little of the taint of extreme nationalism that hung over the sword schools. Quickly these clubs began to reorganize. Judo officials sent petitions to General McArthur explaining that they had now removed mass outdoors training in regimented lines from the judo curriculum. In 1950 the occupying forces gave permission for judo to be reintroduced to the school system.

A Big Blond Foreigner

Judo was the first martial art to make a sustained recovery from the nadir of the 1940s and it also became the first to achieve widespread international acceptance. Small judo groups had been active in several nations as far back as the early decades of the twentieth century. In 1951 thirteen European associations came together to form the International Judo Federation under the leadership of Risei Kano, the son of the founder of judo. In 1956, just eleven years after the end of the war, the first world judo championship was held in Tokyo. The tournament was arranged in the traditional manner as an open-weight competition that allowed small men to engage in combat with much larger opponents. It was a demonstration of Kano's faith in technique over strength. Japanese fighters dominated this world championship and the following competition that was held in 1958.

It was easy for the Japanese to believe that even though foreigners might choose to study the Japanese martial arts they could never surpass the skill of the local experts. But a huge shock rattled the foundations of Japanese judo in 1961 at the third World Judo Championships. It came from a blond Dutchman named Anton Geesink. He was almost two meters tall, weighed 145 kilograms and had trained extensively at the Kodokan in Tokyo. The Japanese knew all about Geesink and respected his power and technique but few expected a foreigner to be able to outclass the Japanese fighters. Judo was, after all, the living interpretation of an old samurai tradition.

But in the final of the World Championships Geesink defeated Koji Sone. It was a result that rocked the foundations of Japanese judo. The senior teachers of the Kodokan had always held unquestioned authority at the summit of the judo world. Now they suddenly looked rather foolish, so foolish that they abruptly responded to the defeat of Sone by pushing for rule changes to ensure that future competitions would be fought in separate weight groups. No longer, the Kodokan instructors hoped, would an overgrown foreigner be able to overwhelm the most skillful Japanese fighters.

In 1964 one of Jigoro Kano's greatest dreams was fulfilled when the Olympics were held in Tokyo. It was a thrilling event for the entire Japanese nation, an event that stimulated great feelings of patriotic pride. And the Olympics came at a time when Japan was entering the period of white hot economic boom that would make it, within a single decade, the world's second economic power. As the host nation Japan was able to secure a place for judo as a demonstration sport at the Olympics.

With the new weight categories in place, Japan dominated most of the judo medals. But when it came to the most prestigious event of all, the open weight final, a second disaster was lying in wait for Japanese judo. After an exhausting nine minute struggle the tall, blond European Geesink finally pinned the Japanese fighter Akio Kaminaga into submission. As Kaminaga shuffled back into his locker room he found that the entire Japanese judo team was in tears. The team's grief was shared by one hundred million Japanese who had been expecting nothing less than a gold medal. Ian Buruma has colorfully described the effect of this shocking defeat on the fragile national morale.

> Judo was not just a national sport, it symbolized the Japanese way — spiritual, disciplined, infinitely subtle; a way in which crude Western brawn would inevitably lose to superior Oriental spirit. A big, blond foreigner had humiliated Japan in front of the entire world, It was as though the ancestral Sun Goddess had been raped in public by a gang of alien demons. (38)

While Kaminaga's team mates and most of the Japanese public were devastated by his defeat at the hands of Geesink the leaders of Japanese judo had long been aware that the foreigner could win and had prepared themselves for the worst. The following day they released a statement declaring that the win by Geesink was "a win for Western science." From this point onwards those in judo circles who had attempted to preserve the legacy of Kano and Mifune by stressing elegant technique over brute force quickly lost their influence. The driving force of Japanese judo became an intense focus on international competition and especially on the Olympics. 'Scientific' programs of physical development were introduced and competition was placed at the pinnacle of the judo world.

By the late sixties judo was booming all over the world but in Japan the sport also became even more popular thanks to the thrilling prospect of regular international competition. By the end of the decade there were very few Japanese schools or universities that could not boast a judo club. And these clubs all had rigorous training programs that involved the young club members in a daily hour of tough physical conditioning before classes and then two hours of training at the end of the day. Japanese judo was soon able to boast of not just a huge population of judo fighters but also of a very large group of elite fighters. The internal competition for places on the national team became so strong that Japan was able to take its pick from a pool of already highly conditioned athletes. Despite the uncertainty of the sixties Japan was able to retain its dominant role in international judo.

The Bear
Among all the Japanese boys who fell in love with judo after the war and kept their nation at the top levels of international competition the outstanding figure was Yasuhiro Yamashita. As a nine year old Yamashita had been an overweight and unruly school bully who had so provoked his despairing mother that she dragged him along to the local judo class. At first the physical workouts did little more than help the youth become a more effective bully but slowly he discovered that competition was another way to express his strength. The turning point came when Yamashita was warned by his teachers that he would have to give up judo if he did not mend his ways. He did, and became a serious, and outstanding, young fighter.

At eighteen Yamashita entered Tokai University, one of the most important breeding grounds for top judo fighters. He soon outstripped his seniors in the university judo club and, at the raw age of 19, won the open weight category of the 1977 all-Japan championships. From that point Yamashita went on to completely dominate Japanese judo, winning the national championships for nine consecutive years and remaining undefeated until his retirement from competition in 1983. Not since Masahiko Kimura had a judo fighter been so commanding.

Yamashita's unbroken reign at the top of Japanese judo was not without incident. His career almost came to a premature end in 1980 in the final of the Japanese championship when his opponent managed to throw Yamashita with an unexpected and dramatic technique, a jumping leg-scissor throw (kani basami) that twisted Yamashita's legs in such an unnatural direction that a bone broke. Yamashita was naturally unable to continue fighting and the judges declared the match a draw. In line with the well established judo tradition of removing dangerous techniques from the curriculum kani basami was quickly banned from competition fighting.

Yamashita was the dominant heavyweight fighter in world judo when the 1980 Olympics came around but, thanks to Japan's boycott of the Moscow Olympics, he was unable to take part. Despite that disappointment he pressed on. By 1984 he had already won the world championships four times and had become a famous man in Japan. Yamashita was offered large sums of money to try his hand at either wrestling or sumo but he simply told anyone who asked about his future that his childhood dream had been to win an Olympic medal. He would allow nothing to get in the way of that dream.

Yamashita arrived at the Olympic tournament in Los Angeles in the shape of his life. At only 180 centimeters he was shorter than most of the other heavyweights but his 128 kilogram frame gave him enormous power in both standing throws and wrestling on the mat. In the run up to the Olympics Yamashita had been undefeated in 196 consecutive competitive matches and had won the great majority of those bouts by full ippon points that were awarded for devastating throws, holds or chokes. He seemed to have no weaknesses.

Hundreds of excited Japanese fans were in the Los Angeles audience and millions more were watching on television at home when disaster struck in Yamashita's second match. At the end of the bout he limped off the mat, his calf muscle shredded. As Yamashita appeared for his semi final match the Japanese supporters were watching through their fingers as their hero, by now moving with great difficulty, seemed to offer an easy target. His opponent immediately attacked the injured leg and Yamashita was thrown. He was down half a point and, for the first time in many years, staring impending defeat in the face. But somehow the determined fighter ignored the pain in his leg and threw his opponent so hard that he was easily pinned in Yamashita's bearlike grip. The Japanese judoka held down his helplessly struggling opponent to win the match by ippon.

As the final began Yamashita walked onto the mat with an almost comical gait, dragging his injured leg across the floor. He did not look like a man capable of putting up much of a fight. When the Egyptian opponent attempted a throw Yamashita managed to slide inside and once again pinned the powerless fighter in a crushing grip. As the referee awarded the victory to Yamashita he broke into a burst of high speed hobbling that took him away from the mats where he fell, in floods of tears, into the arms of his team members. The silver medal winner, Rashwan, had sportingly declined to attack Yamashita's injured leg. When Rashwan helped the unsteady victor climb up onto the medal podium the entire Japanese nation applauded and wept.

Full of Openings
The father of karate Gichin Funakoshi returned to Tokyo in 1947 as an old and saddened man. He had lost the son who could have been his successor and the wife who had patiently waited for him in Okinawa for decades. The building he had erected to serve as a home for Japanese karate had been burned to the ground. Any human being would have been entitled to grieve after these terrible events but not a single note of self-pity can be found in the writings of Funakoshi over the ensuing years. His autobiography, written at the very end of his life, rings with a quiet enthusiasm for the progress of karate and a simple joy in the long life he had been able to lead.

Funakoshi was particularly proud of his physical strength as he entered his eighties, something that he regarded as an advertisement for the benefits of karate. He had a reddish complexion that was not the result, he insisted, of a love for alcohol but was simply the glow of good health. Funakoshi never became wealthy and he spent his last years sleeping in an upstairs room of the house that he shared with his eldest son and his grandchildren. He considered that the regular climb up and down the stairs to his bedroom was good training for his aged leg muscles. Each morning he would tidy his room, carefully comb his hair and wash his face and then he would kneel in prayer in front of images of the Emperor and of Saigo Takamori. Before eating breakfast he would always practice a number of karate kata. Funakoshi had a well developed sense of his own dignity and, in the old fashioned way, he would never allow himself to be seen in a kitchen or to be heard mentioning common items like socks or toilet paper.

Even at an advanced age Funakoshi maintained the vigilance of a karate expert. One night when he was well into his seventies he was walking home alone when a young man jumped in front of him and demanded that he hand over the package he was carrying. When the rude thief grabbed his umbrella the old master decided to act.

> His stance was full of openings. When he swung the umbrella at me, I ducked under and, with my right hand, took a firm grasp of his testicles. The pain was, I have no doubt, very nearly unbearable. (34)

The sprightly Funakoshi handed the robber over to a passing policemen but it was typical of the man that he later felt only sympathy for the thief and a certain shame over his own actions.

The founder of Japanese karate lived long enough to witness the first signs of revival in his art. Karate was being passed on to a new generation that Funakoshi was now too old to take much part in teaching. He continued to oversee one class each week at Waseda University, conducting most of his instruction from a seated position. Funakoshi was a humble man who continued to express deep gratitude to friends like Jigoro Kano who had helped and supported him when he arrived in Tokyo as an unknown outsider from Okinawa. Every time Funakoshi passed the home of judo he would remove his hat and bow deeply to the memory of the departed Kano.

The old karate master had also finally become a distinguished and venerated member of the national community. In 1954 he took centre stage at a large martial arts demonstration in Tokyo. It was an event that publicly celebrated the restoration of the once shameful fighting arts to a position of honor in Japanese society. In front of a crowd numbering in the thousands Funakoshi demonstrated kata in the company of other martial greats that included Kyuzo Mifune from judo and Hakudo Nakayama from kendo. The audience rose to its feet to applaud the little old man who had done so much to establish karate on the mainland.

Scientific Karate

Funakoshi had been too old to do very much to help the young men who had once been his students and who were now finally able to make their way home from the war. Those who had lived through that madness found it hard to remember the details of kata they had learned several years earlier. And the few karate clubs that were still in existence faced a struggle to reignite the energy and discipline that had been the norm in the 1930s. In the universities things were somewhat different. The college karate clubs were wary of the Americans and disguised themselves for some time after the war as boxing clubs. But it was in the university karate clubs that the mix of older returnees who had studied karate before the war and new and energetic young students created the right conditions for karate training to once again be taken seriously.

At the centre of the karate revival was Takushoku University where a group of students formed the Japan Karate Association (Nihon Karate Kyokai) in 1949. Gichin Funakoshi was appointed as the honorary Chief Instructor of this new organization but the real driving force was the thirty-six year old

Masatoshi Nakayama. Nakayama had been a prominent student in the karate school led by Funakoshi and his son Yoshitaka in the 1930s. He then went to China for several years where he served as a colonial administrator. As the war ended he returned to Tokyo and quickly became the outstanding figure in the circle of alumni that made up the leadership of the Takushoku University karate club. With Funakoshi being really too old to lead by example and his son Yoshitaka having died the remaining students naturally looked to Nakayama as the de facto chief instructor of the fledgling Japan Karate Association (JKA). He would hold his position at the head of this rapidly growing organization for almost forty years. Nakayama had outstanding business acumen and leadership skills and used them to transform the JKA into one of the world's leading martial brands.

Nakayama was a rationalist and an innovator who played a huge role in shaping the dynamic of post-war karate. He built on the ideas of Funakoshi's son Yoshitaka by insisting that students train in extremely low stances to develop muscular strength and use high kicks. His karate was a powerful, direct and logical fighting style. Nakayama was profoundly affected by his early attempts to teach karate to the many American servicemen in Tokyo. Quickly he realized that the Americans were very different from Japanese students. They would not simply accept instruction without explanation. Nakayama began to search for ways in which karate teaching could be made more rational and explicit. He introduced body conditioning methods from other sports and ideas from various scientific fields such as body mechanics, anatomy, physics and even psychology.

The emergence of the JKA created a good deal of friction among karate enthusiasts in Tokyo. Before the war the university karate clubs had quite naturally accepted that Funakoshi was the unrivaled authority at the head of the karate world. But the post-war scene was more fractious. Over the course of the long war with China individual interpretations of karate kata and karate practice had diverged and some clubs found it hard to agree with the direction being taken by the JKA. Outside the university clubs many long standing karate students were hostile to the new emphasis on competition and decided not to join the quickly growing new organization.

But by the middle of the 1950s the JKA had clearly become the largest and best organized of all the Japanese karate groups. A permanent headquarters was opened in 1955 and no less a figure than the grandson of Saigo Takamori was appointed as the JKA chairman. The leaders of this group hoped that the various karate factions would eventually unite around their system. Their plans were disrupted, however, by the death of Gichin Funakoshi in 1957. As the corpse of the old man was laid out for viewing fifty of his most senior students gathered to discuss the arrangements for the funeral ceremony.

When the karate men sat down to discuss formalities it became clear that there were two factions in the room, those who supported the reformist JKA grouping and everyone else. The opposition to the JKA was made up of those who were uncomfortable with the changes the JKA had been introducing and this group now named themselves the Shotokai (Shoto's group). As the meeting began the atmosphere was extremely tense. Speakers for both groups insisted that they were the official inheritors of the Funakoshi karate tradition and had the right to organize the funeral. In the end Funakoshi's eldest son, the official heir to his father, cast his lot with the Shotokai faction. In great anger the JKA group rose to their feet and walked out of the meeting. It was the beginning of a bitter rift that was never to be healed. To general dismay the members and clubs associated with the JKA announced that they would not attend the funeral of the great old man who had devoted his life to passing karate on to them.

Just a few months after the funeral of Funakoshi the JKA began preparations for an event that their deceased master would certainly have vetoed, the first all-Japan karate fighting tournament. Funakoshi had always openly doubted the value and even the morality of competitive sparring but even so informal matches between university karate clubs had been common in the 1930s. After the war meetings between university clubs were revived as they offered such an obvious outlet for the energies of the most enthusiastic karate students. They were intensely competitive affairs with very few rules and were commonly marked by broken bones and a good deal of blood on the floor.

There was a real contradiction between the eagerness of the young bloods in the karate clubs for competition and the pacifist mood that still prevailed in the 1950s. Fifty years earlier Jigoro Kano had created a set of rules to make controlled judo sparring safe enough for regular practice. Nakayama now followed in his footsteps by leading a search for a way that young karate men could fight without severely injuring each other. He felt sure that karate would never become as popular as judo or kendo if it lacked a tournament system to add excitement and motivation to regular training. But how could karate men fight each other in safety? Nakayama had seen with his own eyes the brawls at informal karate meetings, matches that ended up with "broken noses and jaws, teeth knocked out, and ears almost ripped off." [39] Nakayama came to the conclusion that fighters would end up being killed if karate competition was not highly controlled.

After a good deal of experimentation a set of rules were agreed on. As in judo competition, the JKA fighters wore no special protective equipment. They were discouraged from applying holds or throws and techniques were basically restricted to kicks and punches. In order to ensure safety the competitors were given points for techniques that were judged to have been delivered with full power but controlled just at the point of impact. Actually hitting or kicking an opponent without control, especially in the face or neck area, was penalized. Teams of referees awarded points and ensured discipline. This new system was not perfectly safe. Young fighters who closed on each other at speed often found it hard to stop their punches in time. But serious injuries did become rare and these new arrangements for fighting would become the dominant competition model as karate spread throughout Japan and then the world.

You Still Have Both Legs

The first all-Japan karate tournament turned out to be a brilliant success for the JKA. Several thousand spectators gathered in Tokyo to roar on the competitors in the first display of karate fighting that was open to the general public. Among those favored to win the title was Hirokazu Kanazawa, a leading protégée of Nakayama. Kanazawa had earned his black belt at Takushoku University, the toughest of all the karate clubs. When he had first joined the club it had been so overcrowded with young students that the instructors made a habit of ordering their charges to race to a local temple and back before training started. The last two to arrive back at the dojo each day were excluded from the club. Takushoku was at the leading edge of the experiments with free sparring and Kanazawa been one of the most talented guinea pigs.

Just before the tournament Kanazawa had graduated from the JKA instructor course, a training program that had been established in 1956 with the aim of creating polished karate teachers who could spread the JKA system throughout Japan. He became the star of the instructor's course. Tall and lean, with razor sharp reactions and outstanding athleticism, Kanazawa was perfectly designed for this new form of competition. As the all-Japan tournament approached Kanazawa began to stay away from the JKA headquarters where most of his main competitors were training. Instead, he spent the last few weeks of preparation at Takushoku, sparring each night at full intensity with the younger students. But after months of hard and dedicated training disaster struck just a few days before the competition. Kanazawa felt a sharp pain in his right forearm and was informed by a doctor that his wrist was broken. Devastated, his arm in a plaster cast, Kanazawa was sure that his dream of winning the first Japanese karate championship was over.

But he had reckoned without his mother. When she arrived in Tokyo after making a long journey from her home in northern Japan his mother looked him up and down and then asked her son, "Do you only use your right hand when you fight?" Having been assured that her son was, in fact, allowed to use both hands as well as both feet Kanazawa's mother, who was clearly of the old school, continued. "I still don't understand. Please ask the JKA why you cannot participate. You still have your left arm and both legs. Only one hand is broken." In the face of this maternal 'support' Kanazawa decided to remove his plaster and apply for readmittance to the competition. He would do his best to win one fight so that his mother's long journey would not have been wasted.

On the day of the competition he fought using his left hand to block attacks and to feint. All of his attacks were made with kicks. To his surprise he won, and then won again. After three fights his mother sent down a message to tell him that enough was enough. But Kanazawa had begun to enjoy himself and he was now feeling as though the movements of his opponents were being played out in slow motion. He reached the final match where he found himself up against another expert kicker. Kanazawa managed to somehow hold off his opponent's attacks by moving in and kicking at the supporting leg each time a kick came his way. Finally, he connected with a roundhouse kick to the head. His opponent staggered back and a point was awarded. Kanazawa was the champion of Japan.

Empty Mind

The athleticism and courage displayed by Kanazawa was typical of the extremely high standard set by the leading ranks of the JKA as they consciously strove to take the karate they had inherited from Funakoshi onto a new plane. The pioneering atmosphere of Japanese karate in those days has been recorded in a wonderful memoir by C.W. Nichol that describes his experience of spending two years training at the JKA headquarters in the early sixties. Nichol, a large Welshman who had extensive experience of judo, wrestling and street fighting, decided to join the JKA after visiting the headquarters of all the main karate styles.

The organization that Nichol signed up to join was, in many ways, unimpressive. Japan was no economic superpower in the 1960s and the JKA at that time was still financially weak and housed in dilapidated premises that it had rented from a movie company. The training, however, was intense and disciplined. Students lined up on their knees on a wooden floor that shone with the polish that they applied after every class. They bowed to the Japanese flag and to a photograph of Funakoshi. For Nichol, who had spent a lot of time in the rather informal surroundings of the home of judo at the Kodokan, the contrast was striking. Here at the JKA headquarters discipline was maintained by senior grades (senpai) who would scold beginners for any infraction of the rules. Inside the dojo no informal talk, physical relaxation or any other casual behavior was tolerated. Nichol was surprised to be slapped across the face on one occasion when he failed to stifle a yawn during class.

The training he experienced began with basic punches and kicks that the students performed in unison as they moved in ranks up and down the floor. These movements were repeated for long periods, periods that often stretched well beyond the point when the students had reached exhaustion. Gasping for breath they were ordered to summon up reserves of mental and spiritual energy to drive their helpless bodies forward. When it came to kata practice Nichol was told to constantly visualize an enemy who was attempting to strike him as he made the set moves.

Finally there were free sparring sessions. The muscular Nichol was quite prepared to give as good as he got but he found that he had little success with the black belts who could counter his strength and size with superior speed and accuracy. He describes in his memoir the experience of sparring with the phenomenal Kanazawa who was so athletic that he could jump over Nichol's head, kick at the back of his neck and then land in perfect balance before Nichol could turn to face him again. Nichol was aiming for promotion to black belt during this period and in preparation for the black belt test he experienced the toughest training of all. Candidates were made to fight their seniors continually in sessions that lasted for over an hour. Often, like the sword students of Yamaoka Tesshu in the nineteenth century, they found that even in the midst of utter exhaustion they could summon up a powerful determination.

Nichol, like the other black belt candidates, supplemented his daily training with sessions of punching a makiwara post and kicking with iron slippers strapped to his feet. He gradually learned to keep his body entirely relaxed until the split second when an attack was either delivered or received. He also learned to relax his mind and emotions. His teachers, echoing the samurai of the seventeenth century, told him that fighters who can keep their mind completely empty are able to respond freely to any situation.

After two years of intense daily training Nichol was allowed to take a black belt examination. Interest in karate had risen quickly during the early sixties and he found that, although he was the only foreigner, he was one among two hundred black belt candidates. The crowd of karate students sat for hours on their knees on the hard wooden floor waiting for their turn to perform basic techniques and kata. When the time came to demonstrate sparring Nichol was warned by his teachers that they would beat him afterwards if he backed off even one centimeter from his opponent. Nichol stood his ground and passed the test, becoming one of the eighty who received a black belt that day. But he was not given long to enjoy his success. At his very next training session Nichol was reminded that a first degree black belt is only one step on the ladder. His seniors lined up to spar with him and, one by one, did their best to thrash him. It was a tough, almost military, training environment but Nichol found it to be a rewarding one. Behind the aggressive discipline he felt that his teachers wanted nothing more than to help their students develop as human beings.

What is True Strength?
The JKA grew in popularity as it attracted crowds to its thrilling competitions. But some of the old students of Funakoshi found the spectacle of karate men facing each other in refereed fights to be anathema. For these hold outs the leading alternative to the JKA was the Shotokai, an organization that claimed to preserve the legacy of Funakoshi. The leader of this group was Shigeru Egami, one of the three younger men, the other two being Yoshitaka Funakoshi and Hinorori Otsuka, who had led the development of a distinctively Japanese karate in the pre-war years. Egami had grown certain that the

JKA was missing the essential point of Funakoshi's teaching. Karate was not a sport, it was a lifelong battle to overcome the self. Defeating an opponent in competition was a direct contradiction, he believed, of everything that Funakoshi had stood for.

The angry row over Funakoshi's funeral drove the two groups that claimed to be his heirs far apart. From that point onwards Egami, who had been badly shaken by a period of serious illness, turned inwards in the search for an alternative approach. He had always been one of the toughest karate men, the expert who was hand picked as a combat instructor for Japan's wartime spies. Now he began to believe that he had been on the wrong track.

> I trained tsuki and keri with the idea of becoming the strongest possible person, investing my life. This helped me attain a remarkable strength. But in time I understood the limits of physical strength and human strength ... and tried to heighten them by exploring and creating new possibilities. He who is weak can become strong, and he who is strong, becomes even stronger, but there is a limit in the search of physical strength. What is true strength that cannot be obtained through a physical training taken to the limit? Is there such a thing? (40)

As he explored the meaning of true strength Egami developed a new kind of karate that preserved the low stances and katas of the Shotokan school but encouraged students to move in a much lighter, more fluid and relaxed way. He regretted the rigorous body toughening he had put himself through as a young man and came to the conclusion that there was another dimension to technique, something hidden, spiritual and infinitely superior. He began to wander in the countryside and to sit for long periods in meditation as he searched for that extra dimension. In the end he told the world that there are magnetic waves that can penetrate a human body and that these waves can be projected as a non-material force, a force that he called toate. Someone with the power of toate, he claimed, can strike without making any physical contact with an opponent.

Egami was a troubled man, both physically and spiritually, until the end of his life in 1981. Most unusually for a martial artist, however, he was extremely open about his own uncertainty and encouraged his followers to make their own explorations of the limits of human potential. One of those who enthusiastically seized on the encouragement to experiment was Hiroyuki Aoki, a student of Egami who eventually moved away from karate to found Shintaido (New Body Way). This organization took a bold leap into the world of mysticism that was much more radical than any of Egami's experiments. Aoki wanted Shintaido to provide a developmental path that was open to people in any physical condition. His groups avoided rigorous training and focussed instead on the creation of an eclectic art that encompassed elements of religion, spiritualism, dance and the martial arts. Nothing could have been further away from the tough, rational path taken by the JKA.

The Quality of the Person

In the years after the war there was a deep spiritual hunger among the Japanese people, a hunger that provided fertile ground for the growth of new religious movements. In creating Shintaido Aoki had been able to tap into the public appetite for a new kind of faith. Another martial artist who benefitted from the general openness of Japanese people in the 1950s to religious experimentation was Michiomi Nakano.

Nakano had lived for more than twenty years in China during the run up to the war and when hostilities commenced had acted as an intelligence officer for the Japanese military. Undoubtedly he had acquired a knowledge of Chinese language and culture that few other Japanese people could rival. On his return to Japan after the war Nakano had an enlightenment experience that he later formulated in the words "Hito! Hito! Hito! Subete wa hito no shitsu ni aru." ('The person, the person! Everything depends on the quality of the person').

Nakano combined his own personal vision of life with elements of Buddhism to create a religious movement that he named as Kongo Zen. At the same time he took on the honorific name of Doshin So and made it known that in China he had been appointed as the twenty first master of a branch of kenpo that was closely linked to the northern Shaolin temple. On the basis of this pedigree he launched a new martial arts organization that he gave the name Shorinji Kempo (Shaolin Fighting Art).

As Nakano's organization grew there were critics who openly cast doubts on his claim to be reviving a Chinese martial arts legacy. Nakano had clearly emphasized the Chinese origins of his art by naming it after the legendary Shaolin temple. But it was suggested that most of the techniques of Shorinji Kempo did not actually seem to be of Chinese origin and had more likely been adapted from Nakano's studies of Japanese jujutsu and karate. There was also concern about the religious dimension of Nakano's movement. Shorinji Kempo seemed to some critics to be a near cult that had more in common with the New Religion movements sweeping Japan in the 1950s than it did with the mainstream martial arts. But Nakano's fighting art proved to be a popular one. It offered a brand of martial training that was less aggressive and more philosophically inclined than most others. Over the years it steadily grew into a substantial organization with an especially strong base in the Japanese universities.

The Cat

Gogen Yamaguchi was another mystically inclined martial artist who had returned to Japan after years of intrigue and danger in China. Yamaguchi went through a period of despair at the hopeless state of postwar Japan but finally decided to dedicate himself to rebuilding the spirit of the nation's demoralized youth by teaching karate. Yamaguchi had made many friends among the Yakuza while he was interned in a Siberian prison camp and he drew on these contacts in 1948 as he laid the ground for the opening of a karate dojo in Asakusa, a tough area of Tokyo. By 1950 Yamaguchi had enrolled a sufficient number of students to be able to launch a national organization, the All Japan Karate Goju Group (ZenNippon Karate-do Gojukai).

Goju Ryu karate had originally been created in Okinawa by Kanryo Higaonna and Chojun Miyagi. But in the years after the war Okinawa was swarming with American troops and there was little chance for Yamaguchi or his students to visit the off-limits southern island. He had far more contact, in fact, with the other karate organizations on the Japanese mainland. As a result, Yamaguchi's karate became somewhat lighter in style than its Okinawan progenitor, with less emphasis on body conditioning. Regular sparring with members of other karate styles encouraged the Japanese Goju fighters to kick more than they had before the war and reduced their use of the less mobile cat stance. What they did retain from their Okinawan heritage was a preference for fighting in close proximity and a liking for short, powerful strikes to central areas, with kicks aimed not at the head but at the instep or the groin.

Yamaguchi's harrowing experiences in Siberia and his post-war enlightenment experience had liberated him from conventional patterns of behavior. He grew his hair long and began to wear a traditional hakama in the dojo. He was a small man but he exuded a powerful aura that led the many American soldiers who took his classes in the 1950s to name him 'the Cat'. It was a nickname that Yamaguchi relished, as he told an interviewer later in life.

> Even today, young man, if you were to face me in combat, I would be able to determine in a second the strength of your Ki. Immediately I would know if you were a good opponent. It is this quality, and no other, which has given me the name of The Cat. (41)

Yamaguchi became a passionate student of Shinto and Yoga and eventually created his own religious system that he named Goju Shinto. He would lay hands on a crystal ball to communicate with the spirit world and performed complex rituals that involved a good deal of chanting, howling and salt sprinkling. But despite Yamaguchi's attraction to the esoteric his karate group did not become a semi-religious organization in the manner of Shintaido or Shorinji Kempo. Instead it found a place in the mainstream of Japanese karate and grew into an association that could boast half a million registered members by the 1970s.

Pulled Into a Dream

At the end of the war Morihei Ueshiba was in his countryside retreat of Iwama farming the land with his family. He was now in his sixties and years of illness had stripped away a good deal of the muscle that he had developed as an army sergeant, wilderness pioneer and leading martial artist. He no longer seemed to be the legendary warrior that many had taken him for in the 1930s and perhaps he felt that those years were over. A few students who had returned from the war made their way to Iwama where they were greeted with warm embraces and fresh food. But there was not a great deal of training going on. The little community in Iwama devoted most of their energies to the struggle to produce enough food from the land to stay alive.

In Tokyo Ueshiba's son Kisshomaru was doing his best to keep the central aikido training hall open in the chaotic, bombed out city. The dojo had somehow survived the devastating bombing raids but now, like every other undamaged building, it was required to open its doors to some of the homeless survivors. Aikido practice went on in one corner of the building while refugee families warmed their meals in another corner. Most of the serviceable floor matting was being used for bedding by these impoverished refugees and the few aikido students had to throw each other onto hard wooden floors.

Kisshomaru, who was a very different personality from his impulsive and romantic father, now became the most important force in the revival of aikido. A key first step toward social acceptance was for aikido to be granted recognition by the Ministry of Education. Like all of the other budo groups in the post-war years the Aikikai was regarded with suspicion. In order to win approval Kisshomaru set about a reinvention of the history of aikido. He presented his group as a cultural society dedicated to promoting healthy lifestyles and personal development. In his letter of application to the Ministry Kisshomaru suggested, somewhat disingenuously, that aikido had avoided any involvement in the war effort and that the art had always been intended to serve only "altruistic and positive uses." Aikido, his document said, was an art that gave priority to "mutual love between human beings." He even took the imaginative leap of suggesting that the 'ai' of aikido could be changed from 合 to the character 愛 which means 'love'. (29)

In 1949 the last of the refugees finally moved out of the Kobukan dojo and there was once again room to practice properly. But only handfuls of students were turning up each day and Kisshomaru was not receiving sufficient income from aikido to be able to employ himself a full-time instructor. He needed an outside job and so he would rise early to teach aikido classes before he began the commute to his post at a bank. This tiring life continued until 1955 when enough students had enrolled to allow Kisshomaru to become a full-time aikido teacher.

In Iwama a small training hall was erected and the students who lived there began to balance long hours toiling in the fields with regular lessons from the master. In time Ueshiba slowly started to move outside his rural base, giving talks and demonstrations at schools, police academies and judo societies. He had been a famous man before the war and his name still had impact but by the 1950s the founder of aikido had been physically transformed into a much older looking white-haired man with a wispy beard.

The twelve years in Iwama had certainly changed the aikido that Ueshiba was practicing. It had become a softer and more flowing art with fewer of the aggressive striking moves and hard throws that had been common before the war. Ueshiba, to the despair of his students, now believed more than ever that aikido techniques should never be preconceived but should descend naturally from the gods. When the students gathered for a training session there often seemed to be no pattern to the classes and Ueshiba rarely gave any indication of what would come next. He preferred to act on the inspiration of the moment.

From the middle of the 1950s aikido was caught up in the general boom in interest in the martial arts. Ueshiba was once again famous and in so much demand that he was obliged to return to live in Tokyo. From his home in the capital he continued to train and teach with great enthusiasm until his death. Ueshiba gave many demonstrations in those years that inspired awe in some spectators and skepticism in others. If surrounded by attackers Ueshiba would throw the healthy young men around the room with only the slightest of contacts, or no contact at all. At times he would emit a brief shout that would knock his opponents onto their backs.

Ueshiba had always been an unusual man and his eccentricities increased with age. He never learned to buy train tickets and made his way around Tokyo's complex train system by walking with great dignity through ticket gates, oblivious to the gaping inspectors. He gave great weight to his instincts and he would often bewilder the students who had been assigned to accompany him on a journey by stepping off a train that was about to depart for an important meeting. It did not "feel right", he would often say.

In his final years Ueshiba was certainly a remarkable man, possessed of both advanced skills and a rich and complex humanity. Kisshomaru's description of his father's final demonstration in 1968 wonderfully captures the sparkling reality of the aged Ueshiba.

> O Sensei wore a gown of pure white, and as he demonstrated his breathtaking technique, the whole hall fell utterly silent, as if they had been pulled into a dream. Then suddenly, for some reason, his gown ripped apart audibly at the seams. He grinned, and shouted, "Ah, I will be scolded by my old wife!" There was a moment of dead silence, followed by a roar of laughter. (30)

A few months later, saying "the gods are calling me," the founder of aikido retired to his bed and soon died. He left behind a booming organization that, under the leadership of Kisshomaru Ueshiba, dedicated itself to preserving the legacy of the founder's post-war teaching. Gradually the importance of striking techniques fell away and weapons training was largely forgotten. Kisshomaru was not as passionate about religion as his father had been and slowly secularized the art. What emerged in the 1970s was a relatively gentle and elegant martial art that had a deep philosophical base. This was an attractive proposition to many and aikido clubs spread throughout the universities and the city centers of Japan.

Rational Aikido
Not all of Morihei Ueshiba's senior students appreciated the changes that were introduced to aikido from the 1950s onwards. To some extent the discontent was contained by the founder's utter lack of interest in imposing organizational discipline, something that offered a good deal of freedom to those of his students who wanted to experiment with their own approaches to training. But when Ueshiba died in 1968 three of his longest serving students at last felt free to follow their own stars.

Kenji Tomiki was the oldest of this elite group. He had been one of the very first judo experts to be drawn to aikido and was already a fourth dan in judo when he first met Ueshiba in 1926. Tomiki was well aware that both judo and aikido had their roots in jujutsu but he came to the conclusion that aikido had preserved many important jujutsu elements that had disappeared from modern judo. Tomiki thought that judo was excellent preparation for the kind of combat that breaks out when two fighters come into close physical contact. But Ueshiba was a true expert in the stage of combat that precedes grappling. Tomiki continued to train in judo, eventually reaching the eighth dan rank and also became an instructor in aikido. Although he greatly admired Ueshiba as a martial artist Tomiki was rather stifled by the atmosphere of spiritualism that surrounded aikido. Intellectually he found the rationalism of his other great influence, Jigoro Kano, much more convincing.

As the war approached Tomiki became a professor in a Manchurian university and toward the end of the war he was captured by Soviet troops and spent three years in a prison camp. When he finally returned to Japan Tomiki found work at the elite Waseda University in Tokyo where he also instructed the judo club. In marked contrast to Ueshiba, Tomiki had little time for the idea that students could learn a martial art properly by watching and copying the moves of a master. Like Kano he looked for ways to break his techniques down into simple elements that could be easily passed on. Tomiki had lived for years in Manchuria, far beyond the direct influence of either judo or aikido, and had enough confidence in himself to take an independent approach.

In 1958 Waseda University gave its approval when Tomiki submitted a request to be allowed to establish an aikido club. But the mood of the time was in favor of competitive martial arts and the university suggested that Tomiki should try to find some way of adapting aikido for competition use. Tomiki was intrigued by the challenge and over a number of years he worked out a system for aikido sparring that involved a defender applying a limited range of aikido techniques against an attacker who was either unarmed or armed with a rubber dagger. These innovations were regarded with general horror by the aikido establishment. Ueshiba had been strongly opposed to any suggestions that aikido should become competitive and had, in fact, announced that such a thing was morally wrong.

Despite finding himself in such open disagreement with most other aikido teachers Tomiki did not formally leave the Aikikai until 1974, well after the death of Ueshiba. From that date, with greater freedom from organizational constraints, Tomiki could more openly emphasize competition and argue for the mental and physical benefits that competition brings to aikido. His brand of aikido evolved into a more direct fighting art with a strong focus on practical self-defense. As he experimented with effective ways of teaching students Tomiki also decided to create a number of kata, a common feature of the Japanese martial arts that is absent from mainstream aikido.

You Cannot Complain

While Tomiki reformed aikido by taking it in a rational, competitive direction his contemporary Gozo Shioda worked to revive the tough, dynamic aikido that had been taught by Ueshiba before the war. Shioda was eighteen years old and had already gained several years of experience in both judo and kendo when he first met Ueshiba. As he watched the master give a demonstration the young Shioda was deeply unimpressed. It all looked like a fake, he thought to himself. When Ueshiba finally asked Shioda to attack him the young man stepped forward with confidence. Shioda was small but Ueshiba was even smaller. He decided to kick the master as hard as possible. Suddenly he found himself crashing onto his back, his head thumping into the floor. Like so many before him Shioda was forced to instantly revise his opinion of Ueshiba. He quickly became a student and spent eight years training with the master in the pre-war years when Ueshiba was at the height of his fame and power.

During the war Shioda spent most of his time in China working as an administrator for the Japanese powers. It was a dangerous world and even in the relative safety of the cities life could still be rather wild. On Shioda's first night in Shanghai he visited a bar where he was surrounded by a dangerous gang that his Japanese friend had made the mistake of picking a quarrel with. The argument quickly escalated into a violent struggle and Shioda had to fight for his life.

> When I jerked open the door at just the right time, one of the men, who seemed to have been caught off guard by this maneuver, fell forward into the room. I hit him on the head with the beer bottle. The bottle broke and I saw the jagged remainder in my hand notched like the teeth of shark. I pushed it forward into the man's face all at once and twisted. It caught him squarely. The pain must have been unbearable. Blood gushed out and he threw himself back immediately. I pulled him back into the room to prevent his escape. It all happened in an instant.
>
> There were still three men left. Then, a big Chinese man came to kick me. I opened my body to the left and slapped down his kicking leg with my right hand while turning my back to him. I just hit his leg naturally without using much strength and he lost control and fell. I learned later that his knee joint and bones were broken.
>
> Having easily taken care of two of the men, I became to feel somewhat calmer. However, as soon as I regained my composure, another man punched at my face. I evaded his punch with an inward turn and applied a variation of shihonage grabbing his hand from underneath. I then put his elbow on my shoulder and applied a decisive pressure and the man fell. His elbow snapped easier than what one might suspect and he flew forward. I handled three men and I don't think the whole struggle lasted for more than a minute. I tied up the three stunned men with my belt and calmly looked up.
>
> I saw Uraoka struggling against the last man...I thought I would test how effective aikido atemi was and told my companion to let me take care of the man. When he got up again after being thrown by Uraoka he came to attack and I executed an atemi to his ribs. He groaned frothing at the mouth and fell backward. (36)

After years of training with the founder of aikido Shioda had still harbored some doubts about how effective his training would prove to be in the real world. But these experiences in China gave him great confidence. When Shioda returned from the war he did not plan to become a martial arts teacher. Things began to change for him in 1950. All over Japan violent confrontations were breaking out between employers and militant labour unions and the Japanese police were regularly overwhelmed and outfought by determined left wingers. Shioda was employed as a security expert by a large steel company with a remit to protect strike breakers. It was dangerous work and business managers were on the look out for the toughest martial artists who would be able to handle rough and tumble confrontations with striking workers.

Shioda soon found himself in demand as a teacher as word spread that he had developed his own brand of aikido. From the beginning Shioda taught a hard edged fighting style that he named Yoshinkan Aikido. He specialized in training police officers in methods for controlling and immobilizing attackers. As his own school developed Shioda was also able to maintain a friendly relationship with the Aikikai and the two organizations never had a formal parting of the ways. Ueshiba himself even awarded Shioda a 9th dan grade in 1961.

But Yoshinkan aikido developed into a very different type of martial art from the elegant practice that could be found at Aikikai headquarters. It acquired a reputation as a style where tough training was the norm and was strongly supported by the police services. Even today a background in the martial arts is required of any Japanese police officer aiming for promotion and every year ten members of the notoriously rugged Tokyo riot police undergo live-in training at the Yoshinkan headquarters.

Shioda was a strong teacher who would go to great lengths to make himself a living example of courage and determination. He followed a highly unusual personal work out routine that included training his pet dog to attack him each morning in the park so that he could practice using his aikido to evade the animal's snapping teeth. His martial art was a very different creature from the mystical aikido of Ueshiba or the rational aikido of Tomiki. Aikido was for fighting, he believed. It is "not a sport but a budo. Either you defeat your opponent or he defeats you. You cannot complain that he did not follow the rules. You have to overcome your opponent in a way appropriate to each situation." (36)

Mind and Body Unified

Kisshomaru Ueshiba, Kenji Tomiki and Gozo Shioda all carried aikido forward after the death of the founder but even these important teachers were overshadowed by the extraordinary talent of Koichi Tohei. Several years younger than both Tomiki and Shioda, Tohei was a close contemporary of the only person who was to be his rival for the leadership of aikido, Ueshiba's son Kisshomaru. These four men all trained together under Morihei Ueshiba and they became close friends but it was the emotional, passionate Tohei who most resembled the master. Although Tohei would finally come up with his own distinctive take on aikido he shared with his master a desire to penetrate the universal principles that lay behind the art.

Tohei had trained in judo as a young man but he was forced to give up sparring by a serious case of pleurisy. As he lay in bed convalescing Tohei read a life of Yamaoka Tesshu and he was gripped by the intensely engaged life of the nineteenth century swordsman. On the spot he decided that he would follow a similar path, even if the challenge ended up destroying his weak body. Tohei found a group that was trying to emulate Tesshu's spiritual approach and he threw himself into their training routine. It was a highly serious group. Beginners were required to undertake intensive zen practice that often involved sitting in meditation through the night. They could then graduate to purification rituals (misogi) which put them on the receiving end of a good deal of shouting and pummeling from the group's senior members.

It was an exhausting process but Tohei gradually recovered from illness and the transformation in his health convinced him that the mind has the power to control the body. He returned to his university judo club but judo, after all he had been through, now seemed to be a rather superficial art. In a search for something deeper he visited the Ueshiba dojo in Tokyo and, like so many other young men before him, did his best to embarrass the master. Tohei found himself flying through the air without any sensation of having been thrown. This, he decided, was something that he needed to investigate.

The year was 1940 and Tohei was one of the most junior of Ueshiba's students. Many of the others had been with the master for more than a decade. But the approach of war emptied the dojo of seniors and Tohei was quickly promoted to assistant instructor. Within a year he was helping Ueshiba to give demonstrations at police academies. He continued to follow his religious studies and he believed that those practices lay behind his rapid progress in aikido. The purification rituals conducted by his group aimed to strip individuals of all of their physical and mental restraints. After this kind of draining practice an exhausted Tohei would make his way to the aikido dojo where he found, to his great surprise, that it was supremely easy to throw his training partners. This, he came to believe, was the secret that lay behind Ueshiba's greatness. The master was clearly a powerful man but, more importantly, he was completely relaxed when facing an attack. Tohei became convinced that the secret of aikido was mental control. A person fully in control of their own mind will find even the most aggressive attacker easy to contain.

Tohei had become an established master in his own right by 1953 when he was chosen to be the first aikido teacher to work overseas. He found himself in Hawaii attempting to teach the massively built locals who very rarely arrived at his dojo with any respect for his reputation or his rank. Tohei was forced to re-evaluate his aikido in this extreme situation where every day felt like a battle, a battle with two meter tall Hawaiians who wanted to test the limits of his strength. It would have been a disgrace for both himself and his teacher Ueshiba if Tohei had been defeated by these outsiders. He set about reorganizing his fighting system, retaining only techniques that he found to be genuinely effective against a determined opponent.

When Tohei returned to Japan Ueshiba was aging quickly and seemed to be rapidly approaching the end of his life. Tohei was now, by some distance, the strongest and most skilled member of the Aikikai dojo and Ueshiba himself seemed to recognize this fact. Up to this point the master had set a limit of eighth dan on the grades he would award to his students but other martial arts were beginning to create ninth and even tenth dan grades. Just before he died Ueshiba gave Tohei the ultimate accolade when he made him the first aikido tenth dan.

But Tohei had already set out on a journey that would take him far away from being simply a follower of Ueshiba's teachings. He was fascinated by ki, the universal force believed by aikido experts to flow through the human body. While Ueshiba had given religious and esoteric explanations for the working of ki, Tohei developed a different, more practical and pragmatic, view of ki energy. He came to believe that there was indeed an extrasensory force that emerges in human action but he shied away from using the occult to explain this force. Tohei, in fact, became scornful of suggestions that aikido involved anything supernatural and angered many in the aikido community by dismissing those among them who believed that Ueshiba had 'godlike' powers. To the end of his life he was full of admiration for the extraordinary ability, the supreme combination of power and relaxation that Ueshiba embodied. But he had spent many years training with the master and, he said, he had never seen anything take place that was remotely supernatural or that lay beyond human explanation. Those who suggested otherwise were doing the master a disservice.

After Ueshiba's death it did seem for a while that Tohei would take on the role of chief instructor to the increasingly large and international aikido family while Kisshomaru Ueshiba seemed to be happy to assume a quieter, more administrative position. But over the following years the principle of heredity won out and it was Kisshomaru who adopted his father's honorific title of doshu. Tohei, who had angered many by his experiments with ki training, left the Aikikai to create his own organization. He named his own group Mind-Body Unified Aikido (Shin Shin Toitsu Aikido) when the final break with the Aikikai took place in 1974.

Unlike the friendly departures of Tomiki and Shioda, the split between the Aikikai and its chief instructor Tohei was a bitter one. Many students were torn over the decision about which side to support and several branches left the Aikikai to join Tohei's new group. After the break Tohei no longer felt constrained in what he could study or teach and he set out on a long journey that involved introducing ideas from Zen Buddhism, Shiatsu massage and yoga into the aikido template. Eventually it was a quest for deep knowledge, rather than the martial arts, that became the main focus of Tohei's life. His Ki Study Group became a large and influential international organization with more than 200,000 registered members. Tohei died in 2011.

The Pliant Art
Among all the Japanese martial ways it was the sword arts that were most seriously affected by the end of the war. To both the Japanese people and the American occupiers it was clear that the way of the sword had been deeply intertwined with the ambitions of the militarists. Kendo was not completely suppressed, a few private dojos continued to meet, but for several years it was impossible for any official sword organization to exist or for competitions to take place.

The first sign of revival for sword fighting came in 1949 when a group of individuals who had been members of university kendo clubs before the war came together as the Tokyo Kendo Club. How, they asked each other, could kendo possibly be revived when Japanese society was so hostile to sword training and all that it had represented? The group decided to reorganize kendo as a sport that would carry as few connotations of the old samurai world as possible. They even created a new name for kendo, shinai kyogi (pliant competition), that disguised the sword based nature of the art. Shinai referred to the bamboo sword used in kendo fighting but the reformers changed the characters used to write shinai so that the name had a much softer appearance. The look of the art was also transformed. The dramatic, dark-colored protective clothing used for kendo was discarded in favor of Western style shirts and trousers. Competitors were not allowed to clash physically and were forbidden to shout with the traditional kiai. Even the practice swords were changed to a softer, leather wrapped bunch of bamboo slats.

Shinai kyogi had a certain success for a short period but quickly became irrelevant. From 1950 onwards there was a dramatic shift in the national mood that made it possible for old-style kendo to reemerge. Sword lovers made representations to the American occupiers that claimed, with some justification, that the wartime militarists had disliked kendo and had thought it to be an ineffective martial art. Unfortunately, they argued, the wartime atmosphere had changed kendo for the worse. The new kendo clubs, the petition promised, would return kendo to the 'wholesome and peaceful sport' it had originally been.

By 1952 the atmosphere had changed sufficiently for an All Japan Kendo Federation to be established. A rather confusing situation continued for a while with two quite different kinds of kendo in existence but the problem eventually disappeared as support for the 'pacifist' shinai kyogi dried up. Schools and universities reopened their kendo clubs and the sport quickly became as popular as it had ever been. But something had undoubtedly changed during the post-war experiments. Kendo after the war was a more dignified art, with fewer of the tough body clashes and leg sweeps that had been common before the war.

Up to the 1930s the direction of kendo had largely been set by the traditional sword schools and by the tough police kendo clubs. Now the life blood of the sport became competitions that were held at high-school, university and national level. The new generation fought in a different way. Before the war the principal focus of kendo had been on delivering powerful strikes that would be lethal if a sword was used. But this now shifted to an emphasis on extremely rapid strikes that made the most of the lightness of the bamboo sword. This change in technique was never completely accepted, especially among the more senior teachers. They had grudgingly gone along with the sport oriented direction of kendo after the war in an environment where the government was strongly discouraging the use of martial arts for character building. By the 1970s, however, there were signs of a general desire among the martial arts community to revive the more spiritual aspects of training. In 1975 the All Japan Kendo Federation had reached a point where it could describe kendo as a method to "discipline the human character through the application of the principles of the sword."

One Heart
In Japan the martial arts found a new energy and direction in the decades after the war. But perhaps the most amazing recovery was that of Okinawan karate. Like so much on the island karate seemed to have been a casualty of the terrible battle of 1945. Many teachers were dead and those who survived had experienced such trauma that the martial arts seemed of little consequence.

At the end of the war the senior karate man on the island was undoubtedly Chojun Miyagi. He had endured the loss of family members, friends and students and it was with a heavy heart that he finally reopened his garden dojo. Miyagi continued to be a teacher of the old school. He showed little interest in creating an international organization, ignored the innovations that had transformed karate on mainland Japan and even refused to award dan grades to his students.

Miyagi was really the last of the great generation of Okinawan masters who had been responsible for bringing karate out of the shadows and into the twentieth century. With his death the torch passed to younger men. Tatsuo Shimabuku was one expert who survived the years after the war by working as a poor farmer. Shimabuku had spent many years before the war learning karate from teachers like Chotoku Kyan and he now combined farm work with karate practice as part of Miyagi's group. After the death of the master in 1953 Shimabuku struck out on his own and created a new style of karate that he eventually named the One Heart School (Isshin Ryu). It was a school that benefitted greatly from the American occupation. Shimabuku was one of several Okinawan karate teachers who were paid a salary of $250 per month, a great deal of money at that difficult time, to teach their art to American servicemen.

Shoshin Nagamine had also learned his karate skills from Chotoku Kyan and from Choki Motobu. At the end of the war he surrendered to the American forces and was working as a prisoner of war transporting casualties through the Okinawan countryside when he came across a copy of Introduction to Karate by Gichin Funakoshi lying on the ground. It was a sweetly ironic moment that inspired Nagamine to create Matsubayashi Ryu, his own modern version of the karate that had been taught by Funakoshi's own teachers.

Shimabuku, Nagamine, and other important teachers such as Kanei Uechi rebuilt Okinawan karate after the war in a way that preserved many of the best elements of the old systems while making room for the introduction of innovations from the karate schools of the Japanese mainland. On Okinawa karate clubs continued to have a relatively small average number of students. They trained in a less regimented manner than the mainland clubs and maintained a particular focus on practical self-defense and body conditioning. The Okinawan teachers had impressive skills and were able to develop several outstanding American students who later returned to the United States to establish Okinawan karate associations. In a strange twist of fate many of the karate masters of this isolated island would end their lives at the head of international organizations that greatly outnumbered their groups in Okinawa. Karate, like the other martial arts of the Japanese islands, was becoming the property of the world.

15. GodHand

Catching Up

Recovery from the long and disastrous years of war began slowly. Even in 1950, five years after the end of the war, the Japanese economy was almost lifeless. In those years the average Japanese person was producing about as much national income as a resident of Ethiopia or Somalia and 40 percent less than an Indian. But in the course of the next eighteen years the dreadful memories of hunger and poverty were to be almost entirely erased. Japan entered a dramatic period of sustained and rapid growth in which the sheer speed of change was astounding. By 1968 Japan had been transformed into the world's second richest economy.

As the boom years began the entire population of Japan was driven forward by complex emotions of love and hate for the great American power that had done so much to humiliate, crush and then rebuild their country. "Catch up with America, overtake America!" (Amerika ni oitsuke, oikose!) became the national catchphrase that encapsulated a new sense of purpose. The people had firmly turned their backs on war and now it seemed that business success was to become the guiding focus of the nation. Those who had lived through the war were well used to personal sacrifice and with little complaint they gave their lives to their companies. These hard working people were determined to build powerful organizations and create effective business methods. Japan became a bustling world, a world in which even the martial arts were drawn into the relentless search for growth, for new products and for marketing expertise.

As recovery of the martial arts picked up pace in the 1950s it soon became clear that there were substantial amounts of money to be made from teaching people how to fight. Before the war there had been very few professional martial artists and most teachers had controlled only a single school. But in the new atmosphere of booming post-war Japan large national organizations headed by the senior teachers began to emerge. These associations gave the leaders of each martial art great power. They could create and control training systems that would be systematically followed by a supporting pyramid of thousands of teachers and their students.

In the new atmosphere it seemed almost natural for the martial arts groups to spread like wildfire. There was a general openness to ideas in the 1950s that encouraged new fighting systems to emerge. These new styles competed with the established groups and were more willing to use modern recruitment techniques. Before the war the relationship between teachers and students had been direct and personal but now it was often mediated through a process of outreach and advertising. In this modern era martial artists who could effectively promote and sell their product were going to have a great advantage.

The most effective martial arts salesman of them all proved to be Masutatsu Oyama. More than anyone he understood the needs of the new marketplace. Oyama created thrilling promotional events and brilliantly exploited the mass media. At the centre of his outreach he placed his own remarkable figure, a living advertisement for the benefits of karate. Oyama turned his martial art into a famous brand that would be adopted by millions around the world during his lifetime.

Young-Eui

The man who would become the most famous face of the Japanese martial arts world began his life in unlikely circumstances. He was born in 1923 in Korea, a nation that had already been a fully annexed part of the Japanese Empire for thirteen years. In their occupied country Korean schoolchildren were required to stand and bow every day in front of a photograph of the Japanese Emperor and then sit down to studies of Japanese language and history. The Korean people had good reason to resent their occupiers and their resentment regularly broke out in demonstrations and riots that were forcefully repressed.

And yet many Koreans had complex feelings about Japan. It was, after all, the most advanced and wealthy nation in eastern Asia. It had been Japanese technology, production methods and educational systems that had made it possible for Korean society to rush into the modern age. And because the Japanese controlled education they had great power to persuade Korean children that Japan was at the leading edge of the modern world, the very fulcrum of progress. But while many young Koreans did hold a grudging appreciation for Japan, the esteem was not mutual. Most Japanese people, in fact, regarded the Koreans as a barely human race whose primary reason for existence was to serve the needs of the homeland.

The boy who would come to be known as Masutatsu Oyama was born as Young-Eui Choi in a south-western farming village near the sea. He was an energetic, athletic boy who had little interest in school. When he was nine years old he attended a village harvest festival where the local men were entertaining themselves, in the traditional way, by wrestling in public. A powerful young man, who had won the competition and had plenty of fight left in him, asked if anyone in the crowd was brave enough to take him on. The watching Young-Eui was surprised when a much older, and smaller, man from the north of Korea stepped into the ring. The boy knew this man well. He was named Yi and had worked on the farm owned by Young-Eui's father. But he had never seen this poor laborer fighting. As the match began the young champion hurried forward to take hold of Yi but he was instantly knocked to the ground by a blow to the face. After several further blows the local champion had to be carted off to hospital. Thrilled by the unexpected victory, Young-Eui learned from the crowd that Yi was an expert in Chabee, a Korean martial art that is closely linked to Chinese fighting styles. On their next meeting the boy pestered Yi until he finally agreed to teach him the basics of Chabee.

Young-Eui spent two years learning to fight with Yi but these combat skills only served to get him into even more mischief than before. The boy was sent to Seoul to enter a junior high school and there made such a nuisance of himself that the police began to take an interest in him. At the age of fifteen his despairing father gave up on the boy and agreed to let him take the long boat ride to Japan in search of adventure and opportunity. The year was 1939 and war between Japan and China had been going on for years. Many Koreans were serving in the Japanese forces, usually in menial positions. But a man named Shin had just made his name in Korea by becoming, against all the odds, a fighter pilot in the Japanese air force. Shin was regarded as a hero by thousands of Korean boys and Young-Eui was eager to follow in his footsteps. As soon as he arrived in Japan he enrolled in a military academy for teenagers where he trained as a flight mechanic.

But even in this more exciting environment the young man was still restless. After two years he suddenly quit the academy without qualifications and found himself alone on the streets of Tokyo, a young Korean in a nation that was boiling with fanatic nationalism. Young-Eui was well aware that he was at the very bottom of society. He struggled to find a place to live in a city where no one wanted to take in a Korean boy as a lodger. Even more than the Okinawan Funakoshi, he was a lonely and despised outsider. After a long search Young-Eui found the Oyamas, a Korean family who welcomed him into their home. He displayed his gratitude for their friendship in the most profound way. In xenophobic Japan a Korean name was nothing but a handicap. His host family had themselves adopted a Japanese name and Young-Eui decided to take their name as his own. He became Masutatsu Oyama.

Life was easier with this new name and Oyama enrolled as a student at Takushoku University where he joined the karate group run by Gichin Funakoshi and his son Yoshitaka. In later life Oyama was highly critical of the father of karate. Funakoshi only taught kata, he said, and did so in slow motion. But he was more appreciative of the younger Funakoshi and especially of his efforts to introduce free fighting to the karate curriculum. According to Oyama, Yoshitaka Funakoshi had taken a team of fighters from the Shotokan dojo to compete with a Goju karate group in Osaka. The Shotokan team had been thrashed by the more experienced Goju fighters and Yoshitaka had, from that point onwards, made a priority of improving the fighting ability of his students.

Among the Goju team of fighters the outstanding figure was Nei Chu So. He was one of the strongest karate men in Japan during the 1930s, heavily muscled and powerful. But, more importantly for Oyama, he was Korean. At last the young man had identified a role model that he could take seriously. He shifted his allegiance away from the Funakoshi group and began a study of Goju karate.

With the war now approaching its climax Oyama was drafted to work at a military airfield near Tokyo. A unit of young kamikaze pilots were based at the airfield and Oyama made friends with these suicide squad members. In the morning he would see the pilots dressing themselves in headbands that displayed the rising sun and belts that were decorated with a thousand stitches that had been sewed one at a time by a thousand different Japanese women. The youthful airmen would compose a death poem in the style of the ancient samurai and then fly off into the morning sky to attack American ships. Many, many of them never returned. Oyama was deeply affected by the profoundly romantic and desperate atmosphere of his airbase. It filled him with a burning hatred for the American enemy and also for the Japanese officers who were so casually wasting these young lives.

At the Bottom
As the war ended Oyama was twenty two years old and had already gained a fourth dan black belt in Goju karate. He was a powerful young man, and rather wild. At that time Tokyo was swarming with gangster gangs who ran the black markets. Oyama was sucked into the periphery of these Yakuza groups where his great strength and fighting prowess were of obvious value. On one fateful evening he was attending a dance competition when a minor gangster started to wave a knife in his face. Oyama maintained a safe distance from the knife until the gangster lunged at him. He blocked the strike and punched forcefully to the man's head with a direct blow. The yakuza member fell to the ground dead.

Oyama expected to be jailed for this killing but he was saved by several witnesses who testified that he had clearly been acting in self defense. Even though he was released from prison the horror of the incident was renewed when the dead man's wife and children turned up on his doorstep. How could they survive in these desperate times, they asked him, without a man in their home to bring in some money? Oyama was so shaken by the visit of the bereaved family that he later travelled to their farm where he made an offer to work on the land to keep them all alive.

But even this nightmarish incident was not enough to shake Oyama out of his reckless ways. He was the archetypal angry young man who swaggered through the streets of Tokyo with his hoodlum friends on the lookout for cash and adventure. More and more often he came to the attention of the American military police as they enforced public safety in the capital. Most Japanese people at that time were eager to accept the direction of the Americans but this young man was made of different stuff. After repeated clashes with the authorities Oyama was finally thrown into jail for six months.

In his prison cell Oyama felt that he had reached the bottom of his life. As a young man from patriarchal Korea it was only natural for his father's face to haunt him. Oyama knew that he had brought great shame on his family. His life was worthless. As these dark thoughts swarmed in Oyama's mind he received a visit from his karate teacher Nei Chu So. The older man angrily attempted to shake some sense into his student. Oyama was now at a turning point, So told him. He was at least as strong as his teacher. Did he plan to use that great strength for evil purposes, to become a murdering gangster? Or would he become a great man? So urged Oyama to get away from the city. He needed to isolate himself and to discipline his body and his mind. He had to find a new direction for his life.

On the Mountaintop
As he emerged from prison Oyama did his best to make a fresh start. He made an attempt to open a karate dojo in Tokyo but the timing was all wrong. Very few people in those days just after the war had the energy or interest to take up karate. In the empty hours Oyama filled his time by reading and rereading Eiji Yoshikawa's romantic novelization of the life of Miyamoto Musashi. The book portrays the great swordsman as a fanatic for self-improvement, as a man who loved his sword so much that he regularly made retreats on distant mountaintops where he could conduct solitary training. Oyama was sufficiently inspired by the book to make a pilgrimage to the home of the author.

After some thought he decided that he would act on the advice of his teacher and follow in the footsteps of Musashi. Oyama travelled to the very same mountain in Yamanashi where Musashi had created his own distinctive sword style. He found lodgings in a Buddhist temple on the slopes of the mountain. In return for the accommodation he performed chores for the monks and practiced karate in the remaining hours. But it was a lonely place and Oyama ended up wondering why he was there. After three months of life on the mountain he was disappointed and discouraged. He made his way back to Tokyo.

At least in the city there was the warmth of other people. Oyama assuaged his loneliness for a while by marrying a beauty queen and fathering his first child. But still the unfulfilled dream that he could become a modern day Musashi ate away at the young man. He had made a promise to both his teacher Nei Chu So and to himself that he would go away and train relentlessly until he could return as a master of karate. Oyama decided to make one more serious effort at a life of isolation. In preparation he visited wealthy sponsors who promised to keep him supplied with food and other necessities. When he had enough backing to be able to train for several months without financial worries Oyama decided to make another desperate attempt to take his karate to a higher plane. Once again he chose an inspiring location, Mount

Kiyosumi, a peak that rises steeply from the shores of the Pacific Ocean in Chiba. This was the place where in 1253 Nichiren had founded the militant sect of Buddhism to which Oyama belonged. The mountain slopes offer magnificent views of the sea and the climate is mild. Oyama took a vow to stay on Mount Kiyosumi for a thousand days.

Along with one of his karate students Oyama settled into a simple hut high on the slopes of the mountain. He had brought along some cooking utensils and hunting equipment but little else. His only concession to relaxation was to carry with him a full set of the Musashi novels. The karate men rose early every day and embarked on a training program that Oyama had designed to make the most of their surroundings. They lifted trees, pounded rocks and raced each other up the hillside. In the midst of this hard physical activity it was quite possible to forget the outside world. But in the evening when the light faded it was terribly lonely and eerie on the deserted hilltop. After a few months of this spartan existence Oyama's training partner had had enough. He made an unannounced getaway during the night. Once again Oyama was on his own.

With a touch of desperation Oyama stepped up his training. He had been advised to plant flax seeds and to make a habit of jumping over the growing shoots fifty times every day. As the plants grew taller his leaps became higher and higher. Mornings were devoted to running and weight lifting while the afternoons were for pure karate practice. Oyama felt almost unbearably lonely, knowing that his wife and child were waiting for him in the great city that was only a day's walk away. He was ready to give up once more but decided to first write to Nei Chu So asking for his blessing to leave the retreat. The answer that arrived one month later was uncompromising.

> Whether a painter seriously studying the concept of beauty, or a martial artist investigating budo, those who become recognized as geniuses work much harder and demonstrate far more perseverance than the average person. ... Oyama, I believe you to be an irreplaceable figure in the world of Japan Martial Arts. Training harder than anyone else will make you invincible. You have what it takes to stand alone, unrivaled as a modern day warrior, and become the example of a true martial artist for the world. If you have the urge to come down from the mountain hut then shave off an eyebrow. You will most likely have very little desire to see anyone until it grows back ... Was there any Master of the martial arts who had not experienced mortification? (42)

Oyama did as he was told, shaving both his hair and his eyebrows. Before long his hair was as bushy as ever but he continued to shave his eyebrows as a sign to himself that he had truly renounced the world. Day by day his power was growing. He found that he could now shatter rocks with his bare fists and could jump over tall bushes. He was feeling immensely strong and confident. For the first time he was sure that he could really become a legend like Musashi. But first he needed to prove to the world just how strong he had become. Many other young men dreamed of becoming famous martial arts instructors. How could he stand out from the crowd?

Controlled Mayhem

Oyama knew that he had to do something dramatic to put himself in the public eye. He was already twenty-six years old and there were hundreds of karate experts in Japan. On his mountain perch Oyama came up with the plan that would launch his reputation. He would fight bare handed against a bull, the very symbol of strength and aggression, and he would subdue the beast with the power of his karate. Coming down from Mount Kiyosumi Oyama sought out a stockyard. After watching the bulls for a while Oyama climbed into a paddock where a large bull was being held and launched a tremendous punch to the animal's forehead, a punch that produced a river of blood from the bull's mouth and nose. A second punch brought the beast to its knees and Oyama then chopped off its horns with two karate strikes.

Or so he described the scene in his later writings. Oyama's personal accounts of his duels with bulls are undoubtedly full of drama but they were subsequently questioned in some quarters. One ex-student, writing well after Oyama's death, described his own understanding of the first confrontation between Oyama and a bull in the following manner.

> Workmen prepared a fat old ox for Oyama by hitting one of its horns with a hammer so that it was quite loose. Oyama did not kill the ox, he only knocked off the loose horn. (43)

Whatever actually happened in that stockyard near Mount Kiyosumi it did prove to be the first step in a publicity campaign that Oyama believed would lift his young family out of poverty and ensure his own fame. There is no doubt that he was, after his long months on the mountain, a powerful, highly skilled and courageous man. But Oyama was also keenly aware that the staged antics and amateur dramatics of professional wrestling had great commercial potential. He was a close friend of the judo great Masahiko Kimura, a man who had himself made a good deal of money on the professional fighting circuit. Oyama wanted some of that action.

In 1952 Oyama embarked on an American tour in which he performed as one member of a tag wrestling team. The tour became a hit in the United States after Oyama was publicized as a representative of the mysterious and unknown Eastern art of karate. Before each match he gave dramatic demonstrations in which he broke planks with karate strikes. The audience was assured that he could crush bones with his bare hands. His publicity outreach was greatly assisted by the American press which described the feats of Oyama, performing under the stage name of Togo, in the most breathtaking fashion.

> ... a terrifying exponent of karate ... perhaps the deadliest form of weaponless self defense devised by man ... It cannot be put to full use without maiming or killing. To demonstrate its lethal characteristics against humans is unthinkable. The deadliness, nevertheless, is demonstrable. Togo can - and has - killed steers by cracking their skulls with one blow of the fist. He also has ripped out the entrails of dogs with a single slashing stroke of his finger tips ... The young (28) expert in controlled mayhem is only 5 feet 8 inches tall and weighs, at the most, 180 pounds. He modestly believes that he can handily dispose of 'maybe 15 or 16' adversaries in an ordinary free for all. (44)

Oyama arrived in Chicago for his first experience of professional wrestling. He began the performance with a demonstration of karate kata and was rewarded with a hail of boos. Oyama quickly switched to smashing up bricks and boards and this proved much more to the liking of the audience who began to applaud him.

These exploits were being closely followed by the Japanese public. Newspaper readers in Japan were eager to make a hero of anyone named Oyama who was willing to face the giants of America on their home turf. Oyama himself recognized just how important these adventures in the United States were for his growing reputation in Japan. For the rest of his life he would describe these matches as an all-conquering tour of America.

In 1955 Oyama published a series of articles in a Japanese magazine that presented his tour of America in the most sensational manner possible. He had won 270 matches against all-comers, the articles claimed, knocking out most of the challengers easily. He described a match in North Carolina where he had fought a man named Becker who quickly punched Oyama out of the ring. Oyama waited for the right moment and then leapt back into the ring where the two men fell into such an intense struggle that they were hurled out of the ring again. They continued to fight outside the ring until Oyama felled Becker with a body punch. Immediately he himself felt a powerful blow on his back. Turning and punching he realized a moment too late that the attacker had been a woman assailing him with a chair. The crowd bayed for Oyama's blood and only the presence of a strong police force allowed him to escape with his life.

On another occasion Oyama had to confront an enraged off-duty policeman who had challenged him to a $1000 match.

> As soon as my mind was made up, I leaned forward, ducking the devastating blows thrown by his enormous arms. Then, almost out of desperation, I unleashed and connected my chudan-zuki; once, twice and three times. Each time my tsuki connected, I heard the dull un-describable sounds. Seven of his ribs were broken as a result of my chudan-zuki. He went down for the count with a KO. I won the match in a mere minute and a half. The match was over, but not the crowd. The whole crowd got up on their feet, and began throwing apples and empty bottles like a rain falling on us. They all screamed, "Don't let Tojo get away. Kill Tojo!" Their screaming of my name all of a sudden became "Tojo!", "Kill Tojo!" The audience was over-excited. They started rushing toward the ring. I knew there was no way out. (44)

Oyama's descriptions of his bouts in America have the unmistakeable ring, to a modern ear, of the comical antics of a pro-wrestling event. But at the time they were received with excitement in Japan and helped to make Oyama famous. After he returned from America Oyama was delighted to learn that another arm of his publicity campaign had paid off. A movie producer had heard of his confrontation with a bull and approached Oyama to recreate the fight so that it could be recorded on film. This was something new for Oyama, an opportunity to prove himself to the Japanese public. The karate man threw himself into training for his match with the bull. He ran long distances to build up his stamina and made regular visits to stockyards to practice his technique on any available animal.

The confrontation between man and beast took place in 1953 in front of several journalists and the camera crew. In his own dramatic account of the incident, written years after the event, Oyama described how he waited anxiously on the seafront dressed only in a pair of leather shorts. Thousands of spectators had gathered.

> Now the huge black bull was released from a rope. I swiftly dodged its attack left and right and finally grasped it by the horns. I tried to twist it down to the ground, but the 1,250 pound bull, spreading its legs, refused to budge ... At last my hands slipped off the horns because of perspiration and the enraged bull rushed at me with terrible force ... Suddenly I missed my footing and fell on my back ... the bull, with a low snort, made a thrust at me. Though I recovered quickly, my skin was torn from abdomen to breast. The blood flowed, but I felt no pain ... Gradually I felt my opponent becoming tired. The moment I noticed this, I twisted with all my might. When it toppled down into the sand making a heavy thud, I jumped in quickly to grip the horns firmly with my hands. Its large abdomen was beating thunderously and both the bull and I were covered with perspiration and sand. ... I concentrated on my right shuto (knife-hand). With a yell I struck at the base of the horn. The bull groaned; its horn, broken at the root, was hanging down from its forehead. I pulled the horn from the forehead and unconsciously held it high over my head. Suddenly the stir of the spectators like a distant thunder reached my ears. I had conquered the bull. (45)

After this brutal display Oyama would go on, according to the legend, to fight no less than fifty two bulls with his bare hands and to kill three of those bulls instantly. Were these real fights or were they stunt fights against small animals that had been prepared to ensure an easy victory for the karate man? Opinions vary. Whatever the truth, the effect on the public of these challenges with bulls was just what Oyama had hoped for. He began to emerge from the pack of karate teachers as an individual with a colorful and startling past. He had trained alone on a mountain top. He had killed bulls with his bare hands. He was the greatest fighter in the world.

Full Contact
Oyama had reached a crossroads in his life. He could choose to have a career as a serious and respected karate teacher, or one as a circus performer. It seemed unlikely that he could wear both hats for much longer but Oyama seemed to want to try. While he was still fighting bulls Oyama also began to teach karate outdoors in a Tokyo park. His high profile attracted a substantial number of students. They signed up for classes that were, at this time in the middle of the 1950s, essentially offering the Goju style of karate that Oyama had himself learned.

After two years of his outdoor karate classes Oyama was taking enough money in fees to be able to rent space in a ballet studio. In this new venue he began to shape his own unique style of karate, a style that was ideally suited to his own powerful physique and his love of dramatic physical confrontation. Most of the other karate groups at this time had followed the lead of the Japan Karate Association in adopting rules for free fighting that minimized the danger and the pain of combat. Oyama took the opposite approach. His students fought each other bare handed and did not try to control their techniques. Instead they punched each other repeatedly with full force, a type of fighting that the JKA believed to be so dangerous that it was likely to end in death. Nobody died in Oyama's dojo but the training was tough. More than ninety percent of those who came to try his karate dropped out. Despite the huge turnover Oyama was determined to stick with his brand of 'tough karate' and he became openly scornful of the other schools who were, he said, teaching a kind of 'dancing karate'.

At first Oyama allowed his students to punch each other to the face without control. No body protectors were allowed. The students would wrap towels around their hands to provide some kind of padding but contact to the face often produced spurts of blood. Matches would continue until one student was so tired or in so much pain that he shouted out a surrender. Eventually Oyama decided to reduce the flow of blood by barring hand strikes to the head and neck but he continued to encourage his students to kick at each other's heads with full power. For the select group who could cope with the rough training Oyama's dojo was an exciting place to be. Black belts in other clubs heard stories about this tough karate and began to wonder if they were missing out. Many paid visits to find out for themselves.

To succeed in Oyama's dojo karate fighters needed to have the same basic skills as fighters from other schools but they also needed to have enough power in their punches and kicks to knock down opponents and a good deal of physical bravery. Over time fighting training at the Oyama dojo became more and more dominant at the expense of the precise techniques that Funakoshi had valued. Kata and basic skills continued to form part of the regular training sessions but they gradually came to represent little more than a warm up for the key aspect of Oyama karate which was fighting practice. In marked contrast to most other karate styles body conditioning, practice of sparring techniques, and sparring itself took up more than half of the training time in Oyama's dojo. Perhaps it was little wonder that the turnover was so high. Inexperienced beginners were expected to train alongside the black belts and to take part in sparring from the very first class. And however tough they might be, newcomers had to be careful. Any new student who displayed too much confidence or aggression risked a sound beating from the senior grades who were loath to lose face to a mere beginner.

By 1957 Oyama felt that the time was ripe to officially launch his own style of karate. He held a ceremony on yet another mountaintop to name the new style Kyokushin (Ultimate Truth) karate. In his new position as the head of a karate association Oyama became ever more outspoken. He was openly disillusioned with the peaceful philosophies that were so dominant in the Japanese martial arts during the years after the war. Oyama had never been a man to accept hardship meekly and he did not see why anyone should have to. "Life is to struggle, life is to fight," he wrote and he proudly championed the value of physical confrontations where nothing was more important than pure strength. For many Japanese teenagers this was a refreshing and attractive world view.

Even as his karate organization grew Oyama still had unfinished business as a showman. He hoped to continue touring the world to fight bulls and break stones. But animal rights activists in both Japan and America now made it clear that they would target his exhibitions. In 1957 Oyama made a disastrous tour of North America and Mexico. He was hounded by demonstrators, failed in several attempts to break boards and stones and was so badly gored in the stomach by a Mexican bull that he had to spend six months recovering. The whole experience was so disappointing that Oyama made a decision to put the publicity stunts behind him. For a while he continued to speculate about the possibility of staging a fight with a bear in northern Japan but increasingly it seemed that his future lay in the leadership of a karate organization.

Get Strong

In 1964 Oyama followed in the footsteps of Japan's other leading martial arts organizations by establishing a permanent headquarters in central Tokyo. At the time this was a risky financial move.

Oyama was by no means wealthy but he had been able to scrape together enough money and land to build a home for his family. Presented with what he regarded as a more important opportunity he gave up on his homebuilding plan and donated the money and land to the headquarters project. Squads of young karate students cleared the ground and carted away rocks. The building that rose on the land that had been set aside for Oyama's home proved to be his greatest investment. He immediately set about using the building to further imitate the Japan Karate Association by establishing a full-time training program for resident students. These young men would become the officer corps for Oyama's growing organization and would help him to spread Kyokushin karate throughout Japan.

The training program for the live-in students was a truly exhausting one, as their daily pre-breakfast routine indicates. Their day began at six with a run of several miles to an outdoor location where kicks and strikes would be performed hundreds of times followed by two hundred push-ups and two hundred squats. The students would then run back to the dojo where they would practice sparring techniques. They finished the early morning session with two or three hundred sit-ups and some stretching. Breakfast would be eaten with Oyama himself at the head of the table. For many of the students this meal proved to be more of an ordeal than the early morning run. Oyama, who had lived through the war years, insisted that the students clear their plates. They needed plenty of energy, he told them, for the hours of training still to come. All were served the same portions as Oyama, and he had a big appetite.

Oyama was now becoming a well known public figure in Japan. His dramatic life story and his tough karate style comprised a package that was easy to promote and Oyama made brilliant use of the media as he worked to broaden his appeal. In 1957 he published his first book, What is Karate? It was a vivid mix of autobiography and explanations of karate that became a best seller in Japan and, in later years, throughout the world. Oyama went on to publish twenty books that made the most of his self-created image as the toughest man from the toughest school of karate. His books were early examples of the personal development publishing genre with ringing titles like Conquer Yourself, Live With Strength, and Get Strong.

In later years Oyama's efforts to mythologize his own life story reached their widest audience with the creation of Karate Baka Ichidai (A Crazy Life in Karate). This was a comic for teenagers that liberally embellished Oyama's life story in its depiction of a fantastic modern day karate hero. The bestselling manga was such a success that it was converted into a television series in the mid seventies. Some of the most dramatic stories were also recreated in a trilogy of movies that featured the greatest star of martial arts acting in Japan, Sonny Chiba. Chiba, who had himself been a student of Kyokushin karate for several years, played a character loosely based on Oyama. The hero of the trilogy was a conflicted, restless character who endlessly confronted and defeated other karate masters, gangsters, bulls and even bears in his quest to protect the weak and to achieve inner peace.

Fighting on the Moon

Oyama was constantly on the lookout for new ways to promote his karate as a more effective and powerful brand of fighting. A golden opportunity to do just that fell into his lap in 1964 after a Japanese boxing promoter attended a Muay Thai tournament in Thailand. The native fighting art of Thailand is a tough, unarmed style that resembles karate but makes a greater use of elbow and knee strikes. It was a professional sport in Thailand that was based around stables of young fighters who lived in training camps where they prepared for matches that attracted crowds of roaring gamblers.

When the Japanese promoter asked his Thai contacts what they thought about karate he was assured that Muay Thai fighters could easily defeat any karate fighter from Japan. Karate, they said, was a dance. It was ridiculous and ineffective. Suppressing his patriotic anger the promoter decided that he would recruit a group of Japanese fighters to take on these boastful Thais. Back in Japan he visited the headquarters of several karate groups to find a team who could challenge the Thais. To his great surprise none of these organizations expressed the slightest interest in sending a team of their fighters into the unknown. Finally the promoter made his way to Oyama.

The master of Kyokushin karate had been an outsider all his life and this opportunity excited him. It was a chance to prove the strength of his own style and to taunt the rest of the Japanese karate establishment for their weakness and lack of patriotism. If we do not accept this challenge, he remarked, then all practitioners of Japanese karate will be seen as cowards. Almost immediately he selected four of the strongest young members of Kyokushin and informed them that they would soon be fighting in Thailand. These four young men were willing to follow instructions but they knew nothing about Thailand, or about Muay Thai. Their teacher might as well have told them to go and fight on the moon. The four representatives did not even have much competition experience. Kyokushin did not yet have its own national tournament and its members had not been encouraged to enter the competitions that were organized by other styles of karate. How, they must have wondered, should they set about fighting against professionals in a distant and unfamiliar land?

The four fighters and their coach Kurosaki set up camp in a rural farmhouse one month before the scheduled match in Thailand. Desperately they struggled to use those few short weeks to make their bodies invincible. Every day they waded into the frigid nearby river where they kicked underwater to strengthen their hips. To Oyama's delight the Japanese media had picked up on the story and were portraying these young men as heroic defenders of the nation's martial pride.

At last the Kyokushin team flew out of wintertime Japan and soon found themselves in the sticky January heat of Bangkok. They were immediately exhausted by the climate and struggled to eat the unfamiliar food. But they discovered, to their great relief, that the tournament had been delayed. They would have more time than they had expected to acclimatize. Knowing that Oyama and much of the population of Japan was anxiously following their progress the young fighters forced themselves to train during the hottest part of the day, often locking themselves into a sealed garage where they would sweat in rivers. As the Japanese team prepared for their challenge the Thai organizers of the tournament saw enough of them to realize that these men were no weaklings. Quietly the original Muay Thai team was withdrawn and three of the strongest fighters in all Thailand were recruited in their place.

The famous first ever match between Japanese karate and Muay Thai took place on a sweltering evening in Bangkok's Lumpinee Stadium in front of ten thousand excited spectators. The first Japanese fighter was the twenty three year old Tadashi Nakamura, probably the strongest of all Oyama's students. Before he could settle into the fight a strong kick to his legs from the Thai fighter sent him flying into the air and onto the mat. With adrenalin pumping through his veins Nakamura climbed to his feet and managed to block another flurry of low kicks. Then he knocked his opponent onto his back with a powerful stomach kick.

As the first round ended Nakamura felt that he was holding his ground but the coach reminded him that the Thai fighters were conditioned to fight through multi-round bouts. They had tremendous stamina and Nakamura would not be able to outlast his opponent. He had to win quickly. As soon as the bell rang Nakamura launched a desperate all out attack and finally he was able to knock out the Thai with a punch to the face. He had won.

Nakamura was elated by his victory but behind the joy he still felt a sense of dread. Two further matches remained and he was afraid of the outcome. If the Kyokushin team lost it would represent a national disgrace. He felt that such great shame would prevent he and his friends from ever returning to Japan. His sense of impending doom deepened when the second Japanese fighter was hit below the eye with an elbow strike that ripped open his face and produced a gusher of blood. The referee stopped the fight and the scores were now even.

The final Japanese fighter came out to fight almost growling with anger at what had happened to his comrade in the previous match. But his determination could not extinguish the great physical disadvantages he faced. The Thai fighter was much taller and used his knees to pound the chest of the Japanese man. If one knee strike reached as high as his chin the competition would immediately be over.

In desperation the Japanese fighter launched his body forward and butted the Thai in the face. It was a dirty move but it was effective. Crawling back to a standing position the Thai fighter was so shaky on his feet that the Japanese man could pound him in the face at will. Before long the fight had ended and the Japanese team hurried away from the stadium, escaping from the angry crowd.

When the victorious team arrived back in Japan they encountered a warm reception from the press but a surprisingly cold one from Oyama. Instead of thanking these young men for their efforts and for the sacrifice of several months of their lives Oyama demanded to know why the second fight had been lost. Had they been spending their time drinking instead of training? Nakamura, who had devotedly followed Oyama for many years, began to lose faith in his idol.

One Hundred Men

Nakamura was an outstanding member of a powerful group of dozens of black belts at the head of Kyokushin karate. Oyama wanted to provide a dramatic focus for the training of his most senior students and decided that he would give them all an almost impossible target to work towards. He had been reading about the life of Yamaoka Tesshu, the great nineteenth century swordsman, and the seigan-geiko test that Tesshu had created as the ultimate challenge for the top swordsmen of his school. In this test a swordsman would face hundreds of opponents in consecutive matches that could last for an entire day or even more.

Oyama decided to create a karate version of Tesshu's challenge, one that would involve one hundred two minute fights without a break. He wanted it to be a truly grueling test of physical endurance, strength and, most importantly, of mental willpower. The master is said to have tested out his idea by personally fighting one hundred of his students in a single day and then repeating the challenge on two consecutive days. In the end so few of the students were willing or able to continue that Oyama stopped fighting.

The first one-hundred man sparring session (hyakunin kumite) for which clear records exist was that undertaken by Steve Arneil in 1965. Arneil, a South African who had been training with Oyama for four years, lived at the Kyokushin headquarters as he prepared for the challenge. The one hundred man kumite became the focus of an entire year of his life, a year in which he trained through every waking moment to get ready. When the day for the challenge arrived Arneil used his enormous strength to knock out several of his opponents quickly and thereby somewhat shortened the test. In the end he remained on his feet, fighting almost without break, for two hours and forty five minutes.

The one hundred man challenge subsequently became the ultimate goal for the small elite group of championship level Kyokushin fighters. The great physical and mental difficulty involved in sparring continuously for around three hours against determined opponents is reflected in the fact that, in the almost fifty years since Steve Arneil completed the test, only twenty more individuals have been able to follow in his footsteps. Successful challengers have included Tadashi Nakamura, who took the test a few months after Steve Arneil, and Naomi Woods who became the first woman to complete the challenge in 2004.

The format for the one hundred fights involves the challenger lining up against a group of opponents that usually includes both powerful and aggressive black belts and a number of nervous colored belts. Challengers must win more than half of their fights. If they are knocked down, they must get to their feet within five seconds. All who undergo the test are enormously strong and skillful fighters but the real challenge takes place during the second half of the hundred matches when collapsing with exhaustion becomes a distinct possibility and great mental energy is required to continue.

Oyama used the one hundred man kumite as yet more evidence of the superiority of his style as he worked to build a national organization for Kyokushin karate. To his undoubted promotional skills he had added an outstanding managerial ability that dovetailed perfectly with the booming Japanese business world of the 1960s and 1970s. He sent senior students, many of them graduates of the headquarters training program, to establish Kyokushin karate branches in regional towns. These young experts would first find a place to live and would then offer free demonstrations of karate in a public building or a civic park until they had gathered a large enough number of interested students to open a dojo. The same methodology was later followed on an international basis as Oyama began to dispatch his very strongest students overseas to form the nuclei of new national organizations. In addition to the work of these pioneers Oyama targeted teachers from other karate groups who had fallen under the spell of Kyokushin karate. Oyama exploited the interest of these teachers by offering them Kyokushin qualifications and teaching licenses by return of post. He believed that quality could be established later. For now the priority was growth.

Japanese Karate Shall Not Be Vanquished
In 1972 a karate world tournament was held in Paris. The competition ended in defeats for the Japanese competitors that were almost as shocking as the loss of the judo heavyweight gold medal at the Tokyo Olympics had been for judo fans. The previously unbeaten Japanese team, which had largely been recruited from the Japan Karate Association, was defeated and the team compounded its disgrace by subsequently withdrawing from the championships entirely. In the wake of this startling debacle Oyama published a remarkable open letter.

> We have concluded that this team went to pieces strictly because all its members and the Federation to which they belong had long come to regard karate, the sole surviving system of our martial arts, as being merely something of a playact ... Our organization, for one, has always striven to be an exception to the prevailing mental climate in postwar Japan. For to us karate has always meant the sole existing form of martial art ... directly based on the dictates of our traditional warrior spirit, or the way of the samurai ... Let us once and for all say that true Japanese karate shall not be vanquished but will continue to prevail ... In two years, we will hold in Tokyo ... the first world championships in name and fact. (46)

Once again the immigrant from Korea was accusing the leaders of Japanese karate of incompetence and cowardice and presenting his own organization as the sole inheritor of the legacy of the samurai. Throwing petrol onto the fire that he had started Oyama next made a announcement that he would commit ritual suicide if the Japanese Kyokushin team did not win the open world karate tournament he was planning. The effect of this radical statement on the world of Japanese karate and on Oyama's own students was profound. His words were greeted with horror, anger and fear.

Oyama had promised that his world championships would be an opportunity for Japanese karate to take on the best of the world and to restore its honor in open competition. In the end, however, the tournament in 1975 was a purely Kyokushin affair. Oyama's threat to respond to failure with suicide hung like a sword of Damocles over the heads of the organizers. In the circumstances it was not surprising that they did everything in their power to ensure the victory of the Japanese fighters. Foreign teams were restricted to a maximum of four members and the visitors from overseas were given no training facilities in central Tokyo. At the same time the eight Japanese fighters were engaged in intense workouts at the Kyokushin headquarters every day.

As the competition began the strongest foreign fighters found that they had been drawn against each other, a situation that meant that the number of overseas competitors was quickly reduced. Oyama, who was acting as chief judge, continually called the referees aside to overrule their decisions. The tournament ended with the top six places having all been taken by Japanese fighters. Oyama, who might have shown some gratitude for having been spared the necessity of killing himself, still found room for complaint. It would have been more pleasing, he grumbled, if the best foreign representatives had taken the second and fourth places.

Thanks to a widespread and aggressive publicity strategy the Oyama brand of karate rapidly expanded throughout the world during the seventies. His books were translated into English and Kyokushin groups were established in many countries. To a large extent the booming interest in Kyokushin karate was a side effect of the international explosion of enthusiasm for the martial arts that had been sparked by the Bruce Lee movies. But Oyama was infuriated by suggestions that a Chinese actor could outperform him as a publicity guru.

> It was my work, and not the popularized fame of a motion picture actor, that brought karate international fame and popularity. (47)

As he aged Oyama achieved all of the success that he had dreamed of as a young man on his lonely mountain retreat. By the time of his death in 1994 he had created an international organization of more than ten million students and was esteemed in many countries for his strength, courage and leadership. His life was certainly an impressive one and yet it had been a study in contradiction. He was an calculating self-publicist who preached in his books about the importance of sincerity; a farm boy from Korea who nominated himself as the inheritor of the Japanese martial legacy; a friend of the Yakuza who led his students in Zen meditation sessions.

There was a dark side to Oyama that drove some of his closest followers and greatest admirers away. But, for all his weaknesses, the founder of Kyokushin karate proved to be a necessary corrective to the passivity that had seeped into the Japanese martial world in the decades after the war. Oyama made it acceptable once more for martial artists to be forceful. He created training methods that produced levels of physical toughness and mental fortitude in his students that put most of the other schools to shame. Throughout his life he was a restless outsider but he died at the centre of a vast circle of followers who revered his name and drew inspiration from his life.

16. Into the World

The Black Belt General

In the years that followed the war the fighting arts of Japan were little more than exotic rumors to people in the outside world. The one exception was judo, a sport that had established strong international roots before the war. Other arts such as kendo, karate and aikido barely existed beyond the shores of Japan. The only international practitioners were small groups of emigrants who quietly maintained their martial skills as an exclusive and secret knowledge.

But in the 1950s this situation changed rapidly. Thousands of American servicemen engaged in the occupation and the Korean War were able to soak up the atmosphere of martial training halls in Japan. When they finally made their way home to the United States it was almost inevitable that stories about the extraordinary fighting arts of the East would spread, and spread quickly. All of the sudden there seemed to be a global fascination with this aspect of Japanese culture. And this was a welcome surprise for the Japanese martial organizations. By the middle of the 1950s they had become strong enough to be able to send highly trained experts to every corner of the globe. Everything possible was done to encourage and exploit the new fascination for judo, karate and aikido.

Perhaps the most important, and most unlikely, figure in the worldwide spread of the Japanese martial arts after the war was Curtis LeMay. If any individual could have been singled out as the greatest scourge of the Japanese nation during the Second World War it was this man. LeMay had been the planner and commander of the devastating firebombing raids that rolled remorselessly over the defenseless skies of Japan in 1945. Half a million civilians are believed to have died in these indiscriminate raids and five million more were left homeless by conflagrations started by the American incendiary bombs that fell among the wooden cities of Japan.

At the war's end LeMay became an assistant to General McArthur. He was a top level occupation official and so could go where he wanted and do as he liked. One thing that fascinated him about Japan was its martial arts and he paid a number of personal visits to the home of judo, the Kodokan. The arrival of such an important American threw the officials who remained in charge of Japanese judo into a certain confusion. Quickly they awarded LeMay a black belt and gave him the rank of Shihan. This was a title reserved for only high level judo experts and ensured that LeMay would be sure to outrank anyone he happened to meet at the dojo. The American general, clearly delighted with this display of deference, made it his business to encourage members of the occupying army to take up judo and to train at the

Kodokan. Many of those who did so arrived in time to have the surprising experience of being thrown around effortlessly by the tiny genius Mifune. This little man was such a remarkable advertisement for the potential of judo that he convinced many Americans to make a lifetime commitment to the sport.

LeMay returned to America at the outbreak of the Cold War and was appointed to be leader of the Strategic Air Command. In this role he was responsible for the nation's rapidly expanding fleet of nuclear bombers and was deeply involved in laying plans for a nuclear showdown with the Soviet Union. LeMay was an aggressive personality who would later go on to campaign for invasion of Cuba and the bombing of North Vietnam "back into the Stone Age". His enthusiasm for a nuclear first-strike policy was lampooned in the character of General Buck Turgidson in Stanley Kubrick's celebrated movie Doctor Strangelove.

As he laid plans for a nuclear offensive LeMay realized that nuclear bomb crews would be required to fly deep into Soviet territory to drop their payloads. But in the early 1950s American bombers could not carry enough fuel to make the return trip from distant targets in Russia. LeMay wanted his aircrews to know how to evade capture if they came down over enemy territory and so he set about creating an in-house personal combat program. LeMay ordered that the training should be based on the judo and karate he had observed during his time in Japan.

The Air Command began to send groups of airmen to Tokyo where they enrolled in an intensive eight week training course that taught them the basics of judo, karate and aikido. It proved to be an immensely popular program, running for fifteen years and introducing hundreds of Americans to the best Japanese teachers. LeMay went on to expand the program by inviting groups of senior Japanese martial arts instructors to tour air bases in America and give demonstrations at nearby cities. One of those who took part in these tours was Masatoshi Nakamura, the leader of the Japanese Karate Association. He found that American students wanted explanations and the process of being forced to give rational justifications for karate movements encouraged his intense exploration of the mechanics and psychology of the martial arts. This was just one example of how constant interaction with American military students during the post war period encouraged Japanese martial artists to modernize their teaching methods and improve their skills.

Just Do It!
Even by the late 1950s only a very few Japanese citizens were able to travel beyond the shores of their homeland. One important exception was the trickle of outstanding martial arts experts who were beginning to make longer visits overseas. Some travelled in response to invitations but more were simply sent into the unknown by their associations to capitalize on what seemed to be a boundless demand for

instruction in their arts. These men found themselves in strange places among strange peoples. They began to work with individuals who had no idea of the cultural routines that lay behind the martial arts and could not understand a single word of the Japanese language. Often, in fact, these Japanese pioneers had almost no language in common with their students.

Teruyuki Okazaki was the first karate instructor sent by the Japan Karate Association to act as a full time teacher in the United States. He was one of their very best, a pillar of the organization who had helped to create, and had headed, the first JKA instructor program. Okazaki was technically brilliant but he spoke almost no English. In 1961 he found himself in Philadelphia trying to teach karate to Americans who, in marked contrast to Japanese karate students, were fond of asking questions and had little inclination to behave formally. Okazaki could rarely understand the questions of his American students and he had not had been trained in Japan to patiently explain the meaning of each movement. When one student finally remarked that it might be better for the beginner students to simply shut up and do as they were told Okazaki was delighted to discover that at least one American felt the same way as he did. From that point on if any student asked a question he would respond, in English, "Shut up! Just do it!" It was only when Okazaki married an American woman that he finally figured out why so many of his students had quit training in disgust.

A Ghost in the Night
One of the first Japanese karate teachers to travel to Europe was Tatsuo Suzuki, the outstanding young expert to have emerged from the Wado style of karate that had been founded by Hironori Otsuka. Like most Japanese who were teenagers during the war Suzuki had grown up with a desire to get into the fight with the Americans and when the war was lost had trembled at predictions that the big nosed invaders would slaughter Japanese men and rape the women. In the midst of the mass unemployment that followed the war Suzuki swallowed his deep resentment of the occupiers and took a job as a cleaner on an American military base. For several months he had been living on a diet of insects and moldy rice. He was astonished to find that the Americans did not torture him but instead gave him presents of Coca-Cola and chocolate. Like so many of his fellow citizens Suzuki had his ideas about the invaders instantly turned upside down.

The young man was sufficiently impressed by his encounters with Americans to decide to learn English. When he visited the local YMCA to inquire about language classes he was surprised to learn that the centre was also quietly offering karate instruction. It was a time when Japanese karate students still feared that their activities would be banned by the occupiers and so the YMCA karate club described itself as a 'Japanese boxing' group. They held training sessions in gardens and fields, places that were hidden from casual observation. Like many others of his generation Suzuki had outsize ambitions and he quickly decided that he would become a great karate teacher who would bring karate to the outside world. Slowly he increased his training schedule until he was practicing for ten hours each day. He would work out late at night in the grounds of a local Shinto shrine where the locals, seeing his white karate suit flickering among the trees, thought that a ghost was at large.

Karate teaching methods in the 1950s in Japan were more marked by their severity than by any great concern for the welfare of students. Suzuki pushed through hard club training sessions and then moved on to after hours workouts. He would practice kicking while wearing heavy iron sandals, strive to blow out candles with superfast punches and take part in long sparring sessions. There were few fixed rules when he began to train in karate and when two university clubs held a meeting it was not unusual to see kicks to the groin, eye strikes and shin stamps being used in a fight. The spectators would bay for blood and would 'encourage' visiting fighters by thumping their backs with sticks if they retreated to the edge of the area. The only referees were senior students who turned a blind eye to all but the most serious injuries. There was no such thing as protection, fists were uncovered, and broken teeth and bloody noses were hardly worth a mention.

Suzuki had lived through years of this kind of intense training when he decided to make his way to London in 1965 to begin a career as a full time karate instructor. There were almost no other Japanese people in the London area and it proved to be a lonely life. Suzuki knew enough English to get around but not enough to teach. He brought a phrasebook to his classes. For a Japanese man it was a miserable life in this strange, damp country. The food was execrable and his tiny bedsit was so cold that he had to do karate exercises in order to become warm enough to sleep. He was on his own among a sea of strangers to whom his years of training and high dan grade meant nothing at all. Soldiers, street toughs and boxers wandered into his dojo to see if the little Japanese man could really fight. Somehow he survived it all, training locals experts and recruiting more teachers from Japan who helped him to build an international karate organization with branches in over twenty countries. Tatsuo Suzuki died in 2011 having spent the greater part of his life in the United Kingdom.

They're Big!
When he first arrived in London Suzuki had been confronted with dangers that had almost disappeared from the martial arts in Japan. In the home country the old tradition of challenging members of a rival martial group to combat as a test of ability had been in decline for decades. But for Japanese instructors overseas the situation was very different. The first generation of martial arts missionaries to travel overseas needed great courage, self-confidence and skill to survive in new and unpredictable environments.

Shigeru Oyama, a karate instructor who first travelled to the United States in the 1960s, had rarely met a foreigner before arriving in America. Later he recounted the learning experience he went through in his early years in that country.

> I studied culture and technique (when I came here) because if I fight a 150-pound man in Japan and a 220-pound man here, the same technique does not work. You have to change how you generate power. Timing is everything. The power changes. I started everything over. If I hit a 220-pound guy - I kick him in the face - he is still standing. If I kick the 150-pound guy with the same kick, he is on the floor. My technique changed a lot when I came to the United States. The people are different - they're big! (48)

While many Japanese instructors found themselves at a substantial height and weight disadvantage to their foreign students Hirokazu Kanazawa had the great benefit of being at least as tall as most foreigners. He was among the first wave of Japanese karate teachers to travel overseas when he arrived in Hawaii in 1961. Kanazawa had not come for a beach holiday. During his first year on the islands he was regularly challenged to combat in the dojo and in the street.

When a stranger demanded a showdown the karate man's standard response was to begin 'warming up' by throwing some of his blindingly fast punches and kicks in the air. Just the sight of his speed was enough to convince most challengers to think again. But occasionally a more determined course of action was required to make an aggressive individual back down. Kanazawa knew that few foreigners had ever seen a head-high kick. He was able to end several impromptu fights quickly as his opponents would be so surprised to be kicked in the head that they would fall over in shock.

Perhaps Kanazawa's most belligerent challenger was a huge wrestler who turned up with the press in tow and proceeded to disparage karate for their benefit. Kanazawa decided to test the strong man's courage. He warned his challenger that they would both have to sign documents giving the other immunity in case one of them was killed. He then shared the information that he could rip out a man's heart with his bare hands. Finally, a sharp blow to the wrestler's ribs convinced the bigger man that Kanazawa was probably telling the truth. The challenge was withdrawn.

Kanazawa would later become the senior Shotokan karate instructor in Britain before returning to Japan. In 1977 he left the JKA to create his own organization, Shotokan Karate International. Kanazawa's peerless reputation has helped the SKI to become one of the largest karate organizations in the world today with affiliated groups in more than one hundred countries and two and a half million members.

Kyokushin karate made its first move towards overseas expansion in 1966 when Masutatsu Oyama sent his best student Tadashi Nakamura to teach full-contact karate in New York. Nakamura was only twenty four years old. He was an expert fighter who had travelled to Thailand as part of the Kyokushin team that defeated Muay Thai, but he was ill prepared for life in America's largest city. New Yorkers lined up to challenge this baby faced and moderately sized Japanese newcomer. The first challenge came just two weeks after his arrival in America and Nakamura dealt with the situation by flattening the man with a straight kick to the lower abdomen. His next challenger was a huge man, a three hundred pound giant who managed to knock Nakamura down with a kick to the legs. The young karate teacher was well aware that he was being closely watched by the handful of students that he had been able to recruit. He knew that his reputation was on the line and that he would have to win the fight. But he also knew that seriously injuring an American would bring a world of unknown troubles. In the end he used a palm heel strike to knock the man out.

In retrospect Nakamura admitted that he was desperate during his first few months in America. Just one defeat would have destroyed his standing as a karate expert. And he would then have been forced to return to Japan to face Oyama and his own father with the taste of failure on his lips. But Nakamura was outstandingly powerful and skillful. He survived the early years in New York to create his own independent and powerful karate style Seido, an organization with branches in eighteen countries and twenty thousand registered students.

Karate Becomes American
Individuals like Okazaki, Oyama, Suzuki, Kanazawa and Nakamura were drawn from the very best talent of the Japanese karate world as it developed in the late fifties and early sixties. These young men dreamed of building an international base for karate that could replicate the worldwide acceptance of judo. Undoubtedly they were driven by individual ambition as they travelled overseas. But these teachers were also patriotic citizens of a land that had lost confidence in itself. They hoped to bring Japanese culture to the world and to win respect for what was an essentially Japanese art.

But while Japanese teachers were aiming to create centers of excellence overseas their plans did not always sync with the irrepressible individualism of the foreigners. Thousands of servicemen from the United States had spent time studying karate in the Far East and some of these men were simply not willing to become the overseas subordinates of Japanese martial arts organizations. At the same time that Japanese karate instructors were working to establish their art in the United States there was a parallel American karate movement led by local teachers. These pioneers may have been less skilled than their Japanese counterparts but they were perhaps better able to provide a learning environment that suited the American mood. Over time the American led karate organizations would come to overshadow groups that were dedicated to following the Japanese model.

One of the very first foreigners to open a karate school outside Japan was Robert Trias. In 1942 he was stationed on the Solomon Islands with the American navy. The young sailor filled his spare time by engaging in boxing sessions with his friends. A Chinese man took to watching Trias as he sparred and began to pester the American to let him try his hand. When Trias eventually agreed to let the Chinese man fight him he was shocked. Although he was a champion middleweight boxer he was astonished to find himself receiving "the biggest thrashing of (his) life." Trias asked the man, who was named Hsing, to teach him what he knew. As a result Trias picked up a mixture of Chinese kung fu and karate techniques that Hsing had learned from Choki Motobu on Okinawa. It was a rather indirect introduction to karate but for Trias it was convincing. During the remaining years of the war he sought out every martial arts expert he could find in the Far East and took in as much as he could.

In 1946 Americans knew very little about karate. The fighting art had been confined almost entirely to Japan before the war and had practically disappeared in the aftermath of the conflict. As a result, there were few limitations for Trias as he set about creating his own and distinctively American version of karate. One year after the end of the war he opened a karate school in Arizona and began to teach students who he fitted out in white karate outfits and colored belts.

Trias was a true pioneer who created the first American karate association, wrote the first English language book about karate and organized the first karate tournaments in the United States. How much all of this activity was based on a deep knowledge of Japanese karate is a matter of some debate. Trias had received very limited exposure to Japanese karate during his war years and, although he did develop links with Okinawan karate groups in later years, much of the karate he taught in his schools was probably the product of his own imagination. Trias was, however, a highly successful administrator. In stark contrast to the tight control the Japanese instructors in America exerted over their students Trias ran his United States Karate Association as an open house where member groups were encouraged to develop their own training programs. By the time of his death in 1989 his Association boasted more than half a million members.

Even before Trias had begun teaching karate on the American mainland there had been a tradition on Hawaii of Japanese expatriates inviting karate teachers from Okinawa to visit. Among the Japanese community in Hawaii was one James Mitose, a man who had been born on the island but who had been sent to study in Japan as a child. On his return to Hawaii Mitose began to teach a martial art that he claimed to be Japanese in origin but named as Kenpo, after the Japanese word for Chinese fighting systems. In fact Mitose's kenpo probably owed a great deal to skills he had picked up from other Hawaiian practitioners of Japanese karate and from his study of Japanese karate textbooks. He proved to be a somewhat eccentric teacher but remains an important figure for his influence on one of the key pioneers of karate in the United States, Ed Parker.

Parker grew up in Hawaii where he studied judo and also learned kenpo from a truly unconventional student of Mitose, William Chow, a man who taught martial arts to his students in a local park. When Parker relocated to a Mormon university in Utah he began to teach self defense classes to the students, laying the foundations of an organization that would finally emerge as the International Kenpo Karate Association. Parker moved to California in 1956 and in that environment he slowly moved his fighting style away from its origins in the melting pot of Hawaiian martial arts. Over time he created a fast moving fighting style that proudly adopted an American terminology and ideology.

Superstars

Parker's position as one of the first martial arts teachers in California almost inevitably brought him into contact with the entertainment industry of that state. Parker became a movie actor, stunt man and the favored martial arts teacher to the stars of Hollywood. Among the many ambitious young actors he encountered was Bruce Lee, an Asian-American who had been born in San Francisco but had spent most of his childhood in Hong Kong. Parker played an instrumental role in helping Lee to achieve fame in the United States by giving him a prominent demonstration spot at a karate competition in 1964. At this pivotal event Lee amazed the crowd with an astonishing display of fitness, skill and speed. Lee had developed a unique fighting system that was shaped by his experiences in Hong Kong and by his encounters in America with taekwondo and karate teachers. Word of this impressive young man quickly spread among Hollywood producers.

In 1966 Lee won the role of Kato in the Green Hornet television series. As an Asian in 1960s America he was naturally cast as a servant, but a servant who possessed such amazing fighting skills that they intoxicated the American youth who watched the series. Even after this first success Lee had to fight his way through layers of racial prejudice to win final acceptance in America. He was initially cast in the lead role for the 1972 television series Kung Fu but the producers lost confidence in their decision to have an Asian play a leading role. At the last moment they switched to the distinctly non-Asian David Carradine who took on the role of a Shaolin monk traveling through the United States.

Bruce Lee had an abundance of drive, skill and charisma, certainly enough to enable him to overcome this kind of setback. He fought his way back into prominence through a series of martial arts movies that were produced in Hong Kong. But just when he had taken a huge stride back into winning acceptance from the Hollywood community with the release of Enter the Dragon, an American/Chinese joint production, his tragically early death brought a brilliant acting career to an abrupt end.

The early death of Lee only served to increase his fame and his movies proved to be almost unbearably exciting for the American teenagers who flocked to see them. After watching a Bruce Lee movie the audience would rush out of the movie theatre to search for someone, anyone, who could teach them how to punch and kick like their hero. Largely thanks to the effect of these movies there was an explosion of American interest in the martial arts during the early seventies. Above all it was the established karate groups, such as those led by Trias and Parker, that reaped the rewards of the Bruce Lee boom.

A very different kind of superstar to form a connection with Ed Parker was Elvis Presley. Presley had first tried his hand at karate during his military service in the late 1950s and was sufficiently enthused by his experiences to approach Parker after watching a demonstration of karate at the exclusive Beverly Wilshire Hotel in 1960. The two men became fast friends with Parker serving as personal bodyguard to Elvis during the singer's final years. Parker helped Elvis to attain a black belt in karate when he sent him to take a short course with a tough military trainer, Hank Slomanski. Slomanski sent a message back to Parker that read: "Your boy ain't pretty anymore, but he's a black belt." Parker also awarded Elvis a black belt in American Kenpo and the two men occasionally performed self defense demonstrations together.

When Elvis moved to his sprawling home at Gracelands in Memphis Parker recommended that he continue his studies with the colorful Master Kang Rhee, a teacher who would give full rein to the singer's need for ego reinforcement. Rhee liked to allow his students to select their own animal names and for a period Elvis adopted the martial title of 'Mr. Panther'. But he quickly dropped that name when someone pointed out that the authorities might infer that the ultra-conservative Elvis had developed an affinity for the Black Panthers. After that he chose to be addressed as 'Mr. Tiger'. Rhee designed a special karate outfit that was trimmed in red satin for Elvis and awarded him an eighth degree black belt. The singer liked to take part in teaching classes and demonstrations but his technique, from the brief recordings that exist of those occasions, seems to have been not much more advanced than that of the beginners he was teaching.

The Deadliest Man Who Ever Lived
By the 1960s the majority of American karate groups had adopted those parts of Japanese karate that they found useful and interesting. But they dispensed with a good deal of the cultural behaviors that, for Japanese karate experts, were an indispensable part of their martial art. In the creation of a new American karate there was a fresh energy but also a real danger. These were decades when the American

public had not yet developed a cynicism about the martial arts and experimentation and myth-making could be carried off more easily than they can today.

One of the wildest and most exotic offshoots of American karate was created by John Keehan, a doctor's son from Chicago. He had served in the marines during the Korean war and was one of the most successful students of Robert Trias, reaching the heights of a sixth degree black belt at a mere twenty three years of age. But in 1964 Trias expelled Keehan from his organization. From that point onwards Keehan, from his base in Chicago, was liberated to indulge in the colorful experiments that would make him the best known and most notorious karate man in the American Midwest. In the sixties karate still had an aura of exotic mystery for most Americans and Keehan played on the ignorance of his new students to the greatest possible extent. He was, he told anyone who would listen to his diatribes, "the deadliest man in the world." Keehan was certainly a master of intimidation and liked to petrify his students by informing them that he could penetrate their ribcages with his fingers or rip out their tongues.

Keehan's training methods were unconventional in the extreme. In the karate dojos of his Black Dragon Society beer coolers were installed to provide refreshments between periods of training. It was important, Keehan argued, for karate students to train in realistic conditions and they needed to know how to fight when drunk. My system he liked to say, "is fuck-em-up waza. Cause what I'm doing is fucking up the other guy's body." (49)

In 1970 Keehan was at the centre of the most disturbing incident in the history of American karate when he decided to bring a group of students to challenge a rival martial arts group at their own dojo. Keehan and his friends made their way to the training hall of the Chicago Green Dragon Kung Fu club but as soon as they entered the hall the door was suddenly locked behind them. Several men holding Chinese weapons emerged from the shadows and surrounded the karate detachment. Realizing that they were outnumbered Keehan's group tried to talk their way out of the situation but they were forced to retreat under a hail of punches. The karate group fought their way through kicks and weapon attacks and were able to knock down the outside door. Just as they crashed out of the club one of the group suffered a spear wound to the neck that punctured his carotid artery. An autopsy on the dead man, Jim Koncevic, showed that he had received thirty six wounds including the hole in his throat that had killed him.

Following the death of his closest friend Keehan moved away from running karate dojos and into attempts to create a business empire. He ran a string of pornography stores, opened a hairdressing salon and bragged that he occasionally turned his hand to moonlighting as a hitman for the Chicago Mafia. After he had changed his name legally to Count Dante Keehan had his greatest commercial success with the creation of a slim instruction manual that he entitled The World's Deadliest Fighting Arts. The booklet was advertised heavily in Marvel comics and in men's magazines. With its chilling promises to induct readers into the secrets of instant killing methods the pamphlet proved to be a runaway bestseller, selling millions of copies.

> Yes, this is the DEADLIEST and most TERRIFYING fighting art known to man - and WITHOUT EQUAL. Its MAIMING, MUTILATING, DISFIGURING, PARALYZING and CRIPPLING techniques are known by only a few people in the world. An expert at DIM MAK could easily kill many Judo, Karate, Kung Fu, Aikido, and Gung Fu experts at one time with only finger-tip pressure using his murderous POISON HAND WEAPONS. Instructing you step by step thru each move in this manual is none other than COUNT DANTE - "THE DEADLIEST MAN WHO EVER LIVED." (50)

The behavior of Keehan represented a strange distortion of the ethical underpinnings of karate that had been established by great Japanese teachers such as Itosu and Funakoshi. Keehan claimed to have killed more than fifty human beings personally, half of them during his military service and half in street fights or private sparring challenges. He boasted that he had taken part in two no-holds-barred competitions, one in Canton and one in Bangkok, that involved fights to the death. Keehan died in his bed at the age of 35, finally defeated by a perforated ulcer.

Wolf Killers

In the United States it was possible for karate to take a distinctly American form while continuing to proudly advertise its origins in a Japanese fighting tradition. But in some other parts of the world there were good reasons for any link with Japan to be disguised or buried altogether. This was the case with Sambo, a Russian fighting style that for several decades entirely disavowed its historical connection to Japan.

In 1911 a young Russian army officer named Vasili Oschepkov was working as an intelligence officer in Tokyo. Just a few years had passed since the defeat of the Russian military at the hands of Japan and the two nations still regarded each other with great suspicion. Oschepkov began to take judo lessons at the Kodokan and was directly coached by Jigoro Kano among others as he worked his way towards winning a judo black belt in 1913. The Russian officer was then transferred out of Japan to the Russian Far East port of Vladivostok where he fell under the influence of the Bolsheviks. In 1917 he returned to Japan for just long enough to be awarded a second dan grade in judo.

Oschepkov became a commander in the Red Army during the revolutionary years and was then employed as an important spy for the Bolshevik government. In this role he travelled throughout Japan and China where he presented himself as a movie distributor. By 1921 he was back in Moscow and teaching judo to elite Red Army soldiers. In that role he made the acquaintance of Victor Spiridonov, a combat trainer at the headquarters of the NKVD, the Bolshevik spy agency. Spiridonov was a war veteran who had lost the use of his left arm. Unable to fight he became a teacher and a thinker about unarmed combat who made a habit of recording and learning fighting techniques from around the world.

In 1923 Oschepkov and Spiridonov were the leading lights in a group of experts that were tasked with creating a hand-to-hand combat program for the Red Army. They designed a wide range of fighting methods for units as varied as police groups, border guards, spies, commandos and the secret police. The two experts had very different approaches. Spiridonov recommended training in deadly techniques that could be used by soldiers of any physical build. But Oschepkov, who had a background of sparring in judo classes, pushed for soldiers to be trained to apply their techniques against fully resistant partners. These two strands were later combined by the students of the two men into a distinctively Russian martial art that is known today as Sambo.

In the 1930s Japan was in control of northern Manchuria and had stationed troops on the borders of the Soviet Union. The two nations were on the brink of war and any hint of Japanese influence in Russian society was bound to be deeply unpopular with the authorities. Oschepkov was pressured to stop talking about the judo origins of his fighting style and in 1937, at the peak of the bloody purges ordered by Stalin, he was arrested and taken to Siberia. Oschepkov was accused of working as a double agent for Japan and ten days later was shot through the head.

But the ideas about the martial arts that Oshepkov had formulated were able to outlive their creator thanks to the brilliant stratagems of one of his leading students. A year after the death of Oschepkov, Anatoly Kharlampiev convened a meeting with the stated purpose of creating a purely Soviet form of 'freestyle wrestling'. Kharlampiev drew a careful veil over the Japanese origin of many of his techniques and instead put forward an alternative and largely fictional history in which his own father had toured Russian villages in order to learn and record traditional wrestling styles. The patriotic and completely Russian fighting style that emerged from Kharlampiev's conference was given the name SAMozashchita Bez Oruzhiya (weaponless fighting system) or SAMBO for short. It was a fighting style that found its first recruits amongst the very toughest units of the Soviet army. One such unit was the group of assassins, nicknamed 'wolf-killers', who were being trained for the incredibly dangerous job of assassinating high level targets in Nazi Germany. If anyone needed survival skills it was these men and Sambo provided them with the personal defense and attack techniques for their work.

After the end of the war Sambo became the officially recognized combat sport of the Soviet nation and was soon popular enough to support a large group of professional fighters. As the 1964 Olympics drew near the Soviet government, in an ironic twist of fate, suggested that Sambo fighters should compete for the judo medals. The government had come to desire international prestige above all things and maintaining a distance from the Japanese was no longer a priority. In the years before the Tokyo competition the best Sambo competitors were gathered and efforts were made to convert their skills so that they could be used to win judo matches.

This was not a particularly complex task as the judo roots of Sambo, however carefully disguised, were still strong. In many ways the two fighting arts had diverged. Sambo fighters did not train in choking techniques and were more likely to try to lift their opponents bodily into the air than a judo competitor. But Sambo was still close enough to judo for its powerful fighters to be highly effective. In 1962 a hastily prepared Soviet judo team thrashed the French team who were at that time the judo champions of Europe. In 1963 the Soviet team toured Japan and demonstrated that it was not far behind the mighty Japanese. When the time came for the first judo Olympics the Soviets took four bronze medals. Since then fighters from a Sambo background have won many judo world championships and Olympic gold medals.

Kicking for the Nation

Korean Taekwondo, one of the world's most popular martial arts, has a similar history of Japanese roots that have largely been erased for the sake of national pride. Koreans had plenty of reasons to resent the Japanese after the end of the Second World War and exulted in their release from thirty five years of subjugation. Aside from Korean wrestling, which strongly resembled Japanese sumo, the traditional fighting arts of the Korean people had been suppressed by the Japanese occupiers as part of the general discouragement of Korean culture. Instead study of all things Japanese was promoted and this included the Japanese martial arts. Japanese teachers gave classes throughout Korea in judo (known as yudo to the Koreans), jujutsu (yusul), kendo (kumdo), and karate (kongsudo). As war approached high school students in Korea were required, like their Japanese counterparts, to take part in 'sports' classes that involved bayonet fighting, sword fighting and basic judo and karate techniques. Many among the large Korean population in Japan were also training in the martial arts.

As the war ended there was an understandably open distaste in Korea for all things Japanese and a move to shake Korean culture free of its long domination by the neighboring power. Quickly several Korean fighting styles emerged, all of them led by individuals who had spent several years training in either Japanese judo or karate. The terminology used by these groups was Korean but they commonly practiced Japanese kata in almost unchanged forms and used very similar basic techniques. However, the atmosphere in Korean martial arts clubs was rather different from the pacifist mood that overtook Japanese dojos in the late forties. The Korean groups continued to employ the hard sparring methods that had been common during the war. This tough, competitive atmosphere led the Korean groups to make pioneering experiments in the use of protective clothing that they fashioned from baseball and kendo equipment.

By the early 1950s the emerging martial arts of Korea found themselves floundering amid the violent turmoil of the Korean War and the partitioning of the nation along the 38th Parallel. Following the war an authoritarian President, Syngman Rhee, took charge of South Korea and he ordered that tough hand-to-hand combat training be given to all new troops. Rhee assigned the implementation of this training to one of his protégés, a North Korean named Choi Hong Hi who had risen to the rank of general in the Southern army during the war. General Choi, like many other Koreans, had studied karate in Japan and had been awarded a second dan black belt in karate by the school of Gichin Funakoshi.

The South Korean army organized a conference of the various Korean martial arts groups in 1955 and at this meeting General Choi was instrumental in pushing for the Korean varieties of karate to be renamed as Taekwondo (the way of hand and foot). This choice of name was a deliberate echo of the traditional Korean combat game known as taekkyon. It was an art somewhat similar to Brazilian capoeira, a martial dance game performed for pleasure in village squares that involved a good deal of high kicking and tripping techniques. Taekkyon had been suppressed by the Japanese and had effectively disappeared by 1955 with only one skilled practitioner still alive in the whole of Korea. But the patriotic feelings of the Korean nation in the mid 1950s made the decision to present taekwondo as part of the national heritage a supremely pragmatic one. In time the choice of name proved to be more than merely cosmetic. Everyone knew that taekkyon had been a kicking art and the sense that kicking was a Korean way of fighting encouraged a shift in Taekwondo towards a greater and greater focus on kicking techniques.

General Choi, with his unsurpassed connections to the senior ranks of the South Korean government, had access to the finances and resources that allowed him to quickly build a large national organization and to dominate the other Korean fighting arts. But his position of unchallenged influence came to an end in 1961 when the government of his protector Syngman Rhee was overthrown by a student uprising and replaced by the administration of the equally authoritarian Park Chung-Hee. The new president regarded General Choi as a political enemy and quickly shipped him out of the country to serve as ambassador in Malaysia. Outside the intense politics of Seoul and in the relative quiet of Kuala Lumpur Choi began to reorganize his Taekwondo system. He discarded the Japanese kata that remained and created new forms to take their place.

On his return to Korea Choi turned his attention to creating an international base for Taekwondo. Many American servicemen had trained in Korean fighting schools during the Korean War and in the subsequent years they had taken these arts back to North America. Choi decided that he would encourage this process by forming an elite group of Taekwondo superstars who would help to promote their art by touring the world giving demonstrations. The spectacular shows given in many countries by this group featured breaking displays and astonishing flying kicks that helped to cement the image of Taekwondo as a primarily kicking art.

But inside Korea the situation was not improving for General Choi. At the instigation of the President he was pushed out of the leadership of the Korea Taekwondo Association. Choi responded by creating a new organization, the International Taekwondo Federation, which he eventually based overseas, at first in Toronto and later in Austria. With Choi out of the way the Korean government asserted even greater control over Taekwondo. In 1971 it was named as Korea's national sport and became a required subject in schools and universities. The Korean Intelligence Service helped to create a new international organization, the World Taekwondo Federation, as a block to the growth of Choi's organization. New official histories of the art were written that gave Taekwondo largely fictional roots in ancient Korean history. At the same time the government used its diplomatic clout to promote Taekwondo as an international competitive sport. To the enormous chagrin of karate administrators in Japan the Korean governmental support eventually led to Taekwondo being adopted as an official Olympic sport in 2000.

Modern Taekwondo has today largely discarded its roots in Japanese karate both in terminology and in form. Some branches of Taekwondo do preserve the militaristic training methods that were prevalent in the 1950s and are therefore much closer to Japanese karate. But modern Taekwondo has largely become a sport oriented combat form that finds its ultimate expression in Olympic competition. Competitors wear extensive body padding and make little use of hand striking techniques. In fact modern Taekwondo has become very similar to the traditional taekkyon that existed before the Japanese occupation. It is a spectacular and athletic martial form that centers around high, dramatic kicks delivered with the use of spins and jumps.

Heroes of the Ring

The arrival in Brazil in 1914 of a senior Japanese judo fighter, Mitsuyo Maeda, sparked the sequence of events that led to the creation of modern Brazilian jiu-jitsu. Maeda had spent years traveling the world giving exhibitions of judo and fighting all-comers. In the process he had developed a highly effective style that focussed on forcing opponents into rapid submission. Maeda taught judo to the son of a business acquaintance, Gustavo Gracie, who had helped Maeda settle in northern Brazil. Gustavo's son Carlos in turn passed on his judo knowledge to his younger brothers. One of those brothers, Helio Gracie, is regarded as being the founder of Brazilian jiu-jitsu.

Gracie developed a theory that all fights proceed through an initial striking phase that later gives way to upright grappling and finally to ground-based grappling. As a result he worked towards the creation of a judo-based fighting style that aims to shift any combat situation quickly to grappling on the floor where arm locks, leg locks and choke holds can more easily be applied. Helio made his style famous throughout Brazil by engaging in a series of vale tudo (no rules) matches that became national sensations. Vale tudo was a concept that had emerged from Brazilian circuses and there was still something of the circus atmosphere about the television show Heróis do Ringue that was hosted by the Gracie family in 1959 and 1960. The program brought fighters from different martial styles together in dramatic confrontations.

In 1993 the oldest son of Helio, Rorion Gracie, introduced the vale tudo concept to America with the creation of the Ultimate Fighting Championship (UFC). This was a pay-per-view televised competition that brought together fighters from karate, judo, jiu-jitsu, boxing, kick boxing and wrestling in what were, theoretically, rule-free confrontations. The dramatic sense of a brutal fight to the finish was heightened by the decision to enclose the fighters in octagonal cages. Most of the early UFC competitions were dominated by members of the Gracie family who were able to engineer rapid shifts to the ground fighting in which they were so skillful and in which fighters from most other styles were relatively inexperienced.

The early UFC matches were often bloody affairs and the gladiatorial nature of the competitions proved to be highly controversial. Senator John McCain described UFC competitions as "human cockfighting" and thirty six American states passed laws banning no holds barred fights from taking place on their territory. But despite such initial concerns the UFC has developed into an enormously popular and profitable television spectacle. Although it advertises itself as the ultimate test of actual fighting ability the UFC has taken significant steps to prevent uncontrolled fighting. Competitors are divided into several weight classes and are restrained in the cage by an extensive list of rules that forbid head butts, groin strikes or any kind of kick to the head of a competitor who has one knee on the ground.

Professional mixed martial arts events have also proved to be enormously popular in Japan. An imitation of UFC, known as Pride Fighting Championship, was established in Japan in 1997 and launched with a match between a Japanese wrestler and a member of the Gracie family that was watched by 47,000 spectators and a huge television audience. Pride was following in the footsteps of the hugely successful Japanese professional kickboxing circuit known as K-1. The K-1 series of tournaments was created by

Kasuyoshii Ishii after he broke away from Kyokushin karate to form the Seidokan organization. Competitors in K-1 events wear boxing gloves and aim for a knockout or a points victory achieved through a combination of strikes or kicks. No grappling is allowed and the tournaments attract fighters from kickboxing, karate, taekwondo and Muay Thai backgrounds.

The modern popularity of mixed martial arts events has greatly muddied the waters for the worldwide martial arts community. Regular televised tournaments have changed the way many young people think about the martial arts and have encouraged the emergence of new organizations that provide training in the kind of competition fighting that can be seen on television. Many martial artists who follow traditional Japanese styles regard the mixed martial arts tournaments as tawdry affairs and feel that the kind of training they promote is unsystematic and potentially dangerous. But the emergence of mixed martial arts has brought yet another challenge to the vision of men like Kano and Funakoshi who believed that the martial arts should be a vehicle for the forging of the human character. The question these new fighting styles pose is a real one. Have the traditional martial arts become so closely wrapped up in promoting sporting endeavor and personal development that they have lost sight of the one thing that a fighter truly requires - the ability to fight?

17. The Modern Age

Zest for Life

Japan in the early decades of the twenty-first century is a profoundly different place from the nation where judo, karate and aikido first became prevalent almost one hundred years ago. In many ways the Japan of today is a wonderful place to live; a nation that finally seems to be at peace with itself. The poverty and crime that disfigured Japan in the years after the war have mostly disappeared and in modern Japanese society a decent education, good quality health care and lifetime employment are, for most of the population, the norm. Japanese people are so healthy, in fact, that they enjoy some of the world's longest life spans and they are proud that their crime rates are among the lowest in the developed world.

And yet many Japanese people look back today with a sense of loss to the decades between 1950 and 1990 when economic growth seemed unstoppable, when Japanese companies flooded the world with an endless output of ingenious machines and the country felt young, restless and confident. Japan today is a cautious place, a nation where pensioners easily outnumber teenagers and where safety is valued more than adventure. There are fewer young people and they often seem to the older generation to be lacking the spark that drove the nation forward for so long.

The martial arts are still a very important component of Japanese society. Around seven million citizens are believed to be practicing one or more of the various fighting arts. But this is a shrinking constituency. Teenagers in Japanese schools can choose from an overwhelming variety of activities to fill up their free time: from Western sports like rugby, volleyball, tennis and soccer to the omnipresent mobile phones and computer games. And fewer young people feel that there is a pressing need to learn how to fight. They have grown up, after all, in a society where violent crime is at historically low levels. Teenagers can wander freely through city centers late at night without experiencing any of the sense of danger that is so often present in other parts of the world. In more violent countries there is an obvious need for self defense skills that helps the martial arts clubs to recruit young members, but this factor is of little significance in contemporary Japan.

These days when Japanese education is discussed the cry of conservative politicians is for a back to basics policy, a return to the long hours of character building and intensive study that were regarded as normal in the boom years. In 2008 the Ministry of Education released guidelines for a national education that promotes zest for living (ikiru-chikara). Education, according to the government guidelines, should enable children to develop scholastic competence, sound minds and sound bodies. Those who argued that some of these aims could be achieved by giving the traditional martial arts a larger role in education have been listened to and classes in either judo, kendo or sumo became compulsory for all junior high school students from 2012. This is an important, and controversial, change that will greatly increase the number of Japanese teenagers, especially the number of girls, who are learning a martial art.

Head First

At present judo is the most popular martial art in Japanese schools and it is generally regarded as a healthy, safe and character building sport. A large number of schools employ full-time judo teachers and offer judo as a regular element in the curriculum. The teenage students practice judo technique, spar with their schoolmates and have the opportunity to progress to black belt level through weekly training sessions. These classes, in which all of the students in the school participate, are often light-hearted and playful.

A completely different atmosphere prevails in the high school judo clubs. In the typical Japanese manner club members meet daily and often twice daily for six days each week. They arrive at school early to take part in physical workouts and stay after school for intensive sparring sessions. Whereas judo classes for all students are led by qualified teachers the judo clubs are normally organized and led by the senior students themselves. These boys and girls 'encourage' the younger students by creating an intensely serious training atmosphere. New members are required to follow instruction without question and can expect to be bullied if they do not.

Despite the fact that most Japanese people think of judo as a healthy sport the dangers of high school judo have been more openly discussed in recent years. It has become clear that judo is, in fact, a dangerous sport. Between 1983 and 2009 108 Japanese students between the ages of twelve and seventeen died from injuries that they received during judo practice. This death rate, four students per year on average, is five times higher than that recorded by any other school sport in Japan. Two thirds of the fatalities resulted from brain injuries that were caused by teenagers being thrown hard, head first, onto a judo mat. More than two hundred other children were seriously injured during this period. Now that judo has become a compulsory sport for junior high school students there is understandable anxiety among parents.

The number of judo related injuries in high schools points to a situation that is more worrying than a rash of sporting accidents. Several incidents in recent years have drawn attention to the way in which some judo teachers are using judo techniques to discipline their students. The great majority of judo teachers are well trained and are excellent instructors but a small minority of short-tempered teachers do take out their anger on their teenage students. In 2004 a fifteen year old boy who had missed judo training was forced to spar with his teacher, who was a former All Japan champion. The teacher choked the boy into unconsciousness, allowed him to revive and them choked him again before throwing him violently. The boy suffered serious internal bleeding from the brain and experienced periods of amnesia for the next two years. The teacher was transferred to another school.

The growing unease over judo coaching came to a head in early 2013 with the resignation of the chief coach of the women's national judo team. Fifteen female judoka had lodged complaints against the coach, indicating that he had regularly struck them and had inflicted undue mental abuse in the run up to the 2012 Olympics. At first the complaints were swept under the carpet by the judo establishment but a general mood of concern over bullying in Japanese society and the approach of Tokyo's bid to host the 2020 Olympics forced the issue into the glare of media attention. Finally, it seems that Japanese judo will be forced into taking coach harassment and bullying seriously.

Judo Renaissance
Japanese judo passed through an intense crisis of confidence in the 1960s and 1970s after the shocking defeats of its strongest fighters in international competition. Japan even lost its place as the nation with the largest number of adults practicing judo, a distinction that is now held by France. But despite the anxiety that overtook Japanese judo in those decades it has continued to be, by some distance, the world's strongest nation in judo competition. In the 2010 World Judo Championships Japan took 23 of the medals while the nearest challenger, France, won only six. Although the total number of judo participants may have increased in other parts of the world Japan remains unsurpassed in its ability to turn out elite level fighters. These outstanding athletes are the product of the extremely large pool of gifted competitors that can be found in Japanese university clubs.

Several universities vie for the leadership of Japanese judo but perhaps the strongest of them all is Tokai University situated just to the south of Tokyo. This university boasts a Department of Martial Arts where students can pursue full-time studies of either judo or kendo. The Department has an outstanding faculty and employs Yasuhiro Yamashita, the greatest living figure in Japanese judo, as a professor. The real judo action, however, takes place in the judo club. Housed in a beautiful, free-standing wooden dojo, the club's regular training sessions are attended by almost 150 black belts. It is a university club that explicitly aims to develop competitors who can succeed at the highest world level and employs a large coaching and physical development staff that includes several former Olympic champions.

The students who train in this club are essentially semi-professional athletes. Many are supported by scholarships and those who are good enough to take part in national competitions receive extensive exemptions from their academic requirements. In a number of ways the academic department is actually subordinate to the judo club. Everything is arranged to allow these young competitors to organize their lives around the three hour long training sessions that take place twice a day on six days of the week. Anyone who turns up for training can work out with elite fighters who are undergraduates or members of the coaching staff. In addition the club attracts regular visits from international delegations that help to keep the standard of training at a very high level. This standard is sustained by the high quality intake of first year students who are recruited to Tokai University through a system of feeder high schools. These schools, in turn, scour the entire country for the best junior judo fighters.

The excellence of judo in the university clubs has somewhat disguised the fact that judo is in overall decline among the adult population. While many companies support their own judo clubs and most towns have a club open to all citizens the number of adults who are registered with the all-Japan Judo Federation has steadily fallen and now stands below 200,000. Many in Japanese judo circles feel that the obsession of their sport with Olympic success has tended to create an atmosphere in judo clubs that can be intimidating for those who are too old or too physically weak to be able to compete themselves.

Yashuhiro Yamashita, one of the greatest judo competitors of them all, has added his voice to those who object that the trend towards sport judo has gone too far. He laments the relative absence of 'beautiful' standing throws in modern competition and worries about the lack of traditional values among young judo players. In 2001 Yamashita was instrumental in creating a 'Judo Renaissance' movement that aims to revive the original vision of Jigoro Kano and to promote judo as a vehicle for balanced physical and mental development.

I Thought I Was Dreaming

While Yamashita is undoubtedly the senior figure of the modern day judo community he is eclipsed in the Japanese imagination by a woman half his size. By some distance the most famous living martial artist in Japan today is the elfin judo competitor Ryoko Tani. She rose to fame through a dramatic career of fighting in the lightest under 48kg category during which she won two Olympic gold medals, two silvers and one bronze and seven judo world titles.

The beginning of Tani's success came at the Barcelona Olympics where she won the silver medal at the age of seventeen. She had an all-action, highly aggressive fighting style that made her almost impossible to subdue. Her dynamic fighting combined irresistibly in the public mind with her tiny 1.46 meter frame and her impish smile. Following her first Olympic medal Tani had an incredible string of victories, remaining undefeated in eighty four successive competitive matches. She soon became one of the most famous faces in Japan, known to the nation as Yawara-chan, a nickname borrowed from a judo animation that featured an indomitable female fighter. By the time of the Atlanta Olympics she was the overwhelming favorite to win gold and millions of Japanese viewers cooed at the sight of her small frame leading the Japanese delegation into the stadium for the opening ceremony. It was a stunning shock for the Japanese television audience when Tani lost in the final to an unknown North Korean woman.

But defeat in Atlanta only seemed to amplify the popularity of Tani as she fought her way back to the top in a series of competition victories, often achieved with the most spectacular throws. Her celebrity made her a fixture on Japanese television commercials where she entertained the nation by throwing much larger men around. By the time of the Sydney Olympics in 2000 she was practically boiling with determination to win the gold medal. She wanted to bring home, she said, "at best a gold, at worst a gold." In the final she began like a whirlwind and thew her Russian opponent for a full ippon to win the match after only thirty six seconds. Japanese sports stars are usually reserved in the extreme when they talk to the press but Tani managed to mark that moment with some exuberant language. "When I received the gold medal on the podium I thought I was dreaming," she announced. "It was like meeting your first love after eighty years."

Tani married a professional baseball player in 2003 in a wedding that was almost royal in its scale and in the sensation it caused. The event was staged in Paris, was rumored to have cost three million dollars and was broadcast live on national television. One year later Tani emphasized her dominance of women's judo by again winning an Olympic gold medal in Athens. When the trials for the Beijing Olympics came around Tani was a mother but she informed the nation that she planned to be the first mother to win an Olympic gold medal for judo. In the end she had to finish her career with a mere bronze medal but her position in the public mind is secure. For the Japanese people Tani exemplifies the drive and the fighting spirit that they value above all else. Few eyebrows were raised when she was nominated for a post in the Upper House of the Japanese parliament, easily winning her seat in the election.

The Most Dangerous Man in Japan

Japanese karate is also strongest today among high school and university students. Almost every university boasts a karate club and many universities are home to several varieties of karate. Student members of these clubs typically train for two hours on six days of the week and take part in a week long gasshuku training camp during the summer vacation. Almost all of this intense effort is directed towards competition and the university based karate fighters have incredibly high levels of fitness, strength and speed. The large quantities of time devoted to competition training have had an inevitable effect on fighting styles. Japanese karate students tend to move almost exclusively in straight lines when they are sparring and avoid more dangerous diagonal or circular movements. Upper level strikes are directed to the throat area of the opponent as this conveys an impression of clear contact having been made while greatly reducing the risk of the disqualification that can follow from uncontrolled strikes to the face. Kata is also largely regarded as a competitive activity and students practice their kata with an emphasis on extremely sharp, cleanly defined techniques rather than on strength. Female competitors often prepare for kata competition by carefully applying makeup.

Outside the universities the large karate organizations founded by Funakoshi, Nakayama, Yamaguchi, Oyama and Otsuka reached their peak membership during the 1970s and 1980s and have since splintered into a number of smaller organizations. Many of these karate groups broke up quickly after the deaths of charismatic leaders who could command unquestioning loyalty from their senior students. Every city has a number of karate dojos that are open to the public and where students pay a monthly fee that entitles them to attend training as often as they like. A high proportion of these fee paying students are children who are signed up by their parents following the Japanese mania for structured after school activities. There tends, therefore, to be an important financial relationship between a professional karate teacher and his students. The presence of so many children has also undoubtedly affected the atmosphere of Japanese karate clubs. Teachers are rarely as tough on their students today as they would have been in the post-war years. Instead most karate instructors aim to create an enjoyable, unthreatening environment that can attract students of all ages. Despite these changes the number of students in Japanese karate is in a long term decline.

A countervailing trend can be seen in the popularity of full-contact karate which is today the most stable brand of karate in Japan. Although the Kyokushin organization created by Masutatsu Oyama has now broken up into several competing groups the vision of the founder has continued to be highly influential. For those Japanese teenagers and young adults who are genuinely interested in developing real fighting skills the full contact clubs with their mix of rigorous group training and intensive body conditioning are often the most attractive option.

While Japanese karate may be in relative decline many great teachers are continuing to work with their students using methods that would have been familiar to the karate pioneers of the early twentieth century. Morio Higaonna, an Okinawan karate expert, is one of those teachers who attracts enormous respect from all quarters. He is a small friendly man who speaks English well and has a constant smile on his face. But his karate practice is deadly serious. Don Draeger, the late expert in East Asian fighting systems, once described Higaonna as "the most dangerous man in Japan if it came to a real fight."

Higaonna began practicing karate as a teenager in the famous garden dojo of Chojun Miyagi, one of the great founders of Okinawan Goju karate. After only a few months the teacher died but Higaonna was able to continue training for years under one of Miyagi's senior students, Anichi Miyagi. He did not have much company. The garden dojo was unpopular with Okinawan youths who thought that the training that went on there was ridiculously hard. Higaonna spent thousands of hours building up his short frame with heavy traditional stone weights, practicing kata and sparring with full contact. On many days he would train for ten continuous hours and would at times cough up blood when he returned to his home.

In 1957 Higaonna was ready to leave Okinawa to take up studies at a Tokyo university. He had worn a white belt since he had started training and had never taken a grading exam. His teachers agreed that he would need some kind of karate grade when he arrived in Tokyo and so put him through a fourteen hour long ordeal to 'test' his ability. Higaonna gave a demonstration of everything he had learned. His test included hundreds of makiwara strikes, dozens of repetitions of all the kata he knew and concluded with three hours of sparring. He was awarded a third dan black belt.

Soon after he arrived in Tokyo to study at Takushoku University Higaonna opened a small karate dojo. He was an atypical karate teacher, relaxed and friendly although undoubtedly extremely tough, and his classes soon became popular with both Japanese and foreign students in the Tokyo area. After twenty years of teaching karate in the Yoyogi section of downtown Tokyo Higaonna had developed a shining international reputation that attracted many overseas karate experts to make pilgrimages to study at his side. He went on to teach overseas in both England and California and established his own organization, the International Okinawan Goju-Ryu Karate-Do Federation.

Now well into his seventies Higaonna has returned to Naha in Okinawa where he continues to spend six hours every day training in kata, body conditioning and zen meditation. His karate is undoubtedly powerful and highly effective but the factor that makes this teacher so popular with students of all ages is his cheerful enthusiasm for the lifetime journey of karate. Higaonna regards every day as a fresh opportunity for learning and tries to find purpose in every situation. A stay in a hotel room, Higaonna says, is a perfect opportunity to practice speed punching against the curtains. A walk on the beach is a wonderful chance to develop the abdominal muscles (hara) by making use of the resistance of the sand.

The Old Ways
Of the seven million Japanese people who are practicing a martial art today the great majority are affiliated to one of the modern fighting arts groups (gendai budo). These arts, dominated by judo, kendo, karate-do, aikido, Japanese archery (kyudo) and sword drawing (iaido) are generally run under the control of large organizations that have national headquarters and many local branches. In most of these groups the students wear white training suits and colored belts. They progress through a series of ranks toward black belt level (shodan) and then to higher grades in a training system that adheres to a

published curriculum. Instruction is usually explanatory in nature with the teacher and senior students providing demonstrations and giving detailed instructions to beginners. Many of the larger gendai budo groups encourage their students to participate in some form of sparring that allows them to freely apply techniques learned in their basic training. The names of almost all modern martial arts end in the Japanese suffix do, implying that the training they offer has the ultimate goal of personal, or even spiritual, development.

But an entirely different world exists within the Japanese martial arts community, the world of old style fighting arts (koryu bujutsu). Several of the older fighting systems that were created before the Meiji Restoration have been preserved up to the present day as living embodiments of Japan's martial history. These are fighting systems that were originally created in the samurai training schools of the provinces or were established by individuals, families or groups of neighbors. Their techniques have been passed down through a chain of teachers who have protected their art for generations in a human transmission from teacher to student and from father to son.

Today approximately one hundred of these old style martial schools are in existence. The largest national association of such groups, the Japan Old Martial Arts Association (Nihon Kobudo Kyokai), has 78 member groups. Most of these styles preserve a form of jujutsu or of sword fighting but there are also a number of spear fighting, stick fighting and even gunnery groups. In addition, several of the koryu bujutsu groups practice comprehensive fighting systems that provide training in both unarmed combat and combat using various kinds of weaponry.

These old schools have largely avoided attempts to modernize their methods or to adapt to the present day environment. Essentially they preserve the character of combat training from the days when combat was a truly deadly experience and preparation for war was a matter of the utmost seriousness. These groups rarely wear white uniforms or colored belts for training. Many conduct their practice in traditional Japanese clothing and some even wear samurai armor on occasion. Few of these groups offer dan grades to their students. Instead they prefer to issue older methods of certification that often culminate in the award of a license to teach (menkyo kaidan).

Training in the koryu bujutsu schools usually involves weapons training and practice of deadly techniques. Some schools practice with real battlefield weapons while other use safer substitutes such as the wrapped bamboo (fukuro shinai) weapon that is employed by some sword schools. In almost all of these schools the techniques being practiced are believed to be highly dangerous and so training is largely restricted to kata practice. Students learn by repeating pre-arranged movements, almost always in pairs. Very few of these schools require students to engage in sparring or any kind of body conditioning.

As a result the old style fighting schools have a very different atmosphere from modern schools that tend to be dominated by younger and more powerful members. Students in koyru bujutsu schools can often be in their sixties and masters will continue to teach into their seventies or even eighties.

Another marked difference from the newer martial arts is that the old styles have avoided the creation of franchises and associations that attract thousands of students. The key element in these schools is the transmission of physical knowledge from the head of the school directly to the students. As a result, most of these groups are based in just one training centre or a small group of closely linked dojo. The total number of Japanese people studying the old fighting arts today is a tiny proportion of the martial arts community, well under one hundred thousand individuals in total.

But the old fighting arts provide an incredible opportunity to come face to face with Japan's samurai past. At public demonstrations, such as the display at Tokyo's Meiji Shrine on Culture Day, crowds of spectators gather to enjoy this richly preserved medieval culture. The visitors can see members of a six hundred year old style like the Takenouchi Ryu demonstrating an extraordinary fighting system. They practice an art that was founded by Takenouchi Hisamori in 1532 after he had a vivid dream in which a mountain demon enlightened him to the secrets of combat. Even today the style is headed by members of the Takenouchi family, now in the fourteenth generation, who preside over a unique syllabus that consists of more than five hundred techniques. Beginner students practice unarmed grappling and striking. They learn how to hold down and tie up an enemy. More advanced students progress to training in the use of the long and short sword, the iron fan, the staff and the naginata. They learn how to attack vital points of the body and how to resuscitate drowned opponents. High level students learn how to combine various stages of combat. They train for encounters that begin with sword fighting, involve the use of daggers, move into grappling and end with the binding of a vanquished opponent.

All of these old style fighting groups place great weight on the preservation of historical ideas and techniques and, for some of the groups, preservation seems to be their primary aim. The Morishige Ryu, for example, is a group that continues to practice samurai musket firing methods from the sixteenth century. The style has broken down the preparation, loading and firing of muskets into a series of kata so that the patterns of old-style gun fighting can be passed on in a systematic way. Their demonstrations, carried out in medieval armor and enlivened with billows of smoke and earsplitting gun blasts provide a colorful climax to many events. In their own very Japanese way the Morishige Ryu seem to resemble an group of American Civil War enthusiasts.

And yet there is clearly more than mere historical preservation at play in the practice of many of these old schools. It is impossible to watch an exhibition by the senior students of a group like the Shinto Muso-

Ryu, a seventeenth century staff fighting style, without recognizing the presence of a living and vigorous martial art. The erect, cat-like movements, the total concentration of the participants, the thrusts of solid wood at high speed to within a whisker of the opponent's face. This is a serious, disciplined and impressive art.

The Problem of Death

Old or new the Japanese martial arts exist today as a vivid reminder of the wild flowering of fighting skills that have been so important to the life of this island nation. The fighting arts preserve in a multitude of ways the spirit, the philosophy and the bodily movements of an almost forgotten time when violence was a fact of everyday life. No single word or thought can adequately encompass this rich history or summarize the complex and storied martial tradition of Japan. It has been expressed in so many ways: the brotherly teamwork of the samurai clans; the individualism of Miyamoto Musashi; the Zen inspired swordwork of Yagyu Munenori and Yamaoka Tesshu; the fanaticism of Yamamoto Tsunetomo; the nobility of Saigo Takamori; the liberal humanism of Nitobe Inazo; the Emperor worship of the wartime militarists; the mysticism of Morihei Ueshiba; the upright decency of Jigoro Kano and Gichin Funakoshi. All of these strands, all of these conceptions of the meaning of bushido, continue to live in Japan today and it is the variety and richness of the tradition that gives it strength. For a nation that has been so shattered by decades of war and so convulsed by economic growth the legacy of the martial arts is one vital way for Japanese people to keep in touch with their past. There is much in martial history that makes these people proud of their nation and confident in their own values.

But what possible relevance can the martial arts continue to have in the twenty first century? Japan is now a peaceful place, a land where few young people have ever been so much as involved in a street brawl. Even arguments that the martial arts can serve as a vehicle for self development and can lead to a better understanding of traditional culture have limits. There are a multitude of other paths that offer the same rewards.

One way in which the martial arts do continue to have real meaning has been suggested by the late aikido reformer, Kenji Tomiki. Tomiki was no lover of violence, indeed he strongly argued that the Japanese should turn away from those elements of martial history that were "simply cruelty." But still, he argued, the martial arts do have a fundamental value and they are unique. There is no other human activity that can do so much to bring us face to face with the ultimate question. What does it mean to be alive?

> Martial arts concern themselves with life or death situations in which the main question is whether one will survive. A number of great people in the past ... exposed their bodies to danger to master

these techniques. But, the more they tried to enter this world of danger and violence, the more they ended up going in a direction that contradicted it all. By putting themselves in the realm of life and death, they found themselves delving deeply into the problem of death.

... we are speaking of a bujutsu that looks death straight in the face. In a fight, we are at the edge of death. The spirit confronting death needs to possess a certain philosophy if it is not to lose its balance or composure ... As soon as human beings are born, they are beset with fears and uncertainty and the horror of death. Bujutsu are very concrete. They take violent power, and with it they plunge into the midst of this uncertainty. (51)

Sources

1. Legends of the Samurai - Hiroaki Sato
2. Heike Monogatari - Arthur L. Sadler (tr.)
3. Records of the Goden Ryu
4. The Onin Ki
5. Hideyoshi - Mary E. Berry
6. Samurai William - Giles Milton
7. Miyamoto Musashi: His Life and Writings - Kenji Tokitsu
8. Heaven and Hell - Aldous Huxley
9. The Sword and the Mind - Hiroaki Sato
10. Hoka no Mono no Koto - Yagyu Munenori
11. Sakamoto Ryoma and the Meiji Restoration - Marius B Jansen
12. Commodore Perry in the Land of the Shogun - Rhoda Blumberg
13. The Last Samurai: The Life and Battles of Saigo Takamori - Mark Ravina
14. The Sword of No-Sword: Life of the Master Warrior Tesshu - John Stevens
15. Yamaoka Tesshu - Hidehiro Kojima
16. Yamaoka Tesshu: A Swordsman for Peace - Eiji Takemura
17. Zen and Japanese Culture - D. T. Suzuki
18. The Taming of the Samurai - Eiko Ikegami
19. Tales of Old Japan - A. B. Mitford
20. Hagakure - William Scott Wilson (tr.)
21. Bushido - Inazo Nitobe
22. Japan: A State Strategy for the twenty-first century - Yasuhiro Nakasone et al.
23. Martial Arts in the Modern World - Thomas Green, Joseph Svinth
24. Canon of Judo - Kyuzo Mifune (tr. Francoise White)
25. Waga Judo - Masahiko Kimura
26. Okinawan Karate - Mark Bishop
27. Okinawa: The History of an Island People - George H. Kerr
28. Okinawa Kempo - Choki Motobu (tr. Seiyu Oyata)
29. Karate-Do Nyumon - Gichin Funakoshi (tr. John Teramoto)
30. A Life in Aikido - Kisshomaru Ueshiba (tr. Kei Iwaza and Mary Fuller)
31. Transmission, Inheritance, Emulation (AikiWeb) - Peter Goldsbury
32. Karate: Goju by the Cat - Gogen Yamaguchi
33. The Art of Peace: Morihei Ueshiba - John Stevens
34. Karate-Do: My Way of Life - Gichin Funakoshi (tr.
35. Nippon Times. Tuesday, August 28, 1945.

36. Aikido Jinsei - Gozo Shioda (tr. Aikido Journal)
37. Invincible Warrior - John Stevens
38. The Missionary and the Libertine - Ian Buruma
39. Shotokan Karate: Its History and Evolution - Randall G. Hassell
40. Histoire de Karaté-dô - Kenji Tokitsu
41. Karate Magazine, April 1977 - Roland Gaillac
42. Sosai Masutatsu Oyama 1923 – 1994 (BKK Magazine) - Liam Keaveney
43. Mas Oyama Stories - Jon Bluming
44. Mas Oyama in America - Graham Noble
45. What is Karate? - Masutatsu Oyama
46. Letter, Black Belt Magazine, Oct. 1972 - Masutatsu Oyama
47. The Kyokushin Way - Masutatsu Oyama
48. Was Elvis really a Black Belt? - Tracyskarate.com
49. The Count Dante Story, Black Belt Magazine, Mar. 1976 - Massad. F. Ayoob
50. History of John Keehan - Black Dragon Fighting Society
51. Aikido Pioneers: Prewar Era - Stanley Pranin

Printed in Great Britain
by Amazon.co.uk, Ltd.,
Marston Gate.